Studies in Church History

Subsidia

10

PROPHECY AND ESCHATOLOGY

PROPHECY AND ESCHATOLOGY

EDITED BY

MICHAEL WILKS

PUBLISHED FOR
THE ECCLESIASTICAL HISTORY SOCIETY

BY

BLACKWELL PUBLISHERS
1994

© Ecclesiastical History Society 1994

First published 1994

Blackwell Publishers
108 Cowley Road, Oxford OX4 1JF, UK

238 Main Street
Cambridge, Massachusetts 02142, USA

British Library Cataloguing in Publication Data

A catalogue record for this book is available from the British Library

ISBN 0–631–19051–1

Typeset by Joshua Associates Limited, Oxford
Printed in Great Britain by Hartnolls Ltd, Bodmin, Cornwall

CONTENTS

CONTENTS

PREFACE

'Surely the Lord God will do nothing but he revealeth his secret unto his servants the prophets' (Amos 3. 7), and it has been said that the theme of prophecy runs 'like a golden thread' throughout the whole history of Israel.[1] Much the same might be said of the new Israel of the Christian Church, for which speculation about Last Things was strengthened by the presence of the *Apocalypsis*, the book of the Revelation of St John the Divine. Few books of scripture have been the subject of such frequent comment and discussion, and for many centuries apocalypticism has been an important element in shaping Christian thought and Western culture in general. The search for signs of the approaching end of the world and anticipation of the Day of Judgement was bound to intensify as time wore on and expectations of 'a new heaven and a new earth' were thought likely to be fulfilled. As these essays indicate, the result was a curious mixture of fear and hope: fear that in a sinful world matters could only get worse until the Antichrist himself was unleashed upon suffering mankind; hope of Christ's imminent return to bring the joys of salvation for the elect of God.

The present volume endeavours to reflect that ambivalence. The idea of the old age of the world and of men themselves, both losing their vigour as they reach the end and final judgement, has encouraged the separation of the contributions into two groups. The first deals specifically with the history of millenarism. The enigmas of the Apocalypse had a particular appeal at times when it was perceived that things were getting worse. Prophecies concerning Last Things flourished luxuriantly in the later medieval period, especially under the powerful influence of Joachim of Fiore. This in its turn raised questions about the other end of time, the age of the world and how the intervening sections of history should be divided up. It also brought forward the issue of just how orthodox apocalypticism really was. It was a subject which had an immediate appeal to individuals and sects in revolt against the established order, and it was therefore one with special relevance for the development of Protestant movements in the Europe of the sixteenth and seventeenth centuries. At the same time its medieval roots ensured a continuing history in Roman Catholic theology well into the eighteenth century until the Enlightenment diminished its significance in the mainstream of Christian thought. This is followed by the second section, which

---

[1] J. F. A. Sawyer, *Prophecy and the Prophets of the Old Testament* (Oxford, 1987), p. 16.

considers specific aspects of death and salvation over the same periods. The volume concludes with a splendid account by Dr Binfield of Victorian Dissent, which neatly combines the topic of millenarian prophecy with the question of the salvation of the Jews, so emphasizing how ecumenical the whole subject should be.

As Professor Bredero points out, this volume complements the publication of papers from the 1984 Louvain conference on 'Eschatology in the Middle Ages'.[2] Our selection originated as papers delivered at the Fifth Anglo-Dutch Colloquium of Church Historians held at Groningen in August 1992 between members of the British and Dutch Sub-Commissions of the Commission Internationale d'Histoire Ecclésiastique Comparée. The British contingent is very pleased to have this opportunity to record our warmest thanks to our Dutch colleagues for their hospitality, including accommodation at the Golden Tulip Hotel, Paterswolde, in a degree of comfort to which British academic life has not accustomed us, and an excellent conference dinner at 't Vergulde Anker. Special thanks must go to Professor Freek Knetsch, who acted as chairman of the conference, and to Professor Frits Broeyer, who shouldered most of the burdens of arranging and administering it. It was a most successful meeting, and a great pleasure to be with so many friends, old and new.

The contributors also wish to express their thanks to the Ecclesiastical History Society for its ready agreement to publication of the papers in the *Studies in Church History*, *Subsidia* series. The editor would also like to thank Mrs Stella Wilks, whose skilful revising solved some of the more intractable problems of translation. All the errors that remain are of course entirely mine.

MJW

---

[2] *The Use and Abuse of Eschatology in the Middle Ages*, ed. W. Verbeke, D. Verhels, and A. Welkenhuysen (Leuven, 1988).

CONTRIBUTORS

VIRGINIA R. BAINBRIDGE
Royal Holloway and Bedford New College, University of London

JOHANNES VAN DEN BERG
Emeritus Professor of Church History, University of Leiden

CLYDE BINFIELD
Reader in History, University of Sheffield

ADRIAAN H. BREDERO
Emeritus Professor of Medieval History, Free University, Amsterdam

JAMES K. CAMERON
Emeritus Professor of Ecclesiastical History, St Mary's College, University of St Andrews

TH. CLEMENS
Lecturer in Church History, Catholic Theological University, Utrecht

JANE E. A. DAWSON
John Laing Lecturer in the History and Theology of the Reformation, New College, University of Edinburgh

EUGÈNE HONÉE
Professor of Church History, Catholic Theological University, Utrecht

SARAH HUTTON
Senior Lecturer, School of Humanities and Education, University of Hertfordshire

DAVID M. LOADES
Professor of History, University College of North Wales, Bangor

JAN R. LUTH
Tutor in Liturgical Science, Faculty of Theology, University of Groningen

NICOLETTE MOUT
Reader in Dutch History and Professor of Central European Studies, University of Leiden

ix

CONTRIBUTORS

PETER RAEDTS
>Lecturer in Medieval and Reformation Church History, University of Leiden

JOHANNA ROELEVINK
>Senior Researcher, Institute of Netherlands History, The Hague

BERT ROEST
>Department of Medieval Studies, University of Groningen

STEPHEN WESSLEY
>Professor of History, York College, Pennsylvania

MICHAEL WILKS
>Professor of Medieval History, Birkbeck College, University of London

ABBREVIATIONS

ActaSS	*Acta sanctorum*, ed. J. Bolland and G. Henschen (Antwerp, etc., 1643ff.)
AHP	*Archivum historiae pontificiae* (Rome, 1963ff.)
AHR	*American Historical Review* (New York, 1895ff.)
AnBoll	*Analecta Bollandiana* (Brussels, 1882ff.)
AV	Authorized Version
BIHR	*Bulletin of the Institute of Historical Research* (London, 1923–86) [superseded by *HR*]
BJRL	*Bulletin of the John Rylands Library* (Manchester, 1903ff.)
BL	British Library, London
BM	British Museum, London
BN	Bibliothèque Nationale, Paris
CChr	*Corpus Christianorum* (Turnhout, 1953ff.)
CChr.CM	*Corpus Christianorum, continuatio medievalis* (1966ff.)
CChr.SG	*Corpus Christianorum, series Graeca* (1974ff.)
CChr.SL	*Corpus Christianorum, series Latina* (1953ff.)
CathHR	*Catholic Historical Review* (Washington, D.C., 1915ff.)
ChH	*Church History* (New York/Chicago, 1932ff.)
CHJ	*Cambridge Historical Journal* (Cambridge, 1925–57) [superseded by *HistJ*]
CUL	Cambridge University Library
CYS	*Canterbury and York Society* (London, 1907ff.)
DNB	*Dictionary of National Biography* (London,1885ff.)
DublR	*Dublin Review* (London, 1836ff.)
EcHR	*Economic History Review* (London, 1927ff.)
EETS	*Early English Text Society* (London, 1864ff.)
EHD	*English Historical Documents* (London, 1953ff.)
EHR	*English Historical Review* (London, 1886ff.)
HistJ	*Historical Journal* (Cambridge, 1958ff.) [supersedes *CHJ*]
HMC	*Historical Manuscripts Commission*
HR	*Historical Research* (London, 1986ff.) [supersedes *BIHR*]
HThR	*Harvard Theological Review* (New York/Cambridge, Mass., 1908ff.)
HZ	*Historische Zeitschrift* (Munich, 1859ff.)
IER	*Irish Ecclesiastical Record* (Dublin, 1864ff.)
InR	*Innes Review* (Glasgow, 1950ff.)
JBS	*Journal of British Studies* (Hartford, Conn., 1961ff.)
JEH	*Journal of Ecclesiastical History* (Cambridge, 1950ff.)
JFHS	*Journal of the Friends Historical Society* (London/Philadelphia, 1903ff.)
JHI	*Journal of the History of Ideas* (London, 1940ff.)
JMH	*Journal of Modern History* (Chicago, 1929ff.)
JMedH	*Journal of Medieval History* (Amsterdam, 1975ff.)
JMRS	*Journal of Medieval and Renaissance Studies* (Durham, N.C., 1971ff.)
JThS	*Journal of Theological Studies* (London, 1899ff.)
LCL	Loeb Classical Library

MGH	*Monumenta Germaniae historica inde ab a. 500 usque ad a. 1500*, ed. G. H. Pertz et al. (Hanover, Berlin, etc., 1826ff.)
MidlHist	*Midland History* (Birmingham, 1971ff.)
nd	no date
NEB	*New English Bible*
NH	*Northern History* (Leeds, 1966ff.)
ns	new series
NS	New Style
ODCC	*Oxford Dictionary of the Christian Church*, ed. F. L. Cross (Oxford, 1957), 2nd edn with E. A. Livingstone (1974)
OED	*Oxford English Dictionary*
OHS	Oxford Historical Society
OMT	*Oxford Medieval Texts* (Oxford, 1971ff.)
os	old series
OS	Old Style
PaP	*Past and Present. A Journal of Scientific History* (London, 1952ff.)
PBA	*Proceedings of the British Academy* (London, 1904ff.)
PG	*Patrologia Graeca*, ed. J. P. Migne, 161 vols (Paris, 1857–66)
PL	*Patrologia Latina*, ed. J. P. Migne, 217 + 4 index vols (Paris, 1841–61)
PS	*Parker Society* (Cambridge, 1841–55)
RHE	*Revue d'histoire ecclésiastique* (Louvain, 1900ff.)
RS	*Rerum Brittanicarum medii aevi scriptores*, 99 vols (London, 1858–1911) = Rolls Series
RV	Revised Version
sa	*sub anno*
SCH	*Studies in Church History* (London/Oxford, 1964ff.)
ScHR	*Scottish Historical Review* (Edinburgh/Glasgow, 1904ff.)
SCH.S	*Studies in Church History. Subsidia* (Oxford, 1978ff.)
Speculum	*Speculum. A Journal of Medieval Studies* (Cambridge, Mass., 1925ff.)
Traditio	*Traditio. Studies in Ancient and Medieval History, Thought and Religion* (New York, etc., 1943ff.)
TRHS	*Transactions of the Royal Historical Society* (London, 1871ff.)
VCH	*Victoria County History* (London, 1900ff.)

PART I THE APOCALYPSE

THE ANNOUNCEMENT OF THE COMING OF THE ANTICHRIST AND THE MEDIEVAL CONCEPT OF TIME

by ADRIAAN H. BREDERO

THE Institute of Medieval History of the Flemish Catholic University at Louvain held in 1984 an International Colloquium on 'Eschatology in the Middle Ages' and in 1988 its University Press published the proceedings of that Colloquium, labelled *The Use and Abuse of Eschatology in the Middle Ages*. Asked to review this volume I gave some special attention in my report to the contribution of Horst Dieter Rauh, entitled (at least in translation) 'Eschatology and History in the Twelfth Century: Antichrist-typology as Medium of Social Criticism'.[1]

The author of this article argued that during the twelfth century eschatological ideas became more interiorized under the influence of monastic spirituality. Eschatology also obtained a greater place in the ultimate destiny of the individual. As a consequence of this development the traditionally accepted signs of the coming of the Antichrist, which were already familiar to Pope Gregory the Great, received at the same time a more political and social interpretation. With this statement I agree, as I noted in my review article. But I also expressed my regrets that the eschatological signs announcing the coming of the Antichrist were neglected by Professor Rauh, and that neither were they given real attention in the other contributions to those proceedings.[2]

Before giving attention to those signs, I have to evoke some eschatological notions, which were generally accepted by the learned and literate part of medieval society, especially during the twelfth century; notions which were exegetically connected with the vision of the end. Those literary people were not only familiar with the usual signs, which were considered as the announcement of the coming of the Antichrist, but they also were all acquainted with at least two exegetical allegories about the end of the world which had originated in early Christianity.

The one which became the most accepted, and which therefore receives the greater part of my attention, was primarily put into words by

---

[1] 'Eschatologie und Geschichte im 12. Jahrhundert: Antichrist-Typologie als Medium der Gegenwartskritik', pp. 333–58.
[2] *Tijdschrift voor Geschiedenis*, 103 (1990), pp. 395–401.

Augustine and Gregory the Great. It concerned the biblical story of creation as it appears in the first book, Genesis.[3] According to this exegesis, which had been repeated and handed down by Isidore of Sevilla to many medieval authors, the six days in which God had created heaven and earth were the symbols of the periods of the life of a man as well, at the same time, of the periods of the *Historia mundi*,[4] which some authors, however, reduced to five periods.

A close relationship was seen between the various periods in the lives of men and the periods of history itself. Since the ultimate period in the life of man, his last years, was indicated as the fifth or the sixth day, so the fifth or sixth period in history was also considered as its last 'day'. In this period the world was growing old and mankind losing its force. This ultimate period would last until the end of the world as it took its beginning with the Incarnation of Christ, since it was said that He would return at the end of time. Living in this period of old age men had to expect the end of time imminently, the more when they discovered signs of decrepitude in the world of their own days. Those who lived in the twelfth century developed this eschatological interpretation of history, which they shared with earlier generations, in a more particular way, especially regarding the more recent past.

Because one's own time belonged to the last period of the history of the world, and because this period, at least according to this medieval conviction, possessed similarities with human old age, it was assumed that the world and mankind also had defects comparable with those which appeared in human seniority. The world appeared more powerless than in previous periods. One must, of course, take this as a figure of speech, but it is revealing that one repeatedly meets with this idea. A poet at the Carolingian court wrote that people in earlier time had greater bodily strength and greater power of the senses since at that time the world was still in its period of youth.[5] At around 1124, William of St Thierry used a similar imagery, when, on account of old age, he intended to abdicate as abbot of his monastery. However since he was at that moment not even fifty years old, he rejected allusions to the example of King David, who

---

[3] Augustine, *De cathechizandis rudibus*, xxii. 39 (*CChr*, *SL*, xlvi. 163–4); Gregory the Great, *Homiliis in Evangelia*, i. 1–2 (*PL*, lxxvi. 1154–5). Gregory applied the allegory of the six days to the parable of the master who hired workers for his vineyard in Matt. 20. 1–7, making the six hours of the day during which the workers were taken into service correspond with the six periods of time symbolizing the six days of the Creation.

[4] *Etymologarium*, V. xxxviii. 5.

[5] Dungal Scott, Letter 1, lines 10–11 (*MGH*, *Epp.*, iv. 577).

even in extreme age continued to reign over his people from his bed. For his rejection William used the argument that the stubborn foolishness of an ageing world was, at that earlier time, not so far advanced that the honour due to grey-haired men, worn out with service, was withheld from them.[6]

This imagery of six days also brought some comfort, at least in the twelfth century, when the eschatological expectation became more individual, mostly in monastic circles where the longing for the celestial Jerusalem became part of daily spirituality. Monks realized that the arrival in this heavenly city coincided with the beginning of the seventh day, with that special Sabbath which would never end, the day about which Peter Abelard wrote that unforgettable Sabbath Hymn, remarkable already by its sonorous beginning *O Quanta Qualia sunt illa Sabbata*, adequately translated by Helen Waddell in her *Mediaeval Latin Lyrics*.[7] I quote here the first strophe:

> How mighty are the Sabbaths, how mighty and how deep,
> That the high courts of Heaven to everlasting keep
> What peace unto the weary, what pride unto the strong,
> When God in whom are all things shall be all things to men.

Next to this imagery we know the learned class of the twelfth century did not exclusively connect its expectation of the Antichrist with the metaphor of the sixth day as being the period after the Incarnation of the Lord. Its eschatological outlook was also influenced, however less directly, by another allegorical interpretation of the Bible, namely the division of the *Historia mundi* into four realms, mentioned in the book Daniel. The fourth imperium would be followed by a realm founded by the Lord of Heaven himself, which will persist into eternity. This periodization was borrowed from the vision of the colossus with feet of clay according to the interpretation given by Daniel (2. 31–44). In their commentaries upon this book of the Bible some Fathers, especially Saint Jerome, had been led by the desire to give this eschatological vision its fulfilment in history.[8] In the days of the late Roman Empire this easily led to an identification of the already old and declining empire as the fourth and last realm, after which the Antichrist would make his appearance.

In the more popular eschatological conceptions of the Middle Ages the

---

[6] *Meditatio*, xi (*PL*, clxxx. 239).
[7] Harmondsworth, 1952, pp. 174–7.
[8] *Commentarium in Danielem*, I. ii. 31–5 (*CChr*, *SL*, lxxviia. 393–5).

idea of the coming of the Antichrist, as an appearance from without and not brought about by the sins of men themselves, became easily accepted. In the West it had been introduced more especially in the tenth century by Adzo, a monk of Montier-en-Der, who on the request of Gerberga, the wife of Louis IV of Francia, wrote a treatise on the place and the time of the Antichrist.[9] She asked him to write his account for political and propagandist reasons, and as we know from the book by Norman Cohn, *The Pursuit of the Millennium*, the idea of such a millenarian period played a great part in popular religious and social movements, which chose its historical interpretation according to their own political options.[10]

But the official Church did not accept the idea that the domination of the Antichrist had to be followed by a terrestrial millennium. This idea of a peaceful and prosperous millennium did not take into account the place of the Church in history. Because of the Church's understanding of her vocation on earth, it was she who gave shape to the millennium. Therefore she appealed to the authority of Augustine who confined himself to a purely spiritual-religious explanation of Daniel's vision of the clay-footed colossus, rejecting also any interpretation of the Antichrist as an appearance coming from without. Augustine also ridiculed all milleniarism by criticizing efforts to calculate the very moment that this realm would dawn.[11]

It is remarkable that learned contemporaries of the downfall of the Western Roman Empire at the end of the fifth century did not consider this event as the eschatological fulfilment of the prophecy of Daniel. The realm of the Gothic king, Theoderic the Great, was for Cassiodor, for instance, rather a continuation of this empire than its decline.[12] And in the opinion of Gregory of Tours, approximately Cassiodor's contemporary, when he compared King Clovis with the Emperor Constantine because of his receiving of baptism,[13] the Merovingians were doing much to renew this realm. Even the pope, who experienced the disastrous effects which Italy had to go through after the conquest of this area by the Byzantine emperor Justinian, refrained from the least comment on the book of Daniel. In his anxieties caused by the besieging of Rome, Gregory I

[9] Adzo Dervensis, *De ortu et tempore Antichristi*, ed. D. Verhelst (*CChr*, *CM*, xlv).
[10] First published London, 1957.
[11] *De civitate Dei*, xx. 9 (ed. D. Knowles, pp. 914–18); *De catechizandis rudibus*, xxii. 39 (as above, n. 3). Cf. B. McGinn, *Visions of the End* (New York, 1979), pp. 26–7.
[12] D. Verhelst, 'La préhistoire des conceptions d'Adson concernant l'Antichrist', *Recherches de théologie ancienne et médiévale*, 40 (1973), p. 76.
[13] *Historia Francorum*, ii. 31 (ed. L. Thorpe, p. 144).

restricted himself to an actualized commentary upon the biblical descriptions of the downfall of the cities of Samaria and Nineveh,[14] sharing the trust of the official Church in the Augustinian interpretation of the eschatological Bible passages.

Still, the announcement of the Antichrist did not remain entirely outside his discussion. So Gregory developed in his *Moralia*, being his commentary on the book of Job, his conviction that before his arrival the Antichrist was still living here and going abroad among us by his presence in the iniquitous. Cain and Judas and later the heretics, for instance, who lived before the time of the Antichrist, were nevertheless members of him and so his harbingers or heralds.[15] But more important was the commentary of this Pope on chapters forty and forty-one of the book of Job, which concerned Leviathan and his monstrosity. Gregory considered its description suitable for the Antichrist, and interpreted the verse 'Want shall go before his face' (41. 13), that is to say, 'Scarceness precedes his appearance', as the announcement of his coming. This event became announced when the signs of virtue were taken away from the Church, when the gift of prophecy was obscured, when the mercy of healing would be withheld, the virtue of voluntary abstinence was undermined, and when miracles would disappear.[16]

There is a lot of evidence that Gregory's commentary about this announcement found general acceptance in the literary-eschatological linguistic usage of the official medieval Church. By the appeal to conversion included in this commentary, it also indicated the chances of postponing the coming of the Antichrist through returning to the virtues. There should be a return to an austere way of life, as conducted by the faithful during the unspoilt days of the early Church. We should be reminded that each effort toward spiritual reform had been presented at that time, at least by its adherents, as a return to these beginnings, and by its opponents, of course, as a dangerous novelty. Signs of revival were, according to those who noted them, greeted by joyous surprise that the ruination of the world, although not turned aside, was at least slowed down. Sometimes there was also the joyful discovery that the idealized antiquity had been equalled or even surpassed by those signs of revival.

Indications of this revival as a postponement of the coming of the Antichrist can be found from the earliest Middle Ages. A synod at Tours

---

[14] *Homiliae in Ezechielem*, cxvi. 22–3 (*PL*, lxxvi. 1010–11).
[15] *Moralia*, XXVIII. vii. 15 (*PL*, lxxvi. 484–5).
[16] Ibid., XXXIV. iii. 5–7 (719–21).

complimented Queen Radigunde (d. 587) with the announcement that the worn-out world approaching its end had awoken to new bloom due to her assiduity in faith, and that which had threatened to die of chill had been made warm by the glow of her love.[17] A similar compliment was given to Charlemagne. According to Alcuin, the entire Church should express its gratitude to God because He had given to the Christians of the latter days of the world such a pious, careful, and just leader and defender.[18] And two centuries later, in 1027, the bishops who participated at the Council of Toulouges-Roussillon declared agreement in a Truce of God treaty: 'because the commandment of God and the entire Christian religion has been reduced to practically nothing and because as well, as has been written, justice spreads and brotherly love grows cold'.[19]

Mostly, however, this commentary of Gregory the Great on the verse from Job, 'Want shall go before his face', we find paraphrased in eulogies of saints as for instance in a sermon on Saint Benedict, held by Odo of Cluny (who died in 942), or in the preface to the *Life* of Gerald of Aurillac, which he also wrote.[20] I mention still another example, given by Bernard of Clairvaux in 1150, when he wrote the *Life* of Malachy, the archbishop of Armagh, who was a friend of his. According to its prologue this holy bishop postponed the coming of the Antichrist by his virtue, being already announced by deterioration of prophecy, virtues, and the gift of performing miracles. Bernard wrote an ingenious paraphrase of this commentary in order to introduce the *Life of Malachy* to its readers and listeners:

> It was always considered praiseworthy to record the illustrious lives of the saints so that they could serve as a mirror and good example; they could be as it were a relish for the life of men on earth (Job 7. 1). In this way they are still alive among us, even after death. They call back to the true life many of those who are dead while they live. Now indeed the very rarity of holiness requires it, since our age is only too lacking in holy men. We are so aware of this need at present that we are all doubtlessly struck by the saying: 'Because iniquity shall abound the love of many shall grow cold.' (Matt. 24. 12). And I suspect that he is already at hand, or at least close by, of whom is written: 'Want shall go before his face' (Job, 41. 13: 'Et faciem eius precedit egestas').

---

[17] *Historia Francorum*, ix. 39 (p. 527).
[18] Alcuin, *Letters* 23 and 121 (*MGH*, *Epp.* iv. 61, 176).
[19] J. D. Mansi, *Sacrorum Conciliorum . . . Collectio*, xix. 483.
[20] *Sermo de sancto Benedicto*, iii (*PL*, cxxxiii. 722); *De vita sancti Geraldi*, *praefatio* (*PL*, cxxxiii. 641).

Unless I am mistaken this is Antichrist, whom famine and sterility of all good precedes and accompanies. Then whether he is the messenger of one already here or a presage of one still to come, the need is all too evident.[21]

This Bernardine text gives the impression that the eschatological commentary of Pope Gregory the Great counted in the twelfth century already as a commonly accepted literary metaphor. Evidence for this impression appears also in a pamphlet of Cardinal Mathew of Albano (d. 1136), a Cluniac diehard who rejected any effort to reform the monastic customs of this religious order after the example of the Cistercians. About 1132 he addressed a violent pamphlet to a group of Benedictine abbots in the archdiocese of Reims, who had come together in a provincial chapter to reform the monastic way of life in their abbeys. With this reform they intended to come closer to the way of life followed in antiquity by the founders of monasticism, the Fathers of the Desert. Therefore they also imitated more or less the hermits and the Cistercians, who were already striving for the same ideal. The opposition of Cardinal Mathew to this reform programme merits some special attention. For in the midst of his other objections to the abbots' reform programme, he applied the metaphor about the announcement of the Antichrist in an ironical way, to ridicule their efforts:

God be blessed. Because although the Antichrist is on his way, as is written: 'Want shall go before his face', God has nevertheless preserved people of quality and placed them before you as bright shining lights and glistening stars to chase away the darkness spread out in a dense cloud which surrounds you in your monastic way of life.[22]

Regarding the use Saint Bernard and Cardinal Mathew made here of their adaptations of this eschatological commentary, we may conclude that both of them were aware of the negative appreciation of all the developments of the recent past which still existed in the twelfth century; in their opinion this could not be presented as a return to the ideal values and norms of antiquity. This conclusion finds a strong affirmation in the

---

[21] *S. Bernardi Opera* (ed. J. Leclercq, iii. 307), but quoting here the translation by R. T. Meyer, *Bernard of Clairvaux: The Life and Death of Saint Malachie the Irishman*, Cistercian Studies 10 (Kalamazoo, 1978), p. 11.
[22] See the Latin text in *William, Abbot of St Thierry: A Colloquium at the Abbey of St Thierry, 1976*, Cistercian Studies 94 (Kalamazoo, 1987), pp. 65–6, lines 8–12.

prologue of Orderic Vitalis to the fifth book of his *Ecclesiastical History*. Orderic, a monk of St Evroul in Normandy, wrote this work with much attention to the history of his own days, that is to say from about 1066. He was born in 1075 in Mercia, but being of French origin, he considered the year 1066 as an important date. It was the beginning of his own time, irrespective of the fact that he wrote the greatest part of this *History* between 1127 and 1136.

In his prologue to the fifth book he mentions also his own history, how his father entrusted him, at the age of five, to a parish priest, from whom he received the first rudiments of learning; and how, six years later, his father sent him to St Evroul to enter into the service of the Eternal King, and where he bore (until his death in 1141) the easy yoke of the Lord and joyfully walked in the way of God to the best of his abilities. He always devoted his mind to work of some worth. Orderic considered the writing of his *Ecclesiastical History*, which he officially composed on the order of his abbot, as an example of this.

In relation to the recent history Orderic described, the end of this prologue contains a clear statement on the Antichrist:

> If our bishops and other rulers were so holy in their lives that miracles might be performed by God's will for them and through them—as they so often were by the Fathers of old—and spread abroad in books to warm the hearts of their readers, reminding men of this age of the glory and wondrous works of their first masters, then I would shake off sloth and exert myself to write down things worthy to be told for the eager eyes of future readers. But indeed since now is the time when the love of many waxes cold and iniquity abounds, miracles, which are the proofs of holiness, grow more rare, whilst crimes and sorrowful complaints are multiplied all over the world. The altercations of prelates and bloody wars provide more material for the historian's pen than the treatises of theologians or the fasts and prophecies of ascetics. The time of the Antichrist draws near, preceded, as God made known to the blessed Job, by a drying up of miracles and a growing frenzy of vices in those who give themselves up to fleshly lusts.[23]

This subject comes up again in two of the prologues and in one of the epilogues to other books of the *Ecclesiastical History*, although here Orderic does not explicitly refer to the coming of the Antichrist. But he does

[23] *Historia ecclesiastica*, v. 1, ed. M. Chibnall (*OMT*, 1972), iii. 9.

complain frequently about the moral decline of the society of his own times, criticising the aberrant and frivolous behaviour of many contemporaries who sought novelties and adopted a disgraceful protest culture. They rejected the tradition of honest men, he said, ridiculing the advice of their priests and indulging in a barbarous lifestyle and forms of dress. But these *moderni* whose frivolous clothing, hair, shoes etc. he condemned so vigorously, were not the younger generation of his age, but were people who could be found already in the days of his youth.[24] This despicable modern behaviour began, in his opinion, in 1066, and so at the beginning of his own times. It was even to be found with members of the Cistercian order, and he accused them of hypocrisy and vanity about their ascetic way of life. He condemned those teachers who preferred modern ways to the traditional customs of the early Fathers, and aligned himself with those who were resisting current forces for renewal. But he could not be totally consistent in his rejection of all things new. So we find him praising a novelty like the First Crusade to Jerusalem, which could be explained away as a restoration and return to a more distant past, and was not therefore to be regarded as a deviation from a previous situation. But as already mentioned, he refused to recognize a revival of ancient monasticism in the rise of the Cistercian order.

In the same way other ecclesiastical historians of the time, such as Guibert of Nogent and Hugh of Fleury, had also to strike a balance between an idealized distant past which they saw as belonging to Antiquity, and the recent past whose events they could remember, and in which they discovered signs of the coming of the Antichrist. The difficulties which they encountered may however explain why William of Malmesbury (who was by comparison a better scholar) was an exception who managed to avoid adopting an eschatological interpretation of this kind.[25] It may also be noted that he was a monk living in an abbey influenced by Cluny, and yet he dared to deliver a far more favourable judgement on the Cistercians than did Orderic at St Evroul.

So whilst many clergy were fearful of the recent past because they thought its moral deviations indicated an eschatological threat, a more positive attitude towards it was to be detected within the literary circles of a restricted social group amongst the student population. These younger men, becoming weary of constantly having to study classical authors,

---

[24] Cf. Bredero, 'Medieval mentalities and their misunderstandings', *Christendom and Christianity* (Grand Rapids and Edinburgh, 1994), ch. 2.
[25] A comparison of these authors is provided by N. Lettinck, *Geschiedbeschouwing en beleving van de eigen tijd in de eerste helft van de twaalfde eeuw* (Amsterdam, 1983).

expressed their opposition to the past in satirical verses known as the *Carmina Burana*. It was a type of protest which was still more clearly articulated by the Oxford cleric Walter Map in his *Triflings of Courtiers*. Map declared that because of the acclaim that was constantly accorded to *antiquitas* an amazing miracle had taken place: 'the dead live and the living are buried'. He produced a remarkable explanation for this statement: 'In foolish farces we celebrate in verse the divine nobility of the Charleses and the Pippins; but about the emperors of our own day no one speaks.' Further on he comments that every period seems to be dissatisfied with its *modernitas*. He suggested that this was a period of about a hundred years, during which the most important events would be remembered, and the memory of them would be transmitted by parents and grandparents. For the same reason he argued that his own writings would only be properly appreciated by later generations after they had achieved the authoritative status of belonging to *antiquitas*.[26]

This generally accepted disapproval of the recent past and the corresponding appreciation of antiquity is to be explained by the eschatological view of history which was completely valid for many historians of the day. Since they were clerics their historical narrative had to follow contemporary theological theories about man's pilgrimage through the world. The main task of history was to confirm this interpretation by providing actual examples to illustrate it, and it was a theology which accepted eschatological expectations about the end of time which would come about with the advent of the Antichrist. The recent past was to be seen in the framework of this religious eschatology as an interval, an eschatological interim period, which marked the initial transition from *antiquitas* to heavenly salvation, but which was separated from it by the time of Antichrist. This explains in large measure why the recent past was treated so negatively by each generation in turn: the moral shortcomings of mankind and especially of the clergy must mark the prelude to the appearance of Antichrist.

Such an eschatological interpretation seems to me to be a basic explanation for our usual periodization of history, and in particular for our term 'Middle Ages'. Both the expression and the negative connotations attached to this terminology go back to medieval beliefs that the recent past had to be an eschatologically frightening interim period, a 'meantime'. This possibly surprising conclusion is in agreement with what has long been

---

[26] *De nugis curialium*, i. 30 and iv. 5, ed. M. R. James; rev. C. N. L. Brooke and R. A. B. Myers (*OMT*, 1983).

known about the origin of the term 'Middle Ages'. I do not want to repeat the negative judgements about the medieval period which one can find in textbooks from the Renaissance and Reformation onwards, but I do want to emphasize that even in the Middle Ages themselves people were prepared to refer to the recent past as a 'Dark Age', a *media tempestas* or *temps moyen*.[27] I should also like to remind you that the Renaissance and the Reformation came in their turn to belong to the Middle Ages, that the people of those times also judged the earlier period from their knowledge of the recent past, and that they condemned it in strongly abusive language derived from this same eschatological vocabulary. This was because of their longing to return to the ideals, values, and norms of a Christian or at least Christianized antiquity: but probably they too were anxious to postpone the coming of the Antichrist, which they anticipated on account of their recognition of eschatological signs occurring in the recent past.

---

[27] L. Varga, *Das Schlagwort vom Finsteren Mittelalter* (Vienna, 1932), pp. 5–35; J. Huizinga, 'Een schakel in de ontwikkeling van de term middeleeuwen', *Verzamelde Werken* (Haarlem, 1949), pp. 437–48.

A NEW WRITING OF JOACHIM OF FIORE: PRELIMINARY OBSERVATIONS

by STEPHEN WESSLEY

WITHIN the last decade noteworthy efforts have been made to provide for a better understanding of Joachim of Fiore through new editions of his work and the establishment of a more exact chronology for the events in his life. Under the direction of Kurt-Victor Selge a *Herausgeberkommission der kritischen Gesamtausgabe der Werke Joachims von Fiore* has been established, a symposium on the manuscript traditions of Joachim's work has been held under its auspices, and new critical editions are expected to be forthcoming soon. Professor Selge has contributed significantly to these efforts with his study of the chronology of Joachim's writings and his edition of the *Praephatio sive Prologus super Apocalypsim*.[1] I am building on this work and, of course, the outstanding work of such scholars as Marjorie Reeves, and hope now to identify a distinctive stage in Joachim of Fiore's career.

When Abbot Joachim wrote in his *Expositio in Apocalypsim* about his noted Easter eve vision, he asserted that he had received an insight into the plenitude of the Book of Revelation and the entire, *tota*, concordance of the Old and New Testaments.[2] He marked this 'revelatio' as the significant turning point in his understanding of John's Apocalypse. His 'revelatio' opened the closed door that had blocked his progress for a year on this exegesis and was an event that made him more bold to write.[3] Similarly, in his *Psalterium decem chordarum* Joachim wrote about a vision at Pentecost of a ten-stringed psaltery that showed him the mystery of the Trinity and served as the source of inspiration for the book

---

[1] Kurt-Victor Selge, 'L'origine delle opere di Gioacchino da Fiore', *L'attesa della fine dei tempi nel Medioevo* (Bologna, 1990), pp. 87–131; and 'Eine Einführung Joachims von Fiore in die Johannesapokalypse', *Deutsches Archiv für Erforschung des Mittelalters* 46 (1990), pp. 85–131, edition on pp. 102–31.

[2] Joachim of Fiore, *Expositio in Apocalypsim* (Venice, 1527; repr. Frankfurt a. M., 1964), fol. 39v: '. . . subito mihi meditanti aliquid quadam mentis oculis intelligentie claritate percepta de plenitudine libri huius et tota veteris ac novi testamenti concordia. Revelatio facta est. . . .'

[3] Ibid., fo. 39r–v, 'Aliquid in libro isto meditanti occurrere pro quo confisus de dono Dei audacior factus sum ad scribendum. Quinimmo in silendo et non scribendo timidior, ne quando tacenti mihi diceretur a iudice. Serve male et piger sciebas quia meto ubi non seminavi, et congrego ubi non sparsi. Oportuit ergo te committere pecuniam meam nummulariis et veniens recepissem utique quod meum est, cum usura.'

itself.[4] In describing his visions Joachim acknowledges two major stages in his intellectual development. Joachim's visions, generally dated between 1183 and 1185,[5] have received renewed attention in the last few years. In one article Robert Lerner stressed the significance of the Easter eve vision for Joachim's pivotal understanding of Revelation 'as a continuous story which revealed the entire history of the Church' and a period of earthly bliss. According to Lerner, this was a breakthrough for Joachim and was one of Joachim's three 'big ideas'; the other two were the concordance of Scripture and the Trinitarian scheme of history. In his discussion of Joachim's overall development Lerner went on to propose that, with Joachim's penchant for threes, something was missing. Since the Pentecost vision supporting a Trinitarian plan is connected with the Holy Spirit and the *Psalterium decem chordarum*, and the Easter eve vision supporting Joachim's reading of Revelation as a continuous story, the history of the Church, is connected to Christ and the *Expositio in Apocalypsim*, Lerner observed, 'The symmetry is almost too neat and falls short of perfection only in the lack of a "patrological" vision . . . inspiring the *Book of Concord* . . .'.[6]

The Pentecost vision and the Easter vision, dated between 1183 and 1185, are regarded by historians as symbols of Joachim's intellectual development and understood by Joachim to be heavenly validation that also inspired in him the confidence to write about his new insights into Scripture. But what had spurred on Joachim's earlier exegetical enterprise? Joachim confessed to working on an interpretation of Revelation before his Easter vision[7] and although he wrote his main texts when visiting the

---

[4] Joachim of Fiore, *Psalterium decem chordarum* (Venice, 1527; repr. Frankfurt a. M., 1965), fo. 227r–v.

[5] For arguments for specific and differing chronologies see Robert Lerner, 'Joachim of Fiore's breakthrough to chiliasm', *Cristianesimo nella storia*, 6 (1985), pp. 489–512, in particular pp. 495–6; Bernard McGinn, *The Calabrian Abbot* (New York, 1985), p. 22; and Kurt-Victor Selge, 'L'origine', pp. 108–13.

[6] Lerner, 'Joachim of Fiore's breakthrough to chiliasm', p. 502.

[7] Ibid., pp. 496–8; Joachim of Fiore, *Expositio in Apocalypsim*, fo. 39r–v. Apparently Joachim worked on his texts over a long period; see Kurt-Victor Selge, 'L'origine', pp. 87–131 for a description of this. At the end of his life Joachim was concerned that the exemplars be safeguarded: 'Rogo ex parte dei omnipotentis coabbates meos et priores et ceteros fratres metuentes dominum et ea qua posse uideor auctoritate precipio, quatinus presens scriptum aut exemplar habentes secum ac si pro testamento opuscula que hactenus confecisse uideor et si quid me de nouo usque ad diem obitus mei contigerit scriptitare quamcitius poterint collecta omnia, relictis in salua custodia exemplaribus, apostolico examini representent recipientes ab eadem sede uice mea correctionem . . .' in *Abbot Joachim of Fiore: Liber de Concordia Noui ac Veteris Testamenti*, ed. E. R. Daniel, *Transactions of the American Philosophical*

Cistercian house at Casamari from early 1183 to late 1184, he had been very busy with analysing Scripture before that period. For this early activity we have as a source the *Vita* of Abbot Joachim written, it is argued by Herbert Grundmann, by a Florensian after Joachim's death (1202), but no later than 1209.[8] If we follow the sequence of events in this *Vita* of Abbot Joachim, it is clear that before Joachim journeyed to Casamari, where he was to have his two famous visions, he had earlier worked single-mindedly on the study of Scripture. As new abbot of the monastery of Corazzo (shortly before 1177) Joachim began as a faithful and prudent manager. After Joachim was elected abbot, the anonymous writer reports, 'A faithful and prudent man, he thus began to dispense the temporal substance faithfully and prudently, but all his prudence turned in the exercise of spiritual growth, not at all did he wish to neglect the grace which he received; but he thought, spoke and commented on the understanding of Scripture that was given to him.'[9] Because it is evident to us from the anonymous text that the two visions mentioned above come later, we need to ask what was the source of Joachim's inspiration to which the anonymous writer referred, i.e. 'the understanding of Scripture that was given to him'.

From the period before 1177 Joachim is commenting on Scripture because he did not wish to neglect the grace he had received in the understanding of Scripture given to him, and he wanted to teach others what had been revealed to him. When and where did Joachim receive this grace or insight? If as outlined at the start of this paper the genesis of his two other 'big ideas' are represented as revelations given to him, what about

---

Society, 73, 8 (Philadelphia, 1983), p. 5. The process of manuscript transmission and, in particular, the correction of the Fiore manuscripts have been studied by Fabio Troncarelli and a detailed article with emphasis on Padua, Biblioteca Antoniana, MS 322, is soon to be published by him. Also, seldom mentioned in regard to the Fiore manuscripts is possible damage from the fire of 1215 that burned the original monastery founded by Joachim and that preceded the move of the Florensians to the present-day site of San Giovanni in Fiore. Unless it was symbolic, as a needed purification after the 1215 condemnation, did the fire result in any damage to their manuscripts and thus produce a possible immediate need for new and quickly produced copies such as Padua, Biblioteca Antoniana, MS 322?

[8] Herbert Grundmann, 'Zur Biographie Joachims von Fiore und Rainers von Ponza', *Ausgewählte Aufsätze, II, Joachim von Fiore* (Stuttgart, 1977), pp. 281–94, esp. pp. 281–2, 293–4, and 297.

[9] The anonymous *Vita*, in Grundmann, 'Zur Biographie Joachims von Fiore und Rainers von Ponza', pp. 345–6, 'Cepit itaque vir fidelis et prudens prudenter et fideliter temporalem substantiam dispensare, sed omnis prudentia eius in spiritalis profectus exercitio versabatur, nullatenus negligere volens gratiam quam accepit; sed meditabatur, eloquebatur et commentabatur in data sibi desuper intelligentia scripturarum. . . .'

the genesis of his first 'big idea'—his understanding of the concordance of Scripture? Was this the result of a separate and distinctive revelation? The anonymous biographer, who also mentions the Easter and Pentecost visions, provides an answer when we read his text with this question in mind. The anonymous biography of Joachim, as we have it, opens with Joachim's pilgrimage in the Holy Land.[10] The Florensian biographer begins with the announcement: 'Our Moses having received the revelation of the two-fold law descended from the mountain.'[11] Receiving the revelation of the two-fold law like a Moses is, for the anonymous biographer, the impetus for Joachim's spiritual odyssey. Thus Joachim is credited with receiving three 'revelations': the Pentecost vision connected to the Holy Spirit, the Easter vision connected to Christ, the Son, and this Mosaic vision of the two-fold law connected to God the Father.[12] Even the wording of the later Easter vision suggests a pattern that includes an earlier vision of a concordance of Scripture. When Robert Lerner studied the Easter vision he asked why did Joachim word his description of his Easter vision such that it was purported to reveal the plenitude of the Book of Revelation and the *entire*, 'tota', concordance of Scripture. It can be seen now that this word 'tota' was necessary because Joachim had long before been exploring and writing about the basic two-fold concordance of Scripture that had been revealed to him in a Mosaic fashion on the mount at the beginning of his journey.

What was the content and form of his Mosaic vision? In Book Two of his *Liber concordie* Joachim speaks about having been shown a vision of the special connection of the two Testaments on a mountain top. Comparing himself to Moses receiving the Ten Commandments on the mount, Joachim claimed he himself through the gift of grace saw the relationship of the two Testaments on the top of the mountain.[13] (Here it should be

[10] Grundmann argued that the anonymous *Vita* has survived only in part; the first and last parts are missing. See Grundmann, 'Zur Biographie Joachims von Fiore und Rainers von Ponza', pp. 292–4.

[11] The anonymous *Vita* in ibid., p. 342, 'Moises noster gemine revelatione legis accepta de monte descendit . . .'.

[12] To see Joachim's intellectual development in terms of these three visions, each connected to one of the three persons of the Trinity, is to understand Joachim according to the programme he and his biographer put forth. These visions can be seen also to have occurred in Trinitarian sequence if one accepts Robert Lerner's dating of the visions in 'Joachim of Fiore's breakthrough to chiliasm', pp. 492–6 and 508.

[13] *Abbot Joachim of Fiore: Liber de Concordia Noui ac Veteris Testamenti*, pp. 145–6, 'Has, inquam, duas arbores sublimes et condenpsas ponamus ante oculos mentis, et sic in eis Patrem et Filium, quorum alius ex alio est principaliter intelligamus; ut tamen cum eis genus hominum secundarie accipiamus, quia, etsi disiuncti sumus a bono deo condictione nature, gratie

pointed out that Joachim and the anonymous biographer each speak about all three visions.) Likewise, Joachim claimed, it was necessary for him, just as for Moses, to make an exemplar of what he saw in order to teach others.[14] The basic relationship of the two Testaments, Joachim tells us, was revealed in an image of one tree growing out of the top of another and he understood also that he received a divine mandate to record this for teaching.

There has long been a general consensus among scholars that Joachim's early ideas evolved out of his understanding of the concordance of Scripture; for Joachim not only are there parallels in what has taken place within Scripture but also between what took place in the Bible and what occurred afterward in ecclesiastical history. In the *Enchiridion* Joachim explained that his early insight into the 'concordiarum sacramenta' was that concordance between the Old Testament and Christ as its head would also apply to Christ's body, the Church.[15] For example, an early

---

tamen ipsius participatione coniuncti. Nunquam enim diceret euangelista scribens dominicam genealogiam: "Qui fuit Ade, qui fuit dei", nisi eundem primum hominem filium esse dei per adoptionem sentiret. In prima itaque cedro—de cuius medulla et ramorum uertice nata est arbor secunda, aut dubium quod similis eius—populus ille antiquus intelligendum est qui, sicut iam superius, diximus creatus est specialius ad ymaginem Patris, sicut et sequens populus ad ymaginem Filii. Si autem secundum illud quod ait dominus Moysi: "Vide ut omnia facias secundum exemplar quod ostensum est tibi in monte", non quasi ex similitudine fingenda est ueritas, sed magis, ueritate perspecta, propter eos qui tardioris sunt ingenii, similitudo significans adhibenda, talem nos cedri huius ymaginem assignare oportet, qualem eam pro dono gratie in montis uertice contemplati sumus, non quales in siluis montium consueuerunt inueniri.' Also *Liber concordie Noui ac Veteris Testamenti* (Venice, 1519; repr. Frankfurt a. M., 1964), fo. 19r. As can be seen, Joachim's comment about his Mosaic vision comes in his discussion of the relationship of the two trees/two testaments, the topic of the chapter. Because this part of Book Two of the *Concordia* was written after his later visions, there is one mention at the very beginning of this chapter of a third tree that grows from these two. The chapter, however, treats only of the two trees and Joachim's mention of his Mosaic vision is immediately related to the two trees/two testaments discussion. See also Marjorie Reeves and Beatrice Hirsch-Reich, *The Figurae of Joachim of Fiore* (Oxford, 1972), pp. 32–3.

   For Joachim's tree imagery also see *Abbot Joachim of Fiore: Liber de Concordia Noui ac Veteris Testamenti*, pp. xxviii–xxxv and 107–12, 145–84.

[14] Ibid., pp. 145–6, 'Si autem secundum illud quod ait dominus Moysi: "Vide ut omnia facias secundum exemplar quod ostensum est tibi in monte", non quasi ex similitudine fingenda est ueritas, sed magis, ueritate perspecta, propter eos qui tardioris sunt ingenii, similitudo significans adhibenda, talem nos cedri huius ymaginem assignare oportet, qualem eam pro dono gratie in montis uertice contemplati sumus, non quales in siluis montium consueuerunt inueniri.'

[15] Joachim of Fiore, *Enchiridion super Apocalypsim*, ed. E. Burger (Toronto, 1986), pp. 47–8, 'Sed quia tempus adhuc parumper distat, ut ille intellectus qui perfecte erit in Spiritu assignari queat, magisque nobis incumbit assignare ea quae in statu secundo completa sunt,

STEPHEN WESSLEY

hallmark of the abbot's thought[16] is the matching of the persecutions of the Jews with the persecutions of the Church that had already occurred, along with some parallels still to be fulfilled. What is considered Joachim's earliest tract, the *Expositio de prophetia ignota* (1184), is held as an example of this approach since it contains such a concordance parallel but no mention of his famous three *status*.[17]

No writing of Joachim, however, has been verified as coming from the period before 1184, before the Easter and Pentecost revelations mentioned above, for us to be able to evaluate the earliest stage of Joachim's intellectual development. The survival of a major work from his early period is unlikely because the anonymous biographer noted that in this period Joachim did not violate Cistercian norms about writing, i.e., Abbot Joachim knew he needed permission of the General Chapter to produce a book.[18] When the biographer described Joachim's exegetical activity what he has described is Joachim instructing, teaching, and speaking to his

---

respondentia operibus testimonii prioris, sicut in opere *Concordiae*, quantum Deus donavit, ostendimus, operae pretium credidi ea ipsa quae consonare veteribus simplici assertione monstravimus, pro eo scilicet quod historiae quas ecclesiasticas dicimus, minus authenticae judicantur, ex libro Apocalypsis qui tantae est auctoritatis ostendere, ut tanto securius illi operi fidem accomodare possimus, quanto concordiam rerum et temporum quae in eo praestante Domino claruisse cognoscitur, nequaquam sensus hominis adinvenit et protulit sed is qui in utroque testimonio loquitur Spiritus edidit prophetiae.

Denique et ego cum librum hunc lectitare coepissem, et adhuc concordiarum sacramenta nescirem, quo illuc impetu a primo ductus sim nescio, Deus scit. Unde scio quod nequaquam historiarum peritia ad concordiae notitiam perductus sum, sed sola praeteritorum operum, hoc est, testimonii veteris comparatione pulsatus, credens discordare non posse in corpore quod in capite concors inveni, nec otiosum fore in reliquis sanctis quod in patriarchis et apostolis concordare perpendi, dedi operam in hoc ipso, ut quantum Deus mihi concederet testimoniorum concordiam compilarem, sed an scrupulosis mentibus satisfecerim nescio.'

[16] See Bernard McGinn, *Visions of the End* (New York, 1979), p. 315, n. 33, where he makes this observation in reference to Joachim's *Expositio de prophetia ignota*.

[17] McGinn, *The Calabrian Abbot*, pp. 22–4, and 'Joachim and the Sibyl', *Cîteaux*, 24 (1973), pp. 97–138.

[18] Grundmann, 'Zur Biographie Joachims von Fiore und Rainers von Ponza', p. 346, '... reverens tamen zelum ordinis, in quo stabat, quia non erat ei licitum scribere sine licentia Capituli generalis'. See also ibid., pp. 307–8, and J.-M. Canivez, *Statuta capitulorum generalium Ordinis Cisterciensis*, 1 (Louvain, 1933), p. 26, '"Si liceat alicui novos libros dictare." Nulli liceat abbati, nec monacho, nec novitio, libros facere, nisi forte cuiquam in generali capitulo concessum fuerit.' As I discussed in chapter two of my book, *Joachim of Fiore and Monastic Reform* (New York, 1990), the anonymous biographer was concerned to show that Joachim followed ecclesiastical regulations consistently, and in this case St Paul's admonition (I Cor. 14. 39–40), 'And so, my dear brothers, by all means be ambitious to prophesy ..., but let everything be done with propriety and in order', carried the watchword.

20

monks, as any good abbot, according to Benedict's *Rule*.[19] What *is* significant, for us, is that the anonymous biographer reported that Joachim did comment on Scripture, instructed his monks, according to the special understanding given to him. Consequently, it is plausible that all that might survive from this period is not any major tract, but, possibly, a short instructional piece or notes[20] that record Joachim's commentary. If such a short piece is found, according to what I have outlined, it would be likely to draw on Joachim's principle of concordance that parallels such events as the suffering of the Jews and the persecutions of the Church, employ the basic tree imagery described above, and betray no indication of a third age of the Holy Spirit, new orders, Joachim's disapproval of the Cistercians—any later concepts developed with or after his Easter and Pentecost revelations. I have found a text that fits these criteria.

This discovery has come in a roundabout way. In 1990 Kurt-Victor Selge edited Joachim's *Praephatio sive Prologus super Apocalypsim*, dated to 1188–92. He used six manuscripts for this edition; there are three additional manuscript copies of this text: Rein, 61, 146v–152v, Valenciennes, Bibl. mun., 516, 162v–165v, and Zwettl, 326, 3r–10r.[21] Rein and Valenciennes are the same as Selge's edition, except that the Valenciennes manuscript contains only the second half of Selge's text. The manuscript from the Cistercian monastery of Zwettl is different.[22] It contains another section that amounts to a separate text embedded within a text identical to Selge's edited *Praefatio*. This text breaks the flow of the *Praefatio* commentary and was apparently copied by mistake within the body of the *Praefatio*. Also, at the end of this manuscript copy of the *Praefatio* from Zwettl is a fragment, Joachim's exegesis of Rev. 6. 6, that is related to his

---

[19] See *Benedicti regula*, ed. R. Hanslik, *Corpus scriptorum ecclesiasticorum latinorum*, 75 (Vienna, 1977), p. 23, '. . . ut capacibus discipulis mandata domini uerbis proponere . . .'.

[20] Joachim's sermons and short instructional pieces were not only not itemized in his corpus to be submitted to the Pope, but even today remain incompletely catalogued.

[21] See F. Stegmüller, *Repertorium biblicum medii aevi*, 3 (Madrid, 1951), p. 226. There is a real need to publish a 'definitive' list of the manuscripts of Joachim of Fiore (and Pseudo-Joachim); one manuscript text, not recorded before, that I wish to note here is Joachim's *De septem sigillis* in Bruges, Stedelijke Openbare Bibl., MS 86, fos 100r–101r. See the edition of this work in Marjorie Reeves and Beatrice Hirsch-Reich, 'The seven seals in the writings of Joachim of Fiore', *Recherches de théologie ancienne et médiévale*, 21 (1954), pp. 239–47.

[22] There is a short description of MS 326 in Stephan Rössler, 'Verzeichniss der Handschriften der Bibliothek des Stiftes Zwettl' in *Xenia Bernardina*, pt 2, vol. 1, *Die Handschriften-Verzeichnisse der Cistercienser-Stifte* (Vienna, 1891), p. 413, but no mention of Joachim of Fiore as the author of the *Praefatio*, which Rössler calls the *Explanatio libri Apocalipsis*, and no notice of this additional new text or the fragment on Rev. 6. 6. He dates Zwettl, MS 326 as 'XII u. XIII Jahr'.

commentaries on the same verse in the *Expositio in Apocalypsim* and the *Concordia*,[23] but is different from them. For some reason this Zwettl manuscript, dated to the twelfth and thirteenth centuries, contains these additional short texts. For us the significant text is the one embedded within the text of the *Praefatio*,[24] extending for three and one-half columns from fos 8v–9v. It contains an explanation of the relationship of the two Testaments similar to but more primitive than that found in Joachim's 'Tree of Two Advents' in his *Liber figurarum*.[25] One-half of the text uses the tree imagery explicitly; the second relates the various persecutions of the Jews to those of the Church. This text is a new version of what has been called the *Epistola subsequentium figurarum*. There are only three other manuscripts of this text extant: two in Paris, Bibl. Nat., Lat. 11864 and 3595, and one in Rome, Vat. Lat. 3822.[26] Using Leone Tondelli's edition and notes to compare the Paris manuscripts with the Vatican manuscript, one can see that the Vatican manuscript has additional material, such as an updating of the end to 1290, that comes from Joachim's followers; the Paris manuscripts, however, reflect concepts found in Joachim's writings.[27] The script of the *Epistola* in Paris, Bibl. Nat., Lat. 11864 has been dated to the first decade of the thirteenth century and the text of the *Epistola* (without this title, as is the case also of Zwettl, 326) is found here with only Joachim's genuine writings.[28] Leone

---

[23] *Abbot Joachim of Fiore: Liber de Concordia Noui ac Veteris Testamenti*, p. 295 and Joachim of Fiore, *Expositio in Apocalypsim*, fo. 115r–v. I am examining this fragment in the light of Joachim's condemned Trinitarian ideas.

[24] A comparison between Selge's edition and the Zwettl text shows that they are extremely close; where there are variants, in as much as I have been able to pursue this aspect of research now, the wording in Zwettl seems to make more sense, i.e., following standards of the internal logic of the text, scriptural reference or Joachim's choice of language in his other writings.

[25] See tavola II in Leone Tondelli, Marjorie Reeves, and Beatrice Hirsch-Reich, *Il Libro delle figure dell'abate Gioachino da Fiore*, 2 (Turin, 1953) and Reeves and Hirsch-Reich, *The Figurae of Joachim of Fiore*, pp. 153–9.

[26] Marjorie Reeves, *The Influence of Prophecy in the Later Middle Ages* (Oxford, 1969), p. 518; Paris, Bibl. Nat., MS Lat. 11864, fos 151v–152v; Paris, Bibl. Nat., MS Lat. 3595, fos 28r–29r; and Rome, MS Vat. Lat. 3822, fos 3v–4r.

[27] The text, in its later version, has been edited by Jeanne Bignami-Odier, 'Notes sur deux manuscrits de la bibliothèque du Vatican contenant des traités inédits de Joachim de Flore', *Mélanges d'archéologie et d'histoire*, 54 (1937), pp. 224–6. See Leone Tondelli, *Il Libro delle figure dell'abate Gioachino da Fiore*, 1 (Turin, 1953), pp. 41–3; Tondelli's footnotes show variants found in the Paris manuscript versions that reflect an earlier version than the Vatican text.

[28] Reeves and Hirsch-Reich, 'The *Figurae* of Joachim of Fiore: genuine and spurious collections', *Mediaeval and Renaissance Studies*, 3 (1954), p. 198; Morton Bloomfield and Marjorie Reeves, 'The penetration of Joachism into Northern Europe', *Joachim of Fiore in Christian Thought*, ed. D. West, 1 (New York, 1975), p. 116 n. 40a.

Tondelli accepted the Paris version as a genuine work of Joachim. Marjorie Reeves and Beatrice Hirsch-Reich rejected the *Epistola* as genuine because, they asserted, apart from background in his main writings, Joachim did not explain his *figurae* separately from the drawings. And in relation to the tree the *Epistola* most closely describes, in the *Liber figurarum* there are differences—such as the term 'Christus Iudex' not found in the *Liber figurarum*.[29] Reeves and Hirsch-Reich give the impression that the text, as presented in the Paris manuscripts, contains Joachim's authentic thought, but not as found exactly in the *Liber figurarum*. Their objections to its genuineness fall away if one sees the *Epistola* as a record of Joachim's thought not from the end of his career but from the beginning.

The text manifestly contains Joachim's language, his concordance parallels, and his unique division of the generations of the Old and New Testaments. Scholarly effort in the past has been to try to relate the text of the *Epistola subsequentium figurarum* to Joachim's very mature writings and the *figurae* which represent the summary of his work. The *Epistola* is intriguing because there is no third age of the Spirit, no future orders, no disapproval of the Cistercians. It has a basic concordance of the Old and New Testaments in the image of one tree growing out of another. The early examples of this work carry no title and the style is that of instructional notes, as Reeves and Hirsch-Reich point out,[30] so it would be better to refer to it simply as an instructional writing rather than as an *epistola*.

The text explains Joachim's concordance in an elemental way: the entire span of time from the birth of Christ to the end is to be forty-two generations of thirty years each. At one point in this text the generations are divided into one group of forty and another of two. The Antichrist and the end of time will come in the last two generations, in the final sixty years, according to our author. Hence, this text has all the characteristics of what we could imagine in a possible early text of Joachim. What made the Zwettl manuscript copy so arresting for me is that when the author explained this structure of generations, within the tree imagery, he dated his own place in his chronology of generations. When he wrote about the future completion of forty generations from the birth of Christ he added that it is 1176 years [from the birth of Christ]. The Zwettl manuscript

---

[29] Reeves and Hirsch-Reich, 'The *Figurae* of Joachim of Fiore', pp. 178–82, and *The Figurae of Joachim of Fiore*, pp. 109–10 and 267–8; and Tondelli, *Il Libro delle figure*, p. 41. Herbert Grundmann, *Neue Forschungen über Joachim von Fiore* (Marburg, 1950), pp. 23–4, apparently did not know about the Paris manuscript from the first decade of the 1200s.

[30] Reeves and Hirsch-Reich, *The Figurae of Joachim of Fiore*, p. 110.

reads: 'When therefore in this period from the birth of Christ forty generations are completed, it is 1176 years, only two generations remain to be completed, that is sixty years, that is two thirties in which whatever is said of the Antichrist and the end of time is to be fulfilled.'[31]

The date, 1176 years from the birth of Christ, MCLXXVI, is too distinctive to be a copyist's error for MCC, that is, a completed forty generations, 1200. Forgery or interpolation does not make any sense because the text has no specific target or patent motivation in this regard and such changes occur in Joachite texts usually only to update and in very obvious ways. (Also Joachite additions usually involve the new orders or the third age.) The only other possible significant miscopyings by a scribe that I could imagine in this case could be adding or dropping an X: therefore rendering the original date 1166 or 1186. If we assume now this is Joachim's writing, neither possibility works. If this is Joachim's text, by 1186, as we know well from his *De vita sancti Benedicti*, his writing was preoccupied with the role of the Cistercian order, the symbol of St Benedict, the third age and the new order of monks that would lead to it.[32] This text is much more basic or primitive. It has no third age,[33] no Cistercian reference, and no new order.[34] The *Praefatio* that envelops this text does show Joachim's later interests and insights.[35] In the other case a date of 1166 would put the text before Joachim's pilgrimage to the Holy Land and

---

[31] Zwettl, MS 326, fo. 9r, 'Cum ergo nativitate Christi complete sint hoc temporum xl generationes, id est mclxxvi anni, non restant nisi due generationes complende, id est anni lx, id est duo terdenarii in quibus oportet impleri quicquid de antichristo dicitur et de consummatione seculi.'

[32] See Stephen Wessley, '*Bonum est Benedicto mutare locum*: The role of the "Life of Saint Benedict" in Joachim of Fiore's monastic reform', *Revue Bénédictine*, 90 (1980), pp. 314–28.

[33] There is no mention of a period of earthly bliss and Joachim lists different interpretations of Daniel's 45 days; this period of bliss is described as short in Joachim's *De ultimis tribulationibus*, ed. E. R. Daniel, 'Abbot Joachim of Fiore: The *De ultimis tribulationibus*', in *Prophecy and Millenarianism*, ed. A. Williams (Harlow, 1980), p. 183: '... ad istam modicam et breuem pacem'.

[34] There is an ambiguous 5/7 numerical relationship here in Zwettl, MS 326, fo. 9v. But in this text one finds no indication of Joachim's subsequent use of this sequence, as for example, when he later indicated the direction of future spiritual development in the inheritor of monastic reform.

[35] See Kurt-Victor Selge's description in his 'Eine Einführung Joachims von Fiore in die Johannesapokalypse', p. 100: 'Die Theorie der drei trinitarischen "Status" in Ergänzung der alten Lehre von den sechs Weltaltern und der jüngeren Lehre von den sieben Zeiten des sechsten Weltalters liegt fertig vor, ebenso die hermeneutische Theorie von der Concordia des Alten und Neuen Testaments und der sich aus ihr in Anwendung auf die Zeit der Kirche ergebenden spiritualis intelligentia.' Also compare the wording in ibid., p. 104, for the sixth age: 'quinta in sacratissimi mundi salvatoris adventu, sexta ab eodem incepta', to Zwettl, MS 326, fo. 9r, 'sexta in iudice'.

therefore before any of his spiritual discoveries.[36] The date in this text, 1176, fits exactly the anonymous biographer's description of Joachim's activity. Elected abbot shortly before 1177, Joachim was hard at work on his commentaries of Scripture, according to his biographer, because he did not wish to neglect the grace he received in the understanding of Scripture given to him.

Other variants in Zwettl, 326 also pull the content of the text to Joachim's early period and enable the text not only to make more sense,[37] but even provide confirmation of what scholars had suggested might have been Joachim's debt to earlier exegetes. Reading this text as Joachim's own writing and accepting its accuracy opens new vistas. For example, one sentence in Zwettl, 326 concerning Daniel's forty-five days calls for particularly close attention. In his edition of the *Epistola*, Tondelli, working with two choices from his manuscripts, XII days and XLV days, chose neither and corrected the phrase concerning the days of Daniel to read 'XLII days in Daniel' to fit Joachim's famous numerology.[38] But there are no forty-two days in Daniel, only forty-two months according to Joachim.[39] There are *forty-five* days in Daniel following St Jerome's accounting for the discrepancy between Daniel's 1,290 and 1,335 days.[40] This idea of a forty-five-day period found in Jerome's writing received much discussion in medieval commentaries.[41] An understanding that the

---

[36] Grundmann, 'Zur Biographie Joachims von Fiore und Rainers von Ponza', p. 298: 'Demnach wäre Joachim 1166/67 nach dem Tod König Wilhelms I. in der Kanzlei zu Palermo tätig gewesen und danach ins Heilige Land gegangen ...'.

[37] Only a publication comparing the manuscripts, with some commentary, can make this clear (I will prepare such a study and edition). Joachim's idiosyncrasy can be seen in part by one calculation of generations: two groups of sixty-three arrived at by counting the latter part of the Old Testament twice. See Reeves and Hirsch-Reich, *The Figurae of Joachim of Fiore*, p. 9, and also p. 6: 'Now he plunges into intricate calculations of generations from which he constructs a framework which is constantly used hereafter: the generations are grouped in series of twenty-one in such a way that the Dispensation of the Old Testament is reckoned as $21+21+21$, while that of the New (which, beginning with Ozias, overlaps the Old by twenty-one generations) will likewise endure for sixty-three generations, and beyond, to the *consummatio seculi*.' See Zwettl, MS 326, fo. 9r, where the two groups of generations are arranged to number sixty-three each. This is done as noted by an overlapping, i.e., by computing the beginning of the New Testament with Isaiah and Ozias. Also, as is typical of Joachim, in this text we see some hesitancy in pronouncing when the end will occur.

[38] Tondelli, *Il Libro delle figure*, p. 42.

[39] Herbert Grundmann, *Studien über Joachim von Floris* (Leipzig, 1927), p. 52.

[40] Robert Lerner, 'Refreshment of the Saints: the time after Antichrist as a station for earthly progress in medieval thought', *Traditio*, 32 (1976), pp. 102–3.

[41] Zwettl, MS 326, fo. 9r; the sequence of day, month, year, age in the text does not seem to refer to specific earlier controversies about the length of time, especially if Lerner's 'Refreshment of the Saints' is reasonably complete, but rather expresses the idea that it is unclear what

numbers are accurate in Zwettl, 326[42] (which reinforces the notion of the integrity of the text), that is, that the reading XLV days in reference to Daniel is correct, opens up a whole new connection to Robert Lerner's noted thesis in his article, 'Refreshment of the Saints'. Lerner presented Daniel's forty-five days as a seminal concept for changes in medieval eschatological expectations and he thought it was probable that the tradition stemming from Jerome's concept had been a starting point for Joachim.[43] This now visible link to prior exegesis, envisioned as a probable starting point for Joachim, helps also to convince us of the text's validity as an early work of the abbot.

Convinced of the significance of the date in the Zwettl manuscript, I realized that the other three manuscripts on which Tondelli based his edition and critical notes and Reeves and Hirsch-Reich their observations must be checked carefully. And, though mentioned by no one else, Paris, Bibl. Nat., Lat. 11864 also has the date 1176.[44] Hence, there are four manuscript copies of this text extant; one half of the total, the two manuscripts that are the earliest and that are found only with Joachim's genuine writings, contain the date 1176.

Using the date 1176 written in this text,[45] I find that the content fits

---

Daniel's forty-five days stand for. Joachim posits in this text that the learned have said that a month can stand for a day, so Daniel's forty-five days could be forty-five months, etc., not that others have proposed this explanation for the meaning of Daniel.

[42] Zwettl, MS 326, fo. 9r, 'Quod tempus a Daniele dicitur xlv videlicet dierum.'

[43] Lerner, 'Refreshment of the Saints', pp. 97–114 and 117. See also Marjorie Reeves, 'How original was Joachim of Fiore's theology of history?', *Storia e messaggio in Gioacchino da Fiore*, *Atti del I Congresso internazionale di studi gioachimiti* (S. Giovanni in Fiore, 1980), pp. 25–41. This period of forty-five days, consonant with the earlier traditions, is a time of penance and conversion to one faith. Careful attention should be given also to the seven ages in this text to appreciate how Joachim changed them in his mature writings. With the sixth age to be that of Christ the Judge, the seventh 'in quiete animarum' in Zwettl, MS 326, fo. 9r, takes on a heavenly dimension. The seventh age is not like the description in Joachim of Fiore, *Expositio in Apocalypsim*, fos 209v–210r. Again, this helps confirm the early period of the text.

[44] Paris, Bibl. Nat., MS Lat. 11864, fo. 152v.

[45] Pietro De Leo, 'Una nuova opera di Gioacchino da Fiore? Il *Super Cantica Canticorum* in un codice cosentino del XII secolo', *L'Età dello Spirito e la fine dei tempi in Gioacchino da Fiore e nel Gioachimismo medievale*, *Atti del II Congresso internazionale di studi gioachimiti* (S. Giovanni in Fiore, 1986), pp. 435–88, and *Gioacchino da Fiore* (Soveria Mannelli, 1988), pp. 58, 129, has proposed that a particular anonymous commentary on the Song of Songs is an early work of Joachim from the last quarter of the twelfth century. Kurt-Victor Selge, 'L'origine delle opere di Gioacchino da Fiore', pp. 91–2, n. 16, thinks that the content of De Leo's text does not allow 'alcuna conclusione sulla paternità di Gioacchino . . .'. De Leo, 'Una nuova opera', p. 440, considers the Codex Cusentinus not an 'apografo, bensì di uno scritto originale'. If one accepts Fabio Troncarelli's conclusions in 'Un codice con note autografe di Gioacchino da Fiore', *Scriptorium*, 43 (1989), pp. 3–34, there is a discrepancy between the script of the two

perfectly to the early period of Joachim's career and am convinced that the text of the so-called *Epistola* as found in Zwettl, 326[46] and Paris, Bibl. Nat., Lat. 11864 should be given further consideration as evidence of Joachim's first period of exegetical activity.

---

texts. Both cannot be in Joachim's hand. An examination of the shape of the letter 'd' in the manuscripts Troncarelli and De Leo examined shows me they were written by two different hands. The notes that Troncarelli ascribes to Joachim in Rome, Biblioteca Apostolica Vaticana, MS Barb. Lat. 627, may be early, but they have been able to be dated only in a general way.

[46] Zwettl, MS 326 has the best readings and seems closest to the original.

FRANCISCAN COMMENTARIES ON
THE APOCALYPSE

by BERT ROEST

IN February 1992 I was invited to present a brief communication about Franciscan Apocalypse commentaries to the summer meeting of the Fifth Anglo-Dutch Colloquium. It is a topic which to a certain extent has a bearing on my own research. The study of Franciscan commentaries on the Apocalypse, in which some Franciscan authors developed their eschatological and apocalyptic ideas, forms part of my research on Franciscan conceptions of history and society as they appear in medieval historiography and in more speculative theological and exegetical writings. This invitation gave me a good opportunity to reflect on the problems which I had just begun to encounter while getting acquainted with Franciscan Bible commentaries. They are in fact rather unmanageable pieces of work. And I have the impression that thus far they have been the object of two fields of research which have developed in relative autonomy from each other. On the one hand, a huge amount of scholarship has been, and still is, devoted to a certain form of Franciscan apocalypticism, namely to Franciscan Joachimism in the thirteenth and fourteenth centuries, whether or not in combination with Franciscan radicalism. In this research some Franciscan commentaries on the Apocalypse and other Franciscan works with an apocalyptic bias have figured prominently, most of all the *Postilla super apocalypsim* of Peter John Olivi (1295). On the other hand there has been a re-evaluation of medieval biblical scholarship on the basis of the seminal works of Henri de Lubac and Beryl Smalley, in which the great Franciscan output of Apocalypse commentaries almost appears as an aberration.

To begin with the first type of research: since around 1880 the German scholar F. Ehrle wrote the history of Franciscan Joachimistic spiritual thought for the first time, and especially after the publication of Ernst Benz's *Ecclesia spiritualis* in 1934, which portrayed the existence of a Franciscan Joachimistic and apocalyptical Church over and against the papal Church, the so-called 'Papstkirche', an undigestible amount of scholarship has been devoted to following the penetration and persistence of Joachimism in Franciscan literature and thought. Generations of scholars—like Herbert Grundmann, Bernhard Töpfer, Marjorie Reeves, Herbert Bloomfield, Raoul Manselli, Delno Cloyd West, Paul Vian, and again Henri du Lubac—have shown the infiltration of Joachimistic thought in the Franciscan order just before 1240, its quick first apotheosis in the work of the Franciscan Gerard of Borgo San Donnino in 1254, and its importance for the intellectual outlook and ideological position of late thirteenth- and early fourteenth-century Franciscan authors such as Peter John Olivi, Ubertino of Casale and Angelo Clareno, alleged leaders of the so-called 'Spiritual' faction within the Franciscan order.[1]

The major questions within this type of research were (1) the exact nature of Joachimistic influence on various Franciscan writers, which led for example to the major disagreement between Marjorie Reeves and Aloïs Wachtel on the Joachimistic character of Alexander of Bremen's *Commentary on the Apocalypse* (written just after 1240); and (2) the relationship between Franciscan Joachimism and the quest for poverty and evangelic renewal by the radical or 'Spiritual' wing of the Franciscan order. Especially concerning this last question Franciscan scholarship recently has seen a considerable change of opinion. David Burr and David Flood have reasoned, and I think quite convincingly, that until the persecution of Peter John Olivi in the 1280s, and even beyond that, no real Spiritual faction with a specified Joachimistically inspired apocalyptic ideology did exist. Alleged mid-thirteenth-century Franciscan zealots of poverty and Joachimism, like Hugh of Digne in southern France and the general minister John of Parma, appear to be much more moderate in outlook and flexible in their ideological position than they once seemed to be.[2] Besides, Franciscan leaders with an established reputation for moderation with regard to poverty and willing to develop the Franciscan order in close cooperation with the papacy, were deeply involved in

---

[1] The following works offer the most authoritative introductions to this scholarly field: E. Benz, *Ecclesia spiritualis. Kirchenidee und Geschichtstheologie der Franziskanischen Reformation* (Stuttgart, 1934); M. W. Bloomfield, 'Joachim of Flora: A Critical Survey of his Canon, Teachings, Sources, Biography, and Influence', *Traditio*, 13 (1957), pp. 249–311; D. Burr, *The Persecution of Peter Olivi*, Transactions of the American Philosophical Society, New Series, 66, 5 (Philadelphia, 1976); B. McGinn, ed., *Apocalyptic Spirituality. Treatise and Letters of Lactantius, Adso of Montier-en-Des, Joachim of Fiore, the Franciscan Spirituals, Savonarola* (New York–Toronto, 1979); H. Grundmann, *Studien über Joachim von Fiore* (Darmstadt, 1975); H. Lee, M. Reeves, G. Silano, eds., *Western Mediterranean Prophecy: The School of Joachim of Fiore and the Fourteenth-Century Breviloquium* (Toronto, 1989); H. de Lubac, *La postérité spirituelle de Joachim de Fiore*, 1 (Paris, 1979); R. Manselli, *La 'Lectura super Apocalypsim' di Pietro di Giovanni Olivi* (Rome, 1955); M. Reeves, *Joachim of Fiore and the Prophetic Future* (London, 1976); J. Schlageter, 'Apokalyptisches Denken bei Petrus Johannes Olivi. Versuch einer fundamentaltheologischen Wertung', *Wissenschaft und Weisheit*, 50 (1987), pp. 13–27; D. W. West, ed., *Joachim of Fiore in Christian Thought. Essays on the Influence of the Calabrian Prophet*, 2 vols (New York, 1975).

[2] See especially David Burr, *Olivi and Franciscan Poverty* (Philadelphia, 1989), pp. 18–24.

Joachimistically inspired speculations, as for example the works of Joseph Ratzinger and Bernard McGinn on Bonaventure's theology of history make clear.[3]

Scholars who devote their time and skills to studying medieval theory and practice of Bible exegesis stress the diminishing importance of Bible commentaries in the output of thirteenth-century religious writers.[4] It seems that they spent more and more of their intellectual appetite and energy in addressing dogmatic and outright philosophical problems in their *Sentences*-commentaries and quodlibetal questions. It is the Dominican Robert Kilwardby, an early exponent of high scholasticism in Paris and Oxford, who says in his *Sentences*-commentary that the Bible provides all knowledge necessary for salvation in various scriptural modes, but that the task of the theologian is foremost to shed light in a systematic way on those problems of faith which man, due to the infirmities of his judgement, can not solve by a cursory reading of the Bible. According to Kilwardby, the framework of this systematic treatment of problems of faith is given by Lombard's *Sentences*. So theologians cope with them in a systematic way in their *Sentences*-commentaries, which form also the place where the philosophical legacy of the pagans may be used to arrive at a better understanding of theological truths.[5] And Kilwardby got full support from the highest Church authorities when Robert Grosseteste, bishop of Lincoln, who was himself one of the stimulating forces behind thirteenth-century philosophical speculation, but who was nevertheless alarmed by this pursuit of a systematically organized and philosophically inspired 'science' of theology, repudiated his approach.

Roger Bacon, writing in the 1260s, could complain in his *Opus Minus* that theologians did not read and comment upon the Bible any more. Instead they had found a new playground in their *Sentences*-commentaries

---

[3] J. Ratzinger, *Die Geschichtstheologie des heiligen Bonaventura* (München-Zürich, 1959); B. McGinn, 'The significance of Bonaventure's theology of history', *Celebrating the Medieval Heritage. A Colloquy on the Thought of Aquinas and Bonaventure, The Journal of Religion*, 58 (1978) Supplement, pp. 64–81.

[4] For this scholarly field see especially: W. Kamlah, *Apokalypse und Geschichtstheologie. Die mittelalterliche Auslegung der Apokalypse vor Joachim von Fiore* (Berlin, 1935); W. Lourdaux and D. Verhelst, eds, *The Bible and Medieval Culture*, Mediaevalia Lovaniensia, Series I, Studia VII (Louvain, 1979); H. de Lubac, *Exégèse médiévale. Les quatre sens de l'Ecriture*, Seconde Parti, I (Paris, 1961); P. Riché and G. Lobrichon, eds, *Le moyen age et la Bible* (Paris, 1984). See also: F. Stegmüller, *Repertorium Biblicum Medii Aevi* (Madrid, 1940–80).

[5] Robert Kilwardby, *Quaestiones in Librum Primum Sententiarum*, ed. J. Schneider (München, 1986). See esp. Q. 7, pp. 18ff.

which, to make things worse, were confused by badly understood Aristotelian and Arabic logic and metaphysics. He blamed Alexander of Hales, the founding father of the Franciscan school in Paris, for the creation of a *summa* which was 'heavier than a horse', and he rebuked the Dominican teacher Albert the Great, who had engulfed Western Christianity with flawed and obscure introductions to Aristotle and Avicenna.[6]

Of course, Roger Bacon was very fond of suitable exaggerations and harsh attacks. But if we can rely on the works of modern scholars like Stegmüller, Riché, and Jacques Verger, then we have to conclude that indeed a considerable decline in pure biblical scholarship took place in the golden era of scholasticism. To be sure, the reading of the Bible still formed a considerable part of the university curriculum, and the great teachers of the Franciscan and Dominican orders, such as Bonaventure and Aquinas, did comment upon parts of the Bible, and their commentaries were, and to some extent still are, highly regarded. But their exegetical works and those of many of their contemporaries cover only a relatively small part of the biblical canon, and these scholars were, as they often stated themselves, foremost concerned with an explanation of the literal sense.

The university-educated Bible exegetes commented most of all on the books which lend themselves best to systematical doctrinal or straight-forward moral or literal comment, such as the Psalms, the books of Wisdom, the Gospels, the letters of St Paul. They hardly commented upon the books which demanded far-reaching historical or mystical exegesis (the books of Moses with the exception of Genesis, the Acts of the Apostles, the Prophets and the Apocalypse), books which had received much attention from twelfth-century biblical scholars.[7]

The stress on the literal sense was partly a reaction against the bewilder-ing spiritual interpretations of some twelfth-century exegesis. At the same time this type of exegesis, as Paul Verger reminds us, was not a judaizing literal interpretation: '. . . le sens littéral inclut la totalité du contenu de la Révélation, c'est-à-dire tout l'enseignement religieux et moral explicite-ment donné par Dieu dans la Bible, que ce soit sous la forme d'un discours obvie ou sous celles, multiples, de la parabole ou de la prophetie . . .'.[8]

---

[6] *Rogeri Bacon Opus Minus*, ed. J. S. Brewer (London, 1859), pp. 326–7. With regard to Roger Bacon's criticism of Albert the Great the editor's marginal glosses are misleading.

[7] J. Verger, 'L'exégèse de l'université', *Le moyen âge et la Bible*, pp. 201–32.

[8] Ibid., p. 216.

Moreover, authors like Bonaventure did elaborate upon various levels of literal meaning: for example the meaning intended by the human author (whether expressed in a straightforward way or metaphorically), the meaning intended by voices in the text, the meaning intended by the divine author, the contextual meaning of sentences and words, etc. Thus, in thirteenth-century Bible exegesis the literal sense included much that we nowadays would subsume under spiritual exegesis.

Scholars like me, who want to engage in a study of Franciscan commentaries on the Apocalypse are thus from the start confronted with an array of questions raised by two different forms of scholarship. There is the question of Franciscan Joachimism, and, connected with it, the question of Spiritual partisanship within the Franciscan order. There is also the question of whether the Franciscan authors who commented upon the Apocalypse were following exegetical traditions, and whether they were in or out of tune with the leading paradigm of literal exegesis.

As far as existing inventories allow us to form a judgement, it seems that commenting upon the Apocalypse was predominantly a Franciscan affair. But maybe this says more about the completeness of our inventories and the hazards of survival of medieval manuscripts than about the state of the art in the thirteenth and fourteenth centuries. I am not able nor do I aspire to give any definite answer on these and other questions in this paper. After all, I have just begun to find my tentative way in this scholarly field. But it seems to me that for answers we have to go to the commentaries themselves, to see what they can tell us about exegetical traditions and methods of Bible-exegesis, historical thinking, Joachimistic influences, polemics about the position and future of the Franciscan order, and the possible function of Apocalypse-commentaries as texts (since texts are and were written with conscious and semi-conscious objectives and assumptions). So I will end this communication with a few introductory remarks about some Franciscan commentaries on the Apocalypse.

The earliest complete Franciscan Apocalypse-commentary handed down to us is that of Alexander of Bremen, written shortly after 1240.[9] This work has been hailed as an early example of Joachimism in the Franciscan order by Marjorie Reeves and other scholars of Joachimism, while its editor, Aloïs Wachtel, was at pains to show that Joachimistic themes played a very subordinate role in this—according to Wachtel—

---

[9] *Alexander Minorita Expositio in Apocalypsim*, ed. A. Wachtel, *MGH*, *Quellen zur Geistesgeschichte des Mittelalters*, 1 (Weimar, 1955).

'first truly historical exegesis of the Apocalypse'. In fact Alexander's commentary is a peculiar mixture of a half-hearted, more traditional mystical interpretation of the various visions of the Apocalypse, combined with a thorough chronological and historical reading of the imagery of these same visions. As the prologue makes clear, his mystical interpretation is lip-service to the exegetical tradition, based on gloss-compilations of Haymo of Halberstadt, Walafrid Strabo, and Anselm of Laon. Far more important for Alexander is the historical reading of the apocalyptical visions. For him the Apocalypse as a whole reveals the history of the Christian Church from the days of Christ to the last judgement.

Although Alexander found for his more exorbitant explanations of apocalyptic imagery some inspiration in the prophecies of the Tiburtine Sybil and in the spurious *Super Hieremiam*, an early thirteenth-century Joachimistic work of dubious origins, I am not so sure whether his exegesis can be called truly Joachimistic in outlook. Unlike Joachim he does not indulge in various kinds of numerical schemes, concordances, and figures; nor does he show an interest in the truly tropological, contemplative, and analogical senses of biblical words and passages. And, more important still, he does not elaborate upon the theme of a *tertia aetas*, the period of the Holy Spirit in which a new understanding of the Gospel and a perfect monastic life invigorates the Church for an indeterminate time-span before the coming of the final Antichrist.

His exegesis gives us a history of the Church defending itself against the numerous forces of evil in the course of time. Alexander discerns a time of persecutions under the pagan Roman emperors until Constantine the Great, a time of strife against various heretical movements until the crushing of the Arian Gothic empire under Justinian, a time of wars against the new pagan empires of the Persians and of Islam, a time of comparatively peaceful development of the Church between Charlemagne and Gregory VII, a period of contest between the religious and secular leaders of Christianity from the excommunication of the emperor Henry IV in the late eleventh century until the excommunication of and the wars with Frederic II in the mid-thirteenth century, and beyond. This last period saw also the emergence of the new mendicant orders of Francis and Dominic, and would end, somewhere around 1315, with the coming of the Antichrist, whereafter the Last Judgement would mark the end of history.

Notwithstanding the fact that Alexander of Bremen placed his own time near the end of the world (a fairly normal thing to do for a medieval writer anyway) and that he sees a rejuvenation of the Church in the works of the mendicant orders, he does not give the Franciscan order the dramatic role in the last tribulations of the world which will be the hallmark of later Franciscan Spiritual thinking.

Modern scholars have observed that the historical exegesis of the Apocalyptical images was to gain a dominant place in Franciscan Apocalypse-commentaries, and this may seem a remarkable phenomenon if we recall that in general thirteenth-century biblical exegesis apparently was moving into a different direction. So these scholars have tried to explain this phenomenon by stressing the Joachimistic influences, and elaborating the link between Franciscan Joachimism and Franciscan radicalism.

For some Franciscan works this makes sense. To a certain degree it is legitimate to read the *Postilla super Apocalypsim* of Peter John Olivi in this light. His work is even far more overtly Joachimistic in its organization and many-layered exegetical method than the work of Alexander of Bremen,[10] and Olivi is far more concerned with the struggle between the pure Franciscan life and the ways of the 'carnal' Church. Such an approach makes even more sense for the sometimes confused and extravagant works of fourteenth-century writers allied with the Spiritual factions of the Franciscan order, such as the Catalonian physician Arnold of Villanova and the Franciscan prophet John of Rupescissa.[11] However, this approach is not able to explain the methods, form, and function of the bulk of Franciscan Apocalypse-commentaries.

It is possible to discern three main groups within the extant Franciscan Apocalypse-commentaries. In the first place there is a large group of commentaries which follow various long-standing exegetical traditions of pre-Joachimistic origin. These commentaries—like those of Vital du Four, John Russel, and William of Meliton[12]—are neglected by most scholars of Franciscan exegesis.

---

[10] As a matter of fact, there is some disagreement among scholars as to whether or not Olivi's outlook was predominantly Joachimistic. Manselli agreed that Olivi was influenced by Joachim, but he saw a fundamental difference between Olivi's christocentric view of history and the speculations of Joachim. However, Reeves emphasizes Olivi's overall debt to Joachim's patterns and figures. See: Manselli, *Lectura*, pp. 165 and 190; idem, 'La Terza Età. "Babylon" e l'Antichristo Mistico (a proposito di Pietro di Giovani Olivi)', *Bulletino dell'Istituto Storico Italiano e Archivio Muratoriano*, 82 (1970), pp. 47–79; Lee, Reeves, and Silano, *Breviloquium*, pp. 19–26.

[11] See esp.: R. Manselli, *La religiosità d'Arnaldo di Vilanova* (Rome, 1951); J. Bignami-Odier, 'Jean de Roquetaillade (de Rupescissa)', *Histoire littéraire de la France*, 41 (1981), pp. 75–240; Lee, Reeves, and Silano, *Breviloquium*, pp. 27–88.

[12] The Apocalypse commentary of Vital du Four was printed repeatedly, under the names of Alexander of Hales and Bonaventura. See *Alexander Halensis, Expositio in Apocalypsim*,

Instead they centre on a second group, the famous 'Joachimist' Franciscan Apocalypse-commentaries, and on the many Spiritual apocalyptical treatises from the thirteenth and fourteenth centuries. In fact, the heavy emphasis on Joachimism as a unifying theme exaggerates the uniformity in mental outlook and exegetical methodology among the various commentators within this group. Moreover, this type of exegesis often is presented as the typical Franciscan way of commenting on the Apocalypse.

Finally, there is a group of historizing Franciscan Apocalypse-commentaries, which indeed follow Alexander of Bremen's historical reading of the apocalyptic visions, but which are free from Joachimist ideas. This is for example the case with the commentaries of Peter Aureoli and Nicholas of Lyra. In my view, this type of Apocalypse-commentary corresponds most fully with contemporary scholastic ideas concerning Bible exegesis.

The commentaries of Peter Aureoli and Nicholas of Lyra were part of an ambitious programme of literal exposition of the whole Bible.[13] That is why they called their works *Compendium Sensus Litteralis* and *Postilla Litteralis* respectively. As real exponents of a university-based exegetical tradition and as real adherents of a Bonaventurean exegetical method, they aimed in the first place at the exposition of the literal sense of the Bible, understood in the broad way mentioned above; thus including, where necessary, historical explanations of prophetical imagery as well as explanations of their overtly doctrinal and moral connotations, but excluding more extravagant concordances and multi-layered spiritual, allegorical, tropological, or analogical readings of the text.

Nicholas of Lyra and Peter Aureoli wanted to provide students with a solid and doctrinally safe understanding of the whole canon of the Bible. They did not champion the cause of an endangered Franciscan order in

---

ed. Johannes de la Haye (Paris, 1647); *Supplementum Operum omnium S. Bonaventurae*, II. 5, ed. Benoît Bonelli (Trente, 1773), Cols 5–1035. For the manuscripts of the commentary of William of Meliton, see Stegmüller, *Repertorium Biblicum*, II, nos. 418–28; IX, nos. 2960 and 2964. For the commentary of John Russel, see Beryl Smalley, 'John Russel O.F.M.', *Recherches de Théologie Ancienne et Médiévale*, 23 (1956), pp. 277–320. John Russel sometimes cited Joachim of Fiore, but he did not adopt any of Joachim's patterns, concordances, or divisions.

[13] Good scholarly editions of these works are lacking. The following passages on the commentaries of Aureoli and Lyra are based on two outdated printings, namely: *Fr. Petro Aureoli Ord. Min. Compendium Sensus Litteralis Totius Divinae Scripturae*, ed. Ph. Seeboeck (Quaracchi, 1896); *Biblia Sacra cum Glossa Ordinaria et Postilla Litteralis Nicolai de Lyra* (Antwerpen, 1617), cols 1457–1704. David Burr will no doubt provide us with a more complete picture of this exegetical tradition in his forthcoming book, *Olivi's Peaceable Kingdom: A Reading of the Apocalypse Commentary*.

their biblical exegesis. Nor did they follow the lead of Joachim of Fiore in his concordances or his many levels of spiritual understanding of the text. They were instead anxious to stay close to the dominant modes of thirteenth- and early fourteenth-century exegesis, and to be in agreement with the major theologians on important doctrinal matters.

Maybe it was therefore almost natural for them to give a consequent historical reading of the visions of the Apocalypse. Both authors explain the Apocalypse as the prophecy of a generally acceptable Church-history: successive visions stand in a straightforward way for successive historical developments. The commentary of Peter Aureoli in particular reads as a convenient abridgement of a textbook of Church history. It is a sober narrative with at the end cautious and orthodox concluding paragraphs about the coming of the Antichrist and the Last Judgement. Nicholas of Lyra shows the same spirit of caution and circumspection. He concludes his *Postilla Litteralis* as follows: 'Et quia non propheta sum, nec filius prophetae, nolo de futuris aliquid dicere, nisi illud quod a scriptura sancta vel dictis sanctorum et doctorum authenticorum elici potest, propter quod expositionem literae dictae sapientioribus dimitto.'[14]

---

[14] Nicholas of Lyra, *Postilla Litteralis*, col. 1662.

WYCLIF AND THE GREAT PERSECUTION

by MICHAEL WILKS

AS has been remarked often enough, Lollardy was the first real English heresy, and its progenitor, John Wyclif, inspired what Anne Hudson has so rightly termed a 'premature Reformation',[1] a reformation which had far more immediate impact in Hussite Bohemia, but in England left Wyclif for a century and a half as a voice crying in the wilderness, a prophet without honour in his own country. Since history is usually studied backwards, his name is most commonly associated with the alleged eucharistic heresy condemned at the Blackfriars Council of May 1382. This was more significant for its timing than its substance. The actual charges were not only a distortion of Wyclif's theory, and Wyclif himself was never specifically named, but any reasonably intelligent scholastic could have worked it out from Wyclif's philosophical principles at least ten years earlier.[2] But the eucharist had the great advantage of being a theological matter, which no one could contest the right of bishops and masters to deal with, and this made it a far more effective stick with which the papalists could belabour their lay opponents—and by 1382 the times were far more propitious. The Peasants' Revolt of 1381, an event with which Wyclif's name was quickly linked,[3] had thrown the regency government of the young Richard II into turmoil: and Lollardy, newly introduced as a term of abuse, could be represented as a recipe for any number of horrors, not least the assassination

---

[1] A. Hudson, *The Premature Reformation: Wycliffite Texts and Lollard History* (Oxford, 1988); and see also her 'Lollardy: the English heresy?', *Lollards and their Books* (London and Ronceverte, 1985), pp. 141–63; and now J. I. Catto in *History of the University of Oxford*, 2, *Late Medieval Oxford*, ed. J. I. Catto and R. Evans (Oxford, 1992), pp. 175–280.

[2] One should not be misled by the tactic adopted by his opponent William Woodford of claiming that Wyclif was for a long time uncertain in his own mind about his theory of the eucharist. He admitted that he had had to change his view, e.g. *De eucharistia* (all references to Wyclif Society editions unless noted otherwise), 2, p. 52, 'Unde licet quondam laboraverim ad describendum transsubstantiationem concorditer ad sensum prioris Ecclesiae, tamen modo videtur michi quod contrariatur, posteriora Ecclesia aberrante'; and for other examples see *SCH*, 5 (1969), pp. 69–98, but he was already aware in his debates with Kenningham in 1371 that the same principles governing philosophy, theology, and politics would have an impact on the eucharist: see *Fasciculi Zizaniorum*, ed. W. W. Shirley (RS, 1858), p. 453. This however raises the still unresolved problem of whether the *De logica* should be dated to the 1360s: see W. R. Thomson, *The Latin Writings of John Wyclyf* (Toronto, 1983), pp. 6–7.

[3] M. Aston, 'Lollardy and sedition, 1381–1431', *Lollards and Reformers: Images and Literacy in Late Medieval Religion* (London, 1984), pp. 1–47.

of bishops. The murder of Archbishop Sudbury in 1381 had opened up the way for his replacement by Wyclif's leading opponent, the very vigorous bishop of London, William Courtenay. All this was however simply the culmination of a long process against Wyclif which had resulted in two abortive heresy trials in 1377 and 1378.[4] In both cases Wyclif was rescued by royal intervention, by John of Gaunt. Wyclif, as he had proudly proclaimed, was a *clericus regis*, a king's clerk, a member of the royal household: and as Christopher Given-Wilson has recently shown, king's clerks might be few in number (and exceptionally cheap to maintain, since they could—as Wyclif was—be paid out of normal pluralism), but they wielded a degree of influence out of all proportion to their numbers.[5]

Although Wyclif and his supporters escaped effective condemnation in 1377–8 and continued to enjoy royal protection, one of the great problems in Wyclif's personal history is that it was precisely at this point that he began to issue a steady flow of horror stories about the tribulations of the faithful and the way that their numbers were being cut down. If we accept his insistence that the number of his followers was but a few, those few must have suffered massively. It was, he said at one point, as if God had gone to sleep: there was a savage wave of repression on a huge scale.[6] Close analysis of his words, however, suggests that the dangers involved may have consisted more of risks being taken rather than actual atrocities suffered. Poor priests, we are told, were *threatened* with excommunication, loss of office, imprisonment, and death;[7] soldiers of Christ should

---

[4] J. H. Dahmus, *The Prosecution of John Wyclyf* (New Haven, 1952; reprinted Hamden, 1970).

[5] C. Given-Wilson, *The Royal Household and the King's Affinity: Service, Politics and Finance in England, 1360–1411* (New Haven and London, 1986), pp. 175–9. Wyclif's statement 'Ego autem, cum sim peculiaris regis clericus, . . . defendendo et suadendo quod rex potest iuste dominari regno Angliae, negando tributum Romano pontifici . . .' in the *Determinatio* against Uthred of Boldon and William Binham, p. 422, may be compared with his arguments of the same period in the *De veritate sacrae scripturae* that to condemn him would be tantamount to an attack on the king, his council, and the law; and that 'clerici regum et homines simplicis literaturae' can preach the faith better than doctors of theology: 3, i. 354; 24, ii. 234.

[6] 'Licet autem Dominus ad tempus dormiat', *Speculum saecularium dominorum*, 3, p. 84. See also *De officio regis*, 11, p. 258, 'et vix paucissimi christiani remanebunt in Ecclesia sub Christo', but note the use of the future tense.

[7] E.g. *De ordine christiano*, 5, p. 139, 'Sed quis est qui audet contra praelatos Antichristi doctrinam istam defendere vel papae aut vicariis suis in hoc contradicere, specialiter cum privatio beneficii, excommunicatio cum censuris aliis consequuntur, et breviter quae secuntur ad hanc fidem suppositam pauci vel nulli audeant pro Christo subicere se martirio? Sed rarenter est hodie invenibile quis sit ille'; *De demonio meridiano*, 1, p. 419, 'Ad quod laborarunt pauperes presbyteri clamando usque ad mortis periculum'; 3, p. 424, '. . . et omnino pessimum est quod fideles in Domino prohibeantur per incarcerationes, privationes et censuras alias dicere palam populo legem Christi'; *Dialogus*, 24, pp. 48–9; 27, p. 56.

expect to be killed, and should *prepare* themselves for martyrdom.[8] One cannot avoid detecting what is almost a note of pride in which he relates the perils facing the movement. Although he occasionally descended to a level of petulant protest about the awful unfairness of the great persecution—they persecute us, but we don't persecute them[9]—nevertheless according to his own account a great retribution was taking place: the faithful were being put to death;[10] his supporters amongst the friars were being incarcerated in foul prisons after secret trials, and presently expired from their maltreatment.[11] The Psalms foretold that the death of his saints was precious in the sight of God, and Wyclif himself would provide an example for them to follow.[12] Like Zachariah,[13] he could prophesy that the people of God would find salvation in Christ, but his own expectation was a new martyrdom, and he assured his followers that he was steeling himself for the coming event. He was under heavy attack: there never had been such a time of peril for the Christian faith.[14]

---

[8] *De veritate sacrae scripturae*, 23, ii. 232, 'Quam gloriosa causa foret michi praesentem miseriam finiendo. Haec enim fuit causa martirii Christi . . .'; *De perfectione statuum*, 4, pp. 466–7, 'Sed quia persecutio est horrenda occisio imminet sic dicenti, ideo cum oratione humili disponamus nos ad martirium, memores coelestium praemiorum'; *Dialogus*, 27, pp. 57–8.

[9] *Opus evangelicum*, iii. 47, pp. 172–3, 'ex hoc prosequitur istos simplices quod publicant istam haeresim et patenter reserant fidem suam. Pars autem huius fidei non persequitur haereticos sibi adversarios, sed humiliter scribit et delucidat viva voce evidentias fidei scripturae quae movent ipsam et moverent cunctos catholicos ad istam partem fidei sustindendum.'

[10] *De ordine christiano*, 3, pp. 133–4, 'Ex hoc enim fingit [papa] se praestare Deo obsequium, occidendo quoscunque huic perfidiae tamquam fidei repugnantes.'

[11] *De incarcerandis fidelibus*, p. 95, 'Sed praelati caesarei . . . ad extollendum suum venenosum dominium incarcerant plus tyrannis. Et idem est iudicium de sectis novellis incarcerantibus fratres suos; et sic Antichristi discipuli in subtillitate et severitate excedunt scolares Luciferi . . . ut legitur *Iohannis*, ix.22 . . .'; also p. 97; *De fundatione sectarum*, 7, p. 40, '. . . fratres professionis eiusdem propter hoc quod detegunt scelera sui ordinis incarcerat et occidit'; 10, p. 51, 'fratres proprios immisericorditer usque ad mortem cruciant'; *De versutiis Antichristi* (ed. I. H. Stein, *EHR*, 47 (1932), pp. 98–103), 3, p. 102, 'de incarceratione fratrum suorum usque ad mortem'; *De quattuor sectis novellis*, 12, p. 285; cf. *De eucharistia* 6, p. 183.

[12] *De amore* (*Ep.* 5), pp. 9–10, commenting on Ps. 115. 16–17, 'Hic dico tamquam mihi probabile citra fidem quod quilibet martir Dei potest pertinenter Deo dicere istos versus.'

[13] *Expositio Matthaei XXIII*, 14, p. 352, part of his commentary on Matt. 23. 34 where Christ predicts that his prophets will be killed; cf. Luke 1. 67f. According to medieval tradition Zacharias was slain by Herod in the Temple.

[14] *De perfectione statuum*, 3, p. 461, '. . . ad tantum enim [dyabolus] caecavit saeculares dominos per suos discipulos Antichristos quod reputarent fidelem clericum, qui diceret sententiam evangelicam in hac parte, esse summum haereticum a praelatis et toto populo occidendum. Ideo, si non fallor, a mundi principio usque nunc non fuit fidelibus ewangelizantibus maius periculum quam est nunc in isto meridiano demonio sic regnante. Nunc enim tam clerus quam saeculares domini seducti reputabunt talem esse haereticum, et sic in suo iudicio tam corpore quam anima condempnabunt.' Complaints about teachers of truth being subjected to false accusations of heresy begin as early as the *De mandatis divinis*, 28, pp. 410–11.

The problem is that we entirely lack historical verification for all this. Quite apart from the fact that Wyclif himself died safely in his own bed, as far as we know no Lollard was actually put to death until the beginning of the next century.[15] The most striking feature of the records of the ecclesiastical courts during the last quarter of the fourteenth century is the really very small number of anti-Lollard cases. This might indicate the very small numbers of Wyclif's supporters. But it is much more likely to demonstrate the very great caution, indeed the positive reluctance, of so many bishops, most of whom were royal appointments, to proceed against a group whose chief heresy was the exaltation of royal power. On the whole captured Lollards were treated with tolerance, and released after making purely formal assurances of good behaviour, to an extent which borders on the ridiculous. It amounted to one of the most restrained campaigns against heresy in history, and this is a discrepancy that requires an explanation.

There is no dispute that the charges in 1377–8 concerned Wyclif's views on civil lordship: that he was to be condemned in other words for his antipapalism. He had appropriated the papal theory of dominion and grace for the benefit of the king, creating a version of the theory which made the king rather than the pope the vicar of God, and therefore the effective owner of all the wealth in the kingdom, fully entitled when necessary to dispossess the possessioners, to disendow the monasteries and religious houses, and to reclaim the lay patronage given over the centuries to cathedral and parish churches.[16] It is not surprising that the Pope, Gregory XI, suggested that Wyclif had gone mad,[17] which was not only an expression of shocked disbelief that a doctor of theology could say such things, but was presumably also intended to invite a plea of insanity in mitigation of the offence. But for what the Pope termed wilful misinterpretation of the Scriptures and for preaching theses likely to overturn the good order of the whole Church, Wyclif was to be imprisoned and forced to confess or, if he fled from justice, to be summoned to appear at Rome itself to be dealt with directly by the papal court.[18] The death of Gregory XI in March 1378 and the outbreak of the Great Schism,

[15] P. McNiven, *Heresy and Politics in the Reign of Henry IV: The Burning of John Badby* (Woodbridge and Wolfeboro, NH, 1987).

[16] See my 'Predestination, property and power: Wyclif's theory of dominion and grace', *SCH*, 2 (1965), pp. 220–36.

[17] There is a convenient translation of the three bulls in Sudbury's register in Dahmus, *Prosecution*, pp. 39–45.

[18] Ibid., p. 42; H. B. Workman, *John Wyclif* (Oxford, 1926), 1, p. 294.

combined with the collapse of the second trial in London, left Wyclif free to continue his campaign for a *reformatio regni et ecclesiae*, a process which he claimed was going to have more impact on England than the Norman Conquest.[19]

The Pope, whose knowledge of what Wyclif had actually been teaching was limited to what he had been told by the English Benedictines, 'Black Dog and his pups' (perhaps a reference to Cardinal Adam Easton),[20] declared that Wyclif had espoused the political theory of Marsilius of Padua and John of Jandun, the worst heresy the papacy had ever heard of.[21] In point of fact Wyclif's political thought owed rather more to William of Ockham than it did to Marsilius and in that Ockham was a leading exponent of the doctrine of apostolic poverty radical Franciscan theory was perhaps the single most important influence in the themes which Wyclif propounded during the 1370s, and for which he might have been condemned far more successfully than he ever was. The influence of the Franciscan Spirituals (for want of a better title) in the courts of England and the Empire, also in Spain and Naples, during the mid-fourteenth century, is still a largely obscure subject,[22] but it needs to be seen as the background to the development of what we might call Wyclif's third heresy, the heresy of the New, or rather the Last, Age.

However unlikely it may seem to us that Wyclif should be credited by his contemporaries as being the prophet of a new age, it would in no way have seemed abnormal in the context of the 1360s and 1370s.[23] It was a period when official government propaganda, no doubt fuelled by the French wars, insisted that England was the new Israel, the land of the book, especially of the Old Testament.[24] It was a wonderfully useful

---

[19] *SCH.S*, 5 (1987), p. 163, referring to *De Ecclesia*, 13, p. 278.

[20] Although according to Bale (*Scriptorum Catalogus*, i. 495) it was Nicholas Radcliffe and Peter Stokes who were denounced by Wyclif as 'the black and white dogs'. But dogs was a favourite term of abuse with Wyclif—e.g. cardinals as the dogs of the Roman church: *De demonio meridiano*, 2, p. 421—and looks back to Hildegard's 'fiery dog of unrighteousness'. See also W. A. Pantin, 'The *Defensorium* of Adam Easton', *EHR*, 51 (1936), pp. 675–80, esp. p. 680.

[21] The description is Clement VI's, on whom see now D. P. Wood, *Clement VI: The Pontificate and Ideas of an Avignon Pope* (Cambridge, 1989).

[22] M. Reeves, *Joachim of Fiore and the Prophetic Future* (London, 1976), pp. 45–53.

[23] See now *The Apocalypse in the Middle Ages*, ed. R. K. Emmerson and B. McGinn (Ithaca and London, 1992), especially the contribution of P. Szittya at pp. 383–4 and 391–6, and here further literature; also R. K. Emmerson and R. B. Herzman, *The Apocalyptic Imagination in Medieval Literature* (Philadelphia, 1992), although one may question the comment that this English apocalypticism was 'thoroughly orthodox', p. 148.

[24] *SCH.S*, 5 (1987), pp. 148–52. For Walter Brut's argument that the Apocalypse applied particularly to England because it was the new Israel see Szittya, in Emmerson and McGinn, eds, *Apocalypse*, pp. 396–7.

conception: every victory was proof of divine favour; every defeat another example of the tribulations to be endured by the chosen people before they could take full possession of the promised land. And what was Israel without its prophets? Moreover Wyclif had, so to speak, been brought up into the business. What is to my mind one of the major advances in recent Wyclif scholarship is the book by Jonathan Hughes which deals with the circle of reformers pursuing the aim of a great revival of spiritual life in Yorkshire, which gathered round John Thoresby, royal chancellor during the 1350s and archbishop of York from 1362 to 1373.[25] The Wyclif family were part (to use a fashionable term) of Thoresby's affinity. It may have been under Thoresby's patronage that Wyclif went to Oxford—if he was not already there—and it was Thoresby's encouragement which led to him being enrolled into government service. The chief agent for this was Richard Scrope, the very pious lord of Bolton and Masham, who became royal treasurer in 1371 and was a companion in arms of John of Gaunt. He shared with Gaunt a special interest in promoting advocates of the spiritual life, notably hermits and mystics. It is probably no accident that the finest collection of prophecies and mystical writings in England was to be found in York. The library of the Augustinian Hermits[26] had over 600 works, of which about a third consisted of John Erghome's collection of prophecies, and which included material by other Joachimite and Franciscan-inspired authors like Vincent of Beauvais, William of St Amour, and Robert of Uzès. It also contained writings by John of Rupescissa, an author recently described as a virtual 'clearing-house of medieval prophecy',[27] and a crucial figure in the formation of a 'Northern visionary school' which spread Joachimite influence extensively in northern Europe. Although it has been suggested that all this was a relatively 'quiet apocalypticism',[28] Wyclif is I think positive proof that it was not quiet at all. Whilst there is no evidence that he personally used the

---

[25] J. Hughes, *Pastors and Visionaries: Religion and Secular Life in Late Medieval Yorkshire* (Woodbridge and Wolfeboro, NH, 1988), esp. pp. 127–66. But it should be noted that Wyclif was ordained, and may have gone to Oxford, under the previous archbishop, William de la Zouche, who was not a royalist appointment. This probably explains Wyclif's well-known change of views after the period of his 'youthfulness'.

[26] M. R. James, 'The Catalogue of the library of the Augustinian Friars at York', *Fasciculus J. W. Clark dicatus* (Cambridge, 1909), pp. 2–96; Claire Cross, 'Monastic learning and libraries in sixteenth-century Yorkshire', *SCH.S*, 8 (1991), pp. 255–69 at p. 265. For this catalogue see now *The Friars' Libraries*, ed. K. W. Humphreys (London, 1991).

[27] For John see J. Bignami-Odier, *Études sur Jean de Roquetaillade (Johannes de Rupescissa)* (Paris, 1952).

[28] M. W. Bloomfield and M. Reeves, 'The penetration of Joachism into Northern Europe', *Speculum*, 29 (1954), pp. 772–93.

York library, it is known that he made extensive use of the Franciscan library in Oxford. Sir Richard Southern has shown[29] how Wyclif went to the Franciscan library (like Roger Bacon before him) during the 1360s to read the works of Robert Grosseteste, the thirteenth-century bishop of Lincoln. Grosseteste enjoyed an enormous posthumous reputation in England as the bishop who had opposed the tyranny of Innocent IV to such an extent that he had declared the Pope to be Antichrist, because he had misunderstood the whole character of the Petrine commission. The true *traditio* or grant made to the apostles was to make them like Christ as suffering servants, who would demonstrate that true lordship consisted in sacrificing oneself and repudiating the regal nature which had corrupted the Jewish priesthood of the Pharisees. This was of course grist to Wyclif's mill, but Grosseteste had much more to offer him: the Aristotelian scientific method which was so crucial in Wyclif's own philosophy; stress on the importance of pastoral care and the duty of preaching by the clergy; a call for a logic of scripture which would return the study of the Bible to the basic requirements of the apostolic life: poverty, humility, and love; and above all for present purposes Grosseteste had declared that the number of false clergy, the number of Antichrists, was multiplying so rapidly that the Last Age of the world forecast by St John (I John 2. 18) must be imminent.[30] Grosseteste has been termed a Franciscan by adoption, but I think he must also have been indebted to the prophecies attributed to Joachim of Fiore (although Professor Southern disagrees).[31] There is no doubt however that by the mid-fourteenth century there was a virtually standardized prophecy current in England which was largely a blend, not always a very successful one, of the main theories of Hildegard of Bingen (popularized by the compilation of her sayings by Gebeno of Eberbach in 1220) and Joachim of Fiore, with numerous other spurious items added in. As Henry of Hassia declared,[32] Hildegard and Joachim

---

[29] R. W. Southern, *Robert Grosseteste: The Growth of an English Mind in Medieval Europe* (Oxford, 1986), pp. 296–305.

[30] Ibid., pp. 296, 307, 317–18; R. C. Petry, 'The reforming critiques of Robert Grosseteste, Roger Bacon and Ramon Lull, and their related impact upon medieval society', *The Impact of the Church upon its Culture*, ed. J. C. Brauer (Chicago and London, 1968), pp. 95–120 at p. 111.

[31] Southern, *Grosseteste*, pp. 281–5.

[32] Henry of Hassia, *Epistola* (*Historische Jahrbuch*, 30 (1909), p. 306): 'Est verum quod Hildegardis et Abbas Ioachim sonant quasi finem mundi et adventum Antichristi praecessurae sint una vel plures reformationes ecclesiae seu reductiones in statum primitivae sanctitatis.' There is an excellent summary of this development in H. Lee, M. Reeves, and G. Silano, eds, *Western Mediterranean Prophecy: The School of Joachim of Fiore and the Fourteenth-Century Breviloquium* (Toronto, 1989). From amongst the now massive bibliography on Joachim and Joachism, to which Marjorie Reeves and Bernard McGinn are major contributors, mention should be

MICHAEL WILKS

between them had pointed the way not only to the end of the world and the coming of Antichrist, but to a whole series of *reformationes Ecclesiae* which would 'reduce the clergy to a state of primitive sanctity'. This framework of prophecies had become established and enjoyed what was to all intents and purposes official sanction. Wyclif was able to function as a self-proclaimed Messiah because this prophetic programme was so familiar to his audiences: they were expecting the advent of the end of time and a new revelation. Wyclif appreciated this and was able to offer them one.

One of the best recent studies of this programme is by Kathryn Kerby-Fulton, although mention should also be made of the book by her Cambridge colleague Wendy Scase on what she calls the 'new anticlericalism' of the fourteenth century: both however are writing not about Wyclif but that great Middle English poem *Piers Plowman*.[33] I often think that life would be much simpler if one could show that Wyclif was a poet and was the unknown athor of *Piers Plowman*: they clearly came out of the same stable, the royal court during a period when it was dominated by John of Gaunt (who would become the brother-in-law of Geoffrey Chaucer). When the anonymous author of *Piers Plowman* urged the need for a new Peter and a new apostolic priesthood—because contemporary clergy, for all their learning, could not use English, the true apostolic language, and so could not communicate properly with their people[34]—he was voicing sentiments that must have awoken a lively response in Wyclif himself. There are of course discrepancies between them. The author of *Piers Plowman* seems to have been opposed to the friars from the beginning, whereas Wyclif relied on mendicant support during the 1370s and only later accused the friars of treachery and turned so violently against them. None the less, both of them were strongly influenced by Franciscan notions. Both authors adopted the idea that they should appear as holy fools, the

---

made of B. McGinn, *The Calabrian Abbot: Joachim of Fiore in the History of Western Thought* (New York, 1985). Note also Fiona Robb, ' "Who hath chosen the better part?" (Luke 10, 42): Pope Innocent III and Joachim of Fiore on the diverse forms of religious life', *Monastic Studies*, 2 (1991), pp. 157–70.
[33] K. Kerby-Fulton, *Reformist Apocalypticism and Piers Plowman* (Cambridge, 1990), although she virtually dismisses any relevance to Wyclif and Lollardy, p. 232 n. 6; W. Scase, *Piers Plowman and the New Anticlericalism* (Cambridge, 1989). Reference should also be made to the seminal study by M. W. Bloomfield, *Piers Plowman as a Fourteenth-Century Apocalypse* (New Brunswick, NJ, 1961); cf. R. Adams, 'The nature of Need in *Piers Plowman*', *Traditio*, 34 (1978), pp. 273–301.
[34] Scase, *Piers Plowman*, pp. 123, 164–7.

46

minstrels of God,[35] a Pauline theme made popular by the Franciscan Spirituals. Even the name Lollard itself, although it rapidly became a term of abuse meaning idle layabouts—and worse—had a respectable Franciscan origin meaning one who hung about singing the truth against all adversity: Christ was the supreme Loller, because he above all hung on the cross.[36]

Robert Lerner has pointed out[37] that by the fourteenth century there were two versions or variants of the apocalyptic idea, although it might be more accurate to say that the fourteenth-century theory was an amalgam of both. On the one hand there was the older traditional theme that once society had assumed an ideal form under the rule of an emperor of the Last Age, assisted by a *papa angelicus*, an ideal pope, then the end of the world was at hand, a situation marked by the appearance of Antichrist. The best society was in other words essentially a prelude to the final struggle between Antichrist and the Christlike ruler, which would precipitate the Second Coming. By the fourteenth century however it had become more usual to assume that things had become so bad that the Last Age and the rule of Antichrist already existed. The pessimism that this induced was tempered by the belief that this state of affairs could not last indefinitely: it must of necessity be eventually replaced by the establishment of the ideal society under the rule of a perfect prince, who would bring peace to his messianic kingdom, redistributing wealth throughout society, paving the way for the Last Judgement. Of particular significance in this second version was the means to bring it about, and it was here that

[35] *The Medieval Mystical Tradition in England*, ed. M. Glasscoe (Exeter, 1982), pp. 1–17, and here further references. In England fools and minstrels were classified together in court records: J. Southworth, *The English Medieval Minstrel* (Woodbridge and Wolfeboro, NH, 1989), p. 167 n. 1. For 'lunatic lollers' as holy fools and divine minstrels in *Piers Plowman* see Kerby-Fulton, *Reformist Apocalypticism*, pp. 128–9, 193–4: the author of the poem comes into this category, although it seems unlikely that the C-text is autobiographical. That *Piers Plowman* was complaining about the failure of friars to live up to the ideals of St Francis rather than friars as such is stressed by L. M. Clopper, 'Langland's Franciscanism', *Chaucer Review*, 25 (1990–1), pp. 54–75. See also P. R. Szittya, *The Antifraternal Tradition in Medieval Literature* (Princeton, 1986).

[36] Scase, *Piers Plowman*, pp. 147–51, 220 n. 21. Note Wyclif's elaborate punning in *Dialogus*, 27, p. 57: he was being suspended; Christ was suspended on the cross; but the real suspension was that of the papalists suspending truth. For the term Lollard see R. E. Lerner, *The Heresy of the Free Spirit in the Later Middle Ages* (Berkeley, Los Angeles, and London, 1972), esp. pp. 40–1, 57, and see here for further references and literature.

[37] R. E. Lerner, 'Refreshment of the Saints: the time after Antichrist as a station for earthly progress in medieval thought', *Traditio*, 32 (1976), pp. 97–144; also 'Medieval prophecy and religious dissent', *Past and Present*, 72 (1976), pp. 3–24; 'The Black Death and Western European eschatological mentalities', *American Historical Review*, 86 (1981), pp. 533–52.

Joachimite theories were so influential. The present Church, the *ecclesia activa*, governed jurisdictionally by St Peter and his successors, was to be replaced by an *ecclesia contemplativa* guided by the doctrines of Christian love committed to St John, creating a spiritual, renovated Church. This was to be achieved by the formation of a new order of poor wandering preachers proclaiming the principles of the Eternal Evangel, the true Gospel of the Scriptures rightly understood in a way which had never happened since the days of the apostolic Church. But it was an essential feature of this new order that they should be small in number, a saving remnant of saints, whose efforts to reform society would be met by horrendous persecution, whose faith would be tested by terrible suffering, but out of whose torment society would be reborn. It would, as it was often suggested, be like a second crucifixion, a prelude or testing time out of which the Christian ideal would be resurrected.[38]

It would be tedious to go through each of these items in turn merely to demonstrate that they can all be found in Wyclif's works. Already by the later 1360s he was citing Joachim as a guide to future events: '... praenosticat Abbas Ioachim multiplices eventus in mundo futuros, ut patet in tractatu suo *De speciebus scripturarum*',[39] and from then on the other elements in this pattern of speculation duly make their appearance. His endless complaints that the world was upside down[40] and that the Church had become an *ecclesia carnalis* which could never be in a worse

---

[38] Reeves, *Joachim of Fiore*, pp. 43–4, 48.

[39] *De ente praedicamentali*, 2, p. 18 (this is the anonymous *De semine scripturarum*, apparently originating from Bamberg *c.*1204/5, which Peter Olivi had attributed to Joachim and which became very popular in England: Kerby-Fulton, *Reformist Apocalypticism*, pp. 183–6), although at this stage he seems to have approved of Joachim's condemnation for his theory of the Trinity: *Purgans errores circa universalia*, 5, pp. 45, 47. Later he sought to excuse Joachim, 'si Ioachim ita dixit', on the grounds of ignorance about the nature of universals: *De universalibus*, 11, ed. I. J. Mueller (Oxford, 1985), pp. 263–4; and would argue that Joachim was wrongly persecuted by Innocent III when, like Wyclif himself, he was willing to be corrected if proved to be in error: *De veritate sacrae scripturae*, 7, i. 140–1; *De eucharistia*, 9, p. 278. For a list of other references to Joachim see Thomson, *Latin Writings*, p. 14, although one may doubt Thomson's assertion that these were all borrowings from Higden.

[40] See his use of Isaiah 5. 20, 'Woe unto those who call evil good and good evil' in *De potestate papae*, 5, p. 87: 'et sic de illorum contrariis perversum est nostrum iudicium maniace in contrarium iudicium rationis, et tam multi ac magni inciderunt in istam rabiem quod maior pars mundi arguet docentes et servantes istam sententiam ut insanos, sic quod generalior, accusatior et perseverantior est persecutio in paucos docentes licet remisse istam sententiam quam olim fuerat in prophetas'. See also *De mandatis divinis*, 28, p. 410, 'Sed notandum est hic quod mundus est tantum positus in maligno quod doctores detegentes sensum scripturae et Christi consilium dicuntur ex hinc inimici veritatis et perversores Ecclesiae'; similarly *De civili domini*, ii. 16 and 17, pp. 232 and 240; *De veritate sacrae scripturae*, 28, iii. 120; *De Ecclesia*, 12, pp. 264–5.

condition[41] are well known. His appeals to the king to perform an *imitatio Christi*, to pursue a peace policy, and to redistribute the wealth of the religious—not because the laity were particularly deserving, but because apostolic poverty and humility were essential to those who would teach the true gospel of Christian love—all fall into place as parts of a pre-ordained programme. Much mirth has been engendered by Wyclif's initial determination to support the English Parliament's decision to accept Urban VI in 1378 by announcing that Urban (of all people) was an ideal pope, a *papa angelicus*[42]—although it is quite true that in later years he preferred to argue that both Roman and Avignon popes were Antichrists[43]—but what mattered here was not what Urban was really like, but that it had been written that the Last Age was at hand. So too it was irrelevant whether this final period should be numbered in one way rather than another. Wyclif went to elaborate lengths to divide up world history according to the Augustinian principle of seven ages,[44] so that he could claim to be living in the Saturn-day of the world week, the worst of all times before the coming of the new Sunday, the day of the Lord, only to wreck the entire scheme by reverting to the tripartite Joachimite theme of a third age yet to come.[45] Such inconsistencies only helped to prove that he was fulfilling a prophecy to whose mysteries he alone had the key.[46]

[41] For *Ecclesia malignantium* or *Ecclesia haereticorum*, *De officio regis*, 11, pp. 251 and 257; *De potestate papae*, 7, p. 139 for the pope as 'caput Ecclesiae malignantium et synagoge Sathanae'.

[42] According to *De potestate papae*, 10, p. 233, the Great Schism was caused by Urban's attempt to bring the cardinals to adopt the apostolic life: 'Quam sententiam audivi de papa nostro Urbano VI ipsum dixisse cardinalibus Gregorii qui excessit decalogum ac quia increpans eorum limitavit eos ad vitam apostolicam primaevam, conspiraverant contra eum, eligendo sibi Robertum Gilbonensem, virum ut dicitur dissolutum, superbum, bellicosum et legis Christi ignarum.' Nevertheless both popes could be accepted if *miraculose* they accepted these principles.

[43] *Supplementum Trialogi*, 4, p. 426, 'Et tunc ista duo monstra cum membris diaboli sibi adhaerentibus sese destruerent, Ecclesia fidelium stante salva. Quod autem istorum capitum sit nequius, est nobis impertinens diffinire, sed creditur probabiliter quod Robertus ... Debemus enim credere ... quod nullus talis papa necessarius est per ordinationem Christi, sed per cautelam diaboli introductus': they are *pseudopapae*, false Christs, and the false prophets of Matt. 24. 23–6 (9, p. 448); similarly *De quattuor sectis novellis*, 3 and 5, pp. 249 and 257, notwithstanding continued use of 'our Urban' (7, p. 265); *De perfectione statuum*, 3, p. 458; *Opus evangelicum*, i. 3, i. 141–2.

[44] Joachim's use of both seven-age and three-age patterns is well known: e.g. Reeves, *Joachim of Fiore*, p. 8. For Chaucer note the interesting suggestions made by P. Brown and A. Butcher, *The Age of Saturn: Literature and History in the Canterbury Tales* (Oxford, 1991).

[45] The threefold division made it easier to accommodate the Donation of Constantine as the turning point between the first apostolic age and the second period which came to an end around 1200 with Innocent III and the *Decretales* on one side and the institution of the friars on the other, making the third age both an age of Antichrist and an Age of the Spirit.

[46] Wyclif's constant insistence that he understood Scripture better than anybody else,

All this suggests that the really dangerous Wycliffite works were less the books on lordship of the first half of the 1370s, nor the *De eucharistia* of about 1380, but his studies of the Bible during the middle years of the 1370s, first in the form of his famous commentary on the whole Bible,[47] followed by his book on the truth of Scripture, the *De veritate sacrae scripturae* of about 1378. From now on he saw himself as expressing Joachim's Eternal Evangel, the true gospel of the Bible understood rightly. These biblical studies not only required him to produce a commentary on the Apocalypse of St John, but also drew his attention to the so-called 'synoptic apocalypse' of Matthew, chapters 23 and 24-5, which he quickly convinced himself contained a special message for himself and his followers, but which the bishops had tried to conceal from the faithful.[48] Discussion of these chapters occasioned numerous pamphlets, and two tracts on the subject were to be included with the Lollard sermon cycle to denote their outstanding significance.[49] As he explained, understanding the Bible required a special gift of knowledge from God:

---

e.g. *De civili dominio*, ii. 10, p. 105, 'Unde audacter non pompatice assero de insolubilitate scripturae sacrae, quae est fides mea, securus quod omnes doctores mundi non possunt veritatem istam dissolvere', would lead him to argue that the rightness of papal and conciliar decrees, as in the case of the eucharist, could be ascertained by measuring them up against his own interpretation: *De eucharistia*, 1, pp. 25-6. The bishops should be grateful to him for teaching them the true nature of the Church: *De Ecclesia*, 1, p. 2.

[47] G. A. Benrath, *Wyclifs Bibelkommentar* (Berlin, 1966); also B. Smalley, 'John Wyclif's *Postilla super totam Bibliam*', *Bodleian Library Record*, 4 (1953), pp. 186-205; 'Wyclif's *Postilla* on the Old Testament and his *Principium*', *Oxford Studies presented to Daniel Callus* (Oxford, 1964), pp. 254-96. Wyclif would also have absorbed Joachimite material through his use of Nicholas of Lyra, on whom see above, pp. 36-7. But the basic character which he assigned to himself came from his extensive use of the biblical text. As J. F. A. Sawyer, *Prophecy and the Prophets of the Old Testament* (Oxford, 1987), esp pp. 1-2, 15-18, 58f., 87f., has pointed out, the Old Testament prophet had a double function, on the one hand interpreting and pro-claiming the truth of Scripture and the nature of righteousness, and on the other hand fore-telling the pattern of events leading to the 'day of the Lord'. As an opponent of current ritual practices, he would be rejected by contemporaries and condemned by false accusations, but would survive under the protection of the royal court to which he acted as an adviser. It might almost be a description of Wyclif himself.

[48] The *Expositio Matthaei XXIII* (or *De vae octuplici*) and the *Expositio Matthaei XXIV* cannot how-ever be earlier than mid-1382 and I would prefer to date them to 1383: parts of the latter re-appear in the *Opus evangelicum*, which can be firmly dated to 1384 but is largely a compilation of earlier material. Note the use of these chapters of Matthew to attack the friars as hypocrites and pseudo-prophets in the *De fundatione sectarum*, p. 16, which dates to about August 1383. But cf. *De officio regis*, 11, p. 252.

[49] Hudson, *Lollards and their Books*, pp. 202-3, referring to the *Vae Octuplex* and *Of Mynystris in þe Chirche: Exposicioun of Matthew XXIV*, ed. T. Arnold, *Select English Works* (Oxford, 1869-71), 2, pp. 379-89 and 393-423. Note *Of Mynystris*, p. 408, 'þer shal be wepynge and gnasting of teeþ: þis laste word, *unexpowned bifore*, is dredeful to prelatis.' See also now *English Wycliffite*

Cum sapientia Dei patris sit nucleus veritatis in foliis verborum scripturae absconditus, et ipsa promittit suis fidelibus, Ecclus. 24. 31, 'Qui elucidant me, vitam aeternam habebunt', fideles Christi, et specialiter quibus dedit Deus donum scientiae, darent operam ad Christi evangelium declarandum. Et cum capitulum evangelii Matt. 23 multis hominibus est obscurum et includit in se multa notanda fidelibus, quidam fideles satagunt secundum notitiam quam Deus eis donaverat illud capitulum declarare.[50]

It was therefore the proper task of an evangelic doctor to prophesy, and he claimed that just as his colleagues used the writings of Merlin, Hildebrand and the like, so too he could foretell that wars, plagues, pestilences and other tribulations would continue until a gentile clergy was punished for its sins:

Cum secundum sanctos spectat ad officium doctoris evangelici prophetare, et socii mei prophetant ex dictis Merlini, Hildegardis et vatum similium extra fidem scripturae de statibus membrorum Ecclesiae militantis, motus sum etiam, sed fideliori evidentia, prophetare. Dico ergo quod quamdiu clerus Ecclesiae manserit sic gentilitati commixtus, et fimo temporalium irregulariter inpinguatus, non deficient ab Ecclesia pugna, pestilentia et alia plagae in evangelio prophetatae.[51]

To protests that he would disturb the peace of the Church, he retorted sharply that Christ has said he did not bring peace but a

---

Sermons, ed. A. Hudson and P. Gradon (Oxford, 1983–93), 1, pp. 49–50, although it seems unlikely that these tracts were ever actual sermons: the English sermons were based on the Latin sermons, which were produced in 1383 as a treatise, ostensibly on preaching, but were never actually preached.

[50] *Expositio Matthaei XXIII*, 1, p. 313; cf. *Expositio Matthaei XXIV*, 1, pp. 344–5.

[51] *De vaticinatione seu prophetia*, 1, p. 165. Hildegard is cited fairly often for her attacks on clerical abuses, e.g. *De fundatione sectarum*, 14, p. 67; *Trialogus*, iv. 26, p. 338; and Merlin is presumably Geoffrey of Monmouth; but it is difficult to date the *De vaticinatione* precisely. Loserth rather hesitantly suggested about 1378, whereas Thomson would prefer late 1382: but since Wyclif still seems to be at Oxford before the Peasants' Revolt and the eucharistic controversy, a date of 1379/80 seems more probable. But he scorned the use of astrology in making prophecies: *De quattuor sectis novellis*, 10, p. 280, 'Nec credatur pseudoloquentibus in ista materia ut victoria regnis et regibus sicut antea ascribebatur, quia iuxta fidem pax et caritas sunt Deo plus placitae quam dominationis acquisitio, famae, victoriae vel honoris; et profitendo quod nec sum astrologus nec propheta, ignoro si istorum planetarum coniunctio, quae proximo est futura, sit benevola regno nostro, cum luna, quae est planeta infimus, dicitur super Anglicos dominari.' On Lollard use of Hildegard see now Anne Hudson, *Two Wycliffite Texts*, EETS 301 (Oxford, 1993), pp. 96–7.

MICHAEL WILKS

sword,[52] and he appealed to the king, *athleta Christi*, to protect the heralds of truth (*veritatis praecones*) and listen to one who was 'consiliarius ut confessor et praedicator christianae fidei'.[53] In his last years he became even more openly apocalyptic. The last three books of the *Summa theologiae* against simony, blasphemy, and apostasy were in themselves indications or testimonies to the existence of the Last Age,[54] and the choice of titles like *De solutione Sathanae* or *De versutiis Antichristi* for later tracts seems self-explanatory. The Great Schism came to be seen in his eyes as a climactic event which offered a unique opportunity, and could be compared to the act of creation which brought order out of chaos. It meant Armageddon, the war of the last age of the world against all the forces of evil.[55]

Despite the great deal of blood and thunder involved in this 'reformist apocalypticism' it should be stressed that it evolved out of, and drew its strength from, contemporary spirituality and embraced such very popular ideals as the imitation of Christ and the doctrine of love. Wyclif constantly complained that ecclesiastical life in his own time had been corrupted by unnecessary humanly-devised formalities, by rites and ceremonies, a continual round of meaningless but elaborate services designed to inflate the pride of the clergy and to emphasize their separation from the laity. All this had served to destroy the inner purposes of the

[52] *De vaticinatione*, 2, p. 170, 'Sed hii tertio garriunt quod ex talibus sententiis frustra perturbatur Ecclesia, sed ipsi nec attendunt ad qualitatem sententiae nec considerant quodomodo Iesu noster dicit Matt. 10. 34 quod non venit pacem carnalem vel mundanam mittere in terram, sed gladium ad ligas huismodi dividendum. Et illud officium executi sunt sancti sequentes. . . .' The king should wage a war of resistance against possessioner clergy in the same way that his predecessors resisted the barbarian invasions: 2, p. 174.

[53] *De vaticinatione*, 1, p. 168. The Pauline notion of the Christian as a champion who wins victory in a race or contest, *athleta* or *pugilis Christi*, is usually applied by Wyclif to his followers generally: *De civili dominio*, iii. 3 and 23, pp. 36 and 564; ironically Gregory XI had told the scholars of Oxford in 1377 that they should be champions of the faith: Dahmus, *Prosecution*, p. 48. For the biblical origins see C. F. Evans, *The Theology of Rhetoric: The Epistle to the Hebrews* (Dr Williams' Library, London, 1988), p. 7.

[54] The point that charity grows cold (Matt. 24. 12) in a three-stage process leading to Antichrist and the end of the world is made by Thomas Wimbledon: see I. K. Knight, *Wimbledon's Sermon: Redde Rationem Villicationis Tue* (Pittsburgh, 1967), pp. 109f. For further examples of Wyclif's use of St Paul (Ephes. 5. 16; II Tim. 3. 1f) to declare that the last days had been reached see *De Ecclesia*, 3, p. 51; *De potestate papae*, 8, p. 193.

[55] In *De officio regis*, 11, pp. 251–2, this is linked to Daniel's prophecy (Dan. 2. 40–5) of the break-up of the Roman Empire, the 'iron monarchy': 'In quo regno oportet, instar ferri, quod terram conterit et seipsum consumit, quod surgat gens contra gentem et regnum adversus regnum, sicut prophetat Veritas xxiii [Matt. 24. 7] . . .'; and see also the use of the Matthew passage to argue that wars, plagues, and earthquakes are evidence of the decline of faith and the advent of Antichrist in *Opus evangelicum*, iii. 31, ii. 113–14. Also Benrath, *Bibelkommentar*, pp. 281, 308.

spiritual life. Accordingly he demanded a simplified form of service, whose prime content was the reading and preaching of the Bible, expounding the true message of Scripture. This message was a message of love: the love of God, love of others, and in particular love of oneself—and love of oneself demanded that a man, a naturally corrupt individual, should subordinate himself and measure himself up to his ideal self. He should become a living exponent of his own greater, truer self as a Christian. To do this he had to perform an *imitatio Christi*, to become what Wyclif termed a *Christicola*,[56] a dweller in Christ in whom Christ himself is to be found. In this way the true Church would become, would be converted into, a society of new men. In its proper sense the Church was nothing but a community of the elect, a *universitas praedestinatorum*, a gathering of those who achieved identity with their true spiritual selves and who would therefore be subsumed into the mystical *corpus Christi* to become one with Christ himself. So the true Christian in his search for salvation was obliged to perform a constant imitation of Christ, a permanent striving to measure and match up his earthly conduct with the pattern of right living defined by his heavenly self. His success would prove that he was indeed one of the elect, and society itself would actually become the Augustinian reflection of heaven on earth. It may be remarked in parentheses that precisely the same lesson was being taught in *Piers Plowman*.

It was a process which men should not undertake unaided. They had to have models to adopt and imitate. They needed Scripture rightly understood, but this itself was something which had to be taught: it needed ministers of the word, a clergy whose aim was not to govern people but to direct by word and deed into the ways of love with learning and humility. This was the function of the poor priests.[57] But the poor priest, the true

---

[56] The term is taken from Marsilius, *Defensor pacis*, I. i. 5. His criticisms of 'rites and ceremonies' are too numerous to specify: e.g. *De civili dominio*, ii. 13, p. 165; cf. I Reg. 15. 22, Isa. 1. 10–17, 66. 3, Jer. 7. 22, Amos 5. 25.

[57] The *sacerdotes simplices* of the *Responsiones ad XLIV conclusiones monachales*, proem pp. 201–2, 'Nec est illis quod vocantur a satrapis ydiotae, quia sic vocabantur apostoli evangelium praedicantes, ut patet Act. 4. 13, . . . non confidunt de ingenio proprio vel potestate humana, sed quod Deus utitur tamquam organis ad hoc opus. Habent autem hoc signum caritatis communicandi altrinsecus quod volunt libenter offere doctrinam suam adinvicem et praedicare populo sine pecunia vel proprietate aliqua acquirenda.' The 'pauperes presbyteri clamando usque ad mortis periculum' only want to preach freely the *evangelium Iesu Christi*: *De demonio meridiano*, 3, pp. 419, 424–5; cf. *De diabolo et membris eius*, 4–5, pp. 371–2, where the *simplices sacerdotes* have the *sensum Christi*, 'sensum ewangelicum divinitus eis datum', and 'qui volunt esse secundum formam ewangelii Dei adiutores' according to I Cor. 3. 9. But they were also to do physical labour, and could teach grammar to children: *Dialogus*, 25, p. 51; and should visit

follower, also had a higher duty: he not only had to preach, he had to suffer. Like Christ himself he was to be the suffering servant of Deutero-Isaiah, the man who sacrificed himself for his people. Just as it was fashionable in the fourteenth century to depict Christ less as a God to be obeyed and more as an example of tormented humanity, so the distinctive feature of the *vita evangelica* for the Wycliffite minister was a denial of self-interest and a willingness to endure suffering in accordance with a predetermined pattern. For Wyclif, the sending out of Lollard preachers into the towns and rural areas was a re-enactment of the great dispersion of the apostles set out in the Bible. Christ's lament over Jerusalem as the city which killed its prophets, juxtaposed to the Olivet discourse on the nature of faithful disciples, was a clear indication to him that the true Church was to be sought by means of the example, preaching, and suffering of a few true men. They would be a church of saints as opposed to the *ecclesia* of the malignants, the false prophets and hypocrites who clustered like vultures round the carcase of the body of Christ, and were inspired by the Roman church, the very synagogue of Satan himself.[58] Salvation was to be looked for from wise prophets sent out as angels with trumpets to proclaim the everlasting Gospel and to prepare the elect for the end of time. But they would first need to endure the ultimate tribulation, the great desolation of a dwindling band of saints who would be vilified, tormented, and crucified like Christ. They should expect nothing except to be persecuted and hounded from city to city.

Wyclif's poor priests were university men: they needed to be highly trained in order to teach. But they were to be classed as simple men, the idiots of God skilled in the ways of unknowing, who like children had come to appreciate the fundamental nature of Christianity as a doctrine of love for others. To be like Christ *in vita et in moribus* was to follow the third

---

widows and orphans (Jas. 1. 27) in the description of them in *De civili dominio*, 1, p. 4, where, in opposition to the 'possessioners', they are secular clergy adopting 'paupertatem, castitatem et obedientiam matri Ecclesiae' and friars following poverty: 'mendicantes vero volentes strictius sequi Christum ... abdicant omnem civilem proprietatem'. See further the valuable comments of M. Schmidt, 'John Wyclifs Kirchenbegriff: Der *Christus humilis* Augustins bei Wyclif', *Gedenkschrift für D. W. Elert*, ed. F. Hübner, W. Maurer, E. Kinder (Berlin, 1955), pp. 92–108. Also Benrath, *Bibelkommentar*, pp. 180, 188–9, 245, 274–305.

[58] For the duty of the prophet to condemn corrupt priests see I Reg. 3. 11–14. A further indication of the time of Antichrist was the loss of supporters: 'Nec confunduntur quod quidam qui inchoarunt, nunc deciderunt, quia sic fuit de Christi apostolis', citing John 6. 66, and I John 2. 18–19. Also Benrath, *Bibelkommentar*, pp. 102, 163, 173, 233, 369.

way, the way of love contained in the hidden gospel of St John,[59] and to realize that doing best of all was to be like Christ in loving all, even one's enemies as they persecuted you,[60] a proposition which Wyclif always maintained he was following the more savagely he denounced them. The ideal apostolic man was by definition an eminently saintly being whose life was bound to be a perpetual struggle against adversity: the *paupertates Christi* proved themselves by their willingness to accept harsh conditions and harsher treatment. They were, he declared, the heirs of the prophets, the sons of the apostles,[61] who committed their lives to the service of God and were stoned for doing so. The Wycliffite had to see himself as an *eroicus*,[62] a member of the heroic order of *pugiles Christi*[63] who would wrestle like champions and endure like soldiers until they had overcome. The Bible could only offer men earthly suffering and urge them to be martyrs for the truth.[64] It is very difficult, he once remarked in later life (and no doubt with John of Gaunt in mind), to understand why men can positively enjoy the miseries and sufferings of making war against the Scots for material gain, and cannot even more joyfully endure the sufferings of the greater Scotland of this world for the sake of the rewards of heaven.[65]

---

[59] On the need for *caritas* 'quae est Dei dilectio', see e.g. *De civili dominio*, ii. 7, pp. 61–2; iii. 23, pp. 492–4, 505; *De fundatione sectarum*, 13, p. 63.

[60] *De civili dominio*, i. 6, p. 46, 'Et tertio exemplificat nobis quomodo debemus inimicis nostris proportionaliter misereri, non contentione tumultuosa scandalisando, sed causam nostram, servando caritatem fraternam, in manu Iudicis committendo'; as required by both divine and natural law, *De mandatis divinis*, 8, p. 69.

[61] *De officio regis*, 11, pp. 256–7. In the Old Testament the sons of the prophets were associations of disciples recording and preserving the teachings of a father figure: I Reg. 10. 5–10; 19. 20; IV Reg. 2. 15; 4.38; Amos 7. 14.

[62] *De veritate sacrae scripturae*, 6, i. 124. For the saints as *eroyci*, *De civili dominio*, ii. 13, p. 156.

[63] *De ordinatione fratrum*, 2, p. 95, 'sacerdotes fideles qui ostendunt in vita et opere quod sunt pugiles legis Dei'; and see above n. 53.

[64] *De veritate sacrae scripturae*, 13, i. 326–7, following a long complaint (pp. 318f.) that the world has fallen into falsehood, making men traitors to the truth and to themselves, and urging them to die for the truth after the example of the martyrs: 'Quomodo, quaeso, sequimur martires vel sanctos confessores qui pro quaestu vel otio non audemus dicere fidem scripturae coram domesticis, quam ipsi ad profectum sui et Ecclesiae confessi sunt coram saevissimis persecutoribus et tyrannis, specialiter cum pro defensione scripturae discernimur a pseudo-apostolis et reportamus ex fide scripturae lucrum beatitudinis' (p. 326); *De mandatis divinis*, 2, p. 8, citing Matt. 5. 10; cf. *De civili dominio*, iii. 3, p. 40.

[65] *Trialogus*, iii. 3, p. 139, 'Quis, quaeso, in Scotia propter legis libertatem et privilegia regis Angliae non laetanter pateretur, si cum hoc foret securus quod integer et vivax rediret in Angliam proportionabiliter ad punitionem a rege Angliae praemiandus? Talis, inquam, gratanter reciperet tribulationes in Scotia pro spe praemii in Anglia consequendi. Et multo magis tribulatus in valle huius miseriae, et transferendus ad locum patriae . . . certaret viriliter pro praemio beatitudinis consequendo, cum certi sumus ex fide quod oportet nos a Scotia ista

The effect of this was to restore martyrdom to a central place in the conception of the Christian way of life, and was a logical concomitant of Wyclif's desire for a rebirth of the *Ecclesia primitiva*, the original Church of apostles and martyrs. As the 1992 conference of the Ecclesiastical History Society demonstrated,[66] the High Middle Ages had become very hesitant about the question of martyrdom. There was no doubt that those who had died for the faith in opposition to a pagan Roman Empire were worthy of the status. But there was a reluctance to accept the blanket description that all those who died fighting the pagans on crusades were to be put into the same category; and by the fourteenth century the notion of martyrdom was being diluted and applied to such things as the joyful agonies of the mystics and other very pious people. Wyclif complained that the traditional belief in Christian perfection as something that included an individual's willingness to be persecuted to death had become lost in the apparent but false security and stability of contemporary society. The faithful were likely to be misled by the highly organized and materially successful form of the Church into thinking that undergoing persecution was an outworn requirement.[67] He accused his opponents of trying to do away with the ideal of martyrdom on the grounds that modern society could offer more comfortable, conventional, and lucrative ways of demonstrating their belief, whilst dying for the faith had been perverted into highly institutionalized forms like crusades and the defence of national kingdoms against each other. *Pro patria mori* had to be understood in a different way appropriate to a church-state on the verge of collapse. The rotting body of the realm could only be revived and revivified as a *corpus Christi* by an immediate act of corporate suffering. The *reformatio regni et ecclesiae* could not be achieved without a community sacrifice. Just as the Old Testament prophecies had foreseen the messiah as one who would

---

recedere, et correspondenter ad gratitudinem pro passione tribulationis coelestis Angliae perpetuo praemiari vel pro ingratitudine perpetuo cruciari'; cf. *Dialogus*, 27, pp. 57–8.

[66] *SCH*, 30 (1993).

[67] *Trialogus*, iii. 15, p. 181, 'Unde luciferina est excusatio qua hypocritae moderni dicunt quod non oportet hodie sicut in primitiva Ecclesia pati martyrium, quia nunc omnes vel maior pars conviventium sunt fideles: ideo non superest tyrannus qui prosequatur contra Christum usque ad mortem membra eius: et haec ratio quare hodie non sunt martires sicut olim.' This, he added, only helped to demonstrate that a perverse clergy was the abomination of desolation prophesied by Daniel according to Matt. 24. 15, and (iii. 17, p. 186) 'probabiliter ponitur quod Romanus pontifex sit praecipuus Antichristus.'

suffer for the sins of men,[68] so the ministers of Christ were to be willing to die to bring about the salvation of the kingdom as a *populus Dei*.[69] They were the voice of God whose prerogative of understanding righteousness made them the true representatives of the community.[70] It would be as if Christ was being recrucified in his vicars:[71] the prophets would be stoned again for the sake of Israel:

> Et si notemus omnia praelatorum ecclesiae et nomine clericorum qui omittendo et commitendo diminuunt, lacerant vel corrumpunt fidem scripturae, inveniretur hodie multi haeretici prophetas et apostolos occidentes. . . . Et propter hoc quod Ecclesia haereticorum quae olim lapidavit prophetas atque apostolos vivit hodie persequens eos in suis filiis.[72]

The 'holy committee' (*comitiva sanctorum*)[73] of himself and the poor priests would be like Christ and the *collegium apostolorum* redeeming the sins of England through their corporate suffering. Because it was the end of time, the persecution and their readiness to endure it would purchase a new kingdom: out of their deaths the *respublica Anglicana* would be born anew.

That there was Franciscan inspiration in so much of this can hardly be disputed, but it may be appropriate to add a comment on the way in which Wyclif's conception of a group of wandering russet-clad[74] ministers owed much to Franciscan precedent. Although in later life he came to regard the mendicants, orders founded by Innocent III, that worst of all devils, as part of a great plot to intrude papal power into every aspect of religious life,[75] his own order was deliberately modelled on the friars.

---

[68] For the 'suffering servant' theme see Isa. 40–66. The duty of the prophet to intervene with God on behalf of the people is laid down in Amos 7. 2–5, cf. Isa. 6. 11.

[69] For Wyclif on the virtues of Christian suffering see Benrath, *Bibelkommentar*, pp. 195–7, although he allowed a limited right of resistance and permitted flight when necessary.

[70] *Cruciata*, 5, p. 606, 'vere dicitur quod vox populi est vox Dei, populi videlicet simpliciter spiritu Dei ducti'.

[71] *De veritate sacrae scripturae*, 29, iii. 164.

[72] *De officio regis*, 11, p. 255.

[73] *Trialogus*, iv. 33, p. 364.

[74] Russet signified virtuous work: 'russetum vero significat laborem suum in illis duabus virtutibus absconditum, ne sint hypocritae', *Supplementum Trialogi*, p. 435; also *De fundatione sectarum*, 4, p. 27, but he condemned friars who claimed that their holy dress was a guarantee of salvation, when they were covered from head to foot in lies: *Expositio Matthaei XXIII*, 3, p. 322; *De oratione et ecclesiae purgatione*, 4, p. 351; *De nova praevaricantia mandatorum*, 7, p. 143.

[75] See the long list of grievances against Innocent III in *De eucharistia*, 9, pp. 274–8, 311–15; where in addition to persecuting Joachim, Innocent claimed unlimited supremacy over the Empire and England, encouraged war with France, prohibited vernacular Bible translation,

He came to see himself (a remarkable concept for a secular master) as the last of a great line of friar reformers[76] and his followers as an order, the *secta Christi*,[77] with Christ as its prior or abbot.[78] He wrote in glowing terms about St Francis himself;[79] he claimed to have numerous Franciscan supporters[80]—or at least before the great persecution began; and he devised schemes for combining all the religious into one order, his own, to do away with the divisive effects of having so many. It was to be an order to end all orders,[81] and in his more hopeful moments he would suggest that this sect of true Christians, the mendicants of God,[82] would spread to universal dimensions: all men were to become friars in the great

established the friars (who then helped to produce the *Decretales*), and of course authorized the false doctrine of transubstantiation, despite the credit he obtained by writing *De contemptu mundi*. In the *Purgatorium sectae Christi*, 4, p. 305, his chief objection to the friars is that they were founded by the pope, 'iste religiosarcha in vita et opere suo ostendit quod est mendaciter et capitaliter contrarius Iesu Christi'; cf. *De perfectione statuum*, 4, p. 463, 'duplex pater istarum fratrum, scilicet dyabolus et papa'.

[76] *De ordinatione fratrum*, 2, pp. 91–5, where he lists his predecessors who have tried to reform the mendicants, including Bonaventure, William of Saint Amour, Grosseteste, Ockham, and 'beatus Richardus' Fitzralph.

[77] The *secta Christi* was a term which clearly began as a reference to his followers, e.g. *De veritate sacrae scripturae*, 14, i. 345, 'ego cum secta mea'; i. 357, 'omnes fautores meos', although he would later argue that they were the only true Christians and therefore the expression meant the whole Church: 'Sic secta christianorum debet includere singulos viatores. . . . Patronus autem huius sectae est Dominus Iesus Christus et regula sua est fides catholica, scilicet lex ewangelica', *De fundatione sectarum*, 3, p. 22; 'Sed quomodo possemus esse in ista caritate confoederati ad invicem nisi Christum et suam sectam principaliter diligeremus, cum ipsum aliter odiremus?' 13, p. 63; cf. 6, p. 37, 'Omnes enim christiani sunt fratres in Domino, et istud nomen est ab istis sectis propter ypocrisim usurpatum'; also *De triplici vinculo amoris*, 8, p. 187, 'Augustinus declarat quod omnis viator est mendicus Dei'. The date of the *Purgatorium sectae Christi* is usually estimated as *c*.1382/3, but it could be earlier. Thomson, *Latin Writings*, p. 295, comments, 'His frequent mentions of the *secta Christi* do not take us any closer in this instance to grasping the dimensions and precise identity of that amorphous group than we were at the outset of this section.'

[78] 'Abbas noster Christus', *Trialogus*, iv. 3, p. 364; 'Christus qui est prior nostri ordinis atque principium, in se virtualiter et exemplariter congregavit', *De civili dominio*, ii. 8, p. 73; also ii. 13, p. 166; iii.1, p. 1; iii. 2, p. 75; *De veritate sacrae scripturae*, 10, i. 206; *De officio regis*, 5, p. 99.

[79] *De veritate sacrae scripturae*, 10, i. 206; and *De civili dominio*, i. 18, p. 129; iii.1, pp. 4–6; iii. 2, pp. 17–18, commending Franciscan poverty. But for a very different view, citing Hildegard as prophesying the friars as diabolical seducers, see *Trialogus*, iv. 26–38, pp. 336–85, especially pp. 361–2.

[80] Note his complaint in *De veritate sacrae scripturae*, 14, i. 354–6, about the Oxford doctor who had been attacking the English Franciscans. According to Walsingham, *Chronicon Angliae* (RS, 1874), p. 118, John of Gaunt appointed a friar from each of the four mendicant orders to help Wyclif at his hearing in 1377.

[81] *De civili dominio*, ii. 13, pp. 164–5; iii. 1, p. 1; iii. 3, pp. 31–6; cf. *De Ecclesia*, 14, p. 308; *De fundatione sectarum*, 4, p. 29; 16, p. 80.

[82] *De civili dominio*, iii. 20, pp. 417–19; *De demonio meridiano*, 3, pp. 424–5; and see above, n. 77.

convent of a reformed world.[83] The whole Church as the house of God would become one huge order, neither monastic nor apostatic but apostolic, whose members would not seek to be enclosed but would go out into the world to perform good works.

Despite these occasional suggestions that he had a universal significance, and his determination that papal power should be destroyed in all kingdoms, Wyclif's prophesies were directed almost entirely towards the prospect of an English reformation. Yet it was this prophetic character which makes it so difficult for the historian to estimate the degree of support that his movement enjoyed. His insistence that he was merely taking his appointed place in a set mystical pattern makes it almost impossible to gauge from his own writings any precise information about the numbers of Wycliffites in the 1370s. If Wycliffism meant essentially the assertion of lay supremacy in ecclesiastical matters, then the chroniclers were perfectly entitled to scream that a substantial proportion of all England had become Lollard by 1380.[84] Given the extent of Lollard support, especially the wide geographical spread of reports of it in the latter part of the century, one might guess that the numbers of Lollard ministers was considerably greater than one would expect. On the other hand it was virtually impossible for Wyclif to admit as much. Not only does he seem to have seen the poor priests as a small group of elite advisers to 'the lords', the crown and the greater magnates, a group which would steer the affairs of the kingdom like a college of apostolic cardinals, but it had become a theological necessity to represent them as a saving remnant,[85] a lodge in the wilderness, a very few amongst the multitudes of the stupid.[86] To the argument that his followers must be heretics

---

[83] *De civili dominio*, iii. 20, p. 417.

[84] But the prize goes to the Austrian chronicler: 'iste draco magister Iohannes Wycleff ... qui plus quam tertiam partem militantis Ecclesiae in suum errorem pervertit', *Fontes rerum Austriacarum*, SS, vi. 124.

[85] E.g. *De civili dominio*, ii. 7, p. 61, 'Et patet quod si omnes tales essent subtracti ab Ecclesia, pauci in retibus remanerent'; cf. *De Ecclesia*, 9, p. 189, 'Christus autem semper reliquit in una parte Ecclesiae suae vel aliqua aliquos fideles qui mundum deserant et in illis forte abiectis primatibus stat fides et continuatio sanctae matris Ecclesiae', although in *De potestate papae*, 11, p. 272, he could not resist adding the Ockhamist point that God could use his absolute potency to frustrate Wyclif's belief ('Ego autem credo quod est necessarium ex suppositione ...') that there must be a continuous line of true believers from the Ascension to the Day of Judgement.

[86] *De Ecclesia*, 15, p. 357, 'ideo propter multitudinem, propter famam et propter terrorem istorum satellitum exterriti sunt pauci simplices dicere veritatem'; cf. the use of the 'many are called, but few are chosen' theme in relation to the friars, *De solutione Sathanae*, 2, p. 397, 'sic pauci fideles qui stant hodie in veritate legis Domini ...'.

because there were so few of them compared to the papalists ('. . . sunt manifesti haeretici et pauci contra cleri multitudinem quae constantius stat cum papa'), he retorted

> Hic dicitur quod argutia illa informis pharisaica dependet super stultitia populari. Cum enim stultorum sit infinitus numerus, ut dicitur Eccles. primo [15], et multi sunt vocati, pauci electi, ut dicitur Matt. 22 [14], idem est ac si Antichristus sic argueret: 'pars dyaboli habet multiplicius falsum testimonium contra Christum, ergo parti illi populus debet credere contra Deum.'[87]

The papalists might be as numerous as the sands of the sea, but this only meant that they required a very wide road to convey them all to Hell.[88] Strait is the gate . . . over and over again we are told how few his supporters were, and how their numbers were constantly declining under the weight of papalist repression. But there was no option in the matter: it was the nature of the saints to be a select few constantly being reduced. They were required to be by definition a permanent minority, regardless of the numbers involved. Wyclif insisted that the opponents could not claim to be a majority simply on the grounds that they had greater numbers:[89] you could not have a majority which was *wrong*. Just as Wyclif's majorities were not to be treated numerically, so his concept of a minority is equally suspect and should be taken with caution. The 'wise and prudent few' who understood their Bibles better than anybody else needed to be underestimated to secure their place in the great eschatological drama.

Massive persecution should have needed massive numbers to be persecuted, but in this context numbers are as mythical as the persecution itself. It was what *ought* to have happened, and so in a sense rightly *did* happen, rather than what actually took place. Prophecy-fulfilling mythology is much more important here than mere history. Wyclif's close connection with contemporary spirituality led him to produce a political theory more akin to the Passion dramas with their elaborate

---

87 *Cruciata*, 5, p. 605.
88 *De solutione Sathanae*, 2, p. 396, citing Matt. 7. 13 and Apoc. 20. 8.
89 *Dialogus*, 11, pp. 21–2, 'Qui autem credit ut fidem communitati vel populo est in ianuis ut stolide seducatur, quia Eccles. primo [15] scribitur "stultorum infinitus est numerus". Et sapiens Daniel cum populus dampnasset Susannam ex falso testimonio sacerdotum si generaliter multitudo testium approbetur. . . . Ideo est stulta evidentia si maior pars militantum sic asserit, ergo verum, cum sit argumentum topicum ad contrarium concludendum, quia Deus scit si nunc militant plures filii patris mendacii quam filii veritatis'; cf. *De potestate papae*, 5, pp. 86–8. One is reminded of Marsilius' *valentior pars*.

embroidery of the details of Christ's trial and crucifixion.[90] Despite some of Wyclif's rude remarks about 'miracle plays', Lollardy was not opposed to the drama as such, and his followers are known to have adapted at least one play to their own purposes.[91] But as has recently been asked of *Piers Plowman*, how far did the author believe in his own drama? Was this apocalyptic speculation simply a cynical manipulation of popular piety to promote royalist propaganda, or do we have here another example of the medieval capacity to believe that enactment of a prophecy would actually bring it about? Should the Lollard persecution be added to the lists of great jousts, the ceremonial battles between the forces of good and evil which often preceded crusades, and might even replace the actual crusades themselves? Whatever the answer, Wyclif takes his place in the long tradition of *ludi de Antichristo*, the plays about Antichrist which were strenuously objected to on the grounds that if one portrayed the end of the world, it was likely to cause it to happen.

If one could ask Wyclif why the Lollard movement eventually failed and became politically helpless during the fifteenth century, I suspect he would answer that it was because the great persecution never happened: the sacrifice was refused. But a more valid answer would be that Lollardy was engaged in the long travail in which its adherents walked in the footsteps of St Paul. Wyclif endless praised the wandering apostle not only for seeking to call St Peter to correction, but also for appealing to Caesar.[92] Wyclif knew that without royal intervention the Reformation would never take place, at least not in England, and his appeals became more and more frenzied as it became apparent that the crown was not willing to act. It weighed little with him that there was a basic contradiction between demanding to be persecuted as a theological necessity in one breath and begging to be saved from it the next. He always accepted that lay supremacy required lay involvement. The saints could declare the truth; they

---

[90] Cf. his comment on the Blackfriars Council: 'Unde in ultimo suo concilio terraemotus in quo illudebant episcopi Christum Dominum nostrum vel membris suis triumphantis Ecclesiae tamquam haereticum condemnando regem nostrum et eius proceres, et per consequens communitatem in castigationem pseudoclericorum haereticando, recoluerunt ex timore patris sui de Romano pontifice . . .', *Supplementum Trialogi*, 8, pp. 445–6.

[91] For the use of the drama as a vehicle for anti-Lollard propaganda see V. A. Kolve, *The Play Called Corpus Christi* (London, 1966), esp. pp. 44–9; and in relation to the Croxton *Play of the Sacrament* see now A. E. Nichols, 'Lollard language in the Croxton *Play of the Sacrament*', *Notes and Queries*, n.s., 234 (1989), pp. 23–5.

[92] *De civili dominio*, ii. 14, pp. 170–1; iii. 2, p. 28; *De potestate papae*, 7, p. 157. St Paul, 'doctor praecipuus', was the ideal of a wandering preacher who was not deterred by popular opposition: *De eucharistia*, 9, pp. 294–5; *Dialogus*, 25, p. 52; *Expositio Matthaei XXIII*, 4, pp. 323–4; cf. *Opus evangelicum*, iii. 6, ii. 22; Benrath, *Bibelkommentar*, pp. 243–4.

could set an example; they could pay the price: but it was the king who had to set his own house in order.[93] Wyclif understood that, like Marsilius and Ockham, he needed the same sort of support from the court in London that the Spirituals had had at Munich. But John of Gaunt was not a Louis of Bavaria.[94] He would gladly employ and protect someone who could be useful in bringing bishops and abbots to heel. Dispossession of the religious, crown appointment of clergy, apostolic poverty and so on, were all things which could find a place in the royal arsenal; even prophecies could be utilized for propaganda purposes: but no government could administer the realm on the basis of apocalyptic speculation. If Wyclif made the mistake of believing himself, we can reasonably doubt whether his patrons did too. As one writer, perhaps Hoccleve, subsequently asked, was the life of a Wycliffite conducive to being a governor?

> Hit is unkyndly for a knight
> That shuld a kynges castel kepe
> To babble the Bibel day and night
> In restyng time when he shuld slepe.[95]

He was asking whether a Lollard knight could be effective: was there not an irreconcilable tension between sanctity and successful politics? Wyclif gave his movement the character of suffering saints, but it meant leaving the real political action to others: people with their minds firmly fixed on the blessed agonies of the prelude to reformation were not likely to be good revolutionaries. And the danger was that what the Lollards professed themselves to be, they were liable to become. A persecuted minority must regard actual success as a dubious asset: a life in which patience under tribulation was a necessary qualification was hardly equipped to handle power and influence. Lollardy therefore accepted far too easily the role it

---

[93] *Opus evangelicum*, iii. 46, ii. 170, 'Pauperes autem presbyteri non possunt aliter facere in ista materia nisi loqui fidem Dei et tangere media per quae regnicolae poterunt esse salvi, quia principum potestas et eorum qui portant gladium debet se extendere ad ista media practizanda'; *Dialogus*, 5, p. 11, 'nec sufficiunt pauperes et pauci fideles sacerdotes resistere, nisi Deus per saeculare brachium vel aliunde citius manus apposuerit adiutrices.'

[94] According to Wyclif the seduction of secular lords by Antichrist was further proof of the end of the world: *Opus evangelicum*, i. 8, i. 26. On John of Gaunt see now A. Goodman, *John of Gaunt: The Exercise of Princely Power in Fourteenth-Century Europe* (Harlow, 1992); S. Walker, *The Lancastrian Affinity, 1361–1399* (Oxford, 1990).

[95] T. Wright, *Political Poems and Songs* (RS, 1861), 2, 244. The point was implicitly raised by Wyclif himself when he remarked that the chroniclers provided few examples of popes who had become martyrs after the papacy obtained temporal power: *De potestate papae*, 7, p. 146.

had given itself of being an underground movement, exciting but in-effective. The notion of the suffering saints sustained the faith and enabled Lollardy to survive the long winter of the fifteenth century, but it had little more to offer. It did not provide a formula for successful government: which is why the Reformation, when it came, sought to abolish Lollardy rather than to revive it.

THE RADICAL GERMAN REFORMER
THOMAS MÜNTZER (c.1489–1525):
THE IMPACT OF MYSTICAL AND
APOCALYPTICAL TRADITIONS ON HIS
THEOLOGICAL THOUGHT

by E. M. V. M. HONÉE

I. INTRODUCTION

THOMAS MÜNTZER's name is inseparably interwoven with the early history of the German Reformation. This reformer was active during the third decade of the sixteenth century and this mainly in Thüringen, an area in the eastern part of the German Empire belonging to the electorate of Saxony. As such it was to come early under the influence of the Lutheran reform movement initiated in Wittenberg.

Three elements from Thomas Müntzer's life bear recalling here. Firstly, he had developed a vigorous pastoral ministry in Zwickau, Allstedt, and other cities in the electorate of Saxony. He was an innovative pastor. He was the first, long before Luther, to create a German liturgy in which the community was actively involved in worship. Secondly, Müntzer's life was marked by his relationship with the Wittenberg theologians. Initially, his contacts with Luther and other Wittenbergers were warm and genial, but they ended in virulent animosity. In Müntzer's opinion, the reformation that Luther and his cohorts promoted was far too moderate; whereas he, in his turn, was regarded in Wittenberg as a *Schwärmer* because of his radical views. Thirdly and finally, at the end of his life Müntzer developed into a political activist. He called upon his followers in Allstedt, Mansfeld, and Sangershausen to join the *Bauernkrieg* just then reaching Thüringen from southern Germany. In his speeches and letters Müntzer referred to this revolt as a special moment in salvation history: he called it a Judgement Day on which the elect would be separated from the wicked. In the spring of 1525 the rulers administered a decisive blow to the army of rebellious peasants gathered in Frankenhausen. Müntzer was taken prisoner at the time. After interrogation under severe torture he was executed in Mühlhausen.

2. PROBLEM AND APPROACH

History has long treated Thomas Müntzer as a second-rate reformer dependent on Luther. Early in this century Karl Holl was the first church historian to study his theology. The guiding attitude of his famous study is revealed in its title: *Martin Luther und die Schwärmer* (1922).[1] Thomas Müntzer is primarily portrayed here as one of Luther's radical students. This typical approach, inaugurated by Karl Holl, continued to exercise its influence even as far as the extensive biography of Thomas Müntzer written by Walter Elliger in 1975.[2]

During the past three decades, other ways of looking at Müntzer have been proffered; these are reflected in the title of this presentation. Some authors have examined what influence Thomas Müntzer may have received from late medieval mysticism, others have referred to his openness toward apocalyptic and chiliastic traditions. These new approaches will be briefly treated here.[3]

Our presentation is divided in two parts. The first gives a rather general outline of the two approaches just mentioned and provides a few illustrations. Then we will look somewhat more closely at the modern discussion, explaining it by using certain insights, some defended by Hans-Jürgen Goertz and others by Reinhard Schwarz.

3. MYSTICAL INFLUENCE

To a reader of Müntzer's writings, it is striking how he demonstrates a special interest in the consciously lived experience of faith, the *experientia fidei*. In ever new combinations he contrasts *erfahrene Glaube* with *erdichtete Glaube*, the fictional faith of all those who have not undergone an inner conversion. Apart from Luther, Müntzer developed his own teaching on *fides*, in which the emphasis lies on the question of how an authentic faith experienced from within comes to be. The result is a description of the *Ankunft des Glaubens*, the process in which the real, the experienced faith arises and develops.

The same thing can also be expressed differently: Müntzer, in his

---

[1] K. Holl, 'Luther und die Schwärmer', *Gesammelte Aufsätze*, 1 (Tübingen, 1923), pp. 420–67.
[2] W. Elliger, *Thomas Müntzer. Leben und Werk* (Göttingen, 1975).
[3] For an all-round overview of modern Müntzer research, see B. Lohse, *Thomas Müntzer in neuer Sicht. Müntzer im Licht der neuern Forschung und die Frage nach dem Ansatz seiner Theologie* (*Berichte aus den Sitzungen der Joachim Jungius-Gesellschaft der Wissenschaften e. V.*, Hamburg; Hamburg Jg. 9, H. 2: Göttingen, 1991). This work also contains several chapters on the Marxist approach to Müntzer's activity, which do not come under consideration here.

writings, repeatedly offers a manual for Christian perfection. Indeed, the dissection of the process of faith is expanded in his writings to encompass a description of the path to salvation which every Christian must follow.[4] The beginning, middle, and end of this path to salvation is portrayed in a way which recalls the mysticism of Tauler, Seuse, and the author of the *Theologia Deutsch*. Müntzer describes inner conversion as a complex process in which a person frees himself from ties to the world, that is to all created things, directing desire ever more toward God, so that in the end an immediate experience of God is achieved. All things considered, the mystics use the same basic outline of spiritual life and also portray it as turning away from all the created world and turning toward God.

It is even striking that Müntzer uses the same terminology as do the mystics. In referring to severing ties with the world, Müntzer uses a series of synonymous verbs all beginning with the prefix *ent-*, such as *ent-fremden*, *ent-werden*, *ent-blössen*, *ent-groben*. Many of these unusual word constructions are also to be found in the writings of the above mentioned mystics. Just as with the German mystics, the experience of God's presence takes place for Müntzer in the *Abgrund* of the soul. Finally, he referred to this very experience of God in a metaphor also derived from the mystical tradition. Müntzer and the mystics understood God's self-revelation analogous to both the eternal birth of the Son from the Father and the historical birth of the Son in the incarnation. In other words, Müntzer and the late medieval mystics know a third birth or emanation of the Son, namely, his spiritual birth in each Christian individually. Once the *homo viator* struggling toward perfection has been purified, there takes place, in Müntzer's words, *dye lebendige rede Gots, do der vater den szon ausspricht im herzen des menschen.*[5]

That Müntzer had read the mystics intensively is beyond doubt. We have biographical indications for this, one of which deserves particular mention. According to a certainly credible tradition he possessed an early edition (1508) of Tauler's sermons.[6] Unfortunately Müntzer's own copy of this Tauler edition has been lost. It had long been preserved in the

---

[4] For what follows see: R. Schwarz, 'Thomas Müntzer und die Mystik', S. Bräuer and H. Jung-hans, *Der Theologe Thomas Müntzer. Untersuchungen zu seiner Entwicklung und Lehre* (Göttingen, 1989), pp. 283–301, esp. pp. 285ff.

[5] This quotation comes from the *Prager Manifest* (1521): see Thomas Müntzer, *Schriften und Briefe. Kritische Gesamtausgabe*, unter Mitarbeit von Paul Kirn; ed. Günther Franz (Gütersloh, 1968), pp. 498, 28f. (According to Schwarz, *Müntzer und die Mystik*, p. 291, n. 98, *anspricht* should be read *ausspricht*.) Müntzer's writings are also available in an English translation: *The Collected Works of Thomas Müntzer*, ed. and translated by Peter Matheson (Edinburgh, 1988).

[6] G. Franz, *Schriften und Briefe*, p. 538.

Kirchenbibliothek in Gera (BRD) until the latter was destroyed by fire in 1780.[7] For the study of Müntzer the destruction of this one book was a catastrophic loss, for it was filled with Müntzer's own handwritten notes, recognized before the fire, but not studied in depth. Were we now to have this book from Müntzer's library, how lovingly and meticulously would these notes to Tauler's texts be studied!

4. APOCALYPTIC AND CHILIASM

Is there similar external evidence for the presupposition that Müntzer also studied chiliastic or apocalyptic literature? There is, but in this case there is but one single, though very significant trail. In one of his letters Thomas Müntzer praises Joachim of Fiore. As a matter of fact, without knowing it he is praising here a pseudo-Joachim. Müntzer lauds the Calabrian abbot for his commentary on Jeremiah which he claims to know and to have read.[8] The work to which Müntzer refers in this context has often been attributed to the abbot of Fiore, but is in fact a radical Joachimist tract from the end of the thirteenth century. It is the so-called *Super Hieremiam Prophetam* in which Joachim of Fiore's original ideas are passed on in an heretically distorted form.

Marjorie Reeves has described the content of *Super Hieremiam* in detail.[9] Two ideas are characteristic for the Joachimistic tradition expressed in it: a vehement anticlericalism and the steadfast conviction that the existing order in the Church and society will be overthrown by a radical revolution and that this order will be replaced by a kingdom of peace and justice.[10] It is precisely these two ideas which we find in Thomas Müntzer. For this reason Richard Bailey has let himself be led to propose the risky hypothesis that Müntzer was a student of the author of *Super Hieremiam*, but consciously kept this dependency a secret. Had he proclaimed it openly he would have paid dearly and been persecuted by the inquisition.[11]

---

[7] M. Steinmetz, 'Thomas Müntzer und die Mystik. Quellenkritische Bemerkungen', in P. Blickle (ed.), *Bauer, Reich und Reformation. Festschrift für G. Franz*, pp. 148–59.

[8] 'Bey mir ist das gezeugnis abatis Joachim groß. Ich hab in alleine uber Jeremiam gelesen. Aber meine leer is hoch droben, ich nym sie von im nicht an, sundern vom ausreden Gotis, wie ich dan zurzeit mit aller schrift der biblien beweisen wil', Müntzer to Heinz Zeiß, Allstedt 2. 12. 1523. (*Schriften und Briefe*, p. 398.)

[9] Marjorie Reeves, *The Influence of Prophecy in the Later Middle Ages* (Oxford, 1969).

[10] Ibid., p. 397.

[11] R. Bailey, 'The sixteenth century's apocalyptic heritage and Thomas Müntzer', *Mennonite Quarterly Review*, 57 (1983), pp. 27–44.

Such argumentation *ex silentio* is not convincing, but what is certain is that Müntzer, like Joachim of Fiore's radical followers, counted on a total change of the world in the immediate future and that this expectation marked his life and work. Müntzer was completely convinced that a radical reorganization was imminent and that it would begin with a separation of the elect from the godless. Müntzer thus became the 'Theologian of the Last Judgement' and Judgement became a 'key concept of his thought'.[12]

5. MÜNTZER'S BASIC SPIRITUAL CONCEPT

So far some contrasting data has been ordered in two series: on the one side evidence for a mystical influence on Müntzer's theology and on the other evidence for its belonging to apocalyptic and chiliastic traditions. In contemporary study of Müntzer's works nearly everyone starts from the complexity sketched above, meaning that the very fact of a double influence is no longer doubted by anyone. But there is much disagreement on the weight to be given to each of the traditions individually. In other words, the discussion has been focused on the question of Müntzer's theological starting point.

Some derive his thought from medieval mysticism and consider the apocalyptic a secondary structural element, while others argue for an apocalyptic chiliastic interpretation, in which mysticism receives a subordinate role.

These two competing approaches have each a great power to convince. For this reason the solution to the problem will probably have to be sought in a synthesis. For clarity's sake we will first glance at the direction along which such a synthesis must be sought and only later present and describe the two approaches more closely.

In a manner of speaking we could say Müntzer creatively integrated two medieval traditions. Mysticism and apocalyptic both determine his theological thought, but—and this addition is essential—with a constantly changing ability to exert influence. Thus the mystical component is dominant in his teaching on faith, and the apocalyptic dominates his views on salvation history. The distinction made here between two fields of theological reflection, two great themes, is anything but arbitrary and does not diminish the unity of his theological thinking. In our view, this

---

[12] See Gottfried Maron, 'Thomas Müntzer als Theologe des Gerichts: das Urteil—ein Schlüsselbegriff seines Denkens', *Zeitschrift für Kirchengeschichte* 83 (1972), pp. 195–225.

unity rests on a pneumatological foundation. Müntzer bases both his concept of faith and that of history on the conviction that God reveals himself to us immediately, that his Spirit addresses us without the intermediacy of priests, sacraments, or scriptures. If the direct working of God's Spirit in people is the central and uniting idea of Müntzer's theology, then we must discover how, that is in what terminology and thought forms, he verbalizes this idea in his teaching on faith and in his teaching on history.

6. THE COHESION OF INTERIOR AND EXTERIOR IN MÜNTZER'S THEOLOGY

According to Hans-Jürgen Goertz, Müntzer made greatest use of arguments from the mystical tradition. In a succession of articles this historian has tried to show that Müntzer's concept of Spirit has a mystical slant or signature and that this specific orientation can be found in all parts of his theology. In 1989, Goertz published an intellectual biography of Müntzer designed according to this insight.[13]

According to Goertz, Müntzer began his activity by working for a renewal of piety. In Goertz' view he shared this struggle with Luther and the Wittenberg theologians, but stood far more than the former in the tradition of Dominican mysticism. Also the late medieval German mystics were mainly concerned with reforming the superficial, overly-externalized piety of the period in which they lived. But the mystics' efforts were aimed primarily at the *praxis pietatis* in the religious orders. Müntzer, and Luther, too, for that matter, expanded their attention to include lay people, ordinary church-goers. In other words, Müntzer set the pace for a broadly oriented *Erweckungsbewegung*.[14]

But this had also a partly critical, undermining impact, since in his sermons and tracts Müntzer spoke ever more harshly of the clergy of his time whom he considered responsible for the abuses in the Church. In his

[13] H.-J. Goertz, *Thomas Müntzer: Mystiker, Apokalyptiker, Revolutionär* (Munich, 1989). The same author devoted his dissertation to Müntzer's spiritual origin in mysticism: *Innere und äusere Ordnung in der Theologie Thomas Müntzers* (Leiden, 1967). Goertz presents the main thrust of his biography in a shorter form in an essay entitled, 'Zu Thomas Müntzer's Geistesverständnis', Bräuer and Junghans, *Theologe*, pp. 84–9. The following is based on Goertz's two 1989 studies.

[14] For the mutual attraction of Luther and Müntzer to Tauler and German mysticism and for the different role of Tauler in their respective intellectual lives see A. Friezen, 'Thomas Müntzer and Martin Luther', *Archive for Reformation History*, 79 (1988), pp. 59–80 and *idem*, *Thomas Müntzer, Destroyer of the Godless. The Making of a Sixteenth-Century Religious Revolutionary* (Berkeley, Los Angeles, and Oxford, 1990), chs. 1, 6, and 7.

view the priests were the cause of Christianity's decline. Müntzer reproached his colleagues for wanting to increase their domination of the laity and for hindering their access to God with rules and ceremonies instead of building a bridge to him. Like the Wittenberg theologians, Müntzer originally opposed the authority of the Holy Scripture to that of the ecclesiastical hierarchy, but later he separated from and even turned against the Wittenbergers.

He became convinced that Luther by no means opened the way to God, but rather barred it; like the papalists the Wittenbergers gave the faithful stones for bread by presenting them with the external created letter of Scripture. Battling on two fronts—against the priests of Rome and the 'scribes' of Wittenberg—Müntzer developed his own reform teaching. Its main thesis is that it is not possible to reach God with the help of creation. Scripture was no more helpful than ceremonies or good works. What counts is that the individual personally experiences the inner working of God's Spirit who produced the Scriptures. The immediate experience of the Spirit is of prime importance. Those who share in this Spirit-aroused faith form the true Church, all others are outsiders.

We need not repeat how Müntzer describes the 'arrival' and further development of this Spirit-aroused faith. As we saw he uses here the metaphors and thought patterns of German mysticism. But according to Hans-Jürgen Goertz, one aspect of Müntzer's pneumatological teaching on faith deserves special attention. Repeatedly, Müntzer tells his students that suffering is essential to the attainment of genuine, experienced faith. How are faith and suffering related? God's self-revelation takes place, in Müntzer's view, in the depths of our inner selves, in the 'ground' of our soul, but this *Seelengrund* is in everyone overgrown with thorns and thistles, that is with desires for the created things of this world. Real believers must be liberated from the *ancleben diser welt*, a process involving pain and effort. In this way suffering is part of the process of faith led by the Spirit since this process is essentially a gradual conquest of our attachment to created things.

What Goertz finds important here is that Müntzer makes no distinction between inner and external, between a person's relation to God and relations in Church and society. Müntzer's mysticism is not an introvert piety: it has not turned away from the world, but turns towards it. In the final phase of his activity, Müntzer even preaches revolution and works with apocalyptic energy for a violent world change. According to Goertz, Müntzer remained also at the end of his life totally under the influence of mysticism. His incitement to revolution is closly bound to the basic idea of his theology. Just as an individual must conquer his inner world through asceticism and accepting suffering, so must he overcome external evil. The order in the world can also keep him from God and must therefore be radically changed. Parallel to mortification in the inner sphere there is revolutionary political activity in the exterior sphere of Church and society.

7. THE OUTPOURING OF THE SPIRIT AT THE END OF TIME

This last point is controversial among those studying Müntzer. Various scholars have questioned the way Goertz explains Müntzer's revolutionary preaching and activity. The most cogent criticism comes from Reinhard Schwarz who published a comparative study fifteen years ago on *Die apokalyptische Theologie Thomas Müntzers und die Taboriten*.[15] Schwarz is concerned with the explanation of that part of Müntzer's theology which treats the salvation to be fulfilled in the world and in history. Schwarz also focuses on Müntzer's ideas about the working of the Spirit. But he approaches this in a totally different way than does his colleague Goertz.

Schwarz sought systematically for elements of apocalyptic theology in Thomas Müntzer. He tried to find these by analyzing Müntzer's use of Scripture. When an inventory is made of Müntzer's numerous references to biblical passages with eschatological meaning, and when attention is given to how Müntzer used and commented upon these texts, we find a myriad of apocalyptic representations.

Schwarz first analyses the relevant texts from Müntzer separately and then, at a second stage, he compares them with chiliastic texts from early in the fifteenth century from ultra-radical followers of John Hus, the so-called Taborite.[16] Schwarz is not concerned with demonstrating a causal relationship between Müntzer's activity and the Taborites. The comparison between Müntzer and the Taborites is pursued mainly to bring the profile of Müntzer's apocalyptic theology into the sharpest possible focus. Schwarz discovers an 'astonishing relationship' between Müntzer and the

---

[15] Tübingen, 1977 (Beiträge zur historischen Theologie, hrsg. v. G. Ebeling, 55). See also the recent study by G. Seebass, 'Reich Gottes und Apokalyptik bei Thomas Müntzer', *Luther-Jahrbuch* 58 (1991), pp. 75–99, in which this author aggressively distances himself from Goertz's interpretation and introduces new arguments for an apocalyptic chiliastic clarification.

[16] See Schwarz, *Theologie*, pp. 3ff. where exact references for the chiliastic sources used in the comparison are provided.

Taborites, both 'in their biblical foundation and in the representative content of various chiliastic expectations'.[17]

The most important chiliastic expectation discovered by this method is that of the 'Spirit's unmediated teaching'. Here we find ourselves again at the main theme of our own search. To find out what Müntzer meant when he speaks of God's immediate revelation, it is not enough, for Schwarz, to note possible agreements between his arguments and the mystical traditions. The same idea also has an apocalyptic basis. Schwarz demonstrates that when developing this idea Müntzer generally refers to biblical passages which play no role in German mysticism but which are frequently called upon in Taboritic tracts. One example will suffice to illustrate this.[18]

Müntzer often refers to the promise in Isaiah 54. 13 that in the new Jerusalem all the children of Zion will be taught directly by Yahweh (*universos filios duos doctos a Domino*). In the New Testament this promise from the old covenant is cited and reinforced in John 6. 45 where Jesus, referring to Isaiah, says to his disciples, 'Et erunt omnes docibiles Dei: And they shall be taught by God.'

For Müntzer, as for the Taborites, these two passages have eschatological meaning. For him, they refer to the future situation of Christianity which will differ fundamentally from the present one which it will replace. In his view, Isaiah 54 and John 6 refer to the same moment in history predicted in Joel 2. 28 which tells of the outpouring of God's spirit on all flesh at the end of time. Like the Taborites, Müntzer lived in the tense expectation of this turning-point in history. Where he differs from the Taborites is that he does not see Christianity's new situation purely and solely as a result of external changes over which mankind has no control whatsoever. For Müntzer the arrival of the Kingdom of God involves an inner conversion of many Christians; this conversion will be one of the signs of its arrival. In other words, Christ's second coming will be preceded by his spiritual 'advent' in the elect, an event to which Müntzer believed himself to be a witness and which he wished to accelerate with all his might.

So far, Reinhard Schwarz's arguments have been unable to convince Hans-Jürgen Goertz. Goertz responded to his analysis by maintaining that certain apocalyptic representations merely give 'a flourish and emphasis' to Müntzer's theological argumentation without enriching his thought

---

[17] Ibid., p. 3.
[18] The following is treated by Schwarz in the first chapter of his book, pp. 10–54.

with 'new content'.[19] This reaction is surprising. Should it not rather be said that the apocalyptic representations which Schwarz discovered have been decisive in determining Müntzer's whole concept of history? And if this is true, should not these apocalyptic representations be taken into consideration when analyzing Müntzer's teaching on faith? An argument in favour of this presupposition is that Müntzer's concept of faith and view of history are extensions of one another. They belong together and both proceed from the conviction that the Kingdom of God will arrive soon in each of the elect individually and at the same time will change the face of the world.

[19] Goertz, 'Geistverständnis', p. 95.

THE APOCALYPTIC THINKING OF THE
MARIAN EXILES

by JANE E. A. DAWSON

POCALYPTIC ideas lay at the very heart of British Protestant
thought throughout the early modern period. They were held by
thinkers from all sections of the theological spectrum within
Britain, and formed part of the mainstream of the different reformed
traditions found within the Tudor state and the kingdom of Scotland.
Most British Protestants viewed their daily lives and the world in which
they lived through the lens of apocalyptic thought. Its key themes helped
create the new Protestant consciousness which emerged in the early
modern period throughout the whole of the English-speaking world.[1]

This broad apocalyptic tradition ranged from extremely sophisticated
concepts to very simple slogans. At one extreme, the academic investiga-
tion of chronological patterns produced complicated schemes which
matched biblical prophecies to historical events or forecast the future by
calculating the numbers of the Beast and dating the end of the world. At
the other extreme, apocalypticism offered direct images and catchphrases
which ordinary people could understand and use. A sixteenth-century
British Protestant could demonstrate which side he supported and
denigrate the opposition by shouting 'The Pope is Antichrist'. These
slogans, like a modern football chant, provided very useful verbal
weapons in the ideological battles between Protestants and Catholics. The
great versatility of the apocalyptic tradition, with its ability to appeal to all
levels within British society, made it a major unifying force helping to
hold together a basic Protestant consensus.

The Marian exile was of crucial importance for British apocalyptic
thought. The reign of the Catholic Queen, Mary Tudor (1553–8),
witnessed the exodus of about 800 Protestants from England to the Continent. Many of the exiles travelled to the South German cities on the
Rhine or settled in Switzerland. There they encountered at first hand the
three main schools of religious historiography which had developed
within Europe: the history of doctrinal continuity in Flacius Illyricus and

---

[1] For general discussions and bibliographies see K. R. Firth, *The Apocalyptic Tradition in Reformation Britain, 1530–1645* (Oxford, 1979); R. Bauckham, *Tudor Apocalypse* (Appleford, 1978);
P. Christianson, *Reformers and Babylon* (Toronto, 1978).

75

the other Magdeburg *centuriators*; John Sleidan's political and religious history of the Reformation and the Protestant martyrologists such as Jean Crespin. At this time, many of the exiles became part of a European-wide community of Protestant historians who exchanged ideas and information and this greatly enriched the British apocalyptic tradition.[2] Although relishing their contacts with fellow European Protestants, the exiles were acutely aware of the situation in England and mounted a full-scale propaganda campaign directed at developments in their homeland. Apocalyptic ideas provided the foundation of their analysis of the unique dilemma facing the English and informed most of their anti-Catholic polemic.[3]

John Foxe's *Acts and Monuments* was the most important and influential of the apocalyptic writings of the Marian exiles. Although not published until Elizabeth's reign, the *Book of Martyrs* (as it became known) was a direct product of the experience of exile. John Bale was the other great founder of the English tradition. Throughout the Marian exile, he produced tracts which built upon the insights of his major work, *The image of bothe churches*, completed in 1547. This book, which was the product of a previous exile, was the first major work to introduce to an English audience the main points of European apocalyptic thought and to give them a distinctively English framework.[4]

In addition to the major contributions of the two Johns—Bale and Foxe—many other exiles wrote directly upon apocalyptic themes or incorporated them into their tracts.[5] John Olde strove to educate his fellow countrymen by identifying the enemy which they faced. In the first instance, he translated Rudolf Gualter's *Antichrist* (1556) and the following year wrote his own *A short description of Antichrist* (1557). Bartholomew Traheron gave a series of lectures on the fourth chapter of Revelation to exile congregations; these were published in 1557. Traheron then brought his vigorous polemical style and his apocalyptic viewpoint to explain the fall of Calais to the French in his tract *A Warning to England to Repent*

[2] Firth, *Apocalyptic Tradition*, pp. 1–31, 69–81.

[3] J. Dawson, 'Revolutionary conclusions: the case of the Marian exiles', *History of Political Thought* 11 (1990), pp. 257–72.

[4] L. P. Fairfield, *John Bale, Mythmaker of the English Reformation* (West Lafayette, Ind., 1976); J. Mozley, *John Foxe and his Book* (London, 1940); W. Haller, *Foxe's Book of Martyrs and the Elect Nation* (London, 1963); V. N. Olsen, *John Foxe and the Elizabethan Church* (Berkeley, 1973).

[5] For a full listing of the polemic of the Marian exiles see E. J. Baskerville, *A Chronological Bibliography of Propaganda and Polemic, 1553–8*, American Philosophical Society, Memoirs, 136 (Philadelphia, 1979); A. Pettegree, 'The Latin polemic of the Marian exiles', *SCH.S* 8 (1991), pp. 305–21.

(1558). In his own earlier *Admonition to the Towne of Callys* (1557), Robert Pownall had used specifically apocalyptic language to warn that English city of imminent disaster. More significant in the longer term than such individual contributions was the way in which the general apocalyptic framework permeated nearly all the writings of the exiles. An apocalyptic understanding of England's plight can be found in William Turner's book on 'spiritual physik', in the prayers of William Samuell, the history of the Jews by Thomas Morwin, the pieces offering consolation by Thomas Becon or Lawrence Saunders, the liturgy of the *Forme of Prayers*, or the revolutionary tracts of Christopher Goodman, John Knox, and John Ponet. One of the most important legacies of the Marian exile was the all-pervasive nature of apocalyptic thought.

The products of the exiles' propaganda campaign achieved relatively wide circulation in England both during and after Mary's reign. They were also known in Scotland, not least because a number of the exiles were Scots, the most notable being John Knox, who was one of the ministers to the English exile congregation at Geneva. The Scottish Kirk adopted two products of that congregation, the Geneva Bible and the *Forme of Prayers* which became known within Scotland as the *Book of Common Order*. By far the most important channel through which the ideas of the exiles reached Protestants throughout the British Isles after 1560 was the Geneva Bible. This magnificent translation was easily the most popular version throughout Britain until the middle of the seventeenth century when the Authorised Version gradually superseded it.

The key concepts of the exiles' apocalyptic thought were conveyed through the impressive exegetical apparatus of the Geneva Bible. It contained 'arguments' or prefaces to each of the books of the Bible giving the main lines of interpretation and copious sidenotes to the text with all manner of linguistic and explanatory material and cross-referencing. The reader was guided through the intricate imagery of the Book of Revelation by these devices. For example, the sidenote at Rev. 9. 11 explained the '"Angel of the bottomless pit", Which is Antichrist, the Pope, king of hypocrites and Satan's ambassadour'. The historical development of this antichristian papacy was firmly fixed when Pope Boniface VIII was identified as the beast with two horns at Rev. 13. 11. In a similar way, the sidenote at Rev. 14. 8 said that Babylon was to be understood as Rome, 'the kingdom of Antichrist'. The note concerning the woman on the beast at Rev. 17. 3 provided a careful decoding of the images, 'The beast signifieth ye ancient Rome, ye woman that sitteth thereon, the newe Rome which is Papistrie, whose crueltie and bloud shedding is declared by skarlat.' The step-by-step exegesis found in the notes for Revelation and Daniel and the other key texts were complemented by the general statements of the apocalyptic framework provided in the 'arguments' of the Geneva Bible. Together they produced a compelling interpretation of the situation which confronted Protestant Britain. Through the influence of the Geneva Bible, the *Book of Common Order* and the other writings of the Marian exiles, British Protestants accepted that apocalyptic analysis and increasingly came to interpret their world through the medium of apocalyptic ideas.

The main outlines of that later apocalyptic framework were developed during the Marian exile when two different strands of thought were brought together. The concepts of the True Church and the People of God which previously remained within entirely separate contexts were tied to each other by the central image of Antichrist.[6] This interweaving of the two strands produced the broad and flexible apocalyptic tradition which lay at the heart of subsequent British Protestant thought.

The first strand of apocalyptic thinking focused upon the idea of the True Church. In common with European Protestants, the English needed to justify the existence of their faith. They had to counter the awkward and persistent Catholic charge, 'Where was your Church before Luther?' In their search for a new ecclesiastical history, the Protestants turned first to their overriding source of authority, the Bible. In its apocalyptic prophecies, they found the key to a historical explanation. This was by no means a new approach and like their predecessors in this field, the Protestants built a composite picture drawn from many different biblical texts. For example, they culled the imagery of the four monarchies from Daniel, the Man of Sin from II Thessalonians, Antichrist from I and II John and the Prophecies of the End from Matthew 24. It was the last book of the Bible which provided the vital ingredient. As well as a wealth of complicated images, Revelation offered an overall pattern into which everything else could be fitted. The pattern of the seven-fold division of ecclesiastical history corresponding to the seven seals, trumpets, and vials gave a framework of historical development to the concept of the True Church. For the Protestants, that Church now had a history of its own and a doctrinal continuity from the Apostolic age to the present which could match their Catholic opponents.

---

[6] C. Davies, '"Poor persecuted little flock" or Commonwealth of Christians: Edwardian concepts of the Church', in *Protestantism and the National Church*, eds. P. Lake and M. Dowling (London, 1987), pp. 78–102.

John Bale seized upon this pattern of historical development and took it one step further.[7] He used the seven seals division to construct a chronology. He was determined to prove that the images from Revelation matched a strict sequence of historical events which could be substantiated by evidence from the past. He searched the histories and chronicles of England for the evidence which would correspond to the seven periods prophesied in Revelation. In his researches, he found the historical working-out of the prophecies in precise and elaborate detail. Although clearly fascinated by his historical discoveries, Bale did not let them determine the chronological pattern. He insisted that it was the pattern prophesied in Scripture which gave the historical events their meaning and not the events which determined the pattern. Bale explained his approach in the Preface to the *Image of bothe churches*:

> A prophecy is the Apocalypse called, and is much more excellent than all other prophecies. . . . It is as full clearance to all the chronicles and most notable histories which have been wrote since Christ's ascension, opening the true nature of their ages, times and seasons. He that hath store of them and shall diligently search them over . . . shall perceive most wonderful causes. For in the text are they only proponed in effect . . . but in the chronicles they are evidently seen by all ages fulfilled. Yet is the text a light to the chronicles and not the chronicles to the text.[8]

John Foxe built upon the historical approach pioneered by Bale for the grand structure of his *Acts and Monuments*. He also drew heavily upon the ancient hagiographical tradition and its more recent adaptation into Protestant martyrologies. Thanks to the assiduous and self-conscious collection of evidence concerning the Marian martyrs by all the English Protestants, Foxe was able to add a great deal of contemporary documentary material. The long-term appeal of Foxe's work lay not simply in the impressive wealth of precise detail about the most recent persecution, but the way in which he had located the Marian martyrdoms within a chronological framework which encompassed the whole history of the True Church.

Both Bale and Foxe had sought to elucidate the rhythms of sacred time for their English audience. They had achieved this by their careful compilation of historical detail which produced a chronological framework

---

[7] Firth, *Apocalyptic Tradition*, pp. 32–68.
[8] Cited in ibid., p. 249.

anchored in recorded historical events, particularly those of significance to England or the British Isles. Although they did present the story in its wider European setting, both authors emphasized the contribution of such 'heroes' as Emperor Constantine (whose mother was believed to be British), King John of England, John Wyclif and the Lollard rebel, Sir John Oldcastle.[9] The English heresiarch was particularly important in Foxe's account because the preaching of Wyclif and of Hus signalled the loosing of Satan who, from the time of Constantine, the first Christian Emperor, had been bound for 'a thousand years'.[10] According to Bale, the earthquake which shook England in the year Wyclif was condemned was the one prophesied in Revelation as part of the sixth seal. This placed the start of the period of the sixth seal which included the whole of the present Age of Reformation at the beginning of the fourteenth century. Wyclif, whose own apocalyptic interpretations were crucial to the sixteenth-century tradition, thus became the morning star of the Reformation.[11] In this schema, the Lollard martyrs could provide a direct continuity with English Protestantism of the sixteenth century.

This doctrinal continuity which had been carefully traced from the Apostles through the Christian centuries to the present was directly linked to the other major characteristic of the True Church: its suffering and persecution. The seven-stage pattern which Bale and Foxe had chronicled revealed that the True Church was persecuted precisely because it maintained the purity of its doctrine. William Samuell, in his 1556 verse prayer, characterized the English Protestants as the suffering remnant who upheld the true faith and would thereby save the whole nation:

> So though there be but fewe on earth,
> that rightly do thee serve
> Yet thou, O Lorde, for their good lyfe
> the residue preserve.[12]

The Protestant polemicists were able to stand on its head the superficially strong Catholic argument that the visible continuity and authority of the papacy proved the legitimacy of the Roman Church. The Protestants asserted that the True Church was to be found in weakness and suffering,

[9] John Bale's first history concerned Oldcastle: ibid., p. 48.
[10] Ibid., p. 102.
[11] See the article by Michael Wilks in this volume; Firth, *Apocalyptic Tradition*, p. 42.
[12] W. Samuell, *A prayer to God for his afflicted church in Englande* (1556), printed in Robert Crowley, *An Apologie or Defence* (1566), Sig. Aii^r.

not in hierarchy and power. Far from preserving the true Christian faith, the drives against heresy in the later medieval period had been the actions of the forces of Antichrist striving to crush the pure doctrine of the True Church.

By highlighting persecution and suffering as its defining feature, the Protestants could explain the shadowy existence of the True Church before the advent of Luther. They adopted the persecuted minorities who had opposed the Roman Church in the preceding centuries. The glib assumption of continuity in doctrine enabled them to tie all these groups to their own cause and treat them as proto-Protestants.

The suffering of the True Church was linked directly to the progressive revelation of the seven seals by means of other biblical prophecies. The special fate of the True Church had been foretold, especially in the Book of Daniel. The Marian exiles who translated the Geneva Bible for their fellow countrymen emphasized this point when they prepared 'The Argument', their brief explanation introducing that book to the reader. They pointed out that Daniel had specifically prophesied the continuous suffering of the True Church.

> ... Daniel above allother had moste special revelations of suche things as shulde come to the Church, even from the time that thei were in captivitie, to the last end of the worlde, and to the general resurrection, as of the foure Monarches and empires of all the worlde, to wit, of the Babylonians, Persians, Grecians and Romaines. ... And as from the beginning God ever exercised his people under the crosse, so he teachethe here, that after that Christ is offred, he wil stil leave this exercise to his Church until the dead rise againe, and Christ gather his into his kingdome in the heavens.[13]

The persecution it endured and its doctrinal continuity gave cohesion to the narrative of the True Church as it unfolded according to the seven-stage chronology. The Marian exiles had broadened the story of the True Church to include the whole of created time, not just the Christian centuries. They placed it firmly within the wide sweep of the history of salvation which stretched from the Creation to the Second Coming of Christ. The True Church was the central focus of the working out of God's providential plan for mankind.

This grand apocalyptic scheme furnished considerable solace to those English Protestants who were facing persecution and death in the reign of

---

[13] Geneva Bible (1560), fo. 357.

Mary. It placed their own immediate suffering within the wider context of the story of the True Church and the chronological framework of providential history. In the face of their ordeal, the Marian martyrs found encouragement in several aspects of the apocalyptic tradition. It gave them the assurance of a guaranteed final victory, since no matter how black the present situation, it was certain that Christ would triumph in the end. Robert Pownall encouraged the martyrs, 'Christ's triumphant coming I assure you is not farre of(f). . . . Wherefore ye holy ones of the Lord reioyce, for the day of your redemption drawethe nyghe.'[14]

The persecution should not simply be endured but welcomed as a sure sign of the presence of the True Church. The martyrs could also feel that the suffering of each individual was important. Every martyrdom had been foretold and was valuable as part of the essential witness of the True Church. The great continuity of Christian saints and martyrs provided a tradition and a series of role models for the Marian Protestants to imitate. Underlying the whole persecution and giving the suffering a direct purpose was the firm belief in God's Providence. He remained in control at all stages and the persecutors were merely fulfilling their assigned roles in the divine plan, though that did not remove their guilt. Despite the heavy dualism of some of the imagery, the Protestants did not slip into a Manichean interpretation of a struggle between independent forces of good and evil. When Bartholomew Traheron lectured to his exile congregation on Revelation Chapter 4, he was careful to stress this point.

> . . . the decay and ruine, the afflictions, and persecutions of the Churche in this latter time, and what soever is done in the worlde by Antichriste and his members, is not tossed at aventure by hap, but governed by the hande, and certayne providence of God . . . there shall bee an ende of the raging of tyrannous persecutors, and that the governor of all, shall tourne all to the iuste destruction of the wicked, to the comforte of hys chosen, and to the advauncemente of hys own glorye.[15]

Apocalyptic ideas had been providing similar consolation to the victims of religious persecution from Jewish times through to the sixteenth century. Protestants in other parts of Europe were also helped by apocalyptic explanations which gave them the assurance that they were part of the True Church and God's providential plan. However, for the English

---

[14] Robert Pownall's Epistle in his translation of Musculus' *The Temporyser* (1555), Sig. A7ʳ.
[15] Bartholomew Traheron, *An Exposition of the 4 Chapter of S. Johns Revelation* (1557), Sig. Aiiiiʳ⁻ᵛ.

Protestants, such comfort was not in itself sufficient. They required a special explanation of their fate because among European Protestants they faced a unique problem. England was the only country which had openly and nationally accepted Protestantism and then equally publicly rejected it. The English Protestants had to understand how 'the miserable condition of England under the tyrannous yoke of Antichrist' had come to pass.[16] They needed to know why God had not allowed the unequivocal Protestantism clearly proclaimed during Edward VI's reign (1547–53) to survive and to prosper.

The knowledge that their country had committed the terrible sin of apostasy was a very bitter pill for the English Protestants to swallow. The exiles, in particular, had abundant leisure to dwell on this agonizing question and ask, as Thomas Becon had done in 1554:

> And whence cometh it to pass that we, which before were blessed of God with so many heavenly benefits, are now most miserably compassed about with all kinds of evils, and become the very bond-slaves of these antichrists and spiritual shameless shavelings, and as men wholly estranged from God and utterly banished from the christian commonwealth of the true Israelites?[17]

The actual language and concepts associated with the suffering of the True Church were of little use when confronted with such a question. They described very well how the light of the Gospel battled against the darkness of ignorance and superstition, but they could not explain how those who had seen the light clearly could then choose darkness.

The English Protestants had to explain why God had permitted the True Church to be defeated and the false church or synagogue of Satan to prevail. However simple and attractive a solution, they could not take refuge in the proposition that the Edwardian Church of England had not been part of the True Church after all. This would have been to cut the ground from beneath their own feet, for it was impossible for the Marian Protestants to deny the validity of the message they had proclaimed so enthusiastically in Edward's reign. They were forced to continue to assert that the Edwardian Church had upheld the pure doctrine of the Gospel. Even though it had not suffered persecution during Edward's reign, the Church of England had adopted the Protestant faith and entered into the doctrinal consensus which characterized the True Church through the

---

[16] John Olde's Epistle in his translation of Rudolf Gualter's *Antichrist* (1556), Sig. A2ʳ.
[17] Thomas Becon, *Epistle* (1554) in *Prayers etc*, ed. J. Ayre (Cambridge, 1854), p. 208.

ages. If the actual Protestant doctrine could not be faulted, its reception within Edwardian England obviously could be.

The English Protestants seized upon this aspect of their failure.[18] It was clear to them that when offered the Gospel, the English as a whole had not accepted it with their hearts. As a result of this lack of sincerity and commitment, God was punishing England by allowing the godly prince Edward to die and be succeeded by his Catholic half-sister, Mary. God was therefore, quite correctly in Protestant eyes, chastizing the sins of the English. In the summer of 1553, John Bradford wrote that God was punishing the English for their previous contempt of true religion. He pointed out the moral, 'in taking his word and true service from us and permitted Satan to serve us with antichristian religion. . . . This should we look upon as a sign of God's anger, procured by our sins.'[19] This explanation of their plight and the language and images which it employed simply could not be accommodated within the concept of the True Church held by the Marian Protestants. This forced them to turn to the second main strand of apocalyptic thought, the notion of the People of God.

The idea of divine punishment which provided the English Protestants with a suitable escape from the dilemma posed by Mary's accession fitted perfectly into the concept of the People of God. Thomas Becon had referred to the previous happy state of affairs under Edward VI as 'the christian commonwealth of the true Israelites'. In that reign, the Protestants had combined the language of the commonwealth with a full comparison of England with Old Testament Israel. They had portrayed England as a new Israel, part of the new People of God. They had identified their young ruler, Edward, with Josias the boy king in the Old Testament who had brought God's law and true worship back to his people. The series of precedents and parallels drawn primarily from the experience of the kingdom of Israel recorded in the Old Testament allowed the Protestants to justify the crown-centred, state reformation which they had accomplished in Edwardian England. The idea of the True Church as a suffering and persecuted minority of the faithful was obviously inappropriate to describe a comprehensive national church. Instead, the English Protestants seized upon the alternative language of the People of God in covenant relationship with God.

The humiliating loss of political power after the death of Edward VI

---

[18] J. Shakespeare, 'Plague and Punishment' in *Protestantism and the National Church*, pp. 103–23.
[19] *Writings of John Bradford*, ed. A. Townsend (Cambridge, 1853), p. 35.

and the success of Mary in securing her accession in 1553 encouraged many Protestants to revert to their definition of the True Church as characterized by suffering and persecution. The former bishop of Worcester, John Hooper, had written from prison to his friend Henry Bullinger on 3 September 1553, 'we now place our confidence in God alone, and earnestly entreat him to comfort and strengthen us to endure any sufferings whatever for the glory of his name'.[20] However, the language of the People of God could not be entirely abandoned. To jettison that concept completely would have involved a rejection of the triumphs of Edward's reign and, as shown above, most English Protestants could not accept that corollary. The language of the People of God and the comparison with Old Testament Israel were retained and linked in a new way to the doctrine of the True Church. When Robert Pownall had warned the city of Calais of impending disaster he employed the concept of the tiny remnant alongside the language of God's people. His extended comparison of England and Calais with Old Testament Israel and Samaria was combined with the imagery of the war against Antichrist. He told the Calais Protestants, 'So hath God likewise reserved some of the nobilitie of thy mother England (although thei be but few in nomber) as sh(e)ildes to preserve his people from the tyranny of Antichrist in his blouddy members'.[21]

In the context of apocalyptic thought, an important series of associations were made which enabled the two strands to be joined. The first link in the chain was made by the explanation of England's present position in terms of the sin of apostasy. This was the sin which had constantly afflicted the 'first' people of God, the Israelites, who had forsaken the true faith and worshipped idols. The English, a part of the new people of God, had themselves turned to false gods and so, like the Israelites, were also guilty of apostasy and the accompanying sin of idolatry. The second link used the conventional Protestant definition of the Mass as idolatry to move the focus to Catholic worship. This part of the chain was attached to the Catholic clergy, who performed the sacraments, and to their head, the Pope. Such a series of associations had immediate contemporary relevance in England which had witnessed the rapid reintroduction of the Mass and other elements of Catholic worship at the start of Mary's reign, culminating in the full restoration of Papal

---

[20] *Original Letters relative to the English Reformation*, ed. H. Robinson (Cambridge, 1846–7), I, p. 100.
[21] Robert Pownall, *An Admonition to the Towne of Callys* (1557), pp. 6–7.

Supremacy in November 1554. The final link was provided by the identification of the Pope as Antichrist, which had been a theme of English propaganda since Henry VIII's break with Rome and a mainstay of Protestant polemic from the very beginning of the Reformation.

The chain of association thus ran from apostasy to idolatry, to the Mass and Catholic worship and on to the Catholic clergy and the Pope ending with the figure of Antichrist. This careful forging allowed the English Protestants to argue that the People of God had always battled against idolatry and Antichrist. In their writings, the exiles frequently referred to Psalm 80 with its picture of the Lord's vineyard being trampled by a wild boar. This biblical image of the destruction of the People of God provided a series of comparisons for 'E.P.', the anonymous author of the *Confutation of unwritten verities*. He saw England trodden down by Antichrist, 'the Boar of Rome'.[22] The exiles could also assert, with the full weight of apocalyptic chronology behind them, that the forces of Antichrist had always persecuted the True Church. By employing the bridge concept of Antichrist with its chain of associations linking it to idolatry and the People of God and equally to the permanent battle against the True Church, the English Protestants could continue to use both concepts and languages. In this way, they brought the two strands together and wove them into a single apocalyptic tradition.

The image of Antichrist formed a venerable and flexible tradition within Christian literature. In Protestant ideology, it had evolved a double character. In addition to being identified with the historical papacy, it also represented the head of the forces of evil or the false church which was constantly warring against the True Church and the forces of Christ. To the Marian Protestants, the dual image of Antichrist, as the current enemy, the Pope and his English adherents, and as the representative of the cosmic forces of evil, was of considerable polemical use. In their propaganda campaign against the Marian régime, the exiles employed the apocalyptic language of Antichrist to great effect. It enabled them to reduce the religious conflict in England to simple black and white terms. They could offer their fellow countrymen a stark choice: to support Christ or Antichrist, to be for or against Protestantism. They could further insist that such a choice was as unavoidable as it was simple. There was no middle ground since anyone who did not actively support the Protestant cause was against it. There could equally be no dissembling or Nicodemism; clear and unambiguous commitment to one or other

---

[22] E.P., *Confutation of unwritten verities* (1555), Sigs A3r–A5r.

religion was the only option. The absence of a middle way also removed any possibility of a compromise settlement between the two sides. Political deals or accommodations were ruled out because the choice involved more than the decision between a Protestant or Catholic England or even the religious complexion of the whole of Europe. The propaganda tracts insisted that the real choice was made in a cosmic dimension between good and evil, Christ and Antichrist. By placing the decision within this setting, the Marian exiles could imply that an individual's choice at this juncture was irrevocably tied to the eternal fate of his immortal soul. Picking the correct side became a matter of salvation or damnation, an anticipation of the Last Judgement.

As well as surrounding the choice with the most momentous of consequences, the Marian exiles emphasized the sharp division between Christ and Antichrist by employing the language of warfare. They described the contemporary situation within England as part of a great battle which had been fought by the True Church in all ages and would continue until the Second Coming of Christ in glory. In a tract written whilst he was one of the ministers to the English exile congregation at Geneva, John Knox explained to his readers:

> . . . from the beginning there hath bene, this day are, and to ye end shall remaine, two armies, bandes or companies of men, whom God in his eternall counsell hath so devided, that betwext them there continueth a battell, which never shalbe reconciled, untill the Lord Jesus put a finall end to the miseries of his Church. . . . The one of these Armies is called the Church of God . . . the other is called the sinagoge of Satan.[23]

For some of the exiles, particularly those who were part of the exile congregation at Geneva, it was easy to confuse the apocalyptic language of spiritual warfare with the real battles of revolution and war. Writers such as Christopher Goodman, John Ponet, John Knox, Anthony Gilby, and William Whittingham seized upon the opportunity to couch their plea for political revolution in apocalyptic terms. They called upon the English to depose their Queen by force because Mary was a traitor and idolator, serving Antichrist, the Pope, by reintroducing Catholic worship and papal allegiance into England.[24]

---

[23] John Knox, *Answer to an Anabaptist* (1560), cited in Firth, *Apocalyptic Tradition*, p. 124.
[24] G. Bowler, 'Marian Protestants and the violent resistance to tyranny', *Protestantism and the National Church*, pp. 124–43; and see n. 3 above.

Although many of the exiles did not follow their radical brethren all the way down this road to political revolution, they did exploit the ambiguous myriad of images permitted by the military language of the fight against Antichrist. The two strands of the True Church and the People of God could be plaited together because both were the enemies of Antichrist and engaged in the fight against him. In their propaganda, the Marian Protestants could utilize both sets of language and move freely between the concepts of the True Church and the Godly People or nation. By concentrating upon the fight against Antichrist, they could shift from the experience of the kingdom of Israel facing its enemies to the persecutions of the Early Church. This permitted them to employ a much more comprehensive range of passages from both the Old and the New Testaments in their polemic. Instead of concentrating solely upon those Old Testament sections which dealt with the Exiles and the faithful remnant and the New Testament imagery which had formed part of the tradition of the True Church as a suffering minority, the English Protestants could retain the parallels with the kingdom of Israel as the People of God.

The flexibility of English apocalyptic thought which allowed the Protestants to move between the twin strands of the True Church and the People of God can be seen most clearly at the time of the death of Queen Mary and the accession of Queen Elizabeth in November 1558. Although Mary had been consistently vilified as one of the main servants of Antichrist, her death was not immediately interpreted as a signal for the overthrow of her master and the final victory of the forces of Christ. Reference to the Second Coming or the dawning of the age of the seventh seal was conspicuous by its absence. Instead, the far less chiliastic imagery of the People of God was employed. England, like Old Testament Israel, having been punished by God for its sins of apostasy and idolatry, was now to return to the true worship of God. The Geneva exiles, when they dedicated their translation of the Bible to the new Queen, chose the Old Testament precedent of Israel's return from exile. They greeted Elizabeth by the slightly incongruous title of 'our Zerubbabel'. They wrote to the young Queen

> ... whome God hath made as our Zerubbabel for the erecting of this moste excellent Temple. . . . Therefore even above strength you must shewe your selfe strong and bolde in Gods matters: and thogh Satan lay all his power and craft together to hurt and hinder the Lordes building: yet be you assured that God wil fight from heaven against

this great dragon, the ancient serpent, which is called the devil and Satan, til he have accomplished the whole worke and made his Churche glorious to him selfe, without spot or wrincle. For albeit all other kingdomes and monarchies, as the Babylonians, Persians, Grecians and Romains have fallen and taken end: yet the Churche of Christ even under the Crosse hath from the begynning of the worlde bene victorious, and shalbe everlastingly.[25]

As this quotation demonstrates, the exiles did not only use the language of the return of the Jews from Babylon and the rebuilding of the Temple. They immediately moved on to a warning to Elizabeth of the hazards which she would face. They explained that Satan, and by implication Antichrist as well, would attempt to hinder her attempts to rebuild the spiritual Temple of Protestantism. The exiles then placed the whole of the forthcoming struggle within the apocalyptic chronology of the prohecy of the four monarchies taken from the Book of Daniel, which foretold the suffering of the True Church. The Dedicatory Epistle set out plainly the merging of the concepts of the People of God and the True Church, within an apocalyptic framework. This fusion which created such a rich, flexible, and varied tradition of apocalyptic thinking was achieved by the Marian exiles and permeated the whole of the Geneva Bible which was the most important, influential, and enduring product of that exile.

This apocalyptic tradition was carried forward into the Protestant ideology of Elizabeth's reign and thence into the seventeenth century.[26] It also travelled into Scotland through the medium of the Geneva Bible and the *Book of Common Order* and in the persons of John Knox and Christopher Goodman.[27] The breadth of the tradition inherited from the Marian exiles allowed apocalyptic thinking to spread out and combine with more general attitudes towards prophecy and providentialism. It encouraged the conviction in Protestant circles within Britain that a single pattern could be found which comprehended all Biblical prophecies whether from the Old or New Testaments, directly apocalyptic or more generally prophetic.

[25] Dedicatory Epistle to Queen Elizabeth, *Geneva Bible* (1560), fos. ii–iiiᵛ; Bauckham, *Tudor Apocalypse*, pp. 125–44.

[26] For the immediate impact of the exiles, see N. Sutherland, 'The Marian exiles and the establishment of the Elizabethan regime', *Archiv für Reformationsgeschichte*, 78 (1987), pp. 253–86.

[27] Professor A. H. Williamson, in his work, *Scottish National Consciousness in the reign of James VI* (Edinburgh, 1979), has concentrated upon the distinctive aspects of the Scottish apocalyptic tradition. Whilst not wishing to minimize the differences between England and Scotland, there were important features which were shared by the two countries and provided a common apocalyptic tradition.

As the sixteenth century progressed, apocalyptic writers within Britain were able to fit that single pattern to precise chronological events in the past. The matching of apocalyptic images to exact historical records provided a sense of security in that single pattern. Armed with this growing confidence in the apocalyptic framework, later British writers felt able to project the pattern into the future. The number of the Beast and the days to the End became matters of precise scientific calculation. This was most obvious in the work of the Scot, John Napier of Merchiston. As a young student at St Andrews University, he had listened to a series of sermons on the Book of Revelation given by the Marian exile, Christopher Goodman. From that time, Napier became fascinated by apocalyptic ideas and later wrote his own commentary on Revelation and invented logarithms as a means of improving the accuracy of his apocalyptic calculations.[28] This extremely important mathematical strand within apocalyptic thinking strengthened in the seventeenth century as can be seen in the detailed and minute calculations of men such as Joseph Mede.[29]

Although they investigated the apocalyptic pattern in both the past and the future, British Protestants were also deeply concerned with identifying that prophetic pattern in the present. John Knox had been peculiarly conscious of his role as a contemporary prophet. He justified his vocation

> I dare not denie (lest that in so doing I should be injurious to the giver) but that God hath revealed unto me secretes unknowen to the worlde, and also that he hath made my tong a trumpet to forewarne realmes and nations yea certaine great personages of mutations and chaunges . . .[30]

Knox was certain that all the changes were part of the apocalyptic pattern. The fight against Antichrist was assumed to be taking place in contemporary events. Most Protestants within Britain found it natural to interpret the political and religious divisions of Europe in these terms. This acute consciousness of the apocalyptic significance of the present became linked to the wider belief in the working of God's Providence within the world. It led to the view that all aspects of daily life, from high politics to domestic decisions, were encompassed within God's plan. Protestants looked to their preachers to interpret the Scriptures. They

[28] John Napier, *A Plaine Discovery of the whole Revelation of St John* (Edinburgh, 1593), Sig. A6ʳ.
[29] See the articles by Sarah Hutton and Johannes van den Berg in this volume.
[30] *Works of John Knox*, ed. D. Laing (6 vols., Edinburgh, 1846–64), 6, p. 229.

wanted to hear and so understand the 'application' of Scripture, the precise matching of the biblical texts to the present situation. This could be an unnerving experience as James Melville admitted when recalling his own reactions to John Knox's series of sermons on the Book of Daniel given in 1571 in St Andrews: 'In the opening upe of his text he was moderat the space of an halffe houre; bot when he enterit to application, he maid me sa to grew and tremble, that I could nocht hold a pen to wryt.'[31] Providentialism and apocalypticism were united in the belief that God intervened directly in the world at every level of human endeavour. The quest to align oneself with God's Plan or pattern became one of the central preoccupations for the 'godly' throughout the British Isles and North American colonies.[32]

By their focus upon the fight against Antichrist and the use of that common enemy to join the two strands of the True Church and the People of God, the Marian exiles had produced a very broad apocalyptic tradition and one capable of considerable expansion. The intensity of their experience convinced them that God's providential pattern was an immediate historical reality and indelibly marked their apocalyptic thinking with that conviction. Later British Protestants sought to match that pattern precisely with the past, project it into the future and, most important, perceive it in the present. By utilizing the language and imagery of both the True Church and the People of God, the providential pattern could be understood within an individual, ecclesiastical, or national context. Each level fitted together into the overall fight against Antichrist. The insistence with which the Marian Protestants had hammered home that message provided the central theme which held together the many-faceted apocalyptic tradition within Britain. Their equal determination to retain both strands of thought gave that tradition its great breadth, variety, and flexibility. The Marian exiles ensured that the apocalyptic tradition which they handed on was one of the most powerful components of Protestant consciousness throughout the early modern period for the whole of the English-speaking world.

---

[31] James Melville, *Autobiography*, ed. R. Pitcairn (Wodrow Society, Edinburgh, 1842), p. 26.
[32] This distinctive attitude is discussed in relation to Scripture in P. Coolidge, *The Pauline Renaissance* (Oxford, 1970), pp. 1–22; J. Dawson, 'Resistance and revolution in sixteenth-century thought', *The Church and Revolution*, eds. J. van den Berg and P. Hoftijzer (Leiden, 1991), pp. 69–79.

CHILIASTIC PROPHECY AND REVOLT IN THE HABSBURG MONARCHY DURING THE SEVENTEENTH CENTURY

by NICOLETTE MOUT

I. INTRODUCTION

THE link between chiliastic prophecy and revolt in the Habsburg monarchy during the seventeenth century was obvious to the government of those times but has been neglected by the rational mind of modern scholars. Most of the cases, ranging in time from the beginning of the Thirty Years' War to the eighties, and in place from the Austrian heartlands to remote corners of Moravia and Hungary, have been studied in isolation. Many cases have, undoubtedly, escaped the eye of the historian altogether.

Chiliasm in the Habsburg monarchy was a predominantly Protestant phenomenon. Although the Catholic Church had never repudiated vaticination as such, a number of theologians attacked divination and prognostication from the early seventeenth century onwards.[1] Nevertheless, Catholic authors never ceased to predict fortune and victory for the Emperors in more or less religious terms. Political prophecy had been a familiar aspect of Habsburg propaganda since the late fifteenth century. As of old, supernatural signs, pointing to the defeat of their enemies—Turks, Protestants, or French—played a role in the extensive body of Habsburg propagandistic literature during the seventeenth century. A Moravian Jesuit, Martin Stredonius (Stridonius, Středa, d.1650), even predicted the early death of Emperor Ferdinand IV and the succession of his brother Leopold to the throne, together with the latter's victories over the Turks and the French. The authorities allowed these prognostications—which happened to be accurate—to be propagated, because they showed the House of Habsburg enjoying divine protection and thus buttressed the prestige of the dynasty.[2]

---

[1] For the importance of prophecy during the Later Middle Ages and the Early Modern period cf. M. Reeves, *Influence of Prophecy in the Later Middle Ages: A Study in Joachimism* (Oxford, 1969), and M. Reeves, ed., *Prophetic Rome in the High Renaissance Period* (Oxford, 1992). In the Middle Ages theologians had also written about superstitious divination; cf. D. Harmening, *Superstitio. Überlieferungs- und theoriegeschichtliche Untersuchungen zur kirchlich-theologischen Aberglaubensliteratur des Mittelalters* (Berlin, 1979).

[2] R. J. W. Evans, *The Making of the Habsburg Monarchy 1550–1700. An Interpretation* (Oxford,

However, the possibility of chiliastic exegesis of biblical, medieval, or contemporary prophecies was strongly denied. Astrology, in all its forms, came to be viewed with great suspicion. In the early seventeenth century Adam Tanner (1572–1632), a Bavarian Jesuit and astronomer, could nevertheless still write on the possible meaning of *novae* and comets for the future, like his Protestant contemporaries, although he clearly rejected the validity of divination. It has even been suggested that judicial astrology found more practitioners among Protestants than among Catholics, *pace* Wallenstein's desire for a horoscope cast by Kepler. One of the features of the Counter-Reformation in the Habsburg monarchy was a sustained and, in the end, successful attack on popular magic, including prophecy, astrological divination, fortune-telling, and the like. The fact that so many authors of and believers in chiliastic prophecy were Protestants made it easier for Catholics to condemn it, and confirmed the propriety of persecuting by the secular and ecclesiastical authorities those who professed their belief in it.[3]

It has been argued that in the course of the Reformation 'prophecy became to Lutherans, and more especially to Calvinists, what miracle was to Catholics: an occult principle which they seized on to justify themselves, but which laid them open to condemnation from confessional rivals'.[4] Perhaps the Protestant perception of immense change, embodied in the revelation of the true reformed faith to them and the building of their no less true Christian Church, led to an peculiarly emphatic view of the future of Christendom, including the Second Coming of Christ, his millenium and the end of the world. Catholics usually kept to a more conservative view of world history, emphasizing the importance of free will, as against the Protestant predilection for the foreordained. Moreover, identifying the Pope with Antichrist and Rome with Babylon, scrutinizing the biblical prophetic texts for clues for the future and listening to contemporary prophets for the same reason certainly became very popular pursuits for a number of Protestants during the second half of the sixteenth century. The immediate roots of Protestant chiliastic prophecy in the Habsburg monarchy during the following century must, however, undoubtedly be sought in the apocalyptic, prophetic mood or fashion

---

1979), pp. 396–8; G. Arnold, *Unparteyische Kirchen- und Ketzer-Historie*, 2, part 3 (2 vols., Frankfurt, 1699–1700), p. 240.

[3] Evans, *Making of the Habsburg Monarchy*, pp. 397–9.

[4] Ibid., p. 394.

prevalent in Central Europe around 1600.[5] It is therefore expedient to discuss this before proceeding to a treatment—however discursive—of chiliastic prophecy and revolt.

The best-known feature of this mood is Rosicrucianism. The much-debated question whether there ever was a Rosicrucian Fraternity need not concern us here. The important thing is that, at the time, it was often assumed that there existed a secret movement bent on bringing about a *renovatio mundi*. Although the contents of Rosicrucian literature pointed to a universal reform of society in a spiritual sense, it was common knowledge—since Luther—that such a phenomenon could easily develop into a movement with serious religious and political consequences. Especially the second Rosicrucian pamphlet, the *Confessio Fraternitatis* (Cassel, 1615) could be read as an announcement of a universal reform with chiliastic overtones.[6] In the Habsburg Monarchy Rosicrucianism found particular support among Protestants in Bohemia and Silesia.[7]

A second aspect of this particular state of mind prevalent in Central Europe around the turn of the century was the widespread interest in biblical prophecy and its topical relevance. The works of the Herborn theologians Johannes Piscator (1546–1625) and his pupil Johann Heinrich Alsted (1588–1638) were avidly read. Particularly the latter's publications on astrological prognostication, in which he tried to predict the future and compute the end of the world with the help of biblical prophecy and the newest findings in astronomy, did much to make chiliasm respectable for adherents of a middle-of-the-road Protestant theology in all denominations.[8] As an English admirer put it decades later: 'Alsted leads the stiffest Presbiters into a kind of Millenary expectation.'[9] Around the

[5] Ibid., pp. 394–5.
[6] W.-E. Peuckert, *Die Rosenkreutzer, zur Geschichte einer Reformation* (Jena, 1928); F. A. Yates, *The Rosicrucian Enlightenment* (London–Boston, 1972); R. van Dülmen, *Die Utopie einer christlichen Gesellschaft. Johann Valentin Andreae (1586–1654)*, 1 (Stuttgart–Bad Cannstatt, 1978); *Johann Valentin Andreae 1586–1986. Die Manifeste der Rosenkreuzerbruderschaft* (Amsterdam, 1986).
[7] R. J. W. Evans, *Rudolf II and his World. A Study in Intellectual History 1576–1612* (Oxford, 1973), pp. 280–1; J. Volf, 'Bratří Růžového Kříže (Roseae Crucis) v zemích českých a proroctví jejich na rok 1622', *Český lid* 17 (1908), pp. 145–9, 161–5, 209–12, 257–61, 305–9, 353–5; 18 (1908–9), pp. 52–5, 132–4, 185–7, 356–60; 19 (1910), pp. 217–21, 261–7, 338–41, 362–6, 401–12.
[8] Ch. Webster, *From Paracelsus to Newton. Magic and the Making of Modern Science* (Cambridge etc., 1982), pp. 233–4; W. Schmidt-Biggemann, 'Apokalyptische Universalwissenschaft. Johann Heinrich Alsteds Diatribe de mille annis apocalypticis', *Chiliasmus in Deutschland und England im 17. Jahrhundert: Pietismus und Neuzeit* 14 (1988), pp. 50–71.
[9] John Beale in a letter to John Evelyn (1668), quoted in Webster, *From Paracelsus to Newton*, p. 34.

turn of the century, he certainly made a profound impression on some Bohemian enthusiasts. They had, for the most part, come into contact with his works during their studies at foreign Protestant universities.[10]

A third, and last, dimension of this preoccupation with prophecy, eschatology, and chiliasm consisted in the many prognostications about the Ottoman Empire. Since the fifteenth century the Turks had played a role in Christian prophecy, whether its nature was chiliastic or not. During the so-called Long War between the Emperor and the Sultan (1593–1606) sombre prognostications, containing eschatological, if not chiliastic elements, about the conquest of the Empire by the latter were rife. They were often founded on the fifteenth-century prediction by the German Franciscan Johannes Hilten, who had prophesied this conquest for the year 1600 or 1606. In some prognostications, on the other hand, the Turks appeared in the role of the defeated, who would be converted to Christianity and so herald the Second Coming and the millenium.[11]

If further proof for the predilection for prophecy in Central Europe is required, one need only consider the endless stream of printed prognostications and almanacs at the time, alongside serious theological works on biblical prophecy. In 1618, the theologian David Pareus (1548–1622) had a vision of the destruction of Heidelberg, which actually happened two years later, and wrote it down in his diary. Kepler's prediction of important changes for 1618 in his prognostication of that year is as typical as the elaborate eschatological work on the Book of Daniel, written between 1609 and 1614, undoubtedly under the impression of István Bocskai's revolt against the Emperor Rudolf II (1604), by the Hungarian Calvinist Alexis János Kécskeméti (d. 1618 or 1619).[12] In the case of Italy in early modern times it has been very rightly observed that there existed no dividing line between 'high' and 'low' prophetic culture as far as eschatological expectations are concerned. The same observation can be applied to the

---

[10] Blekastad, *Comenius* (Oslo–Prague, 1970), pp. 32–3; L. Rejchrt, 'Bratrští studenti na reformovaných akademiích před Bílou Horu', *Acta Universitatis Carolinae: Historia Universitatis Carolinae Pragensis*, 13 (1973), pp. 43–82.

[11] W. Schulze, *Reich und Türkengefahr im späten 16. Jahrhundert* (Munich, 1974), pp. 42–4; K. Vocelka, *Die politische Propaganda Kaiser Rudolfs II (1576–1612)* (Vienna, 1981), pp. 219–79; M. E. H. N. Mout, 'Calvinoturcismus und Chiliasmus im 17. Jahrhundert', *Pietismus und Neuzeit* 14 (1988), pp. 75–6.

[12] Johannes Kepler, *Newe und Alter Schreib Calender* (Linz, 1618), cf. H. Sturmberger, *Georg Erasmus Tschernembl. Religion, Libertät und Widerstand* (Graz–Cologne, 1953), pp. 261–2; Alexis János Kécskeméti, *Prédikációs könyve (Dániel proféta könyvének magyarázata)*, ed. L. Szuromi and O. Lábos (Budapest, 1974); Arnold, *Unparteyische Kirchen- und Ketzer-Historie* 2, part 3, p. 206.

Habsburg monarchy, where members of all social groups could be attracted by chiliastic prophecy.[13] Against this background the relation between chiliastic prophecy and revolt must be examined.

2. THE BOHEMIAN REVOLT (1618–20) AND ITS AFTERMATH

The first rebellion to be considered is the Bohemian Revolt, the first phase of the Thirty Years' War which began with the defenestration of two imperial governors and their secretary by members of the Bohemian Estates in Prague in May 1618 and ended with the defeat of the Winter King, Frederick V of the Palatinate, on the White Mountain near the same city in November 1620. It was a rebellion of the predominantly Protestant Estates of the Kingdom of Bohemia and of Upper and Lower Austria, who were soon up in arms against their overlord the Emperor, seeking foreign assistance against him and eventually electing a new king. The Bohemian Revolt has often been described and analysed in great detail, but only rarely has even a passing reference been made to chiliasm as an important concomitant, both during the revolt itself and its aftermath.[14]

The leaders of this revolt were mostly nobles. Two of them should be singled out here because of their particular interest for the subject: one Bohemian, Václav Budovec of Budov (1551–1621), and one Upper Austrian, Georg Erasmus Tschernembl (1567–1626). Both were Calvinists, educated at foreign universities, widely travelled and worldly-wise men, both were experienced politicians, highly respected in their own countries as well as in the international Protestant camp, and both were men of letters.[15]

Budovec's preoccupation with chiliasm can be gathered from his first treatise, written in Czech, the *Short Work On The Golden Future Age Which Is Already Dawning*, written in 1584 but never printed.[16] Referring to scriptural passages he attempted to find out which stage in history the

---

[13] O. Niccoli, *Profeti e popolo nell'Italia del Rinascimento* (Rome–Bari, 1987). English translation: *Prophecy and People in Renaissance Italy* (Princeton, 1992).

[14] For excellent recent treatments of the Bohemian Revolt cf. J. K. Hoensch, *Geschichte Böhmens. Von der slavischen Landnahme bis ins 20. Jahrhundert* (Munich, 1987), pp. 220–9 and V. Press, *Kriege und Krisen. Deutschland 1600–1715* (Munich, 1991), pp. 195–204; for a reference to the importance of chiliasm cf. Evans, *The Making of the Habsburg Monarchy*, p. 395.

[15] Both have been the subject of biographies: N. Rejchrtová, *Václav Budovec z Budova* (Prague, 1984); Sturmberger, *Georg Erasmus Tschernembl*.

[16] *Krátkej spis o zlatém budoucím a již nastávajícím věku*. It is now available in a modern Czech version in Rejchrtová, *Budovec*, pp. 199–221.

world had reached. This was as much in keeping with the general fashion of the day as with the eschatological Hussite tradition in his own church, the Unity of Brethren.[17] He violently disagreed, however, with those fashionable contemporaries who were practitioners of the occult sciences. They asserted that the 'golden age' had already dawned. Budovec conceded that some periods of history deserved such a term, but only in a strictly non-biblical, non-theological, down-to-earth sense. Thus it could be maintained that the Bohemians had had their 'golden age' in the time of Hus, the Germans, Danes, and Swedes in Luther's time, and the French, English, Scottish, and Dutch in the days of Calvin. The present age was, according to Budovec, certainly not golden, but should rather be called an era of iron, fire, and blood. Nevertheless, he was convinced that he lived in the apocalyptic phase of history and regarded the Pope and the Turk as manifestations of the Antichrist. He considered himself an expert on the Ottomans because he had once visited Constantinople as a member of an imperial embassy and had read Bibliander's translation of the Koran. In his later works—among them an *Antialkoran* (1593, second edition 1614)—he always paid much attention to contemporary prognostications and to the actions of the Turks, interpreting them in an apocalyptic sense. At the same time, he ridiculed the Rosicrucians for their pretensions to perfect wisdom and their belief in an imminent *renovatio mundi* brought about by human, as opposed to divine, intervention. He himself lived in hopeful expectation of the Second Coming and the millenium.[18]

Tschernembl, on the other hand, did not write about eschatological themes. He was primarily interested in political life, and wrote reports on its general state, devoting much attention to the pressing question of the right to resist the prince when there existed religious and political differences between him and the estates. Like Budovec, however, he was convinced the end of the world was near, and looked out for the signs. For him, there was but one Antichrist, the Pope, in conjunction with the Church of Rome in all its manifestations—he especially hated the Jesuits because of their role in re-catholicizing his homeland, Upper Austria.[19]

For both Budovec and Tschernembl their chiliastic beliefs were at the heart of their politics. Every major political and religious development was judged by them in the light of the coming millenium. These beliefs

[17] A. Molnár, 'Eschatologická naděje české reformace', in A. Molnár et al., *Od reformace k zítřku* (Prague, 1956), pp. 11–101.
[18] Rejchrtová, *Budovec*; Volf, 'Bratří Růžového Kříže', 18, pp. 185–7.
[19] Sturmberger, *Georg Erasmus Tschernembl*.

found a place in their respective correspondence and in their published and unpublished works. It is even tempting, though perhaps too speculative, to study their opinions on tyranny, the consequences of tyrannical rule and the right to resist in the light of their chiliastic leanings instead of their knowledge of Calvin's doctrines. It is quite striking to see how a number of Austrian, Bohemian, and Hungarian nobles were simultaneously preoccupied with theories of resistance and with chiliasm. István Bocskai, who rebelled against the Emperor in 1604, presented himself as nothing less than a God-sent liberator from tyranny, preparing the grounds for universal reform and, perhaps, for the millenium.[20]

In the case of Budovec, who was more of a lay theologian than Tschernembl although certainly not more pious, it is quite clear that chiliastic prophecy governed his political life from beginning to end. His hour of truth came during the Bohemian Revolt, when he was one of the thirty *directores* of the rebellious government. It was thought politically expedient to strike up an alliance with the Ottoman Sultan. An embassy to the Porte was prepared and an Ottoman envoy was received at the court of Frederick V in Prague. Budovec, who called himself a 'tautologus'—by which he meant a man who ceaselessly repeated one thing—now had to dissociate himself from his view of the Turk as the Antichrist. He eventually did so, but plainly with great difficulty, because it went against those chiliastic prophecies on which his thoughts and actions were founded. As early as 1614, Tschernembl, whose views on the Turks differed from Budovec's, had advocated the idea of an alliance between Protestant powers and the Sultan against Catholic and Habsburg powers. In 1619, he naturally applauded the decision to seek Ottoman support for the Bohemian Revolt. When he was an exile in Geneva after the revolt, he still recommended such an alliance, because chiliastic prophecies had taught him that the conversion of the Turks was one of the certain signs of the approaching Second Coming. With the help of the converted Turks, he thought, the Antichrist—the Pope—could be definitively vanquished. The defeat of his own party, at the Battle of the White Mountain, he simply interpreted—like many others—as a punishment for the sins of the rebels. The fault is ours, he wrote, and we have to toil on for God's glory 'not sparing the Antichrist and his followers, and expecting ultimate victory from above'.[21]

---

[20] Sturmberger, *Georg Erasmus Tschernembl*, passim; Rejchrtová, *Budovec*, pp. 171–9; K. Benda, 'A kálvini tanok hatása a magyar rendi ellenállás ideológiájára', *Helikon* 17 (1971), pp. 322–30.
[21] '. . . ohne Verschonung des Antichrist und seines Anhangs [. . .] und des Siegs von oben herab

It is not surprising that chiliastic prophecy continued to play a part in the political endeavours of the rebels even after the Battle of the White Mountain. While in the past many events had been interpreted with an eye to eschatology, it was not necessary to shed these convictions after the first major defeat of the rebels. For God moves in a mysterious way and, at first, not all seemed lost. Had not a certain Abraham Schönwetter predicted a felicitous ending to the war in Bohemia, which would be followed by the Second Coming?[22]

While the Winter King lived in The Hague as an exile, his political future was at the centre of several chiliastic prophecies. In 1621, he gratefully accepted the predictions presented to him by the Silesian fuller Christoph Kotter, who promised him a speedy victory and help 'from the north and the east' and prophesied the conversion of his most likely allies, the Turks, into the bargain. It is not known how Frederick V reacted to Kotter's dream, in which the exiled king was walking on the beach at Scheveningen, reading Kotter's revelations. He dropped the book into the water where it was caught by a fish. The fish swam with it to Constantinople, where it spat the book into the Sultan's lap. An exiled Bohemian doctor, Andreas Hoberweschel (Haberweschl, Hobervešl) of Habernfeld, predicted the ruin of both Pope and Sultan for the year 1624 in his chiliastic pamphlet *Hierosolyma restituta* (The Hague, 1622), and was consequently criticized by the Dutch theologian Johannes Hoornbeek in his *Summa controversiarum* (1655). Many years later, the same Habernfeld received envoys from an unnamed Christian empire in India, who promised help to the exiled Bohemians.[23] Another exiled doctor, Šimon Partlic of Špičberk (Simeon Partlicius), published a treatise on the *Metamorphosis Mundi*, in which he computed the beginning of the millenium for the year 1694 and professed his belief in the Winter King's return to Bohemia.[24]

There are similar wondrous storied buried in the sources: a little box of gilded silver was said to have been found in the library of St James's Church in Prague in 1621 and was sent to Christian of Anhalt, one of the

---

endlich zu erwarten': quoted by Sturmberger, *Georg Erasmus Tschernembl*, pp. 391–2. Cf. Mout, 'Calvinoturcismus und Chiliasmus', p. 76; B. Mendl, 'Fridrich Falcký a české naděje pobělohorské', *Český Časopis Historický* 24 (1918), p. 81.

[22] Arnold, *Unparteyische Kirchen- und Ketzer-Historie*, 2, part 3, pp. 206–7.

[23] Mendl, 'Fridrich Falcký'; Arnold, *Unparteyische Kirchen- und Ketzer-Historie*, 2, part 3, pp. 206–14; Blekastad, *Comenius*, pp. 337–8.

[24] Simeon Partlicius, *Metamorphosis Mundi* (nd); for his life cf. J. J. Smolík, 'Šimon Partlic ze Špicberka a jeho literární činnost', *Časopis Českého Musea* 45 (1871), pp. 319–25; 46 (1872), p. 461.

most important politicians in Frederick's circle. It was adorned with inscriptions referring to Hussite eschatology and gave rise to the belief that 1626 would be the year of ultimate victory: '1626: one pastor and one flock', it said—a late echo of Roger Bacon's thirteenth-century image of the coming of the Angelic Pope who would redress all evils in Christendom.[25] In his *Unparteyische Kirchen- und Ketzer-Historie*, however, Arnold mentions that the Prague box was suspected to contain a false prophecy. An anonymous prophet, writing in Rosicrucian terminology, revealed that the Winter King was due to return to Bohemia in 1622 whence he would bring peace to the world, and this would herald the last days. Samuel Martinius of Dražov, the respectable and learned court preacher of one of the Winter King's generals, had different ideas. He predicted the salvation of Bohemia at the hands of the kings of England and Sweden in alliance with the Ottomans. A certain Johannes Plaustratius of Kaiserslautern was, according to Arnold, much ridiculed because he computed the defeat of Rome by the Winter King in a way which was too simplistic for an age which was both used to and fond of complicated occult formulae.[26]

As long as the Winter King was alive—he died of the plague while campaigning in Germany in 1632—hopes for his reinstitution in the Palatinate and in Bohemia survived, and consequently predictions of all kinds, most of them tinged with chiliasm, abounded. Jan Jiří Harant, a Bohemian Protestant noble who lived in exile in Lower Bavaria—close to the borders of Bohemia—faithfully entered the predictions which came to his knowledge in his chronicle. His favourite prophets were Christoph Kotter, Kristina Poniatowská—a Polish woman close to the Unity of Brethren in Leszno—and a local celebrity, Lorenz Pscherer, a schoolmaster in a Lower Bavarian village. He called them 'God's messengers', sent to exhort the people and tell them the last days were near. Poniatowská's visions, like Kotter's, frequently mentioned the Winter King and the fate of the Kingdom of Bohemia. On one occasion, she went to see Wallenstein in order to deliver a letter from the Lord to him, but he was not at home in his Bohemian castle at Jičín. His wife received the message, and Wallenstein is said to have boasted that the Emperor got letters from Rome, Constantinople, Madrid, and other important places,

[25] M. Reeves, *Prophetic Rome*, p. 9.
[26] Mendl, 'Fridrich Falcký'; Arnold, *Unparteyische Kirchen- und Ketzer-Historie*, 2, part 3, pp. 206–14; Volf, 'Bratří Růžového Kříže', 19, pp. 338–41. Cf. also J. Jireček, 'Literatura exulantův českých', *Časopis Českého Musea*, 48 (1874), pp. 190–235.

whereas he got a letter straight from heaven. Harant evidently missed that story, for it is not included in his chronicle, but he did record a rumour of Poniatowská's death in 1629. From then on, he mentioned only a few anonymous visionaries in Bohemia and Austria. He must have found solace in the news that in 1630 a maidservant had a vision of the unnamed potentate who was going to bring down the Emperor Ferdinand II—then at the zenith of his power.[27]

The sudden death of the Winter King two years later was a severe blow, especially to those who had attached credence to the repetitious prophecies of Poniatowská, who, during the twenties, had predicted in great detail his recovery of the Bohemian crown as part of a chiliastic scheme. In her ecstasies, she had received visions about the ultimate victory of the Protestants, which would be realized after much suffering of the faithful. Gustavus Adolphus of Sweden and the Winter King appeared to her as saviours of the true Church, paving the way for the Second Coming.[28]

3. THE LAIMBAUER REVOLT IN UPPER AUSTRIA (1635-6)

It is a big step from the Bohemian Revolt which started off the Thirty Years' War to an obscure peasant revolt in Upper Austria in 1635. At that time, the Counter-Reformation in the Habsburg monarchy had not yet reached its full development. It is true that a firm alliance had been forged between the Emperor and his government and the Catholic Church with the express intent of attacking and subduing the forces of Protestantism and of social and political unrest. But it took a long time before this policy could be brought to fruition. In the Kingdom of Bohemia and in most of the Austrian hereditary lands Protestantism was eventually stamped out or driven underground during the twenties and thirties by means of forced conversion and exile. The Counter-Reformation was helped along by tight control of religious observance and reorganization of education and press censorship. There were two exceptions: Hungary, which long retained its special position for its Protestant inhabitants because of its role as a bridgehead against the Turks, and Upper Austria, which the Emperor

---

[27] J. J. Harant, *Paměti Jana Jiřího Harant z Polžic a z Bezdružic od roku 1624 do roku 1648*, ed. F. Menčik (Prague, 1897), pp. 34–6, 41–4, 45; Mendl, 'Fridrich Falcký'; Arnold, *Unparteyische Kirchen- und Ketzer-Historie*, 2, part 3, pp. 216–18.

[28] J. A. Comenius, ed., *Lux in tenebris* (Amsterdam, 1657); J. A. Comenius, ed., *Lux e tenebris* (Amsterdam, 1665); J. A. Comenius, *Historia Revelationum* (Amsterdam, 1659); cf. also Blekastad, *Comenius*, pp. 140–8 and passim.

had given as security to Bavaria in exchange for military assistance during the Thirty Years' War.[29] There, the Protestant peasants repeatedly rose in rebellion, incensed by a combination of foreign rule, exploitation by the military and re-catholization. The biggest revolt occurred in 1626, when about forty thousand peasants were up in arms and even besieged Linz. In 1631 similar uprisings took place. They were smaller in scale but nevertheless considered dangerous, because in the meantime the Swedes had entered the Thirty Years' War and were fighting in Southern Germany. An alliance between them and the Protestant peasants of Upper Austria would pose a serious threat to the Emperor and his allies.[30]

All these revolts were partly religiously inspired and usually involved protests against the persecution of Protestants, forced conversions, and activities of the Catholic clergy in general. Moreover, there existed a tradition of rebelliousness in Upper Austria, going back as far as the Peasant War of 1525 and sometimes involving prophecies with a chiliastic tinge about a perfect world in which unjust rule would come to an end and the peasants would become lords. Similar prognostications had been a feature of many a peasant uprising in Central Europe since the late Middle Ages.[31]

In the seventeenth century the peasants of Upper Austria repeatedly defended their ancient political, social, and religious liberties not only against their direct overlords, but also against the new absolutist rule of the Habsburgs and its implied threat of religious conformity. However, they were invariably defeated because they never managed to strike up successful and enduring alliances with the towns or the nobility or with other Protestant powers like the Swedes.[32]

The Laimbauer Revolt of 1635–6 was only an insignificant regional event without lasting effects, but it had a markedly sectarian Protestant

---

[29] Evans, *Making of the Habsburg Monarchy*, pp. 67–79; R. Bireley, *Religion and Politics in the Age of Counterreformation* (Chapel Hill, 1981); A. Gindely, *Geschichte der Gegenreformation in Böhmen* (Leipzig, 1894); G. Mecenseffy, *Geschichte des Protestantismus in Österreich* (Graz–Cologne, 1956); M. Bucsay, *Der Protestantismus in Ungarn 1571–1978*, 1 (Vienna etc., 1977).

[30] A. Hoffmann, 'Zur Typologie der Bauernaufstände in Oberösterreich', in W. Schulze, ed., *Europäische Bauernrevolten der Frühen Neuzeit* (Frankfurt, 1982), pp. 309–22; F. Stieve, *Der oberösterreichische Bauernaufstand des Jahres 1626* (2 vols, Munich, 1901); G. Heilingsetzer, *Der oberösterreichische Bauernkrieg 1626* (Vienna, 1976); G. Grüll, *Bauer, Herr und Landesfürst. Sozialrevolutionäre Bestrebungen der oberösterreichischen Bauern von 1650–1848* (Graz–Cologne, 1963), pp. 1–9.

[31] Hoffmann, 'Zur Typologie'; G. Heckenast, ed., *Aus der Geschichte der ostmitteleuropäischen Bauernbewegungen im 16.–17. Jahrhundert* (Budapest, 1977).

[32] Hoffmann, 'Zur Typologie'; G. Grüll, 'Bauernkriege, Aufstände und Revolten im Lande ob der Enns', *Bauernland Oberösterreich*, A. Hoffmann, ed. (Linz, 1974), pp. 76–94.

signature and a chiliastically inspired leader.[33] Martin Aichinger, better known as Laimbauer, was a peasant who had become an itinerant preacher of a religion which was largely of his own invention though based on Protestantism and vehemently anti-Catholic. A Benedictine from Augsburg who travelled in Austria shortly after the revolt and witnessed his execution, described him as follows: 'At first he pretended to be a new prophet and a protector of liberty, later he presumed to claim that the Almighty had ordered him, Laimbaur, to replace His Son, because Christ had found the human race too crude to rule any longer—as well as other outrageous blasphemies.'[34] Laimbauer had been preaching for some years, but the authorities paid little attention to him because they thought he was not quite in his right mind. In 1635, however, he initiated something the authorities termed a 'revolt': he collected a few hundred followers and wandered about with them, preaching against the Catholic religion and the government and predicting the Second Coming with himself as a Vicar of Christ. He attacked forced conversion and tried to keep people from attending mass. The authorities were soon after him but he managed to elude them, as they could not muster enough reliable soldiers. As professional mercenaries were scarce and expensive because of the Thirty Years' War, troops needed for keeping the peace were recruited forcibly from seignorial domains in Upper Austria itself. These soldiers, understandably, were unwilling to fight Laimbauer's followers, who were mainly young men, women, and children—their social equals and their compatriots. By May 1636 Laimbauer had a retinue of about five hundred people and was finally surrounded by troops. The end came in a village church, in which the rebels had barricaded themselves. With their women and children, they were mercilessly slaughtered in the church. Laimbauer, who had hidden himself under the skirts of two women, was taken prisoner, brought to trial, and eventually publicly executed in Linz. 'His beautiful wife', wrote the Benedictine who was present at the execution, 'was secretly abducted by an executioner's assistant the same night while we were there.'[35]

[33] Evans, *Making of the Habsburg Monarchy*, pp. 398–9; F. Wilfingseder, 'Martin Laimbauer und die Unruhen im Machlandviertel', *Mitteilungen des Oberösterreichischen Landesarchivs*, 6 (1959), pp. 136–207; A. Czerny, ed., *Ein Tourist in Österreich während der Schwedenzeit. Aus den Papieren des Pater Reginald Mührers Benediktiners von St. Ulrich in Augsburg* (Linz, 1874).

[34] Czerny, *Ein Tourist in Österreich*, p. 53: 'Hat sich Anfangs vor einen neuen Propheten und Beschützer der Freiheit erzeigt, hernach sich erkünet vorzuegeben, dass der Allmechtige Gott, weilen sein Sohn Christus das menschliche Geschlecth ferners zu regieren zue plump seie, ihme Laimbauren an seines Sohns Statt zuetreten anbevolchen, mit dergleichen mehr Unerhörten Gottslesterungen.'

Laimbauer's attraction to his followers had clearly been twofold: his preaching of the imminent Second Coming and his fierce anti-Catholicism, which added up to resistance against the absolutist government. It was exactly this explosive mixture which was intolerable to the authorities, who were, moreover, frightened by probably unfounded rumours about Laimbauer's contacts with the Swedes. Furthermore, Laimbauer angered the secular and ecclesiastical authorities alike by his heresies and political visions. He claimed not only to be a prophet and a vicar of Christ but sometimes said he was an angel who had visited heaven; he pretended to have the divine power to save or damn souls; he administered the sacraments of baptism and marriage and invented ceremonies of his own; he promised his followers not only eternal salvation but also invulnerability to arms during their earthly existence, while those who rejected him were threatened with death and destruction. When he and his people were finally surrounded by troops in the village church he still conjured up visions of the legendary Emperor Frederick Barbarossa who would leave the mountain where he was asleep until he was needed and come to their rescue with his army of sixty thousand. His political visions included the ultimate victory of the Protestant faith and the reinstatement of the privileges of the Estates. He had planned to realize this through a gradual conversion of the population to his brand of Protestantism: first he had wanted to convince the peasantry, then the towns, and finally the government itself.[36] With these plans Laimbauer deserves a small niche in the pantheon of religiously inspired peasant leaders of early modern times, who rebelled against oppression with the aim of reinstating just and legitimate rule as they understood it.[37]

---

[35] Ibid., p. 54: 'Sein schönes Weib ist noch dise Nacht, weil wir da waren, von einem Henkherskecht heimblich entführt worden.'

[36] Wilfingseder, 'Martin Laimbauer'.

[37] W. Schulze, '"Geben Aufruhr und Aufstand Anlaß zu neuen heilsamen Gesetzen." Beobachtungen über die Wirkungen bäuerlichen Widerstands in der Frühen Neuzeit', *Aufstände, Revolten, Prozesse. Beiträge zu bäuerlichen Widerstandsbewegungen im frühneuzeitlichen Europa*, W. Schulze, ed. (Stuttgart, 1983), pp. 261–85; W. Schulze, 'Herrschaft und Widerstand in der Sicht des "gemeinen Mannes" im 16.–17. Jahrhundert', *Vom Elend der Handarbeit. Beiträge zur historischen Unterschichtenforschung*, H. Mommen and W. Schulze, eds (Stuttgart, 1981), pp. 182–98.

4. REVOLTS IN HUNGARY AND BOHEMIA (1670–80):
THE END OF CHILIASTIC PROPHECY

The last decades of the seventeenth century witnessed a number of insurrections in Hungary and Bohemia which, now and then, also involved the phenomenon of prophecy. The great revolt of the Bohemian serfs in 1680 had political and economic roots. It was directed against the increasing burden of taxes and the corvée, and involved the presentation of petitions to the Emperor Leopold I until he outlawed them. The subsequent series of peasant revolts in Bohemia and Moravia was quelled by military force and the ringleaders were severely punished. The immediate outcome was, however, the imperial letters of patent limiting the *robot* to three weekdays.[38] It seems that prophecies concerning the future of Bohemia, allegedly pronounced by Queen Libuše—the legendary foundress of the Bohemian state and of its capital Prague—were part of the mental world of the rebels. The sources, unfortunately, do not permit us to decide whether these predictions had a chiliastic tinge or whether they were solely mirroring certain patriotic sentiments.[39]

Chiliastic prophecy did, however, play a clear albeit limited role in the Hungarian uprisings of the seventies and eighties.[40] The appearance of comets over Hungary in 1660 had fired the imagination and been interpreted as an announcement of great changes, if not the end of the world.[41] In 1663, the Turkish attack on Transylvania led to war. As a consequence of the Peace of Vasvár (Eisenburg), which was concluded the following year between the Emperor and the Porte—a peace highly favourable to the Turks—a number of Hungarian and Croatian magnates conspired against Leopold I because they felt betrayed by his diplomacy. They unsuccessfully tried to enlist help from Transylvania, the Porte, Venice, and France and in every way proved to be clumsy in the art of political intrigue. This Wesselényi conspiracy was soon exposed and the Emperor had its aristocratic leaders tried and executed. The government feared,

[38] J. Kašpar, *Nevolnické povstání v Čechách r. 1680* (Prague, 1965); J. Purš, 'Der Bauernaufstand in Nordböhmen im Jahre 1680 in neuer Sicht', *Jahrbuch für Wirtschaftsgeschichte* (1968), pp. 383–92.
[39] L. Bauer, 'Berichte des hessen-darmstädtischen Gesandten Justus Eberh. Passer an die Landgräfin Elisabeth Dorothea über die Vorgänge am kaiserlichen Hofe und in Wien von 1680 bis 1683', *Archiv für Österreichische Geschichte* 37 (1867), p. 285.
[40] For an account of these conspiracies and subsequent events cf. P. F. Sugar, P. Hanák, and T. Frank, eds., *A History of Hungary* (London, 1990), pp. 115–20.
[41] B. Köpeczi, *Staatsräson und christliche Solidarität. Die ungarischen Aufstände und Europa in der zweiten Hälfte des 17. Jahrhunderts* (Vienna etc., 1983), p. 116.

with some reason, that these discontented Catholic magnates might eventually form an alliance with the *kurocok*—Hungarian Protestant anti-Habsburg guerrilla fighters, who were active in the remoter parts of the country. Fear of a Protestant insurrection in Hungary, which would be supported by both Transylvania and the Porte, led to the decision to persecute the Hungarian Protestants with renewed vigour. Imperial troops occupied the country, Protestant churches were pillaged, numerous members of noble and patrician families were tried in court for conspiracy against the government, and by way of punishment new high taxes were introduced.[42]

One of the victims of this wave of persecution was Mikuláš Drabík (1587/88–1670), a Moravian, originally a preacher of the Unity of Brethren but now a renowned full-time chiliastic prophet. He had been propagating his anti-Habsburg visions since the forties, predicting ruin for the Pope, the Emperor, and his allies, glory for the Princes of Transylvania, the Ottoman Sultan, and the King of France. He had computed the moment of ultimate defeat of the imperial forces and prophesied the conversion of the Turks as a sign of the Second Coming. Since 1657 his visions had been published in a Latin translation by Comenius in the Dutch Republic, where they had been criticized by Calvinist theologians averse to contemporary prophecy. In the sixties, the Swiss pedagogue Johann Jakob Redinger, who was an ardent believer in Drabík's revelations, travelled through Europe in order to recruit adherents, preferably in high political circles. In the course of time, Drabík had become notorious in Vienna as well and was considered to be a dangerous enemy of the Emperor and his government. When the Wesselényi conspiracy was discovered, the authorities lost no time in arresting him and had him tried and executed in Pressburg (Pozsony, Bratislava) in 1671.[43]

Drabík's death caused something of a stir. People as diverse as the Dutch ambassador in Vienna[44] and the Lutheran Pietist Philipp Jakob Spener wrote letters about his execution. Spener's indignant letter to Leibniz on the subject is worth quoting, for he wrote: 'In order that he [Drabík] could be found guilty of rebellion, they did not put forward any other proofs but these prophecies, which he considered to be divine.'[45]

[42] P. F. Barton and L. Makkai, eds, *Rebellion oder Religion?* (Budapest, 1977); Evans, *Making of the Habsburg Monarchy*, pp. 262–3.

[43] Mout, 'Calvinoturcismus und Chiliasmus', pp. 78–84.

[44] Hamel Bruynincx reported Drabík's death to the States General; he is quoted in V. Čihák, *Les Provinces-Unies et la cour impériale 1667–1672* (Amsterdam, 1974), p. 273.

[45] Quoted by W. Neuser, 'Philipp Jacob Speners Eintreten für die verfolgten Protestanten in Ungarn (1671–1689)', *Rebellion oder Religion?*, p. 136.

The efficient and ruthless persecutions of the Hungarian Protestants in the seventies had the unintended effect of reinforcing the Hungarian opposition to Habsburg absolutism in Protestant and Catholic circles alike. The result was the outbreak of the protracted wars of the *kurucok*, led by the Calvinist magnate Imre Thököly, during the late seventies and the eighties. At the time, Drabík's prophecies were still quoted and perhaps believed, but their chiliastic character receded into the background. In one pamphlet, a particular vision of Drabík was interpreted as a prediction of the vanquishing of Vienna by the Hungarians and the Turks—with the help of the French. Another pamphlet quoted Drabík's prophecy of the elevation of the French King to the imperial throne.[46] Obviously, the public was still thought to be interested in political prophecy, but chiliastic overtones were clearly on the wane. They seem even to have been absent from the last Hungarian revolt in early modern times: the Rákóczi rebellion at the beginning of the eighteenth century.[47]

5. CONCLUSION

The disappearance of the link between chiliastic prophecy and revolt in the Habsburg Monarchy coincided with the definitive triumph of the Counter-Reformation and the establishment of imperial absolutist rule in most of the territories. In a joint effort, the ecclesiastical and secular authorities had succeeded in stamping out both Protestantism and popular superstitions like prophecy and divination during the second half of the seventeenth century. Great rebellions and peasant uprisings virtually came to an end early in the eighteenth century, because by then absolutism had won the day and the concomitant socio-economic conditions had consolidated themselves. Understandably, chiliastic political prophecy only lived on in the circles of those who had lost all contact with the political reality of the late seventeenth century in which the Habsburg monarchy had become an unshakeable power: the Bohemian exiles. They valiantly fought for their political and religious ideals in the diaspora until they died out in the last decades of the seventeenth century.[48] For others, the connection between chiliastic prophecy and revolt had been broken

---

[46] B. Köpeczi, *Staatsräson und christliche Solidarität. Die ungarischen Aufstände und Europa in der zweiten Hälfte des 17. Jahrhunderts* (Vienna etc., 1983), pp. 116, 146, 176, 192.

[47] Evans, *The Making of the Habsburg Monarchy*, pp. 263–72; L. Hengelmüller, *Franz Rákóczi und sein Kampf für Ungarns Freiheit* (Stuttgart–Berlin, 1913).

[48] Mout, 'Calvinoturcismus und Chiliasmus'. Cf. also my forthcoming article '"An exile makes all the world his owne". Comenius and his life in exile', *Acta Comeniana* (1994).

much earlier. It belonged to a past in which a very different mentality existed, involving Protestant religious fervour combined with political aims. The memory of it was quickly buried in the age of the Baroque and thoroughly forgotten—perhaps under the influence of the early Enlightenment. It is left to historians to unearth these episodes in the intellectual and political history of the Habsburg monarchy. To posterity, they represent lost causes; but at the time, they often stood for religious and political expectations, if not always for a sense of reality.

JOSEPH MEDE AND THE DUTCH MILLENARIAN DANIEL VAN LAREN*

by JOHANNES VAN DEN BERG

ON 11 October 1629 William Ames,[1] then at Franeker (Friesland), wrote the following letter to his Cambridge friend Joseph Mede:[2]

> Good Mr. Mede,
>
> I shewed your *Clavis*[3] to one much given unto those Studies, and desired his censure; which having at length received, I send herewith to you, desiring from you to receive what you think fit to be opposed: You shall perceive his full meaning out of the printed Treatise adjoyned. He seemeth to me to carry all to the *Jews*, upon no other grounds than communion of Phrases. Thus with hearty salutations to you and Mr. Chappel, I rest
>
> > Your loving Friend
> >
> > > W. Ames.[4]

Ames was in a position which enabled him to act as intermediary between the leading English interpreter of the Apocalypse and a relatively unknown Dutch millenarian. Like Mede, Ames was educated at Christ's College, where he was a pupil of the leading Puritan theologian William Perkins. In 1601 he was elected a Fellow of Christ's. With the anti-Puritans he was 'persona non grata'. In 1610, a fierce Puritan sermon got

* I thank Dr A. de Groot (Utrecht) for helping me to trace Van Laren's *In Apocalypsin . . . Prolegomena*, Dr W. J. Op 't Hof (Nederhemert) for kindly providing me with a photocopy of it from the Bibliothèque Nationale (Paris), Prof. H. J. de Jonge (Leiden) for helping me to identify 'Lawenus' (see below) as Van Laren, and Dr N. E. Emerton (Cambridge) for her willingness to correct the English text.

[1] For William Ames (1576–1633), see H. Visscher, *Guilielmus Amesius. Zijn leven en werken* (Haarlem, 1894); K. L. Sprunger, *The learned Doctor William Ames* (Urbana, 1972); A. de Groot, 'Guilielmus Amesius', *Biografisch lexicon voor de geschiedenis van het Nederlandse Protestantisme* [hereafter *BLGNP*], 1, pp. 27–31.

[2] For Joseph Mede (1586–1638), see A. Gordon, *DNB* s.v.; for his millenarian opinions: J. van den Berg, 'Continuity within a changing context: Henry More's millenarianism, seen against the background of the millenarian concepts of Joseph Mede', *Pietismus und Neuzeit*, 14 (Göttingen, 1988), pp. 185–202 (with further lit.).

[3] Mede's *Clavis Apocalyptica* (see below).

[4] *The Works of the Pious and Profoundly-Learned Joseph Mede* (London, 1677), p. 782 (hereafter *Works*).

him into trouble.[5] He went over to the Netherlands; as professor of theology at the University of Franeker in Friesland (1622–32) he influenced the strict reform movement in the Dutch church which is known as 'the Further Reformation' ('Nadere Reformatie'). His acquaintance with the Dutch theologian mentioned in his letter, indicates that he had personal contacts in a broader circle than that of his university. In 1633 Ames died in Rotterdam; his early death put an end to the life of an able theologian who acted as a defender of 'the rigidest of Puritans'.[6] That he had not forgotten his Cambridge friends appears from his contacts with Mede and his greetings to the prominent Cambridge Puritan, William Chappell.[7] His activities in connection with the *Clavis* gave rise to a discussion between two contemporary millenarians, which is preserved in Mede's *Works*.

Joseph Mede received his education at Christ's College in the time when Ames was a Fellow; he himself became a Fellow in 1613, a position he held till his early death in 1638. Although he appears to have had good contacts with the Puritan circle in Cambridge, he cannot be considered a Puritan himself: rather he should be seen as a moderate Anglican with perhaps some Puritan sympathies. In 1627 he published the little work mentioned in Ames' letter, the *Clavis Apocalyptica*. As *The Key to the Revelation* it appeared in English translation in 1643, in the time of the Puritan ascendancy. That was the time in which he posthumously became famous, annexed as he was by the Puritans, though after the Commonwealth period Anglicans, too, saw him as one of the representatives of their spiritual culture. Mede's seventeenth-century biographer, anonymous, but probably John Worthington, writes about his apocalyptic studies (after the *Clavis* he published *In Sancti Joannis Apocalypsin Commentarius ad amussim Clavis Apocalypticae*):

> By the fruit of the Studies ... what honour our Author purchas'd abroad (besides what he gained at home) among men studious in this way, and therefore capable of judging, is evident by the many Letters sent him from learned men in several parts, expressing their own and others high esteem of his Writings, As, the ... Primate of Ireland, Archbishop *Usher* ... The Judicious and Moderate *Paulus Testardus*, Pastour of the Reformed Church at Blois in France,[8] *Ludovicus de*

---

[5] Sprunger, *Ames*, pp. 18–24.
[6] A term he used in his preface to William Bradshaw, *Puritanismus Anglicanus* (1610): Sprunger, *Ames*, p. 36.
[7] Sprunger, *Ames*, pp. 14f., 17, 110.
[8] Paul Testard, Sieur de la Fontaine, one of the main representatives of the moderately Calvinistic theology of Saumur: E. and E. Haag, *La France Protestante*, 5 (1858), pp. 356f.

Dieu, a singular ornament of the University at Leiden ...; Dr. *Walaeus*, ... who ... did hugely applaud himself in the happiness he had to be acquainted with Mr. Mede's unparallel'd Commentary upon that mysterious Book [the Apocalypse]. ... And though he [Mede] was *Anonymous* in what he had done upon the *Apocalyps*; yet when Foreiners travelling into England came to visit the University of *Cambridge*, they would carefully seek him out, and endeavoured to gain his acquaintance, as much as any others then more eminent in place.

According to the author, 'his *Clavis Apocalyptica* (if compared with other Keys) seems most worth to be deem'd *clavis non errans*'.[9]

Apart from the two apocalyptic works which were published during his lifetime, Mede's interest in this field also appears from a number of other writings (mostly fragments) and from various letters, posthumously published in the *Works*. Mede was a millenarian, who strongly rejected the traditional Augustinian view of the millennium; a futurist, who expected a first resurrection of the saints at the beginning of the time of the *Regnum Christi*. In this, his views coincided with those of the German Reformed theologian Johann Heinrich Alsted, whose *Diatribe de mille annis apocalypticis* appeared in the same year in which Mede's *Clavis* was first published.[10] Mede based his millenarian position on a literal explanation of the Apocalypse. Two years after the publication of the *Clavis* he wrote to one of his correspondents that the 'Saints of the First Resurrection should reign here on earth in the New Jerusalem in a state of beatitude and glory'. This was a point of view which he had gradually accepted; initially he believed that the resurrection of the martyrs should be taken metaphorically 'as the rising of the Church from a dead estate', but 'more seriously considering and weighing all things, I found no ground or footing for any sence but the literal'.[11] The *Clavis* is neither a continuous commentary nor a fully-fledged millenarian treatise, but rather a hermeneutical introduction to the Book of Revelation, while the *Commentarius* in its turn is a further elaboration of the *Clavis* in the form of a number of 'commentationes'. The idea of the millennium is only dealt with in some comparatively short passages (*Clavis*, Pars. II, Synchronismi IV and V; *Commentarius*: 'De mille annis tubae septimae'), in which Mede does not

---

[9] *Works*, pp. vif.
[10] See W. Schmidt-Biggemann, 'Apokalyptische Universalwissenschaft: Johann Heinrich Alsteds "Diatribe de mille annis apocalypticis"', *Pietismus und Neuzeit*, 14, pp. 72–84.
[11] *Works*, p. 770: Mede to Dr [Samuel] Meddus, 18 August [1629].

express himself as explicitly on the subject as in his private correspondence, but yet to attentive readers his position was quite clear. One of these was the learned Leiden theologian Ludovicus de Dieu, who had borrowed the *Clavis* and the *Commentarius* from a friend of Mede, the English ambassador in the Netherlands, Sir William Boswell, who had an interest in theology.

De Dieu's reaction, which he sent to Boswell together with the *Clavis* and the *Commentarius* ('Tandem ad te redit tuus Medus'), was kind and courteous, and though not uncritical, still full of appreciation for the author, whose erudition and whose knowledge of 'res divinae' he highly praised. The letter contained a number of learned animadversions on exegetical details, together with a more fundamental criticism of a central point, Mede's belief in a return of the Jews to the land of Canaan, which would be the beginning of the day of judgement, identified by Mede with the millennium. De Dieu also rejected the idea of a resurrection of some (the 'saints') at that time. He remarked he could not (or rather, interestingly enough, not yet, 'nondum') be brought to agree with the opinion of the chiliasts. Still, he believed in a future conversion of the Jews and a future most happy time for the world, which in fact brought him near to a moderate millenarian position. He did not condemn those who disputed and examined these things in a modest way, and he declared he would consider himself blessed if it would be given him to arrive 'in felicia ista tempora'.[12] As we saw, Worthington also mentioned a letter from the Leiden theological professor Antonius Waleaus, which he did not include, however, in Mede's *Works*. Whatever may have been Waleaus' appreciation of Mede's exegetical qualities, he will certainly not have agreed with his millenarian views—perhaps even less than De Dieu. In his tract on the opinion of the chiliasts (in which he does not mention Mede), he emphatically rejects the 'chiliast' position. With Beza, Waleaus believed in a future conversion of the Jews, and he refused to interpret the term 'Israel' in Romans 11 in a purely spiritual way. At the same time, however, he seems not to connect the conversion of the Jews with millennial expectations; the only concession he is prepared to make is to leave room for the idea that after the 'eversion' of Antichrist a period of rest for the Church is to be expected.[13]

Mede sent, as he wrote to Archbishop Ussher, 'a Copy or two' of his

---

[12] *Works*, pp. 566–9.
[13] A. Walaeus, 'De opinione chiliastarum', *Opera* (Lugduni Batavorum, 1647), Pars I, pp. 537–58; see esp. pp. 541, 546f.

Clavis to Ames, who sent one copy to Van Laren (latinized: Laretius or, after his time as a student: Larenus; in Mede's *Works* always misspelt as 'Lawenus'), 'desiring his censure of it'. In his letter to Ussher Mede called Van Laren 'an ancient Student in those parts in that Prophecy'.[14] Ames, who apparently on many points agreed with Mede but who held to Mede's earlier belief that 'that Millenary state spoken of may well be understood of the Church raised from a dead condition',[15] transmitted Van Laren's 'censure' to Mede, together with a little work by Van Laren, *In Apocalypsin beati Ioannis theologi prolegomena sive notationes proemiales*, published under the name 'Theocritus Justus' in 1627.

Daniel van Laren was born in 1585 in Antwerp as a son of the Reformed minister Joos (or Jodocus) van Laren, whom the fall of Antwerp soon forced to migrate to Zeeland. Daniel studied at the University of Leiden; after a short ministry in a Zeeland village he became a minister of the church of Vlissingen (Flushing), where he worked from 1609 until 1625.[16] According to the eighteenth-century Vlissingen minister Godewardus Vrolikhert, who in his *Vlissingsche kerkhemel (The firmament of the Flushing church)* describes the lives of his predecessors, he was a beloved minister; in the early twenties, however, he was accused by some 'of propagating the opinions of the chiliasts and of boasting of possessing the gift of prophecy'. Apparently he taught 'a resurrection of the martyrs a thousand years before the general resurrection'; an opinion which concurred with Mede's ultimate opinion. At first he received the support of the church council and of a large part of the population, but gradually the tide turned against him. The fact that he published a sermon without official consent angered the church council; the 'classis' (presbytery) interfered, and though no disciplinary measures were taken he was strictly forbidden to give public utterance to his views regarding the millennium.[17]

Since, because of the commotion in Vlissingen, his position there had become untenable he looked for a call to another congregation. A call from the church of Kalslagen (a little congregation in the Presbytery of Woerden, Synod of South Holland; now no longer extant) seemed to

[14] Mede to Ussher, 4 May 1630, *Works*, p. 783.

[15] Ames to Mede, 27 May [1629], *Works*, pp. 782f. I think Sprunger, *Ames*, p. 185, goes too far in his interpretation of this passage, when he remarks: 'Absent from all of Ames's outlines of the church was any place for the millennium'; I am rather inclined to qualify Ames as a 'moderate millenarian' (in the sense in which the term is used in modern literature).

[16] For Daniel van Laren, see *Biographisch woordenboek van protestantsche godgeleerden in Nederland*, 5, pp. 581–6.

[17] G. Vrolikhert, *Vlissingsche kerkhemel, ofte levensbeschrijving van alle de Hervormde leeraren ...* (Vlissingen, 1758), pp. 73–81.

offer a way out. The call had to be confirmed, however, by Prince Maurice, the Stadtholder, who apparently had the right of patronage. Aware of the problems around Van Laren the prince sought advice from the theological faculty of Leiden 'as we have understood before this that he has some particular opinions on the twentieth chapter of the Apocalypse with regard to the corporeal resurrection of the martyrs before the other dead, and their reign of a thousand years'; do these opinions, the prince asked, affect the foundation of salvation?[18] The archives of Leiden University do not contain a copy of the answer, but from the Acts of the Synod of South Holland, which met in The Hague in July 1624, we know that the advice of the faculty was moderate: Van Laren's particular opinions were neither in a direct way contrary to the foundation of salvation nor to the article of the general resurrection of the flesh. Van Laren asked the Synod, to which the matter one way or another had been referred, to acquiesce in the advice of the faculty. The reaction of the Synod was pragmatic: the Synod did not criticize the answer of the faculty, but thought it very precarious to accept 'in these times' a minister who had been the cause 'of such commotions'. For the church of Kalslagen it would be better to receive a minister without scandal, and the churches in Holland should be relieved of the fear of falling again[19] into disturbances. The road to Kalslagen was effectively blocked.[20] It is clear, however, that neither the faculty nor the Synod considered him a heretic. Doctrinally he was a Calvinist, who agreed with the resolutions of the Synod of Dort (1618–19), though he claimed the freedom to interpret them in the moderate manner of the English delegates at the Synod. Furthermore, he rejected the chiliastic doctrine of an earthly Kingdom, of sacrifices in accordance with the Old Testament law and of carnal pleasures—the so-called 'chiliasmus crassus', which was rejected by all respectable millenarians of that time.[21] The decision of the Synod of

---

[18] Maurice of Nassau to the professors of the faculty of theology at Leiden, 25 March 1624: A. Eekhof, *De theologische faculteit te Leiden in de 17ᵈᵉ eeuw* (Utrecht, 1921), pp. 62f.

[19] Of course shortly after the conflicts with the Remonstrants.

[20] W. P. C. Knuttel, *Acta der Particuliere Synoden van Zuid-Holland 1621–1700*, I, pp. 119f.

[21] *Meditatiën over den Catechismum der Nederlandtscher Kercken* (Arnhem, 1636), 'Tot den Christelicken Leser'. He emphatically asserted he was not 'a Libertine, a Papist, an Anabaptist or any other sectarian, but an orthodox Christian', and with approval he quoted Augustine's attack on the 'chiliastai' or 'miliarii' (*De Civitate Dei* xx. 7). This shows that in his terminology the terms 'chiliasts' and 'millenarians' denoted the adherents of a 'chiliasmus crassus'; it does not imply, however, that his eschatology was 'Augustinian'. The proviso with regard to the interpretation of the Canons of Dort made Vrolikhert (pp. 79f.) surmise that Van Laren fostered unorthodox ideas. Appealing to the British theologians, Van Laren rejected a strictly particularist interpretation of the sacrifice of Christ, and referring to John Davenant, one of

Joseph Mede and Daniel van Laren

South Holland ultimately did not hamper his ecclesiastical career. In 1625 he received a call from the town of Arnhem in Gelderland: from an ecclesiastical point of view, an honourable position which he held till his retirement in 1651.[22] Once, in 1648, he was delegated by the Synod of Gelderland as a deputy to the Synod of South Holland;[23] to Van Laren this will have been a little triumph!

In Arnhem he wrote two Latin tracts on apocalyptical subjects and some works of a more devotional nature, among which was his *Meditations on the Catechism of the Dutch Churches*.[24] Furthermore he translated some devotional works from the English; in the preface to one of these he declared: 'I prefer to translate books by others which are well written and well sold, above writing books of my own, which either could pass for waste paper or stay in the bookshops for a long time.'[25] Among the authors he translated were Arthur Hildersham and Nicolas Byfield, both outspoken Puritans.[26] The fact that he translated Puritan works with evident sympathy makes us surmise that he himself was a man of Puritan or Pietist inclinations. He started translating from the English after his brother Jeremias had become a minister of the Dutch church of Austin Friars, London.[27] Perhaps it was his brother who called his attention to the English Puritans.[28] Their nephew Abraham van Laren, a Vlissingen bookseller, also translated Puritan works. In 1637 Daniel received a gift from the London church[29]—it was in the year of the great tragedy of his life, when he lost six of his children by the plague.

The first Latin work he published, though under a pseudonym, was his *In Apocalypsin . . . Prolegomena*, the book which, as we saw, was sent by Ames to Mede in 1629, together with Van Laren's strictures on the *Clavis*.[30] In the preface Van Laren stated that those who write on the

---

the English delegates at the Synod, he emphasized that good works were necessary to salvation: *Meditatiën*, pp. 332f., 334.
[22] The date of his death is unknown.
[23] Knuttel, *Acta*, 3, p. 71.
[24] See above, n. 21.
[25] *BLGNP*, 5, p. 585, n. 2.
[26] See J. van der Haar, *From Abbadie to Young* (Veenendaal, 1980), part 1 no. 1048, p. 608.
[27] Minister in London from 1632 until 1638: J. Lindeboom, *Austin Friars* ('s-Gravenhage, 1950), p. 199.
[28] For him, see *BLGNP*, 5, pp. 590f.
[29] J. H. Hessels, *Ecclesiae Londino-Batavae Archivum*, 3 (Cantabrigiae, 1897), no. 2459.
[30] The work is very rare; I made use of a photocopy of the 1627 edition (see n. *). It is not among the books which Mede donated or bequeathed to Christ's College: see Christ's College Donation Book (with thanks to Dr C. P. Courtney, Librarian of Christ's College, who kindly

117

Apocalypse should part with all prejudices; a seventeenth-century reader remarked in a marginal note: 'Utinam ipse faciat'.[31] He emphatically rejected the idea that for the understanding of the Apocalypse an extraordinary revelation should be necessary: the ordinary revelation of the Holy Spirit is sufficient, which usually is obtained by prayers and fasting through an assiduous reading and comparing of the Scriptures. Van Laren saw his 'Notationes proemiales' as, indeed, a preamble to a 'paraphrase' of the whole of the Apocalypse, which he had apparently started to write ('caepi paraphrasin quandam instituere totius Apocalypseos') but which was never published, perhaps even not finished. His main thesis is that the whole Apocalypse is almost nothing else but a 'compendium quoddam librorum Sacrorum in his quae ad Prophetiam attinent'; for this, he refers to the preface of Beza's commentary on the Apocalypse. To him, the Apocalypse is 'Clavis totius Scripturae Propheticae'. Those who explain the prophecies as if they had almost all been fulfilled through the first calling of the gentiles preclude themselves from the right understanding of the prophetic parts of Scripture, as Brightman rightly observed.

Thus, the work as such starts with the sentence: 'Tota fere Apocalypsis de rebus tractat futuris'. Furthermore, Van Laren emphatically states that the visions of the Apocalypse deal in particular 'de rebus Judaeorum'.[32] This explains the rather cryptic passage in Ames's first letter: 'He seemeth me to carry all to the Jews.' After having read Van Laren's tract, Mede wrote to a correspondent: '. . . though I am not of the same mind with Theocritus Justus (his name is Daniel Lawenus) to direct all the Apocalypse to the *Jews*, upon no other ground but communion of phrases; yet I know nevertheless, that to compare Scripture with Scripture is none of the least helps to understand Scripture'.[33] To Van Laren, the idea of the conversion of the Jews was of central importance; after the preface he inserted a long quotation from Bucer's commentary on Romans (Ch. 2), on 'plena restitutio Judaeorum', and when he himself quoted Romans 11. 26 ('and so all Israel shall be saved'), he had the words 'omnis Israel' printed in huge capitals.[34] Several passages, which in the Christian tradition were

---

provided me with a photocopy of the relevant pages). A copy of the reprint of 1642 is in the University Library of Utrecht (Collection Thomaasse), published under the title *Lareni in Apocalypsin notationes prooemiales*, together with his *Discursus theologo politicus*.

[31] *In Apocalypsin*, fo. (**)3.
[32] Ibid., fos A 1r, 2r.
[33] Mede to Thomas Hayne, London, 21 Oct. [1629], *Works*, p. 754.
[34] *In Apocalypsin*, fo. B [4]r.

usually explained as relating to the Church, the 'new Israel', are explained literally; so Revelation 7. 4–7 (on 'the number of them which were sealed') refers to the restitution of the Jews and their final conversion.[35] On Revelation 20 he is short, but his intention is clear: the first resurrection is 'famosa ac nota illa resurrectio, cuius Prophetae passim faciunt mentionem in gloriosa Israelis restitutione';[36] here (as elsewhere) he mentions Brightman, whose *Revelatio revelationis* (1609) he had read. Of course he had not yet been able to read Mede or Alsted; it is remarkable, however, that the works of Mede, Alsted, and Van Laren, which essentially had so much in common, appeared in the same year.

Two years later (as we saw), Van Laren received Mede's *Clavis* by the hand of Ames. From his 'strictural' on the *Clavis*, published by Mede as an appendix to the 1632 edition of the *Clavis* and the *Commentarius* (or *Commentationes*) we receive the impression that he read the work of his English fellow millenarian with mixed feelings. Mede was amazed at the tone of Van Laren's strictures; to Ussher he wrote: 'He finding it not to sute with his Notions, wrote presently *Stricturae in Clavem Apocalypticam*, not knowing my name, but calling me *Synchronista*; and sometimes seemed to be very angry with me in his confutation of me, though he agreed with me in the mainest Paradox of all.'[37] Mede supposed it was not Van Laren's intention to have his strictures sent to him, but

> the Doctor [Ames] dispatcheth it to me, together with his [Van Laren's] printed Book, for my better understanding his meaning; desires to receive again from me what I thought fit to oppose by way of defence. Thus unwittingly I made myself work, yet such as in the doing I at length found some benefit by, having my torpid thoughts revived and quickned, and the second time more able to wield any notions than they were at the beginning.[38]

Mede, a modest and peaceful man, perhaps could stand some criticism, as he himself was always trying to improve upon what he had written: '. . . I should never get through that which is my own, without everlasting

---

[35] Ibid., fo. C 3v: 'Et Iudaei sunt qui signantur; quia signantur ex *omni tribu filiorum Israel*: et accurate numerantur quot ex una quaque tribu sint signati: quae mysticis Iudaeis non competunt.'

[36] Ibid., fo. H 1v.

[37] At that time the word 'paradox' was sometimes used in the sense of 'a correction to vulgar error' or 'an opinion maintained contrary to the common allowed opinion', *NED*, s.v. Here, Mede has in mind the synchronistic system (see below).

[38] 4 May 1630, *Works*, p. 783.

mending, blurring, and pausing at every sentence to alter it.' Moreover, in spite of its sometimes unnecessarily sharp tone Van Laren's criticism was not (it was indeed noticed by Mede) of a fundamental nature. To a certain extent Van Laren's method was also 'synchronistical', though with him the emphasis lay upon the synchronic relationship between the Book of Daniel and the Apocalypse. The main point of difference was the interpretation of Revelation 10. 2: the angel 'had in his hand a little book open'. According to Mede's *Clavis*, apart from chapters 1–3, the Book of Revelation was divided into two parts: the part concerning the seals which one after another were opened, and the part concerning the 'biblaridion' (see *Clavis*, introduction to Pars. II). This little book which John had to eat was nothing but a repetition of the revelations which John had received up to the moment of the appearance of the angel. Van Laren, however (whose 'Stricturae' together with Mede's 'Responsio' were printed as an appendix to the 1632 edition of the *Clavis* and the *Commentarius*) stated, referring to his own book, that by 'the little book' of Revelation 10 nothing else could be understood but the book of the old prophets, which was closed and sealed for the blind and obstinate Jews during the time of their rejection. In this context he quoted Isaiah 29. 11: 'And the vision of all is become unto you as the words of a book that is sealed.'[39] For the rest, his strictures mainly deal with exegetical details or with some of Mede's synchronisms. Especially the synchronization of the seventh seal (Revelation 8) with the appearance of the beasts with ten horns and two horns (Revelation 13) evoked his fierce criticism: what to Mede was 'cardo Synchronismorum' to Van Laren was 'cardo vanitatum'. The beast with seven heads and ten horns signifies 'regnum Antichristi', which would start when the fifth trumpet would have sounded (cf. Revelation 9. 11). Van Laren went indeed down to the minutest details of interpretation.

Mede was not deeply shocked. On the whole, his 'Responsio' was quiet and moderate. In a lengthy exposition he refuted Van Laren's criticisms, some of which, according to Mede, resulted from the fact that Van Laren had given insufficient attention to the fundamental arguments of the *Clavis*. In a number of cases, Mede contended, Van Laren had misunderstood the exact meaning of what was proposed in the *Clavis*. Mede sharply retorted to Van Laren's remarks on the 'cardo Synchronismorum': 'In hujus demonstratione Lawenus totus interpretationum praejudiciis occaecatus nihil omnino veri cernere potuit'.[40] Still, there was common ground

---

[39] *Works*, p. 541.
[40] Ibid., p. 562.

with regard to the most important part of the *Clavis*, the four synchronisms which deal with the millennium. On the fourth synchronism of the second part of the *Clavis*, which described the binding of the dragon for a period of a thousand years as synchronous with the sounding of the seventh trumpet (Revelation 10. 7) or the fall of the beast, Van Laren wrote: 'Synchronismum quartum . . . non possum non laudare, cum sit verissimus et certissimus.' Likewise he wrote with regard to the fifth synchronism, the coincidence of the thousand years of Christ with the interval after the fall of the beast, that he praised it and that he approved almost everything which was advanced to confirm it.[41] Mede congratulated himself with the consensus between Van Laren and himself on this crucial point, and he added that he implored God that he might open the eyes of both of them to see his truth and that all prejudices might more and more decrease.[42]

Van Laren's last work on an apocalyptic subject was published in 1641, and again (as we saw, together with *In Apocalypsin. . . Prolegomena*) in 1642; it dealt with the question of the duration of the 'imperium Romanum'. He identified (as Mede also did in a tract on this subject)[43] the 'imperium Romanum' with the fourth Beast of Daniel 7. The 'imperium Romanum', Van Laren asserted, will last till the sounding of the seventh trumpet, when the 'regnum humile Christi' will be replaced by his 'regnum gloriosum'. In the tenth horn of the beast (the Antichrist) the 'imperium Romanum' was re-established as 'regnum pontificum'. It received a lethal wound in the period of the Reformation, but this wound has not yet come to full maturation. From the 'imperium Romanum' Van Laren distinguished the 'imperium Germano-Romanum', embodied in Spain and Germany (the Habsburg powers), which was near to its downfall; he expected the fall of this 'imperium' about 1700. This would as such, however, not imply an immediate downfall of the 'imperium Romanum'. In the sequel of future events, first the Jews would be converted (but their conversion would only take place after a fairly long time); then there would take place a 'restitution of Antichrist', which would result in his final destruction. But Van Laren took care not to predict too many details; it is possibly a late answer to the accusation that he claimed the gift of prophecy, when he wrote that we are prophets indeed; not however in order to predict the future, but to interpret what has been predicted, in which we may stumble and fail.[44] Furthermore, it is remarkable that while

[41] Ibid., pp. 546f.
[42] Ibid., p. 564.
[43] 'Regnum Romanum est regnum quartum Danielis', *Works*, pp. 711–16.
[44] *Discursus*, p. 4.

the work has a millenarian flavour, combined with a strong anti-Catholic bias, he never mentions Revelation 20; but neither does Mede in his tract on the 'imperium Romanum'.

It is difficult to establish the sources of Van Laren's millennialism. He had read many works which dealt with the subject, including on the Catholic side Luis de Alcazar, with whom he fundamentally disagreed— 'totus mysticus est';[45] on the Protestant side Thomas Brightman, with whom he disagreed on some points, as Mede did too.[46] He stood close to Mede, though he was critical: their main difference was that with Van Laren the conversion of the Jews took a central place, while this point was marginal with Mede.[47] Van Laren's critical remarks on a number of details in the *Clavis* are typical of the way millenarians tried to outbid each other in clever interpretations of the Apocalypse. It is begging the question to say that in the sixteen-twenties millenarianism was 'in the air'; at that time it was certainly not rampant in the (at least with regard to this point) rather cool air of the Netherlands. Perhaps we may say that with Mede, Alsted, Van Laren, and others it was the logical outcome of a literal explanation of the Apocalypse (a field into which the Reformers had only reluctantly ventured), combined with a negative view of the Middle Ages (the period of the Beast), an ultimately optimistic expectation of the future state of a purified Church on earth. A millenarian interpretation of the Apocalypse could serve as an instrument in the struggle against Antichrist (the Beast), wounded by the Reformation, but not yet defeated. This made the struggle all the more necessary, the right interpretation of the Apocalypse all the more urgent and inspiring.

[45] *In Apocalypsin*, fo. H 1.
[46] Apparently he had not read the work of Johannes Piscator, *Commentarius in Apocalypsin* (1613).
[47] The difference, however, was not essential. For Mede's views on this point, see his letter to William Twisse, 11 November 1629, *Works*, p. 759–61.

THE COMMENTARY ON THE BOOK OF
REVELATION BY JAMES DURHAM (1622-58)

by JAMES K. CAMERON

I N the seventeenth century the Church in Scotland was for the most part engaged in working out an ecclesiastical polity acceptable to itself and to the civil authorities. Hence matters of Church government and of Church/state relations occupied much of the attention of leading theologians such as Samuel Rutherford (1600–61) and George Gillespie (1613–49). Yet there were others who, while deeply involved in the conflicts within the life of the Church, also devoted their attention to the study of the Scriptures and to contemporary theological debates. Prominent among them, on the Episcopal side, was John Forbes (1593–1648) of Corse, the leading member of that group of distinguished scholars know as the 'Aberdeen Doctors'. Forbes was internationally celebrated for his *Institutiones Historico-Theologicae de Doctrina Christiana*, published in Holland in 1645. On the Presbyterian side, James Durham (1622–58) was at the same time beginning to make a name for himself as an outstanding exponent of the Scottish Calvinist ethic and would undoubtedly have gone on to enhance a rapidly growing reputation had not his life been cut short by death at the early age of 36.[1] Of his works which were subsequently published his extensive commentary on the Book of Revelation is justly one of the most important. Between 1658 and 1799 it went through no fewer than seven editions, one of which was printed in Amsterdam in 1660.[2]

Like Forbes, Durham came from a privileged landed family background. After receiving his early education at St Andrews University, he returned home without finishing his philosophy course, settled on his country estate, married, and began to raise a family. At this stage he had no thought of entering the ministry, but after what can only be described as a

---

[1] *DNB* 16, pp. 255f. On Durham's contribution to Calvinist ethics see Gordon Marshall, *Presbyteries and Profits: Calvinism and the Development of Capitalism in Scotland 1560–1707* (Oxford, 1980), pp. 94–103.

[2] See G. Christie, 'A Bibliography of James Durham' in *Papers of the Edinburgh Bibliographical Society, 1912–1920* (Edinburgh, 1921), pp. 37ff. Durham's commentary was published in Scotland in 1658, 1680 (twice), 1739, 1764, 1788, 1790. See also *A Short-Title Catalogue of Books Printed in England, Scotland and Ireland 1475–1640*, ed. D. Wing, 2nd ed. (New York, 1972), 1, No. 2805.

deeply moving religious experience he decided to take an active part in Church life and to devote much of his leisure to the study of theology. During the Civil War he served in the army as a combatant and narrowly escaped death when he falsely replied to an attacker, who asked if he were a minister, that he was indeed a minister. After this escape from almost certain death, he decided formally to prepare for the ministry and take up the study of Divinity at the University of Glasgow. In 1647 he was elected minister of one of the Glasgow churches. At the age of 28 the General Assembly of the Church appointed him a Chaplain to the Royal Household. Two years later he was called to be Professor of Divinity at Glasgow, and shortly thereafter he was made one of the ministers of the Inner Church of Glasgow Cathedral. These rapid promotions bear witness to the high regard which Durham was acquiring both as scholar and pastor.

At the time of his death, which was said to have been brought about by long hours of intensive study, at the age of 36, he had no publications to his credit, although his commentary on the Book of Revelation was in the early stages of publication. It was seen through the press by John Carstairs, a life-long friend of his student days in St Andrews, and a fellow minister.[3] On publication the commentary was immediately regarded as a masterly and clear exposition of a text that was considered to be a comparatively obscure book of the New Testament. Robert Baillie (1599–1662), the well known contemporary, whose *Letters and Journals* shed so much light on this period, noted that neither the 'judicious Calvin' nor the 'acute Beza' along with many other profound divines were moved to attempt an exposition of it.[4] John Carstairs, the first editor, claimed that one of the reasons for the popularity of the commentary was that it gave 'convincing proof of the Pope of Rome being the Antichrist' at a time when zeal in that direction was on the wane. But as shall become clear that thought was not consistently uppermost in his study.

The clearest explanation for his spending so much time, energy, and learning in commenting on the *Apocalypse* Durham set out in a section in the surviving manuscript which is not found in any of the printed editions. In expounding the letter to the Church at Ephesus in chapter 5, Durham commended the work, labour, and patience of God's people, and the fact that they 'have not failed'. He then turned the attention of his audience to the following phrase, 'Nevertheless I have somewhat against thee, because thou hast left thy first love', and invited them to 'look upon

---

[3] The edition used in the preparation of this article is that printed at Glasgow in 1764.
[4] From 'A Letter to the Reader' written by Robert Baillie, printed on p. vi.

this epistle as if [in it] Christ were writing a letter to Scotland', and complaining that, despite outward appearances, Scotland had fallen from its first love. The country and the Church is being judged. 'We are called to look on this letter as directed to Scotland and to Glasgow, the sin is ours, the duty is ours, and the threatening doth also belong to us.'[5] In other words, Durham was stating that he had decided to compose his commentary in the belief that the Book of Revelation had an undoubted contemporary relevance and significance. In this way he was following in the example set by Scotland's best known commentator on the Apocalypse, the mathematician John Napier of Merchiston.[6]

Napier's study was first published in 1593 and repeatedly thereafter in translation, in several continental countries. In his dedication to King James VI he stated that he believed that the Book of Revelation had been written for 'our age' and that the discovering of the Antichrist and the papistical kingdom is the primary significance of the book. Napier had carefully worked out a detailed chronology of events from the birth of Christianity to the sixteenth century, which has most recently been set out in a masterly way by Dr Katharine R. Firth in *The Apocalyptic Tradition in Reformation Britain*. Following Napier's calculations Durham dated the ending of Roman Catholic domination appropriately enough for Scotland about the year 1560, and predicted that the day of God's judgement would fall some time between 1688 and 1700. But the precise day and hour of this event is, he maintained, unknown. Napier wrote that it may even be as early as 1600.

Durham also shared much of the general outlook of his distinguished fellow countryman, nevertheless his purpose in studying the Apocalypse is to be distinguished from that of Napier. Durham was convinced that the entire book had a practical purpose for the Church of the seventeenth century and as such ought to be welcomed as a 'rich jewel'.[7] It shows that Christ cares for his Church, and that the minister as commentator is required to interpret the book as a means of encouraging the spiritual life of his congregation. In it he has to see practical teaching. Accordingly he found in the early chapters, which contain the letters to the various Churches of Asia Minor, material that has to be expounded for the benefit of his contemporaries. Hence every opportunity was taken by him to

---

[5] P. xv.
[6] On Napier see Katharine R. Firth, *The Apocalyptic Tradition in Reformation Britain, 1530–1655* (Oxford, 1979).
[7] P. 50.

discuss the issues of the day. Chapter 2, which has already been mentioned, was seen as an occasion for discussing and developing the principles of Presbyterian church government and discipline, and in particular one of the great contemporary issues in Scotland, namely, that the authority and power in the Church to exercise self-government and discipline were distinct from those of the civil authorities and independent of them.[8] They were in no way derived from the civil power. An opportunity was also found at this point to discuss the relations between ministers and their particular congregations, and to develop the 'high' doctrine of the ministry of Presbyterianism in opposition to that of contemporary Independency. In expounding these early chapters Durham rejected any form of allegorical interpretation and did not find in them anything of an 'apocalyptic' nature. He emphasized the historical setting and used it to develop practical lessons for the contemporary Church. Some of today's readers may find interest in the discussion of the seventeenth-century practice of covenanting and of the use made of the doctrine of justification.

The 'properly prophetical'[9] parts, for Durham, begin with chapter 4 and continue in those immediately following. They contain the six visions and prophesies, the seven seals, the seven trumpets, and the seven vials. Here the language is regarded as metaphorical and allegorical. The four beasts of chapter 4 represent the ministers of the Church in the days of the Gospel, and the message is that God exercises a special over-ruling providence in the Church, and along strictly Calvinist lines this doctrine is stressed as a great consolation for the Church. This element of consolation is repeatedly mentioned throughout the exposition of chapters 6 to 12. There are in these pages occasional references to the Antichrist, but there is no explicit identification of him with the papacy. Unlike many other commentators of his time, including Napier, he was not at this stage interested in calculating days, times, and seasons. Chapters 12, 13, and 14 are interpreted as 'explicatory prophesies' which describe the rise, reign, and eventual ruin of the Antichrist. Chapters 17, 18, and 19 explain that ruin and the following three chapters the ultimate triumph and well-being of the Church.

In many points Durham does not differ widely in his exegesis from that of other orthodox Protestant commentators, of whose writings he was very well informed. In several passages he followed Joseph Mede's

[8] Pp. 193ff.
[9] P. 282.

synchronisms, set out in his *Clavis Apocalyptica*, but does not always agree with him, for example, about the interpretation of the New Jerusalem. The purpose of these passages in the Book of Revelation on this topic, Durham explained, is to set out the 'glorified state of the Church Triumphant'.[10] He did not, however, fail to emphasize that the Church must expect to suffer and to have to do so patiently in this world. A flourishing gospel must expect to be persecuted. 'The persecutions of the Church of God', he wrote, 'are particularly ordered as well as the preaching of the Gospel, and the thriving and flourishing of the Church.'[11] In a poignant passage that is reminiscent of Luther, he wrote, 'God's people's happiness, and the evidence of God's love to them, does not consist in outward things, their lot is oftener suffering from one seal to another'.[12] Suffering is a gift bestowed by God on some and not on all and even on some of those he loves.[13] The words of the author of the Apocalypse, he argued, are doctrinal rather than prophetical, and are intended to be a consolation to believers and an encouragement.[14] Nevertheless, the ending of the sufferings of God's people here on earth and the coming of the great day of Judgement coincide. That is to say, the final judgement of the world shall immediately follow the suffering of the martyrs. Hence he disagreed with chiliasts and millenarians. There is no temporal peace, no millenary kingdom altogether free from suffering, before that day of Judgement, which is the day of redemption from these sufferings.[15]

As has been said, our commentator was not primarily interested in matters of chronology, as set out by Napier and others. Nevertheless, he is indebted to Napier. They believed that chapter 7 predicted the rise of the Antichrist and the coming Reformation. The fall of the Antichrist, whose slow emergence in the Church is believed to have been about 600, is dated from Luther's 'rediscovery' of the Gospel or even to 1559 when the liberty of professing it was being widely confirmed.[16] Much of Durham's commentary on chapter 9 is taken up with a description of the corruption and decay of the Church in the Middle Ages, and there is here much Protestant antipapalism, typical of the period.[17]

Much that Durham had to say about prophesy as the power to predict

[10] P. 354.
[11] P. 364.
[12] P. 375.
[13] P. 382.
[14] Pp. 375f.
[15] P. 388.
[16] Pp. 418ff.
[17] Pp. 458ff.

future events is also in common with Protestant tradition. He believed with orthodox Calvinists that that gift had ceased.[18] However, prophesy understood as discerning God's mind in regard to particular past events, such as the Reformation, is part of the function of the preacher.[19] But interpreting in any specific way the times and seasons given in the Book of Revelation was, he stoutly maintained, neither necessary nor edifying. Thus there was no justification for taking the one thousand years of chapter 20 literally, nor for interpreting the 1,260 days as so many years.[20] On these matters he disagreed with Mede and Roberts.[21] Yet he is not consistent. It has already been mentioned that he believed that the Antichrist's absolute tyranny fell about the year 1559. In support he cited the Peace of Augsburg in 1555, and the events in France, England, and Scotland in the late 1550s, with references to the *Magdeburg Centuries*, Foxe's *Acts and Monuments*, and the works of Alsted, Ussher, and others. He repeatedly returned to his fundamental belief that one need not be tied down to any particular literal or allegorical or historical interpretation.[22] Yet he firmly maintained when he was commenting on chapter 14 that it predicted that the Pope is the very Antichrist and the papacy is the very Antichristian kingdom, and that its destruction had already begun.[23]

It is not, perhaps, surprising that he found chapter 20 difficult to interpret. In common with many orthodox Calvinists he stressed a purely spiritual interpretation of the millennium. Thus the period of one thousand years refers to a period of unspecified length in which the Church enjoys a relatively good condition, a period that is not absolute either for holiness, purity, peace, or length of time, while believers reign in the world. It is not an absolute freedom, for all Christians have their crosses. 'Whatever it be', he wrote, 'it is not literally to be understood and properly as the words sound, but figuratively and spiritually.' Words about souls sitting and reigning with Christ cannot but be taken figuratively. Scripture promised no early, temporal kingdom to the saints. Rather they should be looking for crosses and affliction. Thus Durham totally rejected the idea that Christ would come to earth in person, that all the martyrs and saints would reign for one thousand years before the general resurrection. He was not perturbed that in this matter he was disagreeing with

---

[18] P. 484.
[19] Pp. 486ff.
[20] P. 494.
[21] P. 509.
[22] Pp. 511ff.
[23] Pp. 519ff.

several Fathers of the Church, Irenaeus, Justin Martyr, and Lactantius among the ancients, and Alsted, Piscator, and Henry Archer among the moderns. He returned to his earlier position, maintaining that 'where days and years and months' are formally mentioned no sound interpreter can take them literally. What did the Psalmist say about one thousand years in God's sight? For Durham the millennium 'is neither fully past nor yet fully to come'. Mede's teaching that it will begin with the fall of Antichrist is rejected. The one thousand years may have begun about the year 1560, and may still be running 'being in part past, but in their vigour to come . . . and bringing on the flourishing of the gospel'.[24]

Durham's commentary was published towards the end of a period of concentrated study, particularly in England, on the Book of Revelation. Common to most Protestant commentaries was the identification of the Antichrist with the papacy or Roman popes. In most it was the institution that was attacked. However much our author disagreed with earlier scholars in interpreting many details he shared with virtually all of them this identification. As far as he was concerned the matter could no longer be open to doubt. Hence he dismissed almost out of hand the innovative work of both Hugo Grotius (1583–1645)[25] and Henry Hammond (1605–60).[26] The fact that they both rejected the traditional Protestant identification of the Antichristian Church and the papacy, or at least did not mention it, was enough for Durham to regard what they had written in other parts of their studies as of little consequence. In a final section, in the nature of an appendix to his commentary,[27] he briefly set out his reasons, but in a way that cannot be regarded as scholarly or convincing. It would seem that provided the anti-papal stance was maintained Durham was prepared to disagree with other distinguished commentators, especially on such matters as the interpretation of the millennium and the day of Judgement. After all he shared with them the fundamental belief that the Bible as the inspired word of God contained practical instruction for the Church of his and every age. The function of the commentator and preacher was to extract that message and apply it to the Church in his day for its admonition, its comfort, and its upbuilding.

---

[24] Pp. 723ff.
[25] On Grotius see his *Annotationes in Apocalypsin, Opera Theologica* (London, 1679), 2, pp. 1158ff.
[26] On Hammond see his *Paraphrases and Annotations on the New Testament* (1653). His 'Interpretation of the Apocalypse' is to be found in the 4th edition (London, 1675), pp. 855ff.
[27] Pp. 797f.

HENRY MORE AND THE APOCALYPSE

by SARAH HUTTON

A N interest in prophecy is a continuing theme of the writings of the Cambridge Platonist, Henry More (1614–87). In his earlier writings, the focus is on prophecy in general, particularly in relation to religious enthusiasm.[1] He did not turn his attention to millenarianism until relatively late in his career, after he had established himself as a philosopher. From 1660 onwards, his writings are characterized by a deepening interest in biblical prophecy generally and in the Book of Revelation in particular. More first discusses biblical prophecy in print in his *An Explanation of the Grand Mystery of Godliness* (1660). His first systematic treatment of the topic appears in his *Synopsis Propheticon* which was appended to his *Mystery of Iniquity* (1664). Aspects of this discussion are elaborated in the fourth and fifth dialogues of his *Divine Dialogues* (1668), and in his *An Exposition of the Seven Epistles to the Seven Churches* (1669). He continued to defend his position in other works to the end of his life.[2] As a millenarian, Henry More belongs within the general Protestant tradition which identifies Antichrist as the Pope, the Apocalypse being an 'aenigmaticall, prefiguration and prediction of the Apostasy thereof [the church] into Antichristianism by the misguidance of the Church-men'.[3] Furthermore, as Jan van den Berg has shown, Henry

---

[1] More's earlier writings are preoccupied with the problem of 'enthusiasm' or the claim to divine inspiration by sectarian prophets such as Hendrik Niclaes or David George. See especially his *Enthusiasmus Triumphatus, or a Discourse of the Nature, Causes, Kinds, and Cure of Enthusiasme* (London, 1656). See also M. Heyd, 'The reaction against enthusiasm in the seventeenth century: towards an integrative approach', *Journal of Modern History*, 53 (1981), pp. 258–80. For More's controversy with Robert Vaughan, see N. L. Brann, 'The conflict between reason and magic in seventeenth century England. A case study of the Vaughan–More debate', *Huntington Library Quarterly*, 43 (1980), pp. 103–26; F. B. Burnham, 'The More–Vaughan controversy: the revolt against philosophical enthusiasm', *Journal of the History of Ideas*, 35 (1975), pp. 33–95; A. Miller-Ginsberg, 'Henry More, Thomas Vaughan and the late Renaissance magical tradition', *Ambix*, 27 (1980), pp. 36–88.

[2] There is further discussion of biblical prophecy in More's *A Plain and Continued Exposition of the Several Prophecies or Divine Visions of the Prophet Daniel* (London, 1681); *An Illustration of those two Abstruse Books in Holy Scripture, the Book of Daniel and the Revelation of S. John* (London, 1685); *Paralipomena prophetica* (London, 1685). For a list of Henry More's writings see Robert Crocker, 'A bibliography of Henry More' in S. Hutton (ed.), *Henry More, Tercentenary Studies* (Dordrecht, 1990).

[3] *Divine Dialogues*, Dialogue 4, p. 201. On the Pope as Antichrist, see B. W. Ball, *A Great Expectation: Eschatological Thought in English Protestantism to 1660* (Leiden, 1975); C. Hill, *Antichrist in*

More was a disciple of the great English millenarian, Joseph Mede.[4] He followed Mede's synchronic reading of events described in the Apocalypse, that is he interpreted them not as one linear sequence but as a series of concurrent events. In large part More accepted Mede's collation of the seals, trumpets, and vials with other events described. None the less, More did not agree with Mede on all points. Although the points on which he differed were small, he defended his view with tenacity, as can be seen from his discussion of prophecy with his life-long correspondent and erstwhile pupil, Lady Anne Conway (1630?–79).[5]

To judge by his letters to her, More's interest in prophecy received new impetus in the 1670s from the combined forces of Anne Conway and the Christian Cabbalist, Francis Mercurius van Helmont. The latter came to England in 1670 as agent for Princess Elizabeth, but stayed on as personal physician to Lady Conway, residing at her home in Ragley until her death in 1679. In April 1671 van Helmont introduced both More and Anne Conway to the millenarian and Cabbalist writings of Christian Knorr von Rosenroth. Although More was frustrated by the fact that his limited knowledge of German made reading very slow,[6] he was excited to find that Knorr's millenarian treatise, whose title in English is *A Genuine Explication of the Visions of the Book of Revelation*, savoured of his teacher Joseph Mede as well as himself: '. . . the method and contrivance of it is

---

Seventeenth Century England (London, 1971); C. A. Patrides and J. Wittreich, *The Apocalypse in English Renaissance Thought and Literature* (Ithaca, 1984); also K. Firth, *Apocalyptic Tradition in Seventeenth Century England* (Oxford, 1979) and R. H. Popkin (ed.), *Millenarianism and Messianism in English Literature and Thought, 1650–1800* (Leiden, 1988).

[4] J. van den Berg, 'Continuity within a changing context: Henry More's millenarianism, seen against the background of the millenarian concepts of Joseph Mede', *Pietismus und Neuzeit* 14 (1988), pp. 185–202. Mede's *Clavis Apocalypticae* was first published in 1627 and reprinted in 1632 with an extensive commentary on the synchronic scheme described in the *Clavis*. This version was translated into English by order of the Parliamentary Committee for Printing and Publishing of Books in 1642. The translation, entitled *The Key of Revelation, Searched and Demonstrated out of the Naturall and Proper Characters of the Visions. With a Comment thereupon According to the Rule of the Same Key*, was done by Richard More and supplied with a preface by William Twisse, Prolocutor of the Westminster Assembley of Divines. See also my 'More, Newton and the language of biblical prophecy' in J. E. Force and R. H. Popkin (eds), *The Books of Nature and Scripture* (Dordrecht, 1994), pp. 39–53.

[5] *The Conway Letters*, ed. M. H. Nicolson, revised by S. Hutton (Oxford, 1992). See especially letters 205, 216a, 217a, and 218a.

[6] '. . . the print of the book is so little, and my skill in the German tongue so little, and my dictionary so defective, that I find it a very thanklesse buisiness for me to go about to read the whole book . . .', ibid., p. 330. The book was translated, possibly by Henry Oldenburg, as *A Genuine Explication of the Visions of the Book of Revelation*. It bears no date, but is normally assumed to have been printed in 1670.

very handsome, and the exposition for the most part much like Mr Medes, and if I mistake not the language, his propheticall exposition of the Church of Sardis is not much different from mine.'[7]

By November 1671, Lady Conway was reading Knorr's book, possibly with the help of van Helmont,[8] and discussing the details with More, who acknowledged that Knorr, referred to by his pseudonym, Peganius, 'has for the maine a very handsome hold on the whole Apocalypse'.[9] More was clearly gratified to find that Knorr agreed with him that St John's Letter to the Seven Churches of Asia was itself prophetical. But he noted that 'there are several thinges in Paganius that are not so exact',[10] among them the fact that 'He agrees also with Mr Mede, in making all the phials but one within the sixth Trumpet, but I believe thay are all belonging to the seventh and that the seventh Trumpet is now already sounding, and that the witnesses risen'.[11] The issue of the timing of the pouring out of the seven vials (Revelation 16) was to become a central topic of More's millenarian letters to Lady Conway. For, apparently motivated by a desire to cheer More up when he was feeling depressed she put to him three objections to his contention that all seven vials were poured out after the sounding of the seventh trumpet.[12] In essence, the objections she raises are consistent with the view of Joseph Mede, re-echoed by Peganius, that six of the vials were emptied during the sounding of the sixth trumpet and only the seventh during the seventh trumpet. Most of the argument takes the form of close textual reading in order to establish the order of events. The vials signify the ruin of the beast, that is Antichrist, but More's letters do not give enough of an interpretative scheme to assess the significance of this placing of the vials or why it should matter so much to him. More does indicate that the issue was not a minor detail of textual reading, but had wide significance for his overall interpretation of the Book of Revelation. As he writes to Lady Conway in January 1671–2:

---

[7] *Conway Letters*, pp. 330–1.

[8] This was not the only book she had read on the subject—indeed, according to More she was more widely read than he on the subject of the Apocalypse, to judge by his remarks, 'I am glad your Ladiship takes so much pleasure in reading Peganius. Questionlesse it must be easyer to you, you having read more voluminous writings on y^t subject', ibid., p. 515.

[9] *Conway Letters*, p. 516.

[10] Ibid.

[11] Ibid., p. 331; Peganius actually dates the rising of the witnesses at 1860, the date of the ushering in of the millennium.

[12] 'I thank you for your kinde and ingenious project of diverting me from my Melancholy as you suppose it, by raising those 3 Objections touching the placing of the vialls after the 6 Trumpett': *Conway Letters*, p. 521.

Thus Madame, I have endeavoured as clearly as I can to demonstrate to you the truth, wch you rightly conceive to be of so weighty concerne, as it is in deed, both for a due Testimonie to the justnesse of the Reformation, and to drive off the Reformed churches from a view which some of them have, yt at ye expiration of ye 1260 dayes such wonderfull thinges will be done from them, live they how they will in the meane time. Whenas in truth they have no time now to reckon by, but must expecte the Ruine of the papall power to approache according to their own progresse toward yt estate wch is the Arc of the Testament the Holy of Holyes or the Philadelphian estate.[13]

It is clear that this was an issue on which More felt very strongly: his two extant letters on the subject are among the longest letters he wrote to Lady Conway. The full significance of his views on the seven vials can only be weighed by putting them in the wider context of More's millenarianism.

MORE'S MILLENARIANISM

By the time More came to discuss the seven vials with Lady Conway he was a seasoned writer on the Apocalypse. The issue of the timing of the outpouring of the seven vials was not the only point on which More differed from Mede. Most of the other differences could be described as refinements of Mede's scheme: first of all, More interpreted the Letter to the Seven Churches of Asia (Rev. 2–3) as a prophecy, the unfolding of which runs parallel to the sequence of seals and trumpets of the main scheme.[14] In so far as Mede had, in his *Remains*, acknowledged that the Vision of the Seven Churches could be interpreted as a prophecy, this was not a major departure from Mede.[15] But where Mede saw the Book of Revelation as containing two prophecies—that of the closed book and that of the opened book[16]—More's scheme allows for three parallel sets of

[13] *Conway Letters*, p. 521.
[14] In *An Exposition of the Seven Epistles to the Seven Churches*, More argues that the Vision of the Seven Churches is as convincing as the other prophecies in the Book of Revelation, and a good deal more accessible; sig. (C4)⁴.
[15] *Observations upon some Passages in the Apocalypse*, in Mede, *Works*, 4th edn (London, 1677), 5, p. 905.
[16] 'The whole Prophetical part of the *Apocalypse* following [the vision of the seven Churches] consists of Two main Prophecies; both of them beginning their race at the same *Epocha* or *Terminus a quo* of time, and concluding together likewise at the same Goal or *Terminus ad quem*;

prophecy. The Seven Churches of Asia represent seven stages in the falling away of the Church from perfection and its re-attainment of its original apostolic purity. In More's scheme the Roman Catholic Church is represented by the churches of Pergamus and Thyatira, each signifying a different stage of its degeneracy. The purer, Protestant church is represented by Sardis. The Philadelphian church is the condition of apostolical purity to which the Church will be restored prior to the millennium.

Secondly, More contributes to the apparatus of the interpretation of prophecy a figurative and rhetorical analysis and codification of prophetic symbols and language: this list includes such figures as Henopaoiea, Zoopoeia, Israelismus, Paranomasia, Metallepsis, etc.[17] He regarded the language of prophecy not as colourful uncontrolled utterance, but, like all language, as conforming to rules and conventions in order to convey meaning. Thus meaning was not to be imposed arbitrarily on the text, but the text itself provided the clues. Codification of prophetic symbols—as indeed the reading of figurative elements as symbols in the first place—has a long history in biblical exegesis. More's scheme is in many ways a kind of humanist equivalent of ancient tropological and typological exegesis, that brings to bear his poet's sense of the different ways in which figurative language works.[18] Codifying these symbols, or 'iconisms' as he called them, was one way of demonstrating the easy intelligibility and fundamental rationality of Scripture, even at its most apparently irrational.[19] Again and again in his prefaces he contests claims that

---

... the first of these is *Prophetia sigillorum*, *The Prophecy of the Seals*, reaching from the 4. Chap. until almost the end of the 10. . . . The second is *Prophetia Libri*, *The Book-Prophecy*, beginning at the 8 verse of the 10. Chap. and reaching to the end of the Book'. *Remains* in *Works*, 3, p. 582.

[17] E.g. '*Zoopoeia* is the Typifying out some inanimate thing by what has Life be it Person, or any other living Creature, or part of that Creature. In which sense the *Seven Hills* being signify'd by the *Seven Heads* of the Beast is a *Zooepoeia*.' So also, the two witnesses represent the Old and the New Testaments by a *zooepoeia*: *Synopsis propheticon* in More, *Theological Works* (London, 1708), p. 529.

[18] Most of his symbols are fairly obviously traditional: balances signify justice; a desert paganism; a beast a state. A frog is 'an Hieroglyphick of Imperfection', an eye is 'an iconism of Knowledge'.

[19] In *Mystery of Godliness* More writes: 'There was never any Book penned with that Artifice as this of the Apocalypse as if every Word were weighed in the Balance before it was set down' (p. v). In *Apocalypsis Apocalypseos*, he argues 'for the Intelligibleness and *Truth* of the *whole* Book of the *Apocalypse*' (p. xix). He insists 'that it is as easie a thing to render a *Prophecy* or *Vision* out of this Prophetick Style into *ordinary Language*, as it is to interpret one Language by another; and that the difficulty of understanding *Prophecies* is in a Manner no greater, when

prophecies are just 'Aenigms and Riddles, utterly uncapable of any solution'.[20] It should also be said that his cabbalistic turn of mind shows itself in his awareness of the expressive power of the text, that the external cortex of the words concealed an interior medulla accessible to those who have the key to decipher it. Indeed he notes in his *Explanation of the Grand Mystery of Godliness* that the style of the writings of St John are 'nearest the Notions of the antient *Cabbala* of the *Jews*'.[21] Furthermore, in his method of interpreting, More was less interested in the chronology and exact computation of times than in the symbolic meaning of the text: style is more important than timings. We should attend to the inner voice of the prophecy, 'not tickling our natural spirit with the gratification of the precise knowledge of the time of the Events'.[22]

Finally, as already indicated, More's scheme diverges from Mede's in some of the details of the synchronization of events. Not only does he subdivide the duration of the sounding of the seventh trumpet into seven thunders, but, as already mentioned, he thought that the seven vials were poured out during the last trumpet. Or rather, to be more exact, he believed that the outpouring of the seven vials coincided with the first thunder of the seventh trumpet. I shall return to the significance of this later.

Although there are these differences and elaborations in More's approach to the Apocalypse, his view of the millennium is not substantially different from that of Mede. Although More was critical of Grotius' spiritual interpretation of the Apocalypse, his own concept of the millennium had, as Jan van den Berg has shown, a prominently spiritual emphasis. He considered that millennium itself would be a state of spiritual regeneration which would come about in an almost quietist fashion: 'we ought with Faith and Meeknesse and Patience to abide till God shall bring us to that good Land'.[23] This view of the millennium is

---

once a Man has taken Notice of the settled Meaning of the peculiar *Icasms* therein, than if they had been penn'd down in the vulgar Speech, in which there are as frequent *Homonymies* of Words as here there are of *Iconisms*', *Theological Works*, p. 557. Cf. More's claim that a person 'can no more fail of the right meaning of a Prophecy, than he will of the rendring of the true sense of a *Latin* or a *Greek* Author, keeping to the Rules of *Grammar*, and the known *Interpretations* of *Dictionaries*', *Theological Works*, Preface, p. vii.

20 *Theological Works*, Preface, p. vii.
21 Ibid., pp. 139–40.
22 *Divine Dialogues*, Dialogue 4, p. 198. The vials themselves may not be a sequence of events so much as seven kinds of plague. Philotheus insists that St John gives us 'an Indication of the time no preciselier then was useful'; p. 200.
23 *Seven Churches*, sig. (C3)v.

one More shared with John Durie who, like More, believed that the prophecies of St John had an outward, historical and an inward, spiritual meaning.[24] According to More, the best preparative for the millennium is to strive for moral and spiritual regeneration. Indeed, it could be delayed if Protestants fail to prepare themselves in spirit, and this is a point which he reiterates to Lady Conway. The question which I should like to address now is why More insisted so much on the differences in the layout between his scheme and Mede's. These differences can be explained in part as divergence of opinion on the timing of the events prophesied by St John. But, as I shall go on to argue, there is a political dimension to More's stance on the millennium, and this may explain why he insisted so strongly on his adjustments to Mede's scheme.

More genuinely believed that the last days were at hand, and that the seventh trumpet was already sounding.[25] The millennium would be ushered in at the third thunder of the seventh trumpet after the outpouring of the vials (twenty-first thunder) and the descent of the new Jerusalem and the binding of Satan (second thunder). Unlike Mede, More did not date the beginning of the millennium with the rising of the witnesses from the dead (Rev. 11. 11). In More's view, the witnesses had not actually died, but had been dead only in spirit and had already risen: for he identified the two witnesses with the spirit of the Old and New Testaments,[26] and the rising of the witnesses as the Reformation, that is the regeneration of the spirit of the Old and New Testaments by the break from Rome initiated by Luther and perfected in the Church of England.[27] This means that the 'thousand two hundred and threescore days' for which St John said the witnesses would prophesy (Rev. 11. 3) have already expired, and the events ushering in the last times are already under way. (It also means that no physical resurrection of the witnesses is to be expected.)[28] The rise of Protestantism of course signals the end of the

---

[24] John Durie to Samuel Hartlib, 28 November 1650, in [Adam von Frankenburg], *Clavis apocalyptica* (London, 1651), p. 17. This letter is printed by way of a disproportionately lengthy preface to this anonymous treatise which, as he acknowledges, owes a great deal to Mede's book of the same name. The terms 'Mysterie of Iniquitie' and 'Mysterie of Godliness' are taken up by More, who uses them in the titles of two books.

[25] *Divine Dialogues*, More's spokesman Philotheus states that they are now in the third vial of the seventh trumpet; Dialogue 4, p. 195.

[26] *Mystery of Godliness* in *Theological Works*, pp. 143–4. Compare *Apocalypsis*, p. xxxvi.

[27] *Paralipomena prophetica*, Preface, p. ii. Compare also *Seven Churches*, sig. (C)r.

[28] More writes of 'the vain conceits of a Rising of the Witnesses to come, whenas that Vision most certainly had its accomplishment many years ago, and joining with the ruine of Anti Christ, the abolishing of Monarchical, if not all Political Government' (*Paralipomena prophetica*, Preface, p. ii).

reign of the beast (or Antichrist) but it does not signal the complete destruction of Antichrist. That is a process to be completed by the pouring out of the vials, which represent the final stages in the overthrow of Antichrist.[29] Thus it is logical that the vials should begin to be poured out at the moment when the Reformation signals the end of the reign of the beast. Furthermore, More's view that the Letter to the Seven Churches of Asia is prophetic reinforces his argument for positioning of the seven vials in the last trumpet. Appropriately, in his scheme, the church of Sardis, that is the Protestant Church, takes its beginning from the rising of the witnesses, and its duration coincides with the outpouring of the seven vials.

Since in More's account the 1,260 days in which the witnesses prophesied, along with the three days and a half in which they lay dead, have already expired, the computable aspect of millenarian prediction is behind us. There are no periods of time left to be computed, 'no fit time being defined for the future'.[30] Therefore it is vain to try 'to compute any Futurities upon the supposall of their expiration [i.e. the 1,260 days] to come'.[31] The vials themselves represent not lengths of time but a sequence of events. More thus eliminates speculation as to *when* the millennium will take place. Although More appears to be bringing the millennium forward, the effect of his scheme is to reduce the ardour of expectation and to transfer the onus of responsibility on to expectant Christians themselves. As he said to Lady Conway, 'the Reformed churches' must 'expecte the Ruine of the papall power to approache according to their own progresse toward yt estate wch is the Arc of the Testament the Holy of Holyes or the Philadelphian estate'.[32] It is an exhortation against complacency which echoes his *Exposition of the Seven Epistles to the Seven Churches* where he writes, 'it is left to Protestants to compute the approach of the final Ruine of Antichrist and the blessed Millenium according to their own progress in the Mysterie of real Regeneration and indispensable Duties of Christianity'.[33] According to how much their behaviour is truly Christian, humble, kind, and loving to one another, considerate of the

---

[29] *Paralipomena prophetica*, Preface, p. ii. The inner meaning of the vials, according to More, is, 'That God will at last destroy and utterly rout that Antichristian Power that has hitherto, *Pharaoh*-like, held the people of God in so great a Bondage', *Divine Dialogues*, Dialogue 4, p. 199.
[30] *Seven Churches*, sig. (C)r.
[31] Ibid., Preface.
[32] BL MS Additional, 23,216 fo. 116.
[33] *Seven Churches*, sig. (C)³.

public good, 'by so much more near they may reckon the approach of the downfall of Antichrist, and the glorious Reign of Christ in his Saints at the happy *Millenium*'.[34] This of course means that they must resolve their differences.[35] So the true message of prophecy is anti-schismatical—one of the chief grounds on which More recommends the study of the Apocalypse in his prefaces.

More's insistence on the anti-schismatic value of biblical prophecy points to a powerful external motivation to More's adjustments of Mede's prophetic scheme. When the Church of England was re-established in 1660, millenarianism and prophesying were tarred with the brush of sectarian republicanism. An episode which underlines this occurred at the execution of the regicides in 1660: the followers of Major General Harrison are reported to have claimed that he was one of the witnesses mentioned in the Apocalypse and would rise from the dead three days after his execution.[36] Besides, the works of Joseph Mede had been taken up with enthusiasm by opponents of the Crown and Church. His *Clavis apocalypticae* had been translated by order of Parliament in 1642. It is therefore somewhat surprising to find More, who had made his peace with the new church order, publicly taking up such an unfashionable and perhaps dangerous subject (on which, I might add, he had not published before). Indeed, given the attacks on his orthodoxy which emanated from high-church quarters at the Restoration (attacks which focused on his latitudinarianism and the theological heterodoxy of his belief in the pre-existence of souls)[37] one could argue that to write commentaries on the Book of Revelation was to invite suspicion of political as well as religious unsoundness. Indeed More appears to be aware of this for he repeats the charge that interpretations of prophecy are conducive to 'Faction and Confusion, to the Trouble and Disettlement of the Affairs of Christendome, and to the Hazard and Subversion of States and Kingdoms, and the Ruin and Destruction of the Church of Christ'.[38] Time and again in his prefaces he dissociates his interpretation from the excesses of the Fifth Monarchists, arguing that though a superficial acquaintance with the

---

[34] Ibid.

[35] The different denominations should have a 'tender regard for how they divide from one another or break Communion for difference of Ceremony or Opinion', *Seven Churches*, sig. (C4)r.

[36] Reported by John Finch to Leopoldo de' Medici, Florence Biblioteca Nazionale Centrale, MS GAL 281, fo. 182v.

[37] Marjorie Hope Nicolson, 'Christ's College and the Latitude-Men', *Modern Philology*, 27 (1929–30), pp. 35–53.

[38] *Theological Works*, Preface, p. vii.

books of Daniel and Revelation 'may incline some to a *Fanatical Unsettledness* and a vain Dream of a *Fifth Monarchy*', deeper acquaintance will 'root out of this Spirit all those vain Pretences to Innovation and Schism'.[39]

More's interpretation of the Book of Revelation drives at the spiritual core of the Apocalypse, neutralizing it against literalistic political interpretation. That is not to say that his interpretation had no political significance. On the contrary, by insisting that the prophecies of St John preach not overthrow of the political order but obedience to the magistrate, More the liberal Puritan and instinctive royalist was making his peace with the new religious order of Charles II's reign. An unkind assessment of this would be that this was a sophisticated form of timeserving. Such an interpretation fails to recognize the common ground between More's interpretation of the Book of Revelation and that of John Durie,[40] the indefatigable campaigner for Protestant unity who had such strong links with the inter-regnum governments that he was obliged to leave England at the Restoration and to live in exile abroad. Rather than viewing More as an apocalyptical conservative, it would be fairer to conclude that in his writings on the Apocalypse, he was motivated by a profound concern to rescue the Book of Revelation as indispensible confirmation of the truth of the Christian message and to rehabilitate the work of its best interpreter, Joseph Mede. Thus More's divergence from Mede is not so much a departure from his master but revisionism that serves a shared objective.

[39] *Theological Works*, Preface, p. x.
[40] See n. 24 above.

THE RESTRICTED ESCHATON OF THE DUTCH ROMAN CATHOLICS IN THE SEVENTEENTH AND EIGHTEENTH CENTURIES

by TH. CLEMENS

1. INTRODUCTION

WHAT did the eschaton of the Dutch Roman Catholics in the seventeenth and eighteenth centuries look like? That is the question I will attempt to answer in this article. Before doing so, I should like to note that it is essential to know the expectations, eschatological and otherwise, of a group to get to know its mentality. It is difficult, however, to gauge the nature of expectations and the way in which they operate and it is impossible to arrive at exact 'measurements'. This article will therefore above all be concerned with the way in which expectations were nourished by doctrinal and devotional books. In addition, it will also refer to the literature about the history of the so-called Dutch Mission—the Roman Catholic Church in the Republic of the United Provinces—in the seventeenth and eighteenth centuries.[1]

2. ESCHATOLOGICAL EXPECTATIONS IN THE LITERATURE

If we are to believe the well-known French historian Jean Delumeau and his *History of Fear in Western Society*, it would be a waste of effort to consult historical sources for our purpose. According to Delumeau, eschatological fears reached a peak at the end of the fourteenth and the beginning of the fifteenth centuries and, again, at the end of the fifteenth and the beginning of the sixteenth centuries. In the seventeenth century, however, he detects a clear diminution of those fears in the territories of the Catholic Reformation. After the Council of Trent had settled Roman Catholic affairs, the fear of an imminent apocalypse abated.[2]

The Republic of the United Provinces was not exactly Catholic territory, but Delumeau's claims may nevertheless also be valid for the

---

[1] For a first orientation see J. A. Bornewasser, 'The Roman Catholic Church since the Reformation', in *Lowland Highlights. Church and Oecumene in the Netherlands* (Kampen, 1972), pp. 40–8.

[2] J. Delumeau, *La peur en occident (XIVe–XVIIIe siècles). Une cité assiégée* (Paris, 1978), pp. 197–231, particularly pp. 230–1.

Roman Catholics living there in considerable number and communicating with surrounding Catholic territories, particularly with Münster and Cologne at the eastern borders and the Spanish Netherlands in the south. The indexes of the most important historical handbooks on the history of the Dutch Roman Catholic Church show no relevant entries on the subject and thus they appear to bear out Delumeau's claims.[3] The same can be said of the highly elaborate indexes of the most important Catholic archives in the Netherlands.[4] Here, too, entries such as 'Antichrist', 'apocalypse', 'apocalyptical', 'eschatology', and 'last day' are either absent or offer hardly any useful information. Moreover, recent literature confirms the existence of eschatological expectations during the first decades of the sixteenth century[5] and also reveals traces of such expectations in documents of the leader of the Dutch Mission, the vicar-apostolic Sasbout Vosmeer, at the end of the same century.[6] The literature about the seventeenth and eighteenth centuries, however, contains hardly any relevant information.[7] This leads us to conclude that *if* the Dutch Roman Catholics in the period under discussion were preoccupied with eschatological expectations at all, then that preoccupation left only few traces in the most important ecclesiastical archives and in the historical literature. This does not mean, however, that there is nothing more to be said about the eschaton of the Roman Catholics in the Dutch Republic.

3. THE POLITICAL ESCHATON

After the revolt against King Philip II, the Republic developed into a multiconfessional society. In this society the Calvinists acquired a dominant position. Those who stuck to the old Christianity became involved, *nolens volens*, in a process of increasing confessionalism. They became Roman Catholics. The Roman Catholics in the new Republic were discriminated against and hindered in the performance of public

---

[3] L. J. Rogier, *Geschiedenis van het katholicisme in Noord-Nederland in de zestiende en zeventiende eeuw* (Amsterdam, 1947); P. Polman, *Katholiek Nederland in de achttiende eeuw* (Hilversum, 1968). Cf. O. J. de Jong, *Nederlandse kerkgeschiedenis* (Nijkerk, 1978).

[4] J. Bruggeman, *Diarium Litterarum O.B.C. Indices*, ed. H. L. Ph. Leeuwenberg (Utrecht, 1991).

[5] W. Th. M. Frijhoff, 'Het Gelders Antichrist-tractaat (1524) en zijn auteur', in *Archief voor de Geschiedenis van de Katholieke Kerk in Nederland* [hereafter *AGKKN*] 28 (1986), pp. 195–6 and 207.

[6] Frijhoff, 'Katholieke toekomstverwachting ten tijde van de Republiek: structuur en grondlijnen tot een interpretatie', in *Bijdragen en Mededelingen betreffende de Geschiedenis der Nederlanden* 98 (1983), p. 444.

[7] A small exception is mentioned by Frijhoff in 'De paniek van juni 1734', in *AGKKN* 19 (1977), p. 196.

worship. They eventually found ways of adapting to the new situation but they also held on to their dreams of change.[8] At first these dreams provided words and pictures expressing their hope of a restoration of the political and religious situation that existed before the take-over of the Calvinists. Later they modified their expectations and restricted them to the hope of recovering the old churches for Roman Catholic worship.

During the first decades these dreams were fed by an eager search for, and interpretation of, signs of imminent change. Later, when those signs had again and again failed to bring about the desired change, they began to take refuge in collecting and reinterpreting old prophecies and even in creating new ones. In those prophecies change was predicted to come from across the borders, irresistibly and apocalyptically. Depending on the appraisal of the possibilities of the moment, the restoration was expected to be brought about by the kings of Spain, France, or England, by the German emperor or by the Knights of Malta. The apocalyptic prophecies turned the universal eschaton into a much more limited and small-scale event: a Dutch Roman Catholic eschaton.

This politico-religious eschatology, however limited, deserves our attention because, according to the Dutch historian Frijhoff, it was an essential part of the cultural and mental inheritance of the Dutch Roman Catholics. Frijhoff even suggests that these eschatological expectations may have played a role in the compartmentalization of the late nineteenth and the twentieth centuries.[9] On this point I have my doubts: the prophecies under discussion were already losing credibility in the eighteenth century, at least in clerical circles and among the better educated.[10]

4. ESCHATOLOGY AND THE CATECHISM

The mentality of the Dutch Roman Catholics was probably much more profoundly influenced by the enormous emphasis that the church put on the Four Last Things: death, judgement, hell, and heaven. This brings us to a further restriction of the Roman Catholic eschaton: it came to be seen as an affair of the individual.

---

[8] This paragraph is based on Frijhoff, 'Katholieke toekomstverwachting', and 'De paniek' and M. S. Dupont-Bouchat, W. Th. M. Frijhoff and R. Muchembled, *Prophètes et sorciers dans les Pays-Bas XVIe–XVIIIe siècle* (Paris, 1978), pp. 263–362.

[9] Frijhoff, 'Katholieke toekomstverwachting', pp. 434 and 458–9.

[10] Cf. Frijhoff, 'Katholieke toekomstverwachting', pp. 457–8. His spokesman for the end of the eighteenth century, St Hanewinkel, was too much a partisan for the cause of the Dutch Reformed Church to be a reliable witness.

Nearly every catechism taught the Roman Catholics in the Republic that the Last Judgement would be terrifying, that only God himself knew when it would come, and that it would come unexpectedly.[11] This was not taught for the purpose of preparing people for an expected imminent end of the world, but to stimulate a permanent 'soul-saving' fear in every individual and thus ensure a Christian way of life. At the beginning of the seventeenth century, famous Dutch Catholic authors such as the Jesuits Fr Coster and L. Makeblyde ended their lessons about God's judgement with the characteristic Catholic admonition: live as you will want to have lived when you are facing God at the moment of your death. Or: live in such a way that the coming of Judgement Day can be awaited with a clear conscience and a peaceful mind.[12] Anyone who felt comforted by the thought that the end of the world was still far away was wrong. Some of the authors of catechisms, too, had their doubts about an apocalypse in the near future.[13] That did not mean, however, that it was not dangerous to lead a careless life, because the Last Judgement was preceded by God's particular, individual judgement immediately after a person's death. The moment of one's own, individual death was the moment of ultimate truth for everyone. At that moment one received either eternal reward or eternal punishment. The Last Judgement at the end had no other function than to confirm and make public what had already been established earlier. That is why most catechisms put more emphasis on the Four Last Things than on Christ's return to judge and it is also the reason why the two judgements are not always treated as separate events. They both served the same purpose, a purpose that had already been formulated in the *Catechismus Romanus*[14] of 1566: to distract from sin and to offer comfort and admonition.

To complete the picture of what influenced the Dutch Roman Catholic mind it is necessary to have a closer look at what was taught about the signs announcing the Last Day. Most of the smaller catechisms are very sober on this particular point. Only the books for the better educated contain more comprehensive information but even their contents can hardly have provoked over-excited expectations. They are, on the contrary, used for apologetic purposes. In the new, multiconfessional

---

[11] A list of consulted catechisms can be found in the appendix at the end of this article.

[12] Fr Coster, *Catechismus* (1604), pp. 35–6 and 179–81; L. Makeblyde, *Den Schat* (1610), pp. 64 and 365.

[13] Cf. P. Van den Bossche, *Den katholyke pedagoge* (1685), p. 70, and S. Schmidt, *Volkomen catechismus* I (1771), I, pp. 206–7.

[14] Cf. *Catechismus Romanus* (1566, translated in 1668), ch. 8, lesson 10.

situation the signs were considered to reveal that doctrinal deviations by false prophets and false Christs had been predicted by the Lord himself. Consequently, there was no reason for doubts: the signs admonished Catholics to stick to the Roman Catholic faith and they confirmed that the Roman Catholic Church was the one and only true Church of Christ. This idea featured especially in the catechisms of the Dutch Mission and in those specifically intended for use in the multiconfessional Republic.[15]

The sermon, another important instrument for the instruction of the faithful, will generally have proclaimed the same message as the catechisms. In a recent study on seventeenth- and eighteenth-century sermons the author states that religious education in the Southern Netherlands was invariably coloured by the certainty of judgement after death.[16] In order to find out whether this statement also holds good for the Northern Netherlands I consulted a number of books explaining the Gospels of the Sundays of the liturgical year. The books are closely related to the sermons and they used to be part of the family library of Dutch Roman Catholic families. I studied the early seventeenth-century Heyman Jacobsz, *Sondaechs-Schoole*,[17] Abr. van der Matt (= A. van Brienen), *Meditatien tot de heylige communie op alle sondagen des jaers* (1667, 1st ed.)[18] and *Den Christelyken vader* (1724–5) by Cornelis Boubereel,[19] paying special attention to the explanations of the Gospel of the first Sunday in Advent and those of the twenty-fourth Sunday after Pentecost. Just like the catechisms they use the theme of judgement as an incentive to leading a better life. As might have been expected, they also show apologetic features. In addition, they sometimes also offer spiritual or symbolic explanations of the signs announcing the coming of the Last Day, for instance by relating them to the coming of Christ in the Holy Communion. Such interpretations lead away from thoughts of a coming apocalypse and even presented the Lord's Presence in the eucharist as a kind of protection from judgement: 'Reflect during the day on your last day of which you do not know when it will be. But if you maintain Your Redeemer

---

[15] Appendix, catechisms of 1622, 1633, 1685, 1771(1), and 1798–1801.

[16] G. Vanden Bosch, *Hemel, hel en vagevuur. Preken over het hiernamaals in de Zuidelijke Nederlanden tijdens de 17de en 18de eeuw* (Louvain, 1991), p. 13.

[17] Cf. for the 'Sunday School' Polman, *Katholiek Nederland*, 1, p. 126.

[18] Third impression, Antwerpen: Jacobus Woons, 1685; cf. for these 'Meditations on the Holy Communion of all Sundays of the Year' Jac. Nouwens, *De veelvuldige h. communie in de geestelijke literatuur der Nederlanden vanaf het midden van de 16e eeuw tot in de eerste helft van de 18e eeuw* (Antwerpen; Bilthoven, 1952), pp. 181–5.

[19] 'The Christian Father', Antwerpen: Joannes Franciscus van Soest, 1724–5, 4 vols.; cf. Polman, *Katholiek Nederland* 1, pp. 344–6.

within you, you will be redeemed and beatified by Him. Put this hope in your bosom.'[20] An approach like this cannot have given much nourishment to apocalyptic fears. It would rather have neutralized such fears.

5. THE PRAYER BOOKS

The teachings of the catechisms and sermons left their traces in the Catholic prayer books of the seventeenth and eighteenth centuries. It is remarkable, in this context, that these prayer books contain hardly any prayers for temporal well-being. By far the majority of the prayers for special occasions or particular needs do not ask for things like more rain or more sunshine but are aimed at obtaining and securing individual salvation.[21]

The message of the catechisms concerning individual and general judgement is reflected in the daily prayers of the period. The prayers encourage awareness of the unexpectedness of death by thanking the Lord every morning for preservation through the night. During the day there are short prayers to remind us that the hour of death is near. At night we are admonished to examine our consciences and to set things right with God. We are here and there even explicitly advised to contemplate, before going to sleep, how we will lie on our deathbeds or in our coffins. When we wake up in the middle of the night we are advised to meditate on the Four Last Things to keep away evil thoughts.

It speaks for itself that the prayer books also contain many prayers for use in times of illness and death. They are frequently combined with prayers and exercises with significant titles such as 'powerful prayer to obtain a blessed death', 'prayer to St Barbara, patroness in the hour of death', 'confession of St Charles Borromeo to his guardian angel to acquire a happy death', 'prayer for a mercyful judgement in the hour of death', 'last will a good christian should pray daily', etc.

Also significant in this context is the fact that we find the well-known medieval sequence *Dies Irae* ('Day of wrath! O day of mourning') in most prayer books. This, together with the fact that several new translations of the sequence were made during the centuries under discussion,[22] shows

---

[20] Van der Matt, *Meditatien* (1685, 3rd ed.), pp. 33–4.
[21] This paragraph is based on my study of Roman Catholic prayer books in the Low Countries, *De godsdienstigheid in de Nederlanden in de spiegel van de katholieke kerkboeken, 1680–1840* (Tilburg, 1988). Cf. 1, p. 168 for the nature of the prayers for temporal well-being.
[22] Maximilianus OFM Cap, 'De Nederlandse vertalingen van het Dies Irae in de 17e en 18e eeuw', in *Ons Geestelijk Erf* 38 (1964), pp. 5–22 and 145–205.

us that *Dies Irae* was much more than just a dusty relic from ancient times.

The apologetic features of the catechisms from the Northern Netherlands have parallels in at least some of the prayer books, especially in those used in the Northern Netherlands. One of the most important among them, *Weg des hemels* (*Way to Heaven*) of 1664, opens with no less than twenty pages of instruction on 'the distinctive marks of the true church'. The *Weg des hemels* also contains prayers for the preservation of the Christian (i.e. Catholic) religion in the Netherlands, 'so that we will not become like those who do not know you'.[23] We also find prayers here in which the Lord is thanked for the gift of Catholic parents, because without them salvation would be much more difficult to obtain.[24]

The last aspect of prayer books that I will go into here is that of the different ways in which the attention of the faithful was directed to the Four Last Things. Time and time again they are recommended to reflect on them. In addition, some of the prayer books offer schemes designed to stimulate and guide contemplation. We even find elaborate meditations for every day of the week or for a number of days of the month. The most striking example is *Kleyn Paradys* (Little Paradise) or *Gulden Paradys* (Golden Paradise), which is only a small prayer book but which is combined with a treatise of over two hundred pages on the Four Last Things.[25]

You may be inclined to ask what is new about all this. The Four Last Things have been meditated on for many centuries and their contemplation was vigorously propagated by the Modern Devotion, and particularly by the Jesuits.[26] That is certainly true. Nevertheless, the development of prayer books like *Kleyn* or *Gulden Paradys* was a new, eighteenth-century phenomenon. Moreover, judging by the numerous reissues of the books in question,[27] it was very successful at the time. Because affective devotion to Christ's Passion diminished at the same time as mysticism was distrusted, the religious life of Catholics of the eighteenth century came to be dominated, almost exclusively, by the concepts of reward on the one hand and the threat of eternal punishment on the other.

---

[23] *Weg des hemels of klare kenteekens van 't opregte en waare geloof. Met een bewys van dat nodig is ter zaligheyt; en eenige deugdelyke oeffeningen*, written and collected by P. T. W[eringa SJ], Antwerpen [= Amsterdam], for the heirs of the widow of C. Stichter (1767), pp. 16–35; 70–1.
[24] S. Verepaeus, *Catholijcke handboecxken van godtvruchtige ghebeden* (Antwerpen: J. Bellerus, 1589), pp. 56–7. Cf. *Weg des hemels* (1767), p. 67.
[25] Clemens, *De godsdienstigheid*, 1, p. 108.
[26] J. Delumeau, *Le péché et la peur: La culpabilisation en Occident XIIIᵉ–XVIIIᵉ siècles* (Paris, 1983), pp. 64–7 and 75.
[27] Clemens, *De godsdienstigheid* 2, nrs 333–8 and 558.

6. CONCLUSION

Summarizing, I think it can safely be said that, certainly during the turbulent initial phase of confessionalization, eschatological expectations played a role of some importance. Later, these expectations were transformed into a political eschatology. Whether this development had a lasting influence on the Dutch Roman Catholic mentality has yet to be established. The influence of apologetic features in sermons, catechisms, and prayer books leaves less room for doubt. It seriously restricted the framework within which the Roman Catholics had to cope with new developments and problems.

However, the most important influence on the shaping of the Dutch Roman Catholic mind may have been the restriction of the eschaton from a universal to an individual event. In the words of a little rhyme found in an eighteenth-century prayer book, in the end everything turns to this:

> The Lord presents you with two things
> and leaves the choice to you:
> whether to be eternally with Him
> or to live forever in the pain of hell.

This individual choice dominated Roman Catholic religiosity and left hardly any room for more general apocalyptic expectations.

LIST OF CATECHISMS CONSULTED FROM THE 17TH AND 18TH CENTURIES

1604   Fr Costerus, *Catechismus, dat is De christelijcke leeringhe / in maniere van t'samensprekinghe tusschen den meester en den discipel* (Antwerpen: Jan Moerentorf, 1607), 186–(vi) pp. (with an approbation of 1604).

1610   L. Makeblyde, *Den Schat der christelicker leeringhe tot verklaringhe van den catechismus vytghegheven voor de catholijke jonckheyt van de provincie des arts-bischdoms van Mechelen* (Antwerpen: Joachim Trognesius, 1610), xxxvi–381–xviii pp.

1622?   *Kleine catholyke catechismus, bekwaam om de eerste beginzelen van het christelyk geloof de kinderen in te planten* (Amsterdam: Widow of F. J. van Tetroode, ± 1810 (1st ed. 1622?)).

1623   *Catechismus, oft christelijcke leeringhe, gedeylt in vijf deelen ende een-en-viertigh lessen* (Antwerpen: M. Verhulst, 1678) (this is the so-called *Mechlin Catechism* of 1623).

1624 *Kleyn cabinet der christelycke wysheydt* with an approbation of 1624.

1633 *Catholycke catechismus ofte kort onderwys vande christelijcke leeringhe, tot profijt vande jonghe jeucht ende alle andere die in het oprecht gheloof qualijck onderwesen zijn*, Vtghegheven by Christaen Vanden Berghe (Leuven: B. Masius, 1657), 158–(ii) pp. (with an approbation of 1633).

1668 *Den roomschen catechismus, ofte het kort begrijp van het christen en catholijck geloof. Uyt-ghegeven door 't bevel van het algemeyn concilie van Trenten.* In het Nederduyts vertaelt door Hr en Mr W. Foppens (Brussel: F. Foppens for Joachim van Metelen [Amsterdam], 1668), (xx)–748–(xlviii) pp.

1675 *Catechismus, dat is: christelyke onderwysinge, seer dienstigh, soo voor oude en jonge persoonen, om deselve te onderwysen in de voornaemste geheymenissen des catholycken geloofs; en in de noodigste regels van de waere godtvruchtigheyt. Verdeelt in vier-en-veertigh lessen* (Antwerpen: for Joannes van Weert [Rotterdam], 1694), 144 pp.

1685 P. Van den Bossche, *Den katholyke pedagoge ofte christelyken onderwyzer in den catechismus verdelyt in vijf deelen uytleggende in honderd lessen den christelyke waerheden* (Antwerpen: H. van Dunwalt, 1685), (xxviii)–645–(vii) pp.

1687? *Het collegieboek, in sessen verdeeld ... door J. D(e) G(root)* (Antwerpen: N. Braau [Haarlem], 1693), 250 pp. (approbation of 1687).

1708/1721 *Kort begrip der byzonderste hoofdstukken van de christelyke leering, met het onderwys tot den biegt, de h. communie en het vormzel. Nieuwe druk, vermeerderd* (Deventer: J. W. Robijns, s.a.), 32 pp. (approbations of 1708 and 1721).

1713 L. Danes, *Institutiones doctrinae christianae, sive catechismus nova methodo concinnatus ad usum studiosae juventutis venerandae Facultatis Artium Studii generalis Lovaniensis* (Leuven: Aeg. Denique, 1713), 471–(iv) pp.

1756 *Christelyke onderwyzing of verklaaring en uitbreiding van den catechismus, verdeeld in vyf deelen en eenenveertig lessen, voor de catholyke jonkheid van het aertsbisdom en de onderhoorige bisdommen van Mechelen.* Door F(ranciscus) C(laus) M(inderbroeder) R(ecollect), Nieuwe druk. Overgezien, verbeeterd, en met fraaie plaaten verçierd (Antwerpen: for Theodorus Crajenschot [Amsterdam], 1772), (xiv)–576–(xvi) pp. (approbation of 1756).

1771 Sebastianus Schmid, *Volkomen catechismus, waer in voor de heildorstige zielen uyt de leer van Christus Jezus, als de waere bron des levens ...*

geschept word, . . . in CXXX onderwyzingen op eene nieuwe manier volgens de vyf hoofdstukken van den klynen catechismus R. P. Canisii SJ. ontworpen. En nu naer den vijfden druk . . . vertaeld. For sale at Reckheim: Maria Alberts, 1771.

1771   M. Vogel SJ, *Roomsch-Catholijke catechismus verklaarende de vyf hoofd-deelen van V. P. Petrus Canisius S.J. bekrachtigende met schriftuurplaatzen de roomsche catholyke leere, en wederleggende de leere der oncatholyken. In het Hoogduitsch uitgegeeven (. . .) en nu in de Nederduitsche taal overgezet, ten behoeve van alle Nederlanders* (Keulen: H. J. Simonis [Amsterdam?] or F. Sundorff [Amsterdam], 1771), 2 vols.

1785   *Kort begrip van de christelyke leringe voor de kleine kinderen als ook voor zulke bejaarde catholyken die de nodige stukken van hun geloof na willen gaan; doch bezonderlyk dienstig om de genen, die niet kunnen lezen, zeer schielyk, en gemakkelyk bekwaam te maken tot de H:H: Sacramenten van de biecht, en van de communie* (Amsterdam: P. van Buuren, 1785), 48 pp.

1795?   (H. Beukman), *Allernoodigste onderwijzingen voor de katholijke jeugd, om aangenomen te worden tot den eerste heilige communie* (Amsterdam: C. L. van Langenhuysen, s.a.), 47 pp.

1798/1801   H. Beukman, *Uitbreiding van den grooten catholyken catechismus*, I (Amsterdam: T. Crajenschot, 1798), viii–320–(ii) + 90 pp.; II (Amsterdam: F. J. van Tetroode and P. van Buuren, 1801), (ii)–455–(ii) pp.

1804   *Kort begrip der christelyke onderwyzing of Napelsche catechismus. Opgedraagen aan de koninglyke princessen der beide Sicilien. Uit het Fransch vertaald* (Utrecht: B. Schelling, 1804), viii–424 pp.

1807   B. Overberg, *Catechismus der christelyke catholyke leere; tot gebruik diergenen, welken den kleinen catechismus hebben geleerd. Uit het Hoogduits vertaald* (Deventer: J. W. Robijns, 1807), viii–336 pp.

IN THE BEGINNING WAS CHRONOLOGY: AN EARLY EIGHTEENTH-CENTURY ATTEMPT TO MODEL THE ESCHATON ON THE CREATION*

by JOHANNA ROELEVINK

WHEN T. S. Eliot contemplated the void and the darkness after the Creation, he assumed that there must have been a predetermined moment through which time was made:

> for without the meaning there is no time, and that moment of time gave the meaning.[1]

We are about to meet an early eighteenth-century scholar who tackled the very same problem, the relation between the lapse of 'historical' time and the ultimate meaning of history. But to him, like so many others, time just started with the movement of the stars, which mercifully also provided adequate means for measuring it. In the beginning was chronology. And in its inexorable progress the lapse of time would also in due course spell the end of the world. But when precisely? The answer of our particular scholar to this question sounds deceptively simple. The Bible teaches that God created the world in six days and rested on the seventh. Again, Holy Scripture reveals that to him one day is as a thousand years and a thousand years as one day. So here, by way of analogy, we have the outline of world history. Once having computed the date of the Creation, we can easily deduce that Our Lord Jesus Christ will return on 11 November 1740 to inaugurate his glorious reign.

The several elements of this conception were not entirely new, but this particular combination, with its rather outrageous practical implications, certainly was. The manuscript, now in Leyden University Library, raises all manner of questions. What did the undertaking have in common with other attempts and why did it nevertheless remain virtually unique at the time? What do we know about the manuscript and who may or may not have been its author?

---

* I would very much like to thank two fellow participants in the conference, Professor Dr Johannes van den Berg and Mrs Drs RieHilje Kielman, for generously sharing their erudition on the subject.
[1] T. S. Eliot, *The Rock*, Chorus VII.

I. ASPECTS OF CHRONOLOGY

Throughout the ages mankind has been lured towards a great variety of eschatological scenarios which link one of a relatively small number of theological and hermeneutical concepts with a more or less tangible kind of chronological computation. These differences came about not so much by trying out entirely new concepts or a fundamental change in arithmetic as by using new combinations and by shifting the emphasis from one element to the other. The aim of the following general remarks on the early modern use of chronology therefore is not to analyse in detail or even to explain, but only to clarify and to put into perspective.

One aspect of the art of chronology consisted of technical computation. In it, 'natural' time, perceived as the true and only backbone of human history, took an overwhelming importance. Its course, the *ordo temporum*, the *continua series rerum gestarum*, had to be reconstructed out of the myriad generations, reigns of kings and princes, olympiads, and years *ab urbe condita* supplied by the Bible and by classical texts. Reciprocally, these texts could only be well understood with a fair knowledge of the meaning of chronological terms and unities. Grafton therefore speaks of the humanistic tradition in chronology as far as the textual angle is concerned and of the systematic tradition in connection with separate technical treatises and general reconstructions.[2] From the early modern historian's point of view one had to use both in order to synchronize facts contained in the Bible with evidence concerning the people of the Orient and of classical Europe. At the end of the eighteenth century new evidence and a change of basic concepts was to undermine the very outcome of this daunting task which was after all nearly completed. But that fact should not bring us to underestimate either the problem or the quality of the solutions. Scholars connected a wealth of diachronically related historical information with the results of modern astronomy, which in itself became increasingly better equipped to define time as a function of the regular movement of celestial bodies. Isaac Newton was just the most prominent scientist in a long line of scholars of all kinds who tried to establish an absolute historical chronology on this basis.

The obvious way to realize an absolute system was to find an Archimedean point in the shape of a well documented historical event, highlighted by an unequivocal celestial phenomenon. Justus Josephus Scaliger

---

[2] A. Grafton, 'Scaliger's chronology: philology, astronomy, world history' in: *Defenders of the text. The traditions of scholarship in an age of science, 1450–1800* (Cambridge, Mass., 1991), p. 106.

did just that with Alexander the Great's battle of Gaugamela and an immediately preceding eclipse of the moon.[3] Others, mainly philologists, developed this thought and the computations that went with it. Among them was the Jesuit Dionysius Petavius, who opposed Scaliger, but improved rather than changed the basis of his computations which were accepted by the great majority of scholars. Only Newton came up with a really different solution, but failed to persuade the philologists. They found a new guide in the Dutchman Jacobus Perizonius, who, from the synchronistic historical point of view in 1711 shed more light on the complicated and dangerous fields of Babylonian and Egyptian chronology.[4] Of course the Bible, still the central source for oriental history, yielded crucial evidence. But essentially these scholars were critical eclectics, trying to get the best synthesis out of all dependable sources.[5] Their ultimate aim was to assign to all single historical facts their proper place within the synchronic *ordo* and the diachronic *series temporum*. In that respect they still belonged to the polyhistorical tradition, be it of a critical brand.[6]

The second aspect of chronology was conceptual. The seventeenth century did inherit, but not use, medieval examples, of which Augustine of Hippo with his seven *aetates mundi* and Joachim of Fiore with the age of the Father, the Son, and the Holy Spirit are only the best known. The Renaissance's contribution, the division of history by states or reigns and a dim view of the *media aetas*, had been basically secular. The first major new contribution of the Reformation was the idea of the Pope as Antichrist, that was as much to assist as to hinder a sense of chronological development. But even more important became covenant theology in general and Coccejanism in particular, with their concept of consecutive covenants between God and mankind. While thus defining the phases of world history, with the main distinction between the Old and the New Covenant, this theology was also fully consonant with the sense of the *ordo* and the *series temporum* of polyhistory because of its voluntarism. For it also described history as a series of divine actions and human reactions. Coccejanism, which attached such an overriding importance to the birth of Christ and the beginning of the Covenant of Grace as the great

---

[3] Ibid., p. 129.

[4] Th. J. Meijer, *Kritiek als herwaardering. Het levenswerk van Jacob Perizonius (1651–1715)* (Leiden, 1971).

[5] Grafton, 'Scaliger's chronology', p. 133. See also A. Th. van Deursen, *Jacobus de Rhoer 1722–1813. Een historicus op de drempel van een nieuwe tijd* (Groningen, 1970).

[6] J. Roelevink, *Gedicteerd verleden. Het onderwijs in de algemene geschiedenis aan de Universiteit te Utrecht, 1735–1839* (Amsterdam & Maarssen, 1986), pp. 220–9, 277–89.

watershed in historical time, was to be extremely influential among theologians.

The third aspect of chronology may be termed apologetic. It linked biblical chronology and the fulfilment of prophecy to prove the truth of Christianity, of the Revelation as such or of orthodox doctrine.[7] Therefore it was not only directed against infidels, sceptics, and Jews but also against scores of fellow Christians. For differences concerning chronology were part and parcel of all major divisions within Christianity. The East and the West differed not only on the computation of the Easter dates, but also on the preference for either the Masoretic text of the Old Testament or the Septuagint. The East, which put the Creation in 5508 or 5509 before Christ, was thereby totally unable to accept any result of western chronology and hermeneutics. Quite apart from this, the Roman Catholics and most Protestants were at loggerheads over the Gregorian versus the Julian calendars. Also Protestants on the whole tended to look for the fulfilment of prophecies to the present or the near future, whereas Roman Catholics put it into a past, where their own Church played a crucial role, or in a very distant future.[8] Later on, both sides would join against those detractors who denied the truth of the Bible in matters scientific and historic directly or indirectly by contending that it was impossible to synchronize biblical and ancient history. They did so, like Isaac de La Peyrère, by postulating the existence of Pre-Adamites or, like Voltaire, by alleging that the Chinese or other nations outside the cultural orbit of Europe had a history much longer than that covered by the Bible.

Among those who entered the arena were famous scholars like Pierre Daniel Huet, the Bishop of Avranches, the Huguenots Louis Capelle and Samuel Bochart, and the Anglican James Ussher, Archbishop of Armagh.[9] He saw his computation of the date of the Creation, 4004 BC, as proof that Christ, actually born in 4 BC, was indeed the Second Elijah of Jewish tradition, the Messiah who would come 4,000 years after the Creation.[10] In Germany, Henricus Altenhovius had computed 4004 well before him, in

---

[7] B. W. Ball, *The English Connection. The Puritan Roots of Seventh-day Adventist Belief* (Cambridge).

[8] Ibid., p. 205.

[9] H. Trevor-Roper, 'James Ussher, archbishop of Armagh', in *Catholics, Anglicans and Puritans: Seventeenth-Century Essays* (London, 1989), pp. 120–65; J. Hughes, *Secrets of the Times. Myth and History in Biblical Chronology* (*Journal for the Study of the Old Testament. Supplement Series*), pp. 261–3; J. Barr, 'Why the world was created in 4004 B.C.: Archbishop Ussher and biblical chronology', *Bulletin of the John Rylands Library* 67 (1985), pp. 575–608.

[10] For the Jewish traditions concerning the second Elijah see Barr, 'Biblical chronology', p. 581, and *Theologische Realenzyklopädie* 9 (Berlin/New York, 1982), p. 502.

1592, but he argued contrarily against the Elijah tradition that one should not predict the second coming of Christ or try to construct an analogy between the days of the Creation and world history.[11] To Johann Albrecht Bengel the combat against Jewish thought was still a strong incentive.[12] Yet there were considerable differences within the apologetical strand of chronology. Whereas Ussher and many others were fully prepared to consider the smallest facts to support their claims, others, like Louis Capelle, contented themselves with providing a handy survey of biblical history without alleging details to prove their point. But to all the *historia sacra* remained the pivot of world chronology.

The fourth aspect of chronology was hermeneutic. Biblical texts, especially the prophets and the Apocalypse, provided many opportunities to discuss both history and eschatology. The variety was virtually endless, not only in the choice of the basic texts and notions, but also in the degree of chronological precision of comment. Exegetical methods also differed widely, ranging from cabbalism to theological commentary and philological *adnotationes*.[13]

In fact, matters became increasingly complicated in the course of time, because more and more requirements had to be met. In the first place, one had to disentangle the intricacies of the Masoretic text of the Old Testament. Secondly, by virtue of the Protestant principle that Holy Scripture be explained only by Holy Scripture itself, the early modern hermeneutic approach had to find an Archimedic point to connect the chronologies of the Old and the New Testaments. To Ussher, for instance, the date of the death of King Nebukadnezar served this purpose.[14] All this was necessary because nobody could do any more without some sort of coherent technical chronological framework. Consequently, in order to establish the unity of historical development, it became necessary first to distinguish between absolute, continuous historical time and the theologically explainable process of salvation. Next, one had to synchronize them on the basis of biblical prophecy to understand the *ordo rerum*. In other words, hermeneutic concepts derived from the explanation of prophetic biblical

[11] H. Altenhovius, *Oratio de temporum intervallis a condito mundi usque ad Christum natum elapsis, in qua ostenditur, quatuor integra annorum millia ante Christi in carnem adventum effluxisse, adeo ut his potius aliquid supersit quam desit* (Servestae [Zerbst], 1592).

[12] R. B. Evenhuis, *De biblicistisch-eschatologische theologie van Johann Albrecht Bengel* (Wageningen, 1931), p. 137.

[13] H. J. de Jonge, *De bestudering van het Nieuwe Testament aan de Noordnederlandse universiteiten en het Remonstrants Seminarie van 1575 tot 1700* (Amsterdam/Oxford/New York, 1980), pp. 39, 40.

[14] Barr, 'Biblical chronology', p. 579.

texts had to be related both to the general process of salvation, God's *oeconomia*, and to the actual course of world history.[15] For the voluntaristic *series rerum gestarum*, in which the acts of God and the works of man lay inextricably intertwined, had to be matched with the technically established *series temporum*.[16]

It may be helpful to stress that this was all the more difficult because there were structural differences between hermeneutical and technical chronology, that turned out to be even more decisive than the use of particular biblical texts and symbols. The technical aspects of chronology forced scholars to concentrate on the interpretation of all single facts and on the determination of their proper place within the entire framework of events. But biblical hermeneutics as applied to history tended to emphasize the diachronic element to the detriment of synchronism. They concentrated on interrelated clusters of facts and tried to explain the interplay of just these facts, prophecy and fulfilment in past, present, and future. This being the case, there was a distinct tendency among both theologians and philologists to evade silently each other's problems.

The distinction between the four aspects of chronology may help us to understand the underlying thought of the manuscript under discussion, to gauge the difficulties encountered by its author and to find out more about his background and identity.

2. THE MANUSCRIPT AND ITS CONTENTS

Leyden University Library owns a Latin manuscript, *Observationes sacrae et commentarius in Genesin*, that is undated and anonymous. To my knowledge it has been completely neglected so far. The binding and the handwriting are those of the early eighteenth century, the paper is Dutch and seventeenth-century. This squares with quotations in the text, which refer to books published up to 1710. But because they fail to mention the supremely important *Origines Babylonicae et Aegyptiacae* of Jacobus Perizonius, published in 1711, it may be assumed that the *Observationes* were written not much later than 1712. There is no contemporary author's name, but nothing indicates that this was deliberate. The text has never

---

[15] G. Möller, 'Föderalismus und Geschichtsbetrachtung im XVII und XVIII Jahrhundert', *Zeitschrift für Kirchengeschichte*, IIIE Folge, L (1931), pp. 393–440; H. Bauch, *Die Lehre vom Wirken des Heiligen Geistes im Frühpietismus. Studien zur Pneumatologie und Eschatologie von Campegius Vitringa, Philipp Jakob Spener und Johann Albrecht Bengel* (Hamburg–Bergstedt, 1974), pp. 61, 62.

[16] Roelevink, *Gedicteerd verleden*, pp. 277–89.

been printed and probably never was intended to be either. Indeed some phrases clearly suggest that here we have a clean copy of lecture notes in theology. The author clearly addresses young and inexperienced theologians. Also he states somewhere that he gladly leaves certain points to philologists, confirming the general impression that he himself is a theologian. Apart from this we know only one other thing. The quotations prove beyond doubt that the writer was conversant with Dutch.

Now let us first turn to the contents of the manuscript. It consists of two parts, the *Sermo preliminaris* and the *Observationes et Commentarius in Genesin* properly speaking. The author first stresses that he just wants to explain selected difficult parts of Holy Scripture with which one may need some help. Then he states his intention to prove the opinion of some Church Fathers that one day of the Creation corresponds to a thousand years of world history. The rest of the preface entirely consists of well known Protestant opinions. David Pareus, the early seventeenth-century professor in Heidelberg University, is quoted time and again—though not always explicitly[17]—to make plain that the Bible is infallible, also in matters of nature, and perfect in containing everything necessary toward salvation. Within it, the First Book of Moses is very important, because it may be regarded as a true compendium of theology. Of course chronology and interpretation also loom large in this introduction. Here again the author relies on Pareus, who—by the way—himself held that the millennium had been fulfilled in the past of the Church.[18] Sacred chronology is introduced as the fountainhead and the substance of universal chronology. In exegetical matters the introduction also leaves an impression of sound orthodoxy. The reader is urged to keep typologies and allegories in mind, but the author stresses that the simple, historical sense of the texts takes precedence. So far, so good. But truly revolutionary is the promise—and this is emphatically not Pareus—to show that God created the earth as and when He did to outline the *idea* and the outcome of the world.

To the historian's eye the body of the commentary on Genesis in itself seems to be in no respect unusual. The really intriguing part is the elaboration of the analogy of the days of Creation and the millennia of world history, encased in so called *collationes* of the days of Creation and the

---

[17] D. Pareus, *Operum theologicorum partes quatuor*, ed. Ph. Pareus (Frankfurt am Main, 1647), Part I, *Commentarius in Genesin*.
[18] Ball, *The English Connection*, p. 214.

millennia of world history. These *collationes*, separate from the commentary itself, each consist of a column of key words or concepts from Genesis
and a corresponding column of persons or events of the millennium. For
instance the separation of land and water on the third day is equated with
the segregation of Abraham from the infidels. There is no obvious source
for these analogies. Every now and then the name of Henry Ainsworth
appears in the margin, but there is no systematical connection with the
commentary on Genesis of this Brownist, who does indeed compare the
sixth day with 'the age after Christ', but never specifies the years of the
sabbath after the coming of Christ.[19]

   The theoretical foundation of the idea of chronological order as
expressed in our preface to Genesis does not smack of heterodoxy. The
author warns that astrology is useless because nobody can predict the
futura contingentia. But the stars—the stars, for the earth does not move—
act as celestial watches which forecast natural events and define the
progress of time. Without them, there would be no memory of the *res
gestae* of the past and no hope for the future. If only for this reason, the
theologian has to be well acquainted with astronomy. But the author does
not elaborate too much on this. In fact, apparently unable to devise his
own parallel system of technical chronology, he concentrates on
arithmetic based exclusively on internal biblical evidence.

   After explaining the difference between the Masoretic calculations and
those of the Septuagint,[20] our author predictably keeps to the Masoretic
ones and indulges in additions concerning the generations of the
patriarchs, the judges, and the kings. He refers to a host of well known
theologians who put the Creation in 3928 BC. On the other hand James
Ussher and others who were not very helpful here were quietly dodged.
The division of world history that does emerge is as follows: the first day
lasts from the Creation to the assumption of Enoch, the son of light; the
second day from this day to the 115th year of Terah, the father of
Abraham. It is interesting to note that the scheme effectively leaves out
the Flood in 1666. The foundation of the Temple of Solomon marks the
end of the third day, the fourth terminating with the destruction of the
Temple by Emperor Vespasian in the year of the world 4000, that is AD 73.
And here, of course, the birth of Christ in the year of the world 3927 is

[19] H. A[insworth], *Annotations upon the first book of Moses, called Genesis. Wherein the Hebrew words
   and sentences are compared with, & explained by the ancient Greek and Chaldea versions, but chiefly by
   conference with the holy Scriptures* (1621). No page numbers; see the comment on Gen. 1. 31.
   There is a Dutch version of this book, edited in Leeuwarden in 1690.
[20] For a modern explanation see Hughes, *Secrets of the Times*, pp. 233–41.

quietly skipped, as well as the Crucifixion and the Resurrection. The fifth day runs up to 1073 with Pope Gregory VII. So far, everything is comparatively straightforward. But the rest of the scheme and its computations gets slightly complicated, for the sixth day does not actually count for one thousand years. Instead, the analogy is like this. Eve was created on the tenth hour of the sixth day. Henceforth Christ will come to his bride, the Church, after 666 years, six months, six weeks, six days, and six hours, this *dies novissimus* being the night of 11 November 1740. The seventh day, the glorious reign, will consequently end one thousand years later, in the year 6666 after the Creation.

The hermeneutic methods underlying this division of history were simple and in tune with the analogies of the *philosophia novantiqua*. The author applied words from the text of Genesis to historical events in the several millenia. But of course there was not really a sufficient number of words, so he had to smuggle in some more. All of a sudden the grass, the herb, and the tree become the fig tree which is David, the vine which is Solomon, those bearing fruit who are the pious and the barren who are the hypocrites. Similarly on the fourth day we find not only the sun and the moon, but also the signs of the zodiac. Here the rationality of the scheme goes slightly awry, because the fourth millennium ends in 73, but the story of the planets rushes through till the very end of the world.

It is worth while to look into this because here many familiar eschatological notions emerge. The twelve signs of the zodiac are the twelve sons of Jacob or the twelve minor prophets. Apparently they also stand for a second division of world history. Aries and so forth correspond with periods from the Creation till the flood, the destruction of Sodom, the exodus, the reign of David, the captivity, the year 36, the destruction of Jerusalem and Constantine the Great. With Sagittarius we again reach the year 1073 or the second beast out of the earth. Capricorn ends with the Reformation or the pouring of the vials. Aquarius runs till the conversion of the Jews and Pisces to the consummation of the world. Yet this is not all. For now we come to the actual constellations of the stars, for instance the Lion signifying the kings of Judah, the Great Bear the reign of the Persians, the Lesser Bear the reign of the Greeks, the Dragon the Roman Empire, Hercules Christ treading the serpent, Andromeda Satan in chains. Typically, the author does not really do anything with this wealth of images.

After all this the comparison of the sixth day with the period up to 1740 is disappointingly vague. It does not really come as a surprise that Pope Gregory VII is the beast with horns like a lamb. Of course the serpent is the

Devil, Adam is Christ, and Eve the Church, the spouse of the Lamb. But these themes are not elaborated. Even shorter is the description of the seventh millennium, from 1740 till the end of the world. Adam and Eve now are in the celestial paradise, the new heaven and the new earth, with the sabbath as the eternal celestial rest. There is no attempt to connect the concepts with the signs of the times.

These views were certainly heterodox in the sense that they ran contrary to the Dutch Confession and to the warning of Calvin not to attach a date to the coming of Christ.[21] On the other hand the author probably does not qualify as a chiliast in the context of his time.[22] He was not a revolutionary, the millennium being Christ's reign and part of a new era. The *Observationes Sacrae* are not a treatise concerned in any way with technical chronology. Sources other than the Bible rarely come in. Also literature on the subject is not often or thoroughly quoted. The *Observationes* are equally weak from the conceptual and apologetical points of view. There are no solid excursions on the concept of the seven days of Creation itself, on its actual application to world history in the light of Jewish and early Christian tradition, on the meaning and purpose of the sabbath, the stages of the history of salvation or the conversion of the Jews. No doubt the chronology of the *Observationes* has a firmly hermeneutic character. But to which particular tradition and time does the manuscript belong?

3. THE LATE SEVENTEENTH-CENTURY CONTEXT OF HERMENEUTIC CHRONOLOGY

Hermeneutic chronology thrived in the Netherlands in the second half of the seventeenth century, the high tide of covenant theology in Coccejan shape. Its backbone was a combination of literal and typological interpretation of the Bible, its hallmark a periodization of world history into

[21] Nederlandse Geloofsbelijdenis art. 37: '... de door de Here bestemde tijd (die aan alle schepselen onbekend is)'. Calvin, *Commentary on Daniel*, cited by J. Kramer, 'J. H. Alsteds "Diatribe de mille annis apocalypticis" und W. Burton's Übersetzung "The Beloved City"', J. H. Alsted, *Herborns calvinistische Theologie und Wissenschaft im Spiegel der englischen Kulturreform des frühen 17. Jahrhunderts. Studien zu englisch-deutschen Geistesbeziehungen der frühen Neuzeit von B. Griesing, J. Klein, J. Kramer* (Frankfurt/Bern/New York/Paris, 1988), p. 18. See also E. Kunz, *Protestantische Eschatologie. Von der Reformation bis zur Aufklärung* (Freiburg/Basel/Vienna, 1980), p. 37.

[22] C. J. Meeuse, *De toekomstverwachting van de Nadere Reformatie in het licht van haar tijd. Een onderzoek naar de verhouding tussen het zeventiende-eeuwse chiliasme en de toekomstverwachting van de Nadere Reformatie, met name bij Jacobus Koelman* (Kampen, 1990), pp. 66, 67, 94.

covenants between God and man. With it went a marked attention to the years after Christ and a smouldering interest in a mildly chiliastic future. In this context the interpreters turned almost naturally to the Apocalypse, so easily applicable to the times of the *foedus gratiae*.

In England both the Book of Daniel and the Apocalypse dominated the discussions of John Napier of Merchiston, Thomas Brightman, Joseph Mede, and Richard Baxter about eschatological matters.[23] But on the continent the Old Testament in general and the Book of Daniel in particular seem to have lost much ground during the seventeenth century, except in some parts of Germany. Secular periodizations of history replaced the Four Empires of Johannes Sleidanus. But Johann Heinrich Alsted continued to use the prophesies of Daniel to predict that the millennium would start in 1694.[24] Johannes Bierman, also from Herborn, professor of theology in Middelburg in the Netherlands, was well within this tradition,[25] but most others preferred to serve the same purpose by other means. Although initially the purely historical approach to the Old Testament was linked with both Arminianism and Socinianism, it became more and more fashionable even in orthodox circles to relate the prophesies of Daniel and other prophets to the period of the Diadochs who became gradually better known. This was in tune with Coccejan theology, which was still centre stage during the first decades of the eighteenth century, Campegius Vitringa senior, professor in Franeker,[26] being the main protagonist. Because Coccejanism attached so much importance to the first coming of Christ and the beginning of the Covenant of Grace, it almost naturally concentrated on the Apocalypse to provide the best explanation of the past, the present, and the future within this era.

As a result, eschatology was for some considerable time almost entirely predominated by the images and numbers of the Apocalypse, the time and half a time, the seven churches, the vials, and the seals. A manuscript which turns to Genesis is therefore more in the German tradition of Heidelberg and Herborn than in the line of either Coccejanism or Dutch theology.

Also it was not at all fashionable among Dutch orthodox theologians to compute dates, notwithstanding their interest in millenarian ideas.

[23] Ball, *The English Connection*, pp. 197–200; J. Escribano-Alberca, *Eschatologie von der Aufklärung bis zur Gegenwart* (Freiburg/Basel/Vienna, 1987), p. 12.
[24] J. Kramer, 'J. H. Alsteds, "Diatribe"', p. 17.
[25] J. Biermannus, *Sermo primordialis de regno servatoris glorioso* (Middelburg, 1710).
[26] K. M. Witteveen, 'Campegius (Kempe) Vitringa', *Biografisch Lexicon voor de Geschiedenis van het Nederlandse Protestantisme*, 3 (Kampen, 1989).

Vitringa, who was an extremely prudent man, explicitly warned people not to try and calculate future dates[27] and those who tried it ran into trouble with the Church. In this respect our manuscript does not belong to the mainstream of Dutch theology either.

It does not come as a surprise that there are not many references to the particular Genesis-concept of history used by our author in Dutch theological literature of the late seventeenth and early eighteenth centuries. In his commentary on the *Letter of Barnabas* published in 1685, Stephen Lemoyne mentions that the Church Fathers, together with Platonists and Pythagoreans state that the world will last 6,000 years. But Lemoyne dismisses this thought as Jewish and cabalistic, without referring to any modern theologian.[28] Vitringa is more explicit. In his *Hypotyposis historiae et chronologiae sacrae a Mundo Condito usque ad finem saeculi I, Aetatis V*,[29] he states that it is useless to credit the unpolished and popular chronology of Moses with too much mathematical exactitude, although the questions are legitimate in themselves.[30] In lecture notes on the Mosaic story of the Creation, published in Dutch in 1725, Vitringa quotes Lemoyne. But he strongly rejects the scheme of 2,000 years without the law, 2,000 years with the law, and 2,000 years with the Messiah. He first objects that chronology does not answer the scheme, but his main argument is that the works of Providence in world and Church do not show six major acts that match six days. Vitringa himself stresses that from Christ starts a new order and series of centuries, a new rank and series of facts, a new time.[31] The foundation of his own explanation of Genesis is the analogy of two mystical worlds, two economies of the Church, the one from Moses, the second from Christ.[32]

[27] H. Bauch, *Die Lehre vom Wirken des Heiligen Geistes im Frühpietismus. Studien zur Pneumatologie und Eschatologie von Campegius Vitringa, Philipp Jakob Spener und Johann Albrecht Bengel* (Hamburg–Bergstedt, 1974), p. 25.

[28] S. Lemoyne, *Varia sacra seu sylloge variorum opusculorum Graecorum ad rem ecclesiasticam spectantium*, 2 (Leiden, 1685), pp. 848ff. For the rabbinic and early Christian interpretations: *Theologische Realenzyklopädie*, 3, pp. 270ff.

[29] Published in Leeuwarden, 1716.

[30] Vitringa, *Hypotyposis*, p. 12, 'Ut enim Moses Chronologiam rudiore et populari modo in historia sua tradidit: sic forte eadem ad extremam exactitudinem mathematicam inde erui non potest: etsi hae quoque quaestiones probabili ratione definiri queant.'

[31] In Dutch: 'Een nieuwe ordere en rey der eeuwen; een nieuwe rang en rey van saken; een nieuwe tijt.'

[32] C. Vitringa, *Verklaringe en heilige bedenkingen over de verborgen sin der miraculen van Jesus Christus: als meede allegorische en mysticque uitbreidinge van het Mosaisch verhaal nopens de sesdaagsche scheppinge; en verklaringe over eenige propohetische schriften, als II Sam. XXIII vss. 1–7, Psalm LXVIII, PS VIII en XLV. Voormaals opgegeven in de Latijnsche Tale aan de voesterlingen van de Academie tot Franeker—en nu in 't Nederduitsch vertaalt. Met een voorreden over de sin van de H. Schrift door—*

Later on neither Agge Haitsma, in his very elaborate commentary on Genesis, published in Franeker in 1753[33] nor Herman Venema, the authority on biblical chronology of the middle of the eighteenth century, refers obliquely to the analogy of days and millennia.[34] Kornelis Grebber, in his *Tyd-rekenkundige aanmerkingen* of 1748 did discuss the dates of the Creation, the Flood, and the Resurrection, but he only looked for a geometrical proportion between them based on very detailed computations and abstract biblical concepts of unities of time.[35] In 1817 the Roman Catholic H. Nüse used astronomical computations to establish the date of the Creation. Then he tried to prove that the world would last 7,049 years, analogous to the seven days of Creation and the eighth day until the fall of Adam.[36] But none of them referred to the particular ideas contained in our manuscript. Even the immensely erudite Johannes Ernestus Jungius, who tried, on the basis of the prophecies of the Apocalypse, to compute mathematically that the Day of Judgement would be in 1808,[37] apparently was not aware of our manuscript.

On the whole, I think that our manuscript was not known to official Dutch theology, or entirely ignored by it. This will have been all the easier because, as Vitringa pointed out, the scheme of the six days did not square with chronological knowledge. Indeed, even from the systematical point of view it was much easier to combine the Apocalypse with a historical framework than to use Genesis as a basis. The Apocalypse indicates the signs of the times without actually attaching a specific length to the seven periods. As it was, the scholar could single out important moments in history almost at will. Similarly, the manifold theological explanations of

---

H. *Venema* (Franeker, 1725), pp. 237–362; *Allegorische uitbreidinge over het Mosaische verhaal nopens de eerste scheppinge der dingen*, pp. 260–6.

[33] A. Haitsma, *Curae philologico-exegeticae in Genesin sive explicationes difficiliorum per omnia fere capita locorum* (Franeker, 1753). Also A. Haitsma, *Commentarius exhibens curas philologico-exegeticas in Pentateuchum Mosis . . . Pars Prima ad Genesin* (Franeker, 1765).

[34] H. Venema, *Dissertationes ad vaticinia Danielis emblematica* (Leeuwarden and Harlingen, 1745), pp. 69, 70, 607. H. Venema, *Praelectiones de methodo prophetica seu de argumento prophetarum veteris et novi testamenti ac utriusque periodis* (Leovardiae, 1775), p. 45, only mentions an analogy of the days of Creation and seven stages in the life of the Church of the New Testament.

[35] K. Grebber, *Tyd-rekenkundige aanmerkingen; aanwijzende een verband tusschen de dagen van ouds, de jaren der eeuwen en de tegenwoordige tijd, met deszelfs gebeurtenissen in Nederland tot een grond van bemoediging gelegt voor de kerke Gods in de Seven Vereenigde Provintïen* (Amsterdam, 1748).

[36] H. Nüse, *Sleutel van de verborgenheid der laatste tijden of de zegepraal des Christendoms over alle volken der aarde* (Rotterdam, 1817).

[37] J. E. Jungius, *De verborgentheit der laatste tyden die aanstaande zijn, geopent, in een volgens den betoogtrant der wiskundigen ingerichte Verklaaring van de eerste twee versen van het XIVde hoofdstuk van den propheet Zacharias* (Zutphen, 1749).

the Apocalypse left the interpreter of history every possible opportunity to decide whether he liked to insert a millennium or not and in what way. It was also his to choose whether he located it in the past, in the present, or in an unspecified future. Countless scholars have taken the opportunities offered in this direction.

Genesis was altogether different. It had indeed served both Jews and some Church Fathers in that they applied a theological concept of seven days and seven analogous millennia to world history, but this happened within the context of the Septuagint. The birth of Christ in *annus mundi* 5500 was equated with that of Adam halfway through the sixth day.[38] Nobody bothered with detailed hermeneutics or exact dates. At the other end of the scale many later Seventh-Day Adventists and various other groups advocated a direct combination between the theological concept and some form of genuine or faked technical, astronomical computation. In between there were several possibilities, of which the apologetic ones against the Jews were the most interesting.

But the difficulties with Genesis started when somebody tried to combine a Protestant hermeneutic approach, based on the Masoretic text, with astronomical and historical chronology in order to pinpoint the eschaton in real time. In the first place the Genesis-concept as applied to history in such a radical way requires absolute certainty about the exact date of Creation. In fact, in the seventeenth century a reasonable consensus had been reached by most scholars, who had come to accept the view that God created the world at about 4,000 years before Christ, give or take a few years or even centuries. But this is not nearly precise enough for somebody who wants to establish the millennia of world history in order to know the very date of the coming of Christ. For a difference of a few centuries in early chronology remains a gap that size in the present life-time. The concept absolutely requires as an Archimedean point the precise moment in astronomical time of the first day of the Creation. Therefore the technical computation, relating absolute time to actual history, has to be correct on all levels. But this is not all. Because both the Old and the New Testament periods are covered, this chronology also has to match the Masoretic text of the Old Testament. Essentially the concept carries with it an all-out defence of the literal tradition of the biblical text.

Even so, this is not all. Indeed, a concept of seven ages, with not only a fixed beginning, but also of a specified equal length and on the systematic theological level of equal importance, in itself poses more than enough

---

[38] Hughes, *Secrets of the Times*, p. 255.

problems when confronted with actual history. The theological implications were absolutely daunting. Even if the Incarnation or the Crucifixion coincided with the beginning of a millennium—which strictly speaking was not the case—theoretically these all-important events would still only be on the same level as the start of any of the other days. Last but not least, some form of millenarianism is virtually unavoidable. Worse, the historical analogy of the days of Creation was conducive to a millenarianism of a much more tangible kind than the polite murmurings of the average Coccejan, if only because of the impossibility of dodging the Sabbath as a historical and a chronologically sharply defined period.

Who was the author who honestly, but unsuccessfully, tried to overcome all these problems?

4. THE AUTHOR

A nineteenth-century hand has written on the fly-leaf of the *Observationes Sacrae et Commentarius in Genesin*: 'Manuscriptum Wesselingii'. Some other kindly soul added, as it turns out correctly, the words 'auctione de Groot'. Unfortunately the catalogue of this auction of the library of Cornets de Groot van Craayenburg in 1879 is extremely unhelpful, even misreading the name as 'Wisseling'. But Leyden University Library, which acquired the manuscript in the middle of this century, identified this person as Petrus Wesseling. He was born in 1692 in Burgsteinfurt, in the German county of Bentheim which borders on the Netherlands. After a spell at the Gymnasium Arnoldinum there, Petrus went to Leyden in 1712. Two years later he moved to Franeker to continue his studies in philology and theology under guidance of Vitringa in a most brilliant fashion. Then he left the university to embark on a successful career, first as a teacher at the Latin School of Middelburg, then returning to Franeker in 1723 to take up a professorship in history and Greek. In 1735 he went to Utrecht University where he became a scholar of international fame and a teacher in history, classics, and law. But during his professional life Wesseling never touched anything smacking of theological periodization in history, let alone something as controversial as chiliasm.

Wesseling left no male issue. His son-in-law, the theologian Gisbertus Bonnet, presumably inherited the bulk of his papers, but Bonnet himself died childless. Auction catalogues do not help us to reconstruct the fate of the family papers. Those of Bonnet are in Utrecht University Library, and a large part of Wesseling's correspondence in Leyden. But these letters were acquired much earlier than the manuscript of the *Observationes*

Sacrae. The handwriting of the manuscript does not provide a strong clue either. In general it rather resembles Wesseling's, but there are some telling differences which prevent me from stating categorically that it is the same. All in all, it is possible, but by no means certain, that Wesseling wrote the text.

But even if we assume that the manuscript is indeed in any way connected with Wesseling, there are several options. Either he merely owned it, or he copied or took down somebody else's text or his teacher's lectures, or he did indeed compose and write the manuscript in his late teens and changed his handwriting afterwards. My quest to find another matching handwriting has failed so far.

The conclusions concerning a German theological tradition, combined with the knowledge of Dutch, do tally with Petrus Wesseling. If he did indeed write the text, he did so in 1710, presumably in Burgsteinfurt, when he was only eighteen. But, apart from the difficulties with the handwriting and the doubtful attribution, it does not make sense that an intelligent and daring young man of that tender age came up with a reasonably erudite, but decidedly weakly structured treatise. One would expect it to be the other way round. Also, he would not present himself as a theologian who is going to direct others. So if the manuscript was Wesseling's at all, the most likely solution seems to be that it contains lecture notes.

If we bear in mind that Wesseling lived in Burgsteinfurt till 1712, the most obvious candidate for the job is his professor of theology at the Gymnasium Arnoldinum and vicar of Burgsteinfurt, Arnoldus Visch. This man, a native of Cleves, took an honorary degree at the university of Harderwijk in 1695.[39] Presumably he studied there for some time as well. It is not impossible that he was imbued at that university with rabbinic theology and probably even some cabalism by the professor of history at Harderwijk, Johannes Meier (1651–1725),[40] who was an expert in the field, and probably also influenced Jungius, who was to incur the anathema of the Dutch Church with his own computation. But there is as yet no proof of this either. It might be anybody else connected with a Dutch faculty of theology at the time. In the meantime we are left with a most intriguing manuscript which deserves its place in the history of the hermeneutics of Genesis and among the more interesting attempts to solve the insoluble.

[39] O. Schutte, *Het album promotorum van de Academie te Harderwijk* (Zutphen, 1980), p. 84.
[40] H. Bouman, *Geschiedenis van de voormalige Geldersche Hoogeschool en hare hoogleeraren* (1844–7), I, pp. 237–42; II, pp. 16–20.

PART II: DEATH AND SALVATION

ST BERNARD OF CLAIRVAUX AND
JERUSALEM*

by PETER RAEDTS

ALTHOUGH Jesus wept while mourning the inevitable destruction of the city (Luke 19. 41), and St Paul taught the Christians of Galatia to look for it not on earth, but in heaven (cf. Gal. 4. 25–6), the Christian imagination has always been haunted by the city of Jerusalem. As early as the second century Melito of Sardis travelled to Jerusalem to see for himself 'the place where these things were preached and done'.[1] And as soon as Christianity became a licensed religion under the protection of the Emperor, Christians from all parts of the Empire began to flock to Jerusalem to see for themselves the holy sites *ubi steterunt pedes eius*, where once his feet stood (Ps. 132. 7).[2] Churches were built to mark all the places mentioned in the Gospels, monasteries were founded to receive the pilgrims, and stories began to circulate about the spectacular conversions which happened to pilgrims while visiting the Holy Places, such as that of St Mary of Egypt who turned from a nymphomaniac into a desert mother on the very doorstep of the church of the Holy Sepulchre.[3] Quite soon earnest Church Fathers like St Jerome and St Gregory of Nyssa, both of them pilgrims to Jerusalem, had to issue dire warnings that true Christianity was a matter of the heart and not of geography, and that a trip to Palestine might perhaps be helpful but certainly not necessary in order to find Christ.[4]

But despite their warning, and, indeed, that of St John's Gospel that true

---

* I would like to thank Mrs Erna van Wijngaarden-Raben, who helped me to collect and evaluate the passages from St Bernard's works used in this article.

[1] Eusebius of Caesarea, *Historia Ecclesiastica*, iv. 26. 14, cited in E. D. Hunt, *Holy Land Pilgrimage in the Later Roman Empire AD 312–460* (Oxford, 1984), p. 3.

[2] On the origin and use of this expression see Robert L. Wilken, *The Land Called Holy: Palestine in Christian History and Thought* (Newhaven/London, 1992), pp. 97–8, 147.

[3] Sophronius of Jerusalem, *Vita S. Mariae Aegyptiae*, iii. 22–3 (*PG* 87. 3713).

[4] St Jerome, *Tractatus de Ps. xcv*: 'By the Cross I mean not the wood but the Passion. That cross is in Britain, in India, in the whole world.... Happy is he who carries in his own heart the cross, the resurrection, the place of the nativity of Christ and of his Ascension', as cited in Hunt, *Holy Land Pilgrimage*, p. 92; St Gregory advised Christians to 'make a pilgrimage, but out of your bodies to the Lord, and not from Cappadocia to Palestine', cited in J. Prawer, 'Jerusalem in the Christian and Jewish perspectives of the Early Middle Ages', *Gli Ebrei nell'alto Medioevo, Settimane di studio del centro italiano di studi sull'alto medioevo* 26 (Spoleto, 1980), pp. 745–50, 772.

worship was not to be found on any one mountain but only in spirit and truth (John 4. 21, 24), Christians throughout the early Middle Ages kept going to Jerusalem to visit the Holy Places.[5] It was a thin trickle but just enough to establish a tradition and to keep the memory of Jerusalem alive in the West. And so it could happen that when after the year 1000 Western Christianity came to life again and started to flex its muscles, it was the cry of Jerusalem which, more than any ecclesiastical or spiritual reform, rallied the crowds and led to the recapture of the Holy City in 1099.

The tension I have just tried to describe seems quite straightforward. On the one hand there is the city of Jerusalem in Palestine, once centre of worship of the one God, but now, since the coming of Christ, desolate and no longer of interest to right-minded Christians; on the other there is the 'holy city, new Jerusalem, coming down from God out of heaven' (Rev. 21. 2). It is the tension between literal and spiritual, between Law and Grace, between prophecy and fulfilment. True Christians should not hark back to the past but look forward to the future, to things to come. It is such an attractive and simple dichotomy that quite a number of modern scholars have used it as an explanatory device to chart the ever-changing attitudes of Western Christianity to Jerusalem, forever hovering between crude literalism and an elitist spiritualism. What they all seem to agree upon is that at the time of the Crusades Western Christians, once again, did not heed St Paul's warning that it is the Jerusalem from above which is free and the mother of us all (Gal. 4. 26). They reverted to a far too literal understanding of biblical prophecies about Jerusalem, which they now applied to the city in Palestine instead of to the Church or the future kingdom, as if all that Scripture had predicted had now been fulfilled in the reconquest of the city.[6] All this is usually said with a hint of reproach, particularly by Prawer whose brilliant essay is in fact a political statement on the status of Jerusalem in historical disguise.

It is obvious from all sources that the capture of Jerusalem posed a problem to contemporaries. To some it seemed as if a new page had been written in the book of the history of salvation. That was rather Guibert of Nogent's view; he saw the re-establishment of the Christian Empire in the

---

[5] For a thorough discussion of Christian views on the Holy Land up to the capture of Jerusalem by the Muslims (638) see Wilken, *Land Called Holy*, esp. pp. 82–100, 108–25, 143–92, 216–46 where Wilken argues that Christians, despite all warnings to keep their eye on their spiritual destination, became ever more attached to the Holy Land and the Holy Places as time went on.

[6] K. D. Erdmann, *Die Entstehung des Kreuzzugsgedankens* (Stuttgart, 1935), pp. 279–82; S. Mähl, 'Jerusalem in mittelalterlicher Sicht', *Welt als Geschichte*, 22 (1962), pp. 11–26; Prawer, 'Jerusalem', p. 745.

East as the first sign of the coming of Antichrist.[7] Others were not so sure; St Anselm, repeating the words of St Jerome and St Gregory, warned a monk that going to Jerusalem was contrary to his profession and to the obedience he owed the Pope and his abbot.[8] In other words, the Church and the monastic life provided all the means necessary for salvation, there was no need to go to the Holy Land. What then could be the meaning of the extraordinary events of 1099?

The man to whom both his contemporaries and modern scholars might look for an answer is, of course, St Bernard. As no one else he knew the ancient Christian and the monastic traditions, and so he was fully aware of the fact that going places had never saved a soul; on the other hand he preached the crusade and wrote a book in praise of the Knights of the Temple. So, he must have felt the tension in his own person. It is all part of the chimaera-complex of St Bernard, which has puzzled so many scholars for so long.[9]

Some time ago a German scholar, Michaela Diers, published an important study in which a new solution of this tension in St Bernard's person is offered.[10] Although it is not the thesis of the book as such which concerns us here, but only in so far as it reflects on St Bernard's attitude to Jerusalem and the Holy Land, it is perhaps better to summarize it, before becoming more specific. Dr Diers claims that St Bernard, when calling himself the *Chimaera mei saeculi*, did not want to suggest that he was torn between the cloister and the world, between mysticism and politics, as most scholars seem to suppose. She agrees with all others that St Bernard was a mystic and a contemplative, a man who was deeply convinced that, as a monk, he had, through prayer and fasting and, of course, God's grace, already become a co-citizen of heaven here on earth. But she suggests that it was not despite his mysticism but because of it that he began to think of himself as God's mouthpiece, a man who had received a mission to go out of the cloister into the world to reform the Church, both the clergy and the laity, and to model their lives as far as possible on that of the monks, and above all of the Cistercians. So it was mysticism that led St Bernard

---

[7] Guibert of Nogent, *Gesta Dei per Francos* (*RHC Occ.*, 4), pp. 138–9.

[8] G. Constable, 'Monachisme et pélerinage au Moyen Age', *Revue Historique*, 258 (1977), pp. 19–20.

[9] *Epistolae* (= *Ep*), ccl. 4, ed. J. Leclercq and H. Rochais, *S. Bernardi Opera* (= *SBO*) 8 (Rome, 1977), p. 147: 'Clamat ad vos mea monstruosa vita, mea aerumnosa conscientia. Ego enim quaedam Chimaera mei saeculi, nec clericum gero nec laicum. Nam monachi iamdudum exui conversationem, non habitum.'

[10] Michaela Diers, *Bernhard von Clairvaux; Elitäre Frömmigkeit und begnadetes Wirken*, Beiträge zur Geschichte der Philosophie und Theologie des Mittelalters, ns 34 (Münster, 1991).

into politics, and the problem which tore him apart was not action versus contemplation, but how to reach out to all these lower beings, how to make them understand what constituted a true Christian, without sullying or demeaning the pure vision of Christian life which he had contemplated in the cloister.

It will come as no surprise that in all this Jerusalem was uppermost in St Bernard's mind. Diers says, and I fully agree with her, that St Bernard had no doubts as to where the true Jerusalem was: it was in heaven: 'Deum habet auctorem, de caelo ducit originem.'[11] Its original citizens were the angels.[12] Even the devil and his companions were once sons of Jerusalem.[13] And it was their fall that made God create man so that man might fill the empty places and restore the ruins of the heavenly city.[14] From then on, the true Jerusalem, although still one, is partly in heaven, partly on earth. In heaven it is firm like a house, here ramshackle like a tent, there it is a house of praise, here of prayer. Here on earth Jerusalem is the fortress of our strength, in heaven it is the city of our rest.[15] As long as man cannot join the angels in seeing God, he must strive to conform to them through his way of life, singing rather with his virtues than with his voice: 'Lord, I have loved the habitation of thy house, and the place where thine honour dwelleth' (Ps. 26. 8).[16] Of all men on earth none are closer to the heavenly Jerusalem than the monks: they were first in the Church, one might even say that with them the Church began. They are very close to the order of angels, because of the sweetness of their chastity and the ardour of their love.[17] St Bernard summed it all up when he called himself, in the 55th sermon on the Song of Songs, a monk and a Jerusalemite in one breath.[18]

In that same sermon, however, he warned that there is nothing automatic about all this: it is not the habit which makes the monk. The difference between the Babylon of the world and the monastic Jerusalem is not

---

[11] Diers, *Bernhard*, p. 11; *Sermones super Cantica Canticorum* (= *SC*), xxvii, *SBO* I (Rome, 1957), p. 185; quotation from *De consideratione ad Eugenium Papam*, iii, *SBO* 3 (Rome, 1963), p. 445.

[12] *SC*, xxvii, *SBO* I, p. 186; *S. de diversis* (= *Div*), xix, *SBO* 6. I (Rome, 1970), pp. 162–3.

[13] *SC*, xxix, *SBO* I, p. 207; *S. in Quadragesima*, v, *SBO* 4 (Rome, 1966), p. 373.

[14] *SC*, lxxviii, *SBO* 2 (Rome, 1958), p. 267; *S. in adventu Domini*, i, *SBO* 4, p. 164.

[15] *S. in dedicatione ecclesiae*, ii, *SBO* 5 (Rome, 1968), p. 378.

[16] *SC*, xxvii, *SBO* I, p. 184.

[17] *Apologia ad Guillelmum abbatem* (= *Apo*), *SBO* 3, p. 101: 'Cur adhuc vivo videre ad id devenisse Ordinem nostrum [i.e. monachorum], Ordinem scilicet qui primus fuit in Ecclesia, immo a quo coepit Ecclesia, quo nullus in terra similior angelicis ordinibus, nullus vicinior ei quae in caelis est Jerusalem mater nostra, sive ob decorem castitatis, sive propter caritatis ardorem, cuius apostoli institutores, cuius hi, quos Paulus tam saepe sanctos appellat, inchoatores exsisterunt.'

[18] *SC*, lv, *SBO* 2, p. 112.

the difference between sin and virtue, but merely between manifest and secret sin. Both will be scrutinized carefully and no sin will remain unpunished in either.[19] One always has to bear this sermon in mind when quoting the bold statement in St Bernard's letter to the Bishop of Lincoln that Clairvaux is Jerusalem.[20] Jerusalem it may be, but not yet quite, and only in so far as its monks realize that they must now hold on in faith to what they cannot yet capture completely in mind.[21]

And just as there are no groups which are the embodiment of the true Jerusalem, so there are no places which are intrinsically holy. Even when talking about heaven St Bernard warned that the expression of the psalm that God stretches the heavens like a curtain (Ps. 104. 2) does not mean that heaven is a place but that it is made up of all the loving affection of the angels.[22] And what is true in heaven is even more so here on earth, even in the *claustralis paradisus*: it is life which confers merit; a place is not the making of a saint.[23] The monk's way of life is a very privileged one: it is the right way, it is an undefiled way to the heavenly city on high which is our mother, but it remains an arduous ascent, because the path goes straight to the top of the mountain.[24]

The conclusion must be that neither status nor place can confer holiness; it is only the heart which counts. It is the impeccable doctrine of the Church Fathers, more in particular of St Augustine who more than anyone else had stressed that it was the choices of the heart, not institutions, or places, which made man holy. The question then is what St Bernard can possibly have to say about the Holy Places in the Holy Land to whose defence he repeatedly called the knighthood of Western Europe.

There can, after what has been said before, be no doubt as to what the Holy Land could mean to monks: nothing. St Bernard even disapproved of Cistercian monasteries over there. When the abbot of Morimond left his monastery, together with some of his monks, to journey to the Holy Land to found a monastery there, Bernard wrote a strong letter to Pope Calixtus II (dating from Dec. 1124–Jan. 1125) in which he requested the Pope to put an end to such a nonsensical project: the Holy Land was in need of soldiers and not of monks.[25]

[19] *SC*, lv, *SBO* 2, pp. 112–13.
[20] *Ep*, lxiv, *SBO* 7 (Rome, 1974), pp. 157–8.
[21] *SC*, lxxvi, *SBO* 2, p. 258.
[22] *SC*, xxvii, *SBO*, 1, p. 184.
[23] *Sententiae*, iii, *SBO* 6. 2 (Rome, 1972), pp. 140–1: 'Vita confert meritum; locus non facit beatum.'
[24] *Div*, xxii, *SBO* 6. 1, p. 170.
[25] *Ep*, ccclix, *SBO* 8, pp. 304–5.

But to soldiers the Holy Land and the Holy Places could be important. And it is at this point that I must disagree with Dr Diers. Her argument starts from the premise that St Bernard always adapted his message to his hearers, as befitted an accomplished speaker such as he was. So when he left the cloister and went out into the world to let the laity share in his vision of Christian life, he felt that he could not expect them to comprehend as fully as monks did that the true Jerusalem was spiritual and invisible and that the way thereto was the way of that love which asks nothing for itself; he had to show them an easier way to reach their final destination. To catch their ear he had to promise them things which they could see and touch, and he had to promise them gain (*lucrum*). Both were to be found in the crusade. So, whenever he addressed the laity he reverted to a very literal understanding of the meaning of Jerusalem, as if, in the case of the laity, biblical prophecy referred to the city which had just been reconquered and must now be defended. And in that Holy War Christian soldiers stood to gain a lot: if they killed, Christ won, if they were killed they themselves won. To put it bluntly: Jerusalem was the bait, heaven was the reward.[26] No wonder that Diers comes to the very pessimistic conclusion that in the end St Bernard betrayed his glorious vision of Christian life, because he regarded laymen as little better than heathen, as people whom he could only get interested in their salvation by using the crudest of devices. She also implies that St Bernard was quite aware of the fact that he was selling out, and that this was the real reason for his complaint that he was the chimaera of his age, that although he still wore the habit of a monk, he had long since stopped being one.[27]

I disagree with this conclusion because I think that it is based on too simple and too absolute a distinction between spiritual and literal understanding, as if there were nothing in between. It will be my point that St Bernard is much more subtle in his appreciation of human understanding in general and of the divine mysteries in particular, that to him most of man's knowledge is somewhere between the literal and the spiritual. If Dr Diers had been the only one to base her conclusions on such a simple distinction, a review of her book would have been sufficient to put matters right. But she is not; many scholars see the effort of twelfth-century theologians to give the reconquest of Jerusalem its rightful place in the unfolding history of salvation as a relapse into crude literalism, an accusation which, incidentally, says more about modern qualms about the

---

[26] Diers, *Bernhard*, pp. 349–69.
[27] Ibid., pp. 368, 397–8.

Crusades than about medieval understanding of Scripture, and, indeed, of
the Christian faith and of reality in general.

To St Bernard, as to most medieval men, only the angels had perfect
understanding: only they fully enjoyed the river, the stream whereof shall
make glad the city of God (Ps. 46. 4).[28] That is to say only the angels have
direct knowledge of God ('praesentem habent Dominum') and only they
can see God as he is in himself, because they are the original and the true
citizens of Jerusalem.[29] On the feast of St Michael, St Bernard almost
stammered when he asked himself what a worm could possibly say about
the angelic spirits: 'We believe that these happy ones endlessly enjoy that
presence and vision of God, which no eye has seen, nor ear heard, neither
has entered into the heart of man' (I Cor. 2. 9).[30]

Here on earth all knowledge and understanding of spiritual things is
indirect. In other words, on earth man only gains knowledge by recogniz-
ing that all visible reality has a sacramental character: visible things are but
shadows of that more glorious, more perfect, world, which the angels
inhabit, or in the words of C. S. Lewis: 'the world which we mistake for
reality is the flat outline of that which elsewhere is in all the round of its
unimaginable dimensions'.[31] It was a way of understanding adapted to the
present condition of man, which is now also highly ambivalent. In the
27th sermon on the Song of Songs St Bernard explained the verse (1. 5) in
which the bride compares herself both to the tents of Kedar and to the
curtains of Solomon. It is because she is still in the flesh of sin and in her
fragile body that she is in the tents of Kedar, and because of her immortal
soul that she already is in Solomon's curtains, in the company of the
angels. With them she now only shares devotion, but once she hopes to
share their glory as well.[32] And in the first sermon on Septuagesima he
resumed an Augustinian theme, when he complained that he feels very
sorry for himself, because in his present condition man can only receive
the heavenly goods in weight, measure, and number. So little of it do we
receive here and now that it is like drops so tiny that we cannot even
swallow our spittle with them. And whereas Jerusalem from on high is fed
with the finest of the wheat (Ps. 81. 17), we have to be happy with the

---

[28] *Div*, xix, *SBO* 6. 1, pp. 164–5.
[29] Quotation from *S. in Nativitate B.M.V.*, *SBO* 5, p. 284; also *Div*, xxii, *SBO* 6. 1, p. 176; *S. in
festo S. Michaelis* (= *Mich*), i, *SBO* 5, pp. 294 and 296.
[30] *Mich*, i, *SBO* 5, p. 294.
[31] C. S. Lewis, *The Allegory of Love* (Oxford, 1936; repr. 1973), p. 45.
[32] *SC*, xxvii, *SBO* 1, pp. 185–6.

crumbs that fall from the rich man's dish.[33] In his present body man is tied down to earth, whereas his soul draws him to heaven, a struggle no man can escape from, not even monks, an important point to remember.

If such is man's condition, then his way to knowledge and understanding must be characterized by the same uneasy relation between the visible and the invisible, the literal and the spiritual. In the fourth sermon on the Gospel of the Annunciation St Bernard illustrates that relation when he gives a few rules about the right interpretation of Scripture. He wonders why the angel says to Mary that the Lord God will give to her Son the throne of his father David, whereas Christ later on told off Pontius Pilate by saying that his kingdom was not of this world. St Bernard's answer is:

> We know that a Jerusalem quite different from the one which is now and over which David reigned is meant here, much nobler, much richer. And I think that it is that [nobler city] which is signified here, because it is a common way of speaking in Scripture to put the sign for the signified. . . . So: 'The Lord God shall give unto him the throne of his father David' (Luke 1. 32) means not the symbolical but the true throne, not the temporal, but the eternal, not the earthly but the heavenly. And the reason to call it thus, as I said, is that the throne on which David sat for a time carried the image of the eternal [throne of Christ].[34]

In other words in the Bible spiritual meaning is revealed by cracking the nut of the letter, the invisible can only be reached through the visible.

It is a view which is, of course, not original: St Bernard shared it with all his contemporaries. But unlike at least some of his contemporaries, such as Hugh of St Victor, St Bernard did not think that the recognition of this sacramental quality of visible reality was given with nature.[35] It was not until the voice of the turtle was heard in our land, i.e. not until Christ came on this earth, that man's eyes were opened and his true destination was revealed to him:

---

[33] *S. in Septuagesima*, i, *SBO* 4, pp. 346–7.
[34] *Homiliae super Missus est*, iv, *SBO* 4, pp. 46–7.
[35] Hugh of St Victor, *De sacramentis christianae fidei*, I.ix.2: 'Habet autem omnis aqua ex naturali qualitate similitudinem quamdam cum gratia Spiritus Sancti', as cited in Lewis, *Allegory*, p. 46. The next sentence is even more relevant to Hugh's views: 'Et ex hac quidem ingenita qualitate omnis aqua spiritalem gratiam repraesentare habuit, priusquam etiam illam ex superaddita institutione significavit' (*PL*, 176. 318). See also J. van Zwieten, 'The Place and Significance of Literal Exegesis in Hugh of St Victor' (thesis, Amsterdam, 1992), pp. 30–4.

As long as men accepted only an earthly reward, a land flowing with milk and honey, they did not feel like exiles on earth, nor did they sigh like the turtle at the thought of his homeland, but they mistook their place of exile for the homeland and they gave themselves to eating delicacies and drinking sweet wine. . . . When, however, the promise of the heavenly kingdom was made, men recognised that on this earth they had no lasting city, and they began avidly to seek the city which is to come (Heb. 13.14). And that happened when the voice of the turtle was heard, loud and clear, for the first time here on earth.[36]

Recognition of the ambivalent character of visible reality was not given with human nature, it was the consequence of Christ's coming, it was a gracious act of God, through which the eyes of all followers of Christ were opened as to the true character of this earth: a place of exile, a shadow of the world to come.

It was the tragedy of the Jews that they stubbornly refused to see this and clung to a very literal interpretation of God's promises in the Bible instead. The cause of that tragic error was, according to St Bernard, that the Jews had refused to recognize Christ in his humiliation, in his earthly body, and that, therefore, they were also unable to recognize him in his heavenly glory.[37] Because of this refusal they were struck with blindness and the true character of the whole of reality, as revealed in Christ, escaped them as well. It was this blindness which was typical of the Jerusalem of the letter, the unhappy city in Palestine. Christians should be glad that they had been expelled from that Jerusalem, in which the Law was harsh and the reward was so small, nothing but a miserable piece of land.[38] In his second sermon on Christmas Eve St Bernard touched on the same subject. There he called his hearers true Jews, not according to the letter, but in spirit, sons of promise, not of the flesh; inhabitants of the new city which comes down from heaven, and not of that Jerusalem which killed the prophets and over which Christ wept.[39] That Jerusalem was the city of the Law, the city of blindness from which Christ had been expelled, when He came into what was his own.[40] St Bernard made that point, with a wealth of images, in his sixth sermon on Christmas Eve,

[36] *SC*, lix, *SBO* 2, p. 137.
[37] *SC*, xxv, *SBO* 1, p. 168.
[38] *SC*, xxx, *SBO* 1, p. 213.
[39] *S. in vigilia Nativitatis Domini* (= *NatV*), ii, *SBO* 4, p. 203.
[40] *SC*, ii, *SBO* 1, p. 13.

where he told his hearers that although, somehow, the earthly Jerusalem was the mother of Christ, she had not treated him with a mother's affection, but had thrown him out of the city. Therefore, Christ had left his mother and cleft to his bride, the true daughters of Sion, the Church.[41] In other words, whenever St Bernard spoke about Jerusalem to Christians, whether they were learned monks or simple laymen, he always spoke, somehow, about the heavenly city, and never about the purely historical city, the Jerusalem of the letter.

This brings us to the conclusion that knowledge of God and understanding of the divine mysteries was possible on three different levels. In Old Testament times knowledge had been literal and limited to the visible, because of man's immaturity. With Christ's coming man gained a first understanding of his true destination, but it was still veiled in visible signs, just as Christ himself had hidden his divine glory in a fragile body. Only the angels in heaven had full knowledge. Jews remained stuck in literalism, their Jerusalem was the desolate city in Palestine, at least until the end of times; angels had immediate, spiritual vision in the true Jerusalem; Christians were somewhere in between. So, both ontologically and epistemologically the distinction between Jews, Christians, and angels was much deeper than that which separated laymen and monks.

And yet, when St Bernard addressed laymen, he spoke of Jerusalem in another manner than when he addressed monks: he added what one might call an intermediate level. Whenever he preached to monks, he rushed them, he made them impatient with their bodies and with this earth, he focused their eyes on heaven. Nothing here on earth could possibly satisfy a monk who had tasted the first drops from 'the river, the streams whereof shall made glad the city of God' (Ps. 46. 4). Not once did St Bernard mention the city of Jerusalem or the Holy Land when speaking to monks. That on this earth even monks needed visible signs was a nuisance, an obstacle to that immediate, direct vision for which a monk yearned with all his heart. But to laymen visible signs were not an obstacle but a great help. So much is obvious from the famous passage in the *Apologia* in which St Bernard described the devotion of the laity as that of carnal people, who had to be roused by visible ornaments, because they cannot be tempted by spiritual ones, and contrasted it with that of monks,

---

[41] *NatV*, vi, *SBO* 4, pp. 243–4: 'Et tu quidem, impia Synagoga, hunc nobis filium peperisti, officio quodam matris, sed non matris affectu.... Undique enim egrediuntur filiae Sion, ut videant regem Salomonem in diademate quo coronasti eum. Relinquens matrem adhaeret uxori suae, ut sint duo in carne una, et civitate pulsus atque exaltatus a terra, omnia trahit ad se.'

who had left all this visible beauty far behind them. That was the reason why the laity needed churches with images and pictures.[42] So when St Bernard addressed the laity on the subject of Jerusalem he could not confine himself to a description of the pleasures of heaven, he had to use images and describe the delights and sweetness of that country and that city where once his feet stood. That is exactly what he did in his famous crusading encyclicals which he wrote to encourage people to participate in an expedition to defend the Holy Land after the fall of Edessa in 1144. In those letters, written in about 1146–7, St Bernard waxed lyrical when he got on to the subject of the Holy Land:

> The earth trembles, because the Lord of heaven has now begun to loose his own land, the land in which he was seen for more than thirty years, as a man conversing with men. The land, his own, which he honoured with his birth, set to light with his miracles, consecrated with his blood, enriched with his burial. The land, his own, in which the voice of the turtle was heard when the Son of the Virgin commended the quest for chastity. The land, his own, in which the first flowers of the resurrection appeared.[43]

This was the land which Christian soldiers must now defend. St Bernard described it as a golden opportunity, because what once was a vice in the West became a virtue in the East.[44]

The reason that it became a virtue to defend that land was that the coming of Christ had changed its character completely, just as much as man's understanding of reality and of his own destination had changed since Christ and through Christ. Now Christ's followers knew that what they saw was just a shadow of things to come. Because of that change of perspective the nature of the land and of the city of Jerusalem had also changed. They were no longer of any importance as such: that was the mistake of the Jews; they had now become a sign, a sacrament. When writing to Patriarch William of Jerusalem St Bernard explained this change of character by comparing the Holy Place of which William was bishop with the holy place in which Moses had taken off his shoes. The place of the burning bush was holy, but Jerusalem now is holier. It is not really possible to compare shadow with truth, there is hardly any likeness

---

[42] *Apo*, SBO 3, pp. 104–5.
[43] *Ep*, ccclxiii and cccclviii, SBO 8, pp. 312 and 435.
[44] *Liber ad milites Templi de laude novae militiae* (= *Tpl*) ii–iii, SBO 3, pp. 216–17; *Ep*, ccclxiii, SBO 8, pp. 314–15.

between what was then seen through a glass darkly, but now that the veil has been rent is seen face to face.[45] It is interesting to note that St Paul is talking about heaven as the place where man shall see face to face, whereas St Bernard uses the expression to describe the happy state of the present city of Jerusalem, at least suggesting by this misquotation that Jerusalem is more or less a heaven on earth, in other words that it has a truly sacramental character.

That special character of Jerusalem, and the great opportunities it offered, became a special theme in St Bernard's treatise in praise of the new militia, of all his works perhaps the most disagreeable to a modern ear. St Bernard was quite sure that the soldiers of the Temple were doing God's work: the reconquest of Jerusalem had been foretold by the prophets, for example by Isaiah when he exclaimed: 'Break forth into joy, sing together, ye waste places of Jerusalem: for the Lord hath comforted his people, he hath redeemed Jerusalem' (Is. 52. 9).[46] But he went on to warn that reconquest as such was not enough; the liberation of the city, although to a certain extent a fulfilment of biblical prophecy, was not an end in itself. It offered Christian knights a unique opportunity to become more alive to the fact that the visible city was but the image of that which is in heaven and our mother. If they could see it in that light the present glory of Jerusalem would certainly make them more aware of their heavenly reward.[47]

That such was the true purpose of the crusade in St Bernard's eyes becomes obvious when we look at the last part of De laude, which, perhaps not accidentally, is also by far the largest, and consists of a tour of the most important Holy Places. It is as if St Bernard wanted to show the soldiers and pilgrims in what spirit the Holy Places ought to be visited, to teach them how these visible remains are not of any importance as such, but must be seen as signs of an invisible reality, and how they can help people to gain a better understanding of their true destination, which is not of this world. In his meditation on the Temple St Bernard exclaimed how this land of promise, that once gave only milk and honey to its inhabitants,

---

[45] *Ep*, cccxciii, *SBO* 8, p. 365.

[46] *Tpl*, iii, *SBO* 3, pp. 218–19: 'Videsne quam crebra veterum attestatione nova approbatur militia?'

[47] *Tpl*, iii, *SBO* 3, p. 219: 'Dummodo sane spiritualibus non praeiudicet sensibus litteralis interpretatio, quominus scilicet speremus in aeternum, quidquid huic tempori significando ex Prophetarum vocibus usurpamus, ne per id quod cernitur evanescat quod creditur, et spei copias imminuat penuria rei, praesentium attestatio sit evacuatio futurorum. Alioquin terrenae civitatis temporalis gloria non destruit caelestia bona, sed astruit, si tamen istam minime dubitamus illius tenere figuram, quae in caelis est mater nostra.'

now offers the remedies of salvation and the food of life to all the world. And meditating on Nazareth he comes to speak of Isaac, the patriarch who tragically mistook Jacob for Esau, because he relied too much on touch and smell. Isaac stands for the Jews who also relied on their senses and could not see the Word hidden in the flesh. But whereas Jews were satisfied with the smell, Christians know that the smell is not more than the promise of solid food to come.[48] Because they are not so far advanced as monks, laymen need the smell of the Holy Land, but it is the solid food of heaven which they really want, just as much as monks.[49]

It seems to me that St Bernard was more consistent than he is given credit for, and that he did not defile his mystical insights when preaching to laymen. He did not recommend the heavenly Jerusalem to monks, and the earthly city to laymen; he spoke of the one heavenly city, but in two different ways. All Christians are on the road to the true Jerusalem, all recognize that it is the heavenly city which is their true destination. So both monks and laymen share a spiritual understanding of Scripture, because Christ's coming in the flesh has revealed to all Christians that what we see is but a shadow of a glory we cannot fathom. Only the Jews had remained blind to that obvious fact and stuck to what they could see. The difference between monks and laymen is but a difference in degree, certainly if one compares it with the abyss that separates Jews from Christians on the one hand, and angels and Christians on the other. Monks were far advanced on the way to the heavenly Jerusalem, they hardly needed visible signs, and most of them were an obstacle to them. Laymen on the other hand needed many, to them they were a great help. And because laymen needed so much help, St Bernard was grateful that in his days the Holy Land was once more in Christian hands. It was a gift of God, a *tempus acceptabile*,[50] because laymen could now fight the invisible enemy, the devil, in waging war on the visible enemies of God, the

---

[48] *Tpl*, vii, *SBO* 3, pp. 225–6.

[49] See also F. Cardini, 'Bernardo e le crociate', *Bernardo Cistercense*, Atti del XXVI Convegno storico internazionale, Centro di studi sulla spiritualità medievale dell'università degli studi di Perugia, Accademia Tudertina (Spoleto, 1990), pp. 191–2.

[50] *Ep*, ccclxiii, *SBO* 8, pp. 312–13: 'Ecce nunc tempus acceptabile, ecce nunc dies copiosae salutis. Commota est siquidem et contremuit terra, quia cepit Deus caeli perdere terram suam. ... Miseratur enim populum suum Deus, et lapsis graviter providet remedium salutare.' I cannot accept the thesis of H. D. Kahl, 'Crusade Eschatology as seen by St. Bernard in the years 1146 to 1148', M. Gervers, ed., *The Second Crusade and the Cistercians* (New York, 1992), pp. 36–41, that St Bernard's preaching of the crusade may have had apocalyptic overtones, as it is largely based on the assumption that crusading in general was an apocalyptic enterprise, which I doubt.

heathen, and they also had the unique opportunity to visit the terrestrial Jerusalem, which was the image on earth of the heavenly city: both Holy War and the Holy Places were sacraments, visible signs referring to an invisible reality. Distasteful as it may be to us, to St Bernard crusading and visiting the Holy Land did not constitute a relapse into a literal understanding of Scripture, but a unique opportunity to bridge the gap that separated monks from laymen, and give to laymen that one extra chance to gain the same foretaste of the heavenly glory which monks already saw so clearly in the seclusion of the cloister.

THE MEDIEVAL WAY OF DEATH:
COMMEMORATION AND THE AFTERLIFE
IN PRE-REFORMATION CAMBRIDGESHIRE

by VIRGINIA R. BAINBRIDGE

ASIDE from learned conjecture about the nature of the afterlife, the men and women of the late Middle Ages were as fearful as we are of what lies on the other side of death.[1] They too were afraid of dying, afraid of what was beyond, of their own aloneness in facing death. They too had their euphemisms for the process of dying. Some went the way of all flesh: 'Viam universe carnis ingredi', while others migrated from this light, or from this age, to the Lord, 'ab hac luce migraverit', 'ab hoc saeculo emigraverit', 'ad Dominum migraverit'.[2] To comfort themselves they held up a mirror to their own society, which reflected the network of relationships which bound them in life to their lords, their tenants and servants, their families and benefactors, their fellow religious, their fellow gild brethren, townsmen, and parishioners. This image they projected into the void beyond the grave.[3]

Unlike us, consensus of opinion in their society over preceding centuries of Christianity had mapped out the continents of hell, purgatory, and heaven, and the path through purgatory to the presence of God and eternal salvation.[4] This map enabled them to make the crude

[1] Scholarly interest in the subject of death grew out of the work of art and literary historians on such striking representations as 'the Dance of Death' and the 'Ars Moriendi', for example, A. Tenenti, 'La vie et la mort à travers l'art du xve siècle, *Cahiers des annales*, 8 (Paris, 1952); *Il senso della Morte e l'Amore della vita nel Rinascimento* (Turin, 1957). The debate widened to the discussion of western attitudes towards death and dying, and many publications on this subject followed: P. Ariès, *Western Attitudes towards Death* (Baltimore, 1974) and *L'Homme devant la Mort* (Paris, 1977), translated as *The Hour of our Death* (New York, 1981).

[2] Public Record Office C47/38/7; C47/38/14, 15, 24, 36; C47/38/3, 20, 23, 33; C47/38/8; *Cambridge Gild Records*, ed. M. Bateson, Publns Cambridge Antiquarian Society, 39 (Cambridge, 1903), 24, St Mary's Gild prayer for the dead; J. Chiffoleau, *Le Compatabilité de l'au Delà: Les Hommes, La Mort et la Religion dans la Region d'Avignon à la fin du Moyen Age vers 1320–1480*, Collections de l'École Français de Rome 47 (Rome, 1980), p. 114.

[3] S. Reynolds, *Kingdoms and Communities in Western Europe 900–1300* (Oxford, 1984), confirms the importance of collective activity in the Middle Ages; J. Bossy, 'The Mass as a social institution 1200–1700', *Past and Present*, 100 (1983), pp. 29–61, esp. 37–46, the obligation of the living to pray for the dead to whom they were bound.

[4] P. Camporesi, *The Fear of Hell: Images of Damnation and Salvation in Early Modern Europe* (Oxford, 1991), esp. ch. 1 on the organic horrors of hell; J. Le Goff, *The Birth of Purgatory* (Chicago, 1984); C. McDannell & B. Lang, *Heaven: A History* (Yale, 1988).

assumption that the vast majority of people who had been neither very bad nor very good must be living out their sentences in purgatory.[5] Thus, it was imperative upon the living to do all in their power to ensure that the sentences were curtailed, particularly for those to whom they were bound by ties of loyalty and fellowship. The significance of the bond between the living and the dead has now become almost a commonplace of social history.[6] The belief that the deeds of the living can affect the progress of their dead in the afterlife is extremely ancient, and is to be found in many cultures.[7] Images of the afterlife in western Christendom were deeply rooted in the common stock of Indo-European mythology and some ideas may have been renewed with the Crusades and greater contact with the East.[8] Historians influenced by sixteenth-century Church reformers are apt to take too rationalist an approach to medieval Catholic practice.

Social obligations were as pressing at the moment of death and beyond as they had been in life. Mortmain licences and the foundation documents of chantries, wills, and the records of the corporate devotion of gilds or boroughs cite prayers for the sovereign, the founders' feudal lords, and other benefactors or relatives as the recipients of the spiritual fruits of the chantry or other commemorative practices.[9]

The obligation to provide prayers for the departed members of one's family was passed down together with the title to the estate. The commemoration of one's ancestors, both through the endowment of monastic houses and lesser foundations, such as chantries, was an important aspect

[5] Le Goff places the emergence of the third place where venial sins were sloughed off in the twelfth century; A. H. Bredero, 'Le Moyen Age et le Purgatoire', *RHE*, 78 (1983), pp. 429–52, a review and useful counter-balance to Le Goff, emphasizes the period between antiquity and the twelfth century when prayer for monks and laymen evolved in monasteries; the emergence of towns and money economy in which the concept developed from the eleventh century, and its popularization through preaching and indulgences from the thirteenth century on; C. Burgess, '"A fond thing vainly invented": an essay on purgatory and pious motive in late medieval England', *Parish, Church and People: Local Studies in Lay Religion 1350–1750*, ed. S. J. Wright (London, 1988), pp. 56–84, esp. 56–70; E. Duffy, *The Stripping of the Altars: Traditional Religion in England c.1400–1580* (Yale, 1992), section D, pp. 299–376.
[6] J. Bossy, 'The Mass', pp. 29–61, esp. p. 42; and *Christianity in the West 1400–1700* (Oxford, 1985), esp. pp. 26–34.
[7] R. J. E. Boggis, *Praying for the Dead: An Historical Review of the Practice* (London, 1913), traces the history of this practice from Judaism to the Reformation: *Death and the Regeneration of Life*, eds M. Bloch and J. Parry (Cambridge, 1982), Intro. pp. 10–11. Such beliefs are still widespread in twentieth-century Western society.
[8] *The Tibetan Book of the Dead*, ed. W. Y. Evans-Wentz (Oxford, 1957, 3rd edn 1960), Intro. pp. v, xiii–xiv, xx; the Tibetan judgement pp. xxx–xxxiii. 165–9; pain experienced in the spiritual body after death p. lxxix.
[9] PRO C47/38/24; J. Bossy, 'The Mass', pp. 36–46, the spiritual power of the mass could be directed to confer benefit on friends, and indeed to harm enemies.

of the maintenance of family tradition and identity.[10] Ancestor worship pre-existed Christianity among the German peoples and is one of the strands from which the custom of praying for the dead emerged.[11] In a primarily oral culture, just as the heralds were witness to aristocratic lineage and noble prowess, so the mass-priest embodied the memory of ancestral souls and their spiritual deeds. This may be seen in the wills of the gentry family of Ingaldesthorp of Burgh in Cambridgeshire. In 1456 Edmund Ingaldesthorp, knight, requested his executors to amortize a manor in Burwell, 'for his chantry in Burgh, according to the intention and effects of the last will of Lady Catherine de Burgh', his ancestor who had died in 1409, 'for two suitable chaplains, to pray in perpetuity for his soul, and for the soul of the said Lady Catherine and the souls of their parents'.[12]

The accretion of obligations to dead forbears multiplied as they were handed from generation to generation, and the living were obliged to re-endow foundations which had become impoverished. The duty to continue these observances was passed on by will to the executors, who often included the heir, and even to the executors of the executors.[13]

Sir Thomas Randis, chantry priest of Our Lady Gild in Tydd St Giles, left a messuage and garden to 'The priest serving the Gild of Our Lady and to his successors without end' on condition that he kept an anniversary mass and obit for him.[14] John Savage, chaplain and fellow of King's College Cambridge, left a breviary for the use of Master John Hogekyns. He was to give this and a psalter to Nicholas Burnham *alias* White, when he became a priest, who was to pray especially for John Savage's soul and the souls of Thomas Brown and John White. On his death he was to leave the breviary to another priest who was to do likewise for the term of his life, and he to another priest for his, on pain of excommunication.[15] There was a passing on of spiritual obligations with material wealth, for the priesthood just as for the laity. A priest would expect spiritual services

---

[10] J. Rosenthal, *The Purchase of Paradise: Gift Giving and the Aristocracy 1307–1485* (London, 1972), p. 16, Table 1; Le Goff, *Birth of Purgatory*, pp. 11–12, 233, the strength of family and corporate ties; p. 293, the likeness of the bond between living and dead to 'feudo-vassalic' contracts.

[11] A. H. Bredero, 'Le Moyen Age', p. 448.

[12] PRO Prob. 11/4/7, fos 54r, 1456.

[13] M. Hicks, 'Chantries, Obits & Almshouses: the Hungerford Foundations 1325–1478', *The Church in Pre-Reformation Society*, eds C. M. Barron & C. Harper-Bill (Woodbridge, 1985), pp. 123–42, esp. 124–36.

[14] PRO Prob. 11/14/32, fos 255r and v, 1504.

[15] King's College Ledger Book, 1451–1558, fol. 78r, 1474.

from the inheritor of a spiritual position, or of religious books or ornaments.

It was not only kinsmen for whom one was bound to pray, but one's benefactors: all those who had shown one favour, whose patronage had assisted one in the life of this world. In 1472 Geoffrey Sprynge, Citizen and Draper of London (with connections with Downham in the Isle of Ely), expressed his obligations in this way:

> To have an honest and well-disposed priest for to pray and sing for my soul all divine service, as such priests ought for to do: with the great trental of St. Gregory with all manner of prayers, fastings and other observances belonging, and also to pray for the souls of John and Agnes, my father and mother *and in especiall for the souls of all them that I am most bound to pray for*, and all christian souls.[16]

Duties to the dead not only bound one to those above in the social hierarchy, but also to those below. John Ingaldesthorp, knight, who died in 1420, ordered his executors to distribute money among his tenants 'in order that they might pray for him'.[17] Nicholas Hughson left two of his grandchildren 'five marks to pray for him and for their mother',[18] and Master Robert Fowlmere, rector of Fowlmere and canon of Westminster, left money for five priests to pray for one year 'for his soul, his parents, all faithful departed, his benefactors, and for the souls of his parishioners'.[19]

It is easy for us in our individualistic society to focus on the desire of individuals to be commemorated, particularly when so much evidence comes from documents such as wills.[20] It must be remembered, however, that the will was only the written record of a public act which took place, in ideal circumstances, at the deathbed of the testator surrounded by the family and household.[21] Those bequests not immediately coming into effect would generally be administered by the dead person's family and the expenses for funeral and commemorative rites would come out of

---

[16] PRO Prob. 11/6/15, fos 114r and v, 1472; R. W. Pfaff, 'The English Devotion of St. Gregory's Trental', *Speculum*, 49 (1974), pp. 75–90.

[17] PRO Prob. 11/2b/48, fol. 379, 1420.

[18] PRO Prob. 11/17/20, fol. 160r, 1512.

[19] PRO Prob. 11/2a/1, fos 7r and v, 1401.

[20] M. M. Sheehan, *The Will in Medieval England* (Toronto, 1963); C. Burgess, 'By quick and by dead: wills and pious provision in late Medieval Bristol', *EHR*, 102 (1987), pp. 837–58. Wills give only limited evidence for pious provision.

[21] G. Duby, *William Marshall: The Flower of Chivalry* (London, 1986), pp. 3–27. The poem depicts an ideal death-bed scene, with the hero divesting himself of his worldly possessions one by one to his family and household.

property which would otherwise have been theirs.[22] In some cases an element of coercion was necessary: some sixteenth-century testators reminded their children that they would answer before God on the day of Judgement for the fulfilment of their parent's dying wishes.[23] This illustrates that although they might break these, the responsibility was held in some awe. These things were done for the dead as members of a kin grouping which had sustained them in life and now did so in death.[24]

Commemoration was a collective activity carried out by the various groups to which a person had belonged during the course of his life: the family; those so-called surrogate families: brotherhoods, fraternities, gilds;[25] trade or professional groupings.[26] Some of these represented the ties of neighbourhood and social or occupational status, and others cut across such divisions, thereby lending cohesion to the society of town or parish.[27] Commemoration at once affirmed corporate identity, transcending the boundary between the living and the dead, and issued a direct challenge to the negation of human endeavour by the finality of the grave.

Entry into the fellowship of a gild or other society might entitle new brethren to have their names registered on a bede roll. These documents, sometimes inadequately described as membership lists, were not drawn up primarily for administrative convenience, but so that those named would receive the prayers of their parent institutions.[28] The accounts of St

---

[22] M. Hicks, 'Chantries, Obits & Almshouses', p. 126: some bequests were never paid due to the financial embarrassment of the testator; C. Burgess, 'By quick and by dead', pp. 844, 855. Objections by relatives to the alienation of property for commemorative rites led to their endowment in the testator's life-time rather than relying on their last will being carried out.

[23] There are 22 examples in Ely Consistory Court Wills 1544–58 and one in Ely Archdeaconry Court in 1546. Nine of these come from Willingham, a village where Protestant ideas took root early in the sixteenth century; see M. Spufford, *Contrasting Communities: English Villages in the 16th and 17th Centuries* (Cambridge, 1984), pp. 320–44.

[24] P. Ariès, *Western Attitudes*, ch. ii. Ariès, and those who follow him, perhaps overlook the extent to which commemoration was a collective activity.

[25] J. Chiffoleau, *Le Compatibilité de l'au Delà*, ch. 3. One of his theses is that fraternities grew up as people moved away from their families to the towns of the eleventh and twelfth centuries; H. F. Westlake, *The Parish Gilds of Medieval England* (London, 1919), p. 9 and passim, asserts that the chief function of the fraternities was to pray for their dead.

[26] C. Gross, *The Gild Merchant: A Contribution to British Municipal History* (Oxford, 1890); E. Coornaert, 'Les Ghildes Médiévales (ve-xive siècles) Définition-Évolution', *Revue Historique*, 199 (1948), pp. 22–55, 208–43.

[27] R. F. E. Weissman, *Ritual Brotherhood in Renaissance Florence* (New York, 1982); R. Trexler, *Public Life in Renaissance Florence* (New York, 1980).

[28] N. Orme, 'The Kalendar brethren of the City of Exeter', *Report & Transactions of the Devonshire Association for the Advancement of Science, Literature & Art*, 109 (1977), pp. 153–69; A. Kettle,

Mary's Gild, Great St Mary's Church, Cambridge, 1298–1319, record the entry fines paid by the living on entry into the fraternity, and paid on their behalf for the dead. The three rolls of the same period record the same practice. Single women, men, priests, husbands and wives, and family groups joined the fellowship, and along with them were joined dead parents, spouses, and others who had been important to them.[29] In 1389 the gild of St John the Baptist, Wisbech, ordained that the priest of the fraternity should have a tablet on which were written the names of the living and the dead, so that he was able to pray for both at mass and in his prayers.[30] Ten Cambridgeshire gilds at this date specified that the living and the dead were to be prayed for together at festive occasions. This was also the case in the statutes of three fifteenth-century gilds in the town of Cambridge: St Clements, St Peter and Paul, and All Saints, in the parishes of those names. They had special arrangements with the priests of their respective churches:

> Also it is ordained by all the common assent that every year the vicar of the foresaid church should have 3s.4d. for a centeyne of masses, that is to say to have in mind both the quick and the dead every Sunday in the year and also to pray at the Bedes time for all the company, both for them that ben living and also for them that be passed out of the world.[31]

The dead and the living were prayed for together: they stood as one company before God.[32]

Like the family, societies such as gilds or fraternities, town councils and parishes, religious houses, and colleges of secular priests had a collective identity which would survive an individual member. In this respect they enshrined not only the memory of that individual's existence and his/her

---

'City & close: Lichfield in the century before the Reformation', *The Church in Pre-Reformation Society*, pp. 143–57, 161.

[29] *Cambridge Gild Records*, ed. M. Bateson (Cambridge, 1903), pp. 1–13 minutes, pp. 14–25 bede rolls; J. R. Banker, *Death in the Community: Memorialisation and Confraternities in an Italian Commune in the Late Middle Ages* (University of Georgia Press, 1989), pp. 59–68. There are far fewer women than men on the bede rolls of the Confraternity of San Sepolcre 1269–1309. Banker thinks that they are widowed heads of households which suggests a different system of memorialization, p. 64.

[30] PRO C47/38/39.

[31] British Library, Add. MS 5846, pp. 5–13, St Clement's Gild Statutes 1431; Cambridge University Lib. MMI 36: Baker MSS vol. 25, Item 10, pp. 361–6, St Peter and St Paul Gild Statutes 1488; pp. 367–71, All Saints Gild Statutes 1473.

[32] E. Duffy, *Stripping of the Altars*, pp. 334–7, bede rolls.

deeds and benefactions, but also provided an administrative framework through which memory could be carried forward into future generations. This was recognized in England by the legislative authorities in the application of the Statute of Mortmain, first in 1279 to monastic foundations and chantries, in 1391 to corporate bodies such as gilds merchant, town corporations, and fraternities, and in 1536 to the parish.[33]

Bede rolls or 'liber vitae' were monastic in origin and carried the names of dead brethren to sister houses where they would also receive prayers.[34] As the eucharist took on a central role in late medieval Christianity, the emblem of Christ's passion for mankind and his triumph over the grave, that ancient theme of love and death, became a vehicle for transferring spiritual power to the dead when celebrated in their name.[35] Institutions which were more typical than monasteries as the administrators of commemorative rites in the later Middle Ages were chantry colleges and gilds or fraternities.[36] They provided services for those with less wealth and social connections on a sliding scale, according to the resources of the departed.

In Cambridgeshire this may be seen in the practices of the colleges of the university. These were primarily endowed as chantries for the souls of their benefactors and only secondarily as educational establishments, a fact that is often overlooked due to their secularization at the Reformation. They included the college of Corpus Christi, which had been founded by two gilds of Cambridge burgesses and their aristocratic associates: the gilds of St Mary and Corpus Christi in 1352.[37] They followed the pattern of all chantry colleges at this time, a group of secular priests living a common life, and commemorating through their prayers and masses their benefactors and their fellow priests. Wills proved under the peculiar jurisdiction of King's, one such college, give evidence of

---

[33] S. Raban, *Mortmain Legislation and the English Church 1279–1500* (Cambridge, 1982), p. 170; A. Kreider, *The English Chantries: The Road to Dissolution* (Harvard, 1979), p. 84. The Crown was hostile to the alienation of lands for intercession, even before the abolition of intercessory institutions in the mid-sixteenth century.

[34] G. H. Cook, *Medieval Chantries and Chantry Chapels* (London, 1963), Intro. pp. 1–6.

[35] M. Bloch and J. Parry, *Death and the Regeneration of Life*, Intro., p. 1; J. G. Fraser, *The Golden Bough* (London, 1890); M. Éliade, *The Myth of the Eternal Return* (Princeton, 1965); J. Bossy, 'The Mass', pp. 29–61; M. Rubin, *Corpus Christi: The Eucharist in late Medieval Culture* (Cambridge, 1991).

[36] G. H. Cook, *English Collegiate Churches of the Middle Ages* (London, 1959).

[37] M. Bateson, *Cambridge Gild Records*, Intro.; *VCH Cambridgeshire*, ed. J. P. C. Roach (London, 1959), 3, pp. 371–6; J. Josselin, *Historiola Collegii Corporis Christi et Beatae Mariae Cantabrigiae*, ed. J. Willis (Cambridge, 1880).

this.[38] They have an advantage over the wills of the laity for our understanding of beliefs about the afterlife, as they are in general more articulate where religious ideas are concerned.

In 1509 Richard Hatton, fellow of King's College, left books for his soul, 'in recompensiam omnium neglectorum aut male gestorum et perpetratorum per me in adolescentia mea.'[39] A priest there was to say masses for him and his benefactors for one year. He was also a fellow of the chantry college of St Mary and St Stephen, Westminster, where he was to be buried and an anniversary kept. In 1517 John Sampson, who described himself as 'indignus sacerdos et peccator penitens', commended his soul into the hands of the Trinity, the Blessed Virgin, Jesus Christ his redeemer, a number of saints whom he named, all other saints and the elect of God, 'that through their holy prayers and through the passion of Jesus Christ, he might gain remission of all his sins'. His body he commended to Christian burial.[40] He was not taking any chances, for he continued:

> I will that immediately after my death there shall be celebrated for my soul 30 masses according to the order of the Trental of St. Gregory;[41] and 5 masses for the 5 wounds of Jesus Christ at a certain altar at Scala Celi;[42] and ... that a priest shall celebrate for a whole year for the safety of my soul and all those souls whom I hold dear; ... and that two fellow priests shall celebrate in college for a year ...; if it happens that I die in Cambridge there are to be due ceremonies on the day of my death, and a mass the following day at which the officiating priest shall have 12d., each fellow 8d., each priest 6d., clerks and scholars 4d., choristers 2d., and in alms to the poor 10s.

In 1528 Robert Hacumblen, provost,[43] commended his soul

> into the hands of the Holy Trinity and Jesus Christ my saviour, by whose bitter passion, and through continually worshipping his five

[38] King's College Cambridge, King's College Ledger Book 1451–1558, 39 wills in this period, on the whole made by fellows of the college with some college servants and their widows.
[39] King's College Cambridge ledger, fos 219v–20v.
[40] King's College Cambridge ledger, fos 247v–8r.
[41] R. W. Pfaff, 'St. Gregory's Trental', pp. 75–90. A custom based on St Gregory's release of his mother's soul from purgatory, through his intercession, having just seen a vision of her in torment pleading for help, and afterwards a beatific vision of her release and subsequent joy.
[42] E. Duffy, Stripping of the Altars, pp. 375–6.
[43] King's College Cambridge ledger, fos 278v–9r.

wounds I trust mercifully to be saved . . . and through the intercession and prayer of the Blessed Virgin . . . (and other named saints) . . . through whose prayers and the long worshipping and devotion which I have had of them, God willing the same I trust verily to obtain everlasting joy.

His body was to be buried in the new church (King's College Chapel) and the goods given to him by the grace of Almighty God went to the college in return for provision for his soul, including a gilt chalice and patten engraved with 'Orate pro Anima R.H.' On the day of his burial or within two days, a trental was to be sung with placebo and dirige.[44] A dirige was to be held in the university at which the vice-chancellor, doctors, priests, regents and non-regents, and bedells were to have sums of money graded according to their status, to pray for him. A dirige was to be kept in the college by his 'company', at which the vice-provost, fellows, undergraduates, priests, clerks, choristers, ringers of bells, and college servants likewise were given money. At the burial the executors were to provide torches and eight poor men to carry them, each to have for their labour a black gown and 8*d.* in money. Other mourners were to be dressed in black gowns to the sum of 26*s.*8*d.*, and £6.13*s.*4*d.* was to be distributed to the poor in alms for his soul. A 'month day', or mass thirty days after death, was to be kept, and there was provision for other prayers as well.[45]

These three wills illustrate the extensive range of late medieval funeral and commemorative rites. Jacques Chiffoleau comments on the multiplication of masses and prayers which went hand in hand with the computation of the number of years one was likely to spend in purgatory, and the remission these were likely to provide.[46] Robert Hacumblen's death was commemorated by his college and the university, as he had been a member of both institutions, and Richard Hatton's by both colleges to which he had belonged.

Gilds or fraternities provided funeral and commemorative rites for

---

[44] A trental (from Latin Triginta) was 30 masses; Placebo (from the first Latin word of the service) was evensong; and Dirige (from the first Latin word of the service) mattins; C. Burgess, 'By quick and by dead', pp. 840–1; R. C. Finucane, 'Sacred corpse: profane carrion: Social ideas & death rituals in the later Middle Ages', *Mirrors of Mortality: Studies in the Social History of Death*, ed. J. Whaley (London, 1981), pp. 40–60, gives a brief summary of funeral rites.

[45] *New Catholic Encyclopaedia* (New York etc., 1967), 12, p. 384. Requiem mass was usually celebrated the day after burial, and on certain other days, the third, seventh, thirtieth days after death and the anniversary; C. Burgess, 'By quick and by dead', pp. 840–1; R. J. E. Boggis, chs viii and ix.

[46] J. Chiffoleau, *Le Compatibilité de L'au Delà*, part II, le Mathematique du Salut.

their dead and records of their rituals reveal much about contemporary belief and practice. Early gild historians described them in the language of their times. Toulmin Smith likened them to the 'burial clubs' or funeral savings schemes of the nineteenth century.[47] His critic Westlake, asserting that pious motives were uppermost, labelled them 'co-operative chantries'.[48] Both descriptions are limited and thus misleading. They were not simply the 'poor man's chantry' but one type of social group which kept alive the memory of those who had died in their company: the wealthier the company, the more elaborate the range of practices they were able to provide.

According to the royal survey of these institutions in 1389, thirty-nine (65 per cent) Cambridgeshire gilds undertook some service for their dead brothers and sisters.[49] Attendance at these occasions was compulsory in twenty-one (35 per cent) gilds, enforced by a system of fines to ensure company solidarity, ranging from 1d. to 1s., or 1lb. of wax paid to the light burning before their patron saint. Members were summoned to funerals by a gild officer, sometimes with the title of dean or apparitor.[50] The tasks of the apparitor of the Purification Gild, Great St Mary's Church, Cambridge, were 'to inform brethren of funeral services, meetings and other gatherings; to preside over the offices of the dead and to organise the torches and the carrying of the body to the church.'[51] The fraternity of the Assumption of the Virgin in Tydd St Giles had a 'Bellman' who was 'to go around the village ringing his bell to cause men to pray for the soul of the departed and to cause all others to come to the funeral rites . . .',[52] thus both eliciting prayers from the community at large at the time the soul left the body and reinforcing a sense of gild identity by the special summoning of the brethren to the gild rites.[53] Other companies expressed their solidarity by wearing gild livery or badges to such occasions.

Thirty-two (53 per cent) gilds stated that they organized funerals for

---

[47] *English Gilds*, ed. J. Toulmin Smith, EETS 40 (London, 1870), Intro. by L. Toulmin Smith, p. xxxvi.

[48] H. F. Westlake, *Parish Gilds*, p. 40, contradicts the 'Burial club' idea; p. 44 labels them 'Co-operative chantries'.

[49] Sixty returns for Cambridgeshire are extant.

[50] E. Durkheim, *The Elementary Forms of the Religious Life*, transl. J. W. Swain (2nd edn. London, 1976), p. 399, 'when someone dies the family group to which he belongs feels itself lessened and, to react against this loss, it assembles'.

[51] PRO C47/38/9.

[52] PRO C47/38/36.

[53] A. Van Gennep, *The Rites of Passage*, transl. M. B. Vizedom and G. L. Caffee (London, 1977), esp. ch. viii, p. 165: 'convocation by drum crier or messenger gives the meal even more of the character of a collective ritual'.

their members. This included the provision of lights or torches and in one case a hearse.[54] Thirty-four (57 per cent) organized commemorative rites, fifteen holding requiem masses or prayers for the group as a whole, often on the feast-day of their patron saint. Nine organized commemoration of individual members, a requiem mass, a trental of masses or an anniversary mass, but these were more likely to be for founders or substantial benefactors of the gild. At such occasions, it was obligatory for the brethren to offer soul pennies or halfpennies or for the alderman to do so on behalf of the company. Thus funeral and commemorative rites reinforced notions of hierarchy as well as collectivity.

People with more money had greater opportunity for commemoration.[55] The statutes of Holy Trinity Gild, Holy Trinity Church, Cambridge, a fraternity for the wealthy elite of the town and surrounding area offered the whole spectrum of funeral and commemorative rites.[56] On the death of a member of the gild lights stood around the body to ward away evil spirits at the night's vigil kept by mourners. Brethren were to attend the placebo on the eve and the dirige and mass on the day of burial. They were to accompany the body in a solemn procession to the church and there to make prayers and offerings for the soul, at mass on the day of burial, and on the seventh and thirtieth days following. Elsewhere prayers were said on the third day after burial. The soul was believed to remain in proximity to the body for a few days after its separation at death; the appropriate rites and prayers at this liminal point aided its journey to the other world. The Trinity gild supported a chaplain to say a hundred masses for each departed member and to celebrate mass daily for its brothers and sisters. The gild purchased two indulgences from the Bishop of Ely. One in 1378 granted forty days' remission from purgatory to its benefactors, and one in 1384 another forty days' remission to benefactors or to those who took part in the gild celebration of the feast of the Holy Trinity 'mente pia', with pious intent.

The Holy Trinity Gild, Wisbech, was another wealthy gild.[57] It acted as de facto corporation for the town with the approval of the Bishop of Ely,

---

[54] PRO C47/38/6. The small sums left to gilds in wills of the fifteenth and sixteenth centuries are probably to pay for the hire of such things.

[55] The medieval view was that they also had greater opportunities for sin and therefore less chance of redemption, as exemplified in the story of Lazarus and the rich man.

[56] PRO C47/38/10.

[57] *VCH Cambridgeshire*, 2, ed. L. F. Salzman (London, 1948), pp. 92, 320, 327; 4, ed. R. B. Pugh (London, 1953), pp. 254–6. This gild leaves a number of sources so it is possible to gain a broader picture of its activities.

for whom Wisbech was the administrative centre of many of his estates.[58] In 1389 the gild employed various chaplains and clerks to sing commemorative masses for brethren and benefactors in its private chapel in the church.[59] Income from land endowed these services, and by the time of its abolition the gild employed four perpetual chaplains, one of whom had additional responsibilities as local schoolmaster.[60] The gild purchased a mortmain licence for various bequests of land in 1453 under the aldermanship of John Masse,[61] who left the gild, among other things, the sum of five marks to purchase an indulgence from the Pope.[62]

The smaller and poorer fraternities offered a narrower range of funeral and commemorative practices according to their funds. Not all could support a perpetual chaplain and so contented themselves with hiring a priest for particular occasions when funds allowed, or relying on the intercession of their patron saint for whom they burned a light in the church.

Within a gild, some funeral and commemorative customs were performed for all brothers and sisters, and others only for certain individuals according to a number of factors: age, gender, status, and wealth. The gild, like a microcosm of society at large and like other social groups, made a greater public display of mourning people, generally men, who had played a larger part in public life.[63]

Trentals of masses were celebrated only for the brothers and sisters of the Assumption Gild, St Mary's Church, Ely, who were aged over sixteen.[64] In 1389, although eight gilds buried poor brethren at gild expense, this was an act of charity, akin to burying strangers, rather than an automatic right. The Assumption Gild, Holy Trinity Church, Cambridge, expressed the reduced status of brethren whose funerals were paid for from gild funds by burning only two candles at the offices of the dead, not the customary four.[65]

---

[58] *Wisbech Corporation Records*, vol. 1. This document in the Wisbech & Fenland Museum started life as the Trinity Gild Register and became volume 1 of the corporation records at the incorporation in 1547.

[59] PRO C47/38/43.

[60] PRO Prob. 11/20/8, fos 55v, 56r and v, 1520, will of Robert Smythe; Prob. 11/20/24, fos 190v–2r, 1521, will of Thomas Wyth, gentleman.

[61] PRO C66/478, 32 Henry VI, membrane 23, patent roll licence to found a chantry.

[62] PRO Prob. 11/5/14, fos 112r and v, 113r, 1466, will of John Masse.

[63] Bloch and Parry, *Death and the Regeneration of Life*, Intro. p. 4; Van Gennep, *Rites of Passage*, p. 148, mourning is greater for those of higher social standing.

[64] PRO C47/38/17a, b.

[65] PRO C47/38/5.

So that a brother might not be buried as a stranger in another town, twelve (20 per cent) gilds in 1389 made arrangements to counter this. If a brother died within ten leagues of Stretham, the warden and two brothers of the Assumption Gild would bring the body back to the town, where it was to be buried among the brothers of the fraternity with due ceremony.[66] Other gilds in the rural communities of Stretham, Stowe Cum Quye, and March also imposed a distance limitation on such activities, whereas the gilds of the major towns of the county, Cambridge, Ely, and Wisbech, took it for granted that some members would die while away on business. This is also a feature of gilds in the trade centres of Norwich and Lynn in Norfolk.[67] The statutes of St Katherine's Gild, St Simon and St Jude's Church, Norwich provided for the body to be buried wherever lawful, illustrating the practical as well as the religious aspects of dying away from home. Gilds in the larger towns had members from the surrounding region,[68] who gained limited benefit from the burial customs. Attendance at their funerals was not compulsory, although two Cambridge gilds, the Annunciation, Great St Mary's Church, and St Katherine's, St Benet's Church, arranged for mass to be held as if the corpse were present.[69] In such cases membership of a gild in a town where one had business dealings would ensure a burial appropriate to one's status if one died there.

The widows of the brethren of the Purification Gild, Great St Mary's Church, Cambridge, who had fallen into poverty, were denied burial at gild expense.[70] Poverty brought no recompense for the status they had once enjoyed as the wives of the wealthy burgesses of Cambridge. Women generally received individual commemoration only as the wives of founders, or as widowed benefactresses.

Founders undertook the expense of setting up a gild, in part for their own commemoration, but over the course of time, these institutions came to need re-endowment. Men who had been prominent in gild affairs, such as John Masse, alderman of Holy Trinity Gild, Wisbech, often made substantial gifts so that memory of their deeds would continue. Such commemorative practices were assured on payment of a certain sum: 40s. for an anniversary mass for brothers and sisters of St

[66] PRO C47/38/32.
[67] *English Gilds*, ed. J. Toulmin Smith, pp. 19–20, gild of St Katherine, St Simon and St Jude's Church, Norwich, pp. 51–3; gild of St Leonard, St James Church, Damgate, Lynn.
[68] PRO C47/38/4; C47/38/9.
[69] PRO C47/38/4; C47/38/7.
[70] PRO C47/38/9.

Clement's, St Peter and St Paul, and All Saints Gilds in fifteenth-century Cambridge.[71] Some commemorative practices were administered by the gild on behalf of a wealthy person who had made an endowment for that specific purpose. Lord Robert de Scales of Haslingfield endowed the Assumption Gild to administer his chantry in 1344, and Thomas Whiskyn in 1528 left 12d. a year for 12 years to the Resurrection Gild, Chesterton, for a mass and dirige.[72]

Wills are an additional source of material to augment the scant records which most of the fraternities leave behind. Out of a sample of around 2,000 Cambridgeshire wills (1383–1588), about 1,000 were proved prior to the abolition of the gilds or fraternities in 1547. Only 150 (14 per cent) mentioned gilds or fraternities. Half of these wills were proved nationally in the Prerogative Court of Canterbury and so were made by richer people who could afford to pay for a number of forms of commemoration. Indeed, half did request commemoration by groups besides the gilds to which they had belonged. Wills illustrate multiple membership of the gilds, especially in the later fifteenth and early sixteenth centuries. This caused no apparent conflict of loyalty but merely increased opportunities for commemoration. In 1529 Margaret Pepis of Cottenham left 8d. to every gild within the town keeping a light within the church 'So that they come with their banners to bring my body to burial.'[73]

Town corporations such as that of Cambridge were nominated in the wills of their former aldermen and burgesses as the guardians of their memory and administrators of their commemoration. These follow the same pattern as the exequies kept by the university and the colleges for their fellows.[74] Just as the small sums of money given to participants in the ritual imitate the monastic 'pitancia' given to the monks for their prayers, as money or extra food at the anniversary of a benefactor, so also the gradation of the sums disbursed reflected the ordering of the social hierarchy of the town. In 1545 John Chapman, 'one of the Aldermen of the town of Cambridge', died.[75] After the death of his wife he requested his messuage and tenement to be sold, and the money delivered to the mayor

---

[71] BL, Add. MSS 5846, pp. 5–13; Cambridge University Library, MM 136: Baker MSS, vol. 25, pp. 361–6, 367–71.

[72] PRO C47/38/24; Ely Consistory Court Original Wills 1528 (ECC/1/3/4).

[73] W. M. Palmer, *Village Gilds of Cambridgeshire* (Ely, 1904), p. 348, quotes this will. This goes against the emphasis of the 1389 ordinances on loyalty and keeping gild secrets: J. Chiffoleau, *La Compatabilité*, part II.

[74] P. Michaud-Quantin, *Universitas: Expression du Mouvement Communautaire dans le Moyen Age Latin* (Paris, 1970).

[75] Archdeaconry Court of Ely 2/1/12, 1545, will of John Chapman.

and burgesses on condition that they kept an annual obit,[76] with a placebo and dirige and a mass of requiem for his soul, his wife's, their friends', and all Christian souls. On that occasion the parish priest was to have 8*d.*; every fellow of the same house 4*d.*;[77] the mayor or deputy being present 3*s.*4*d.*; the aldermen present 20*d.*, with 2*d.* or 1*d.* for their offerings; 16*d.* to the town clerk and the town sergeant, with 1*d.* for their offerings; and 4*d.* for the bell-ringers, and 12*d.* for lights about the hearse. The poor were to feast on 13*s.*4*d.* worth of bread, 7*s.* worth of cheese, and 2*s.* worth of ale, while the mayor and corporation were to be entertained to a breakfast or dinner costing 5 marks a year.

The parish, an institution to which technically every person belonged, had emerged into prominence in the course of the later Middle Ages, in recognition of which the Tudor dynasty endowed it with greater local powers. Nearly everyone was buried in the parish churchyard, their funerals conducted by the parish clergy. The parish church possessed a stock of liturgical ornaments and paraphernalia, donated by the parishioners over the years and, like that owned by the gilds, hired out on these occasions. These included hearse, coffins, palls, and lights. Holy Trinity Church, Cambridge, owned a variety of lights, standers, large and small tapers, and torches.[78]

The parish was a repository for collective memory and furthermore provided continuity of administration for memorials to its dead. Wills requested the administration of commemorative rites most commonly by family members, churchwardens, or executors who were generally family members, or men prominent in parish affairs. As with the gilds, age, gender, status, and wealth determined the extent of commemoration. In Norwich at this time

> Notice is given of the death of such a person by the great bell of the parish where the deceased dwelt and died . . . continued a greater or less time according to the estate and reputation of the deceased, and for persons of note half an hour or more; for poor persons only a short time. Also less for children than men or women . . . the bell thus ringing is by some called a soul bell. . . .[79]

[76] Obit—commemorative services on the anniversary of a death.
[77] I.e. college of the University.
[78] Cambridgeshire County Record Office P22/5/1, Church Wardens' Accounts, Cambridge, Holy Trinity parish 1504–58, fol. 6r, and passim.
[79] W. Rye, 'The Order of funerals, ringings &c. at Norwich', *The East Anglian, or Notes and Queries*, ns 2 (1887–8), pp. 389–92. The number of strokes would inform the hearers of the exact status of the deceased.

Because such 'superstitious' practices lingered on, the removal of church bells was still under way when Edward VI died in 1553.

Out of the sample of 2,000 wills, 627 (32 per cent) made specific requests for certain funeral or commemorative rites. Added to this a further 499 (25 per cent) left details of such arrangements in the hands of their executors, bringing the total to 57 per cent.[80] The will itself was intimately associated with the death of the testator: most were written when they were on their death-beds, judging by the short time between the date of the will and the date of probate, and many testators refer to themselves as 'sick in body but of good and perfect remembrance'.[81] The standard bequests of a few pennies to certain causes listed below the preamble, sometimes dismissed as convention, must be viewed in association with the death of the testator. The sums left to the mother church or the churchyard or fabric of the parish church were to pay for burial; to the bells and torches for their hire at the funeral. Bequests for tithes forgotten were so the soul would not be hampered on its journey. Bequests to altars, lights, or gilds within the church invoked the intercession of the saints for the soul, and bequests to secular or regular clergy invoked their prayers. All these disappeared from wills between the mid-1540s and the mid-1550s.

Chantries have received much attention in existing research. They have been studied primarily as architectural or institutional forms and in relation to the aristocratic or gentry families with which they are associated.[82] This has concealed the variations in their administration and their connections with other aspects of late medieval life.

Work on perpetual chantries in Cambridgeshire by Edward Ventris, supplemented by the *Victoria County History*, records sixty-six, founded between the late thirteenth and early sixteenth centuries.[83] This figure includes two chantry colleges: one at Newton St Mary and one at Ely,[84] but does not take into account the many colleges of Cambridge University endowed primarily as chantries.

---

[80] J. Scarisbrick, *The Reformation and the English People* (Oxford, 1984), pp. 5–6: two-thirds of testators in the 1530s requested some prayers for their soul.

[81] This phrase is more common in the sixteenth than the fifteenth century.

[82] G. H. Cook, *Medieval Chantries and Chantry Chapels*; K. L. Wood-Leigh, *Perpetual Chantries in Britain* (Cambridge, 1965); J. Rosenthal, *Purchase of Paradise*, ch. 3; M. Hicks, 'The piety of Margaret, Lady Hungerford', *JEH*, 38 (1987), pp. 19–38, an excellent study of a foundress' pious motivation.

[83] *VCH Cambridgeshire*, 2–6, 8; E. Ventris, 'Notes upon chantries and free chapels', *Proc. of Cambridgeshire Antiquarian Society*, 1 (1859), pp. 201–40.

[84] The 'Cantarie de la Grene' at Ely is not mentioned in either of the above, and is known only through wills: e.g. Ely Diocesan Archives, HK 2751/A, fos. 10v, 40r, 46v.

Early foundations were administered by monasteries, either within their precincts or by providing chaplains to celebrate in a parish church. This was the case in Barton where, from 1278, two canons of Barnwell Priory lived, serving God and St Mary and saying masses for their benefactors.[85] By the later Middle Ages other corporate bodies, gilds or fraternities, parishes or townships were being entrusted with chantry management. Ten (15 per cent) were either wholly or partly funded by fraternities. Henry Cyprian of Whittlesford had endowed a chantry there, but failed to obtain a mortmain licence: the township, through its administrators, recovered the land and put it to other use.[86] Perpetual chantries were expensive, an option open only to the extremely wealthy who could guarantee landed income in perpetuity to sustain them. There has been much debate on whether they were in decline on the eve of the Reformation.[87] However, Alan Kreider has demonstrated that the further away they were from their date of foundation the greater the likelihood of their decline.[88] For example, the chantry at Barton had fallen into abeyance by the late-fourteenth century. There was a pragmatic approach to uneconomic institutions: once the founder had been forgotten, unless there was re-endowment by a new benefactor, as for eight (12 per cent) of the Cambridgeshire chantries, the foundation was dissolved and the revenues transferred elsewhere.[89]

For perpetual chantries to be fully understood they must be set within the context of temporary chantry provision, as revealed in wills and parish records. Out of 254 wills proved in the Prerogative Court of Canterbury, drawn from twenty sample parishes, ninety-eight (38 per cent) requested some form of chantry.[90] The late medieval church catered for every pocket. Great wealth bought 'perpetual' commemoration: fourteen (5 per cent) people requested perpetual chantries to be administered according to the chronological pattern set out above: one by Walsingham Priory, Norfolk, one by a Cambridge college, five by family or executors, six by religious gilds, and one by the Hedborowes or officers of the

[85] *VCH Cambridgeshire*, 5, ed. C. R. Elrington (London, 1973), p. 172.
[86] *VCH Cambridgeshire*, 6, ed. A. P. M. Wright (London, 1978), p. 272.
[87] J. A. F. Thompson, 'Piety & Charity in late Medieval London', *JEH*, 16 (1965), pp. 178–95; R. B. Dobson, 'The Foundation of Perpetual Chantries by the Citizens of medieval York', *SCH*, 4 (1967), pp. 22–38. Both argue against the line put forward by W. K. Jordan and G. C. Coulton.
[88] A. Kreider, *The English Chantries*, p. 89.
[89] R. B. Dobson, 'Foundation of Perpetual Chantries', pp. 22–38.
[90] C. Burgess, 'By quick and by dead', pp. 837–8, esp. 840, 842, reminds us of the inadequacy of wills as a source. Nevertheless they express intention if not actuality.

township of Chesterton. Those with moderate wealth could pay eight marks a year for a secular or regular priest to say mass for them daily,[91] thirty-seven (15 per cent) people requested the services of one or more priests for between two and twenty years, and forty-seven (18 per cent) for one year. Thirty-three (13 per cent) people endowed an anniversary mass or obit for a number of years. These varied in expense and elaboration and were a fashionable practice particularly in the early sixteenth century, often in addition to other commemoration.[92] For those with lesser means a trental costing about 10s. could be sung shortly after death.

Others had to content themselves with a mass of requiem at their funeral or the prayers of their friends and the poor who had enjoyed the funeral dole. Countless others went to their graves with none of these spiritual resources, but were remembered, nevertheless, by the wealthier who made provision for all Christian souls along with those to be specifically commemorated. The same groups which administered perpetual chantries administered temporary ones. They were less cumbersome than the perpetual institutions which may partly explain their popularity. Their numbers and the diversity of commemorative practices attest not only to the vitality of pre-Reformation Catholicism, but also to the resources available to medieval men and women facing bereavement.[93]

Commemorative activities were not merely for the benefit of the dead, but to assist those left behind with their grief.[94] The different stages of the funeral, the vigil, the placebo and dirige, and mass and burial; and of the commemorative rituals, the third, seventh, and thirtieth days and anniversaries may be seen as markers in the passage of grief.[95] Indeed, the commemoration of the dead by the living was an affirmation of their continuing affinity. This may be seen with particular clarity in the commensality or sharing of food provided by the dead at their funeral or com-

---

[91] Ely Diocesan Archives HK2791/A, fos 56v–57r, 1458, wills of Margaret Ffarnham. A priest to sing for a year cost eight marks.

[92] C. Burgess, 'A service for the dead: the form and function of the anniversary in late medieval Bristol', *Trans. of Bristol & Gloucester Arch. Soc.* 105 (1987), pp. 183–211.

[93] P. Ariès, *Western Attitudes*, ch. iv, draws on recent sociological studies to underline the impoverishment of twentieth-century Western society in this respect.

[94] E. Kubler-Ross, *On Death and Dying* (New York, 1969); and *Death: The Final Stage of Growth* (Englewood Cliffs, NJ, 1975).

[95] M. Bloch and J. Parry, *Death and the Regeneration of Life*, Intro. pp. 3–4, the two phases of mortuary rituals enable society to recover and to locate death, an arbitrary event, within time; A. van Gennep, *Rites of Passage*, p. 147. Mourning is a transitional rite for the survivors.

memoration.[96] Wills show that bread and ale and sometimes cheese or barrels of herrings were regularly consumed, sometimes by all who were gathered there and sometimes specifically by the poor, those on the margins of society who represented the dead at the feast. Colleges, gilds, towns, and parishes ate and drank the health of their dead on appointed days, the expenses of which they recorded carefully in their accounts. In Bassingbourne, a herd of 'obit cows' and 'obit lands' funded the anniversaries of those who had left them for this purpose.[97] The cows were hired out as milk beasts and breeding cattle to the poor and the lands to those who could afford them, thus becoming a feature of agricultural life in the community. Grain left as pious bequests to the church was regularly brewed and consumed at 'church ales' to make money for parish funds. In these ways the commemoration of the dead and their gifts to the living were part of the tissue of communal life and endeavour, rather than confined to the elaborate carved forms of the chantry chapel.

The performance of funeral and commemorative rituals was a deed of charity done for the souls of the dead by the living, who in return would gain spiritual reward in the next life. These rituals contained the enactment of the dead divesting themselves of their material goods through the distribution of food, thus symbolizing the complex reciprocities between the living and the dead. For the population in general the Reformation period was a time of doctrinal change and uncertainty which had a profound effect on this nexus of relationships.

In the 1520s the doctrine of purgatory, the belief that the living could help the dead, began to be discredited along with the authority of the papacy, under the attacks of continental reformers. In the early 1530s legal changes prevented the foundation of perpetual chantries.[98] In 1536 Henry VIII issued a declaration against purgatory and by 1540 institutions which had catered for commemoration, not only monasteries but friaries which had been popular for prayers, trentals and other masses, had gone. Other commemorative groups, gilds, colleges, chantries, and hospitals were to follow them in 1547.

In wills this is reflected in changes in the pattern of bequests.[99] From

---

[96] Bloch and Parry, *Death and the Regeneration of Life*, p. 28: commensality is associated with sexuality and therefore birth with death; Van Gennep, *Rites of Passage*, pp. 164–5: commensality unites the survivors with the dead.

[97] CCRO P11/5/1–2, Bassingbourne churchwardens' accounts 1490–1540, passim.

[98] A. Kreider, *The English Chantries*, pp. 84–5, the end of chantry foundation; chs iv. and v. on the demise of purgatory.

[99] From work on the sample of 2,000 wills, it is my opinion that they are not suitable for

the late 1530s, money for prayers, masses, and anniversaries was entrusted to family or executors in preference to public bodies such as gild or parish, presumably due to fear of confiscation. Some anniversary doles to the poor shifted from the date of death of the testator into association with Christ's death and were made during Lent, at Easter, or at Christmas. Prior to these religious upheavals on average one-third of the will was taken up with the disposal of the testator's material wealth for the health of his or her soul. By the mid-1540s, testators requested elaborate funerals and commemoration only 'if it be lawful'. By 1547 and the more thorough-going Protestantism of Edward VI's reign all this was absent from the will, and the testators' personal tastes were marked by the opaque phrases 'at the discretion of myne executors', 'according to the laudable custom of the realm'. Between the mid-1540s and mid-1550s the only continuity was of bequests to the poor at the funeral to pray for the dead man or woman, and annual doles for a number of years after death, with no explicit request for prayers, but perhaps with the hope among those who still held the old beliefs that the poor held them also. However, even this relationship was interrupted by the mediation of the poor men's box into which many bequests now went, thus severing the link between donor and recipient. Traditional Catholic funeral and commemorative bequests reappeared in wills after Mary I had returned England to papal allegiance, but only in any numbers from 1556, and even then fewer in proportion and for a shorter number of years than before.

It seems that medieval belief about the nature of the afterlife had been struck a mortal blow in the one or two generations since the outset of the Reformation. More importantly all the bodies, except the family, which had administered commemorative practices, both the small number of perpetual institutions and the rich undergrowth of temporary provision, had either been secularized or were simply no longer there.

When attempting to understand late medieval perceptions of death, certain things are plain; there is no sense in which death was an annihilation of the individual: he or she was merely translated to the other side of a divide, retaining the status and identity which they had held in life. The dead were still a part of the various bodies to which they had belonged in life and these communities mourned their forbears as their social standing required and to the extent that their resources allowed.

---

measuring the growth of confessional faith, either Protestantism or post-Reformation Catholicism, as too many use neutral wording at this difficult period. They do show, however, the broad outline of response to government initiatives on religious matters.

The swift and apparently uncontested decline in practices identifiable with the belief in purgatory are less well understood. John Bossy suggested that the system became an overwhelming burden on the living and simply collapsed under its own weight.[100] This is a practical suggestion, but does not go far enough to explain the changes in mentality which accompanied it. The tearing apart of death and charity, the reciprocity between the living and the dead and the poor, their substitutes, struck a blow at the very core of medieval concepts of community.[101]

There were some continuities however: those benefactions which were not confiscated by the Crown were re-absorbed and re-deployed by the secular groups which administered them: the family, secular colleges, the town, the parish.[102] The 'elect', once petitioned for spiritual succour on behalf of the faithful departed, were now the champions of the Protestant faith: they hoped to be saved by 'the merits of Christ's passion' and 'his redeeming blood' just as these very symbols had been central to the devotional practices of a generation before.[103] The poor were still given alms at funerals and on church festivals as a pious memorial to the wealthy, who still commissioned elaborate effigies of themselves, now with their eyes open as if alive, rather than closed as if in sleep.[104] Death remained a preoccupying theme for the writers of Jacobean tragedy and metaphysical poetry, and death itself through plague or famine or other mishap continued to carry many to an untimely grave.

So, whither purgatory? How deep-rooted had belief ever been among the laity and how far just an insurance policy? We must view these things in the 'longue durée'. Historians such as Ariès and Le Goff may have underestimated the cyclical nature of eschatological belief,[105] and the renewed emphasis on the imminence of the Last Judgement which accompanied the Protestant Reformation, supplanted the temporary judgement of souls newly arrived in eternity and waiting out their sentences for that last great distant moment. This must be set against the long-term

---

[100] J. Bossy, 'The Mass', pp. 29–61.
[101] E. Duffy, *Stripping of the Altars*, p. 8.
[102] C. Kitching, 'The quest for concealed lands in the reign of Elizabeth I', *TRHS*, 5th series, 24 (1974), pp. 63–78.
[103] The use of these phrases in the preambles of wills takes on a particular ambiguity in the 1540s and 1550s.
[104] P. King, 'The Iconography of the Corpse'. Paper delivered at the Institute of Historical Research, London, 29 May 1991.
[105] C. McDannell and B. Lang, *Heaven: A History*, pp. 353–8, describe the cyclical prominence of various beliefs about the afterlife at different times. Ariès and Le Goff tend to view changes on a linear model.

VIRGINIA BAINBRIDGE

decline in belief in the supernatural. The existence of purgatory became widely doubted in the course of the sixteenth century, and the existence of hell by the late seventeenth century;[106] and the supernatural itself became less able to intervene in everyday life, a realm increasingly remote from the cosmology of the early modern world.

[106] R. Wunderli and E. Broce, 'The final moment before death in Early Modern England', *Sixteenth-Century Journal*, 20 (1989), pp. 259–75, at p. 275 quotes D. P. Walker, *The Decline of Hell: 17th Century discussions of Eternal Torment* (Chicago, 1964): by the late seventeenth century belief in hell had declined, by the eighteenth century it was under open attack; P. Camporesi, *Fear of Hell*, part I, gives details of the outrageous descriptions of hell the Jesuits made in the eighteenth century to try to gain the attention of their sophisticated audience.

RITES OF PASSAGE AND THE PRAYER
BOOKS OF 1549 AND 1552

by DAVID M. LOADES

NOWHERE were the doctrinal ambiguities of the English
Church more evident than in its attitude to prayers for the dead.
The problem had become evident well before 1549, in the
policies of a king who claimed to be more Catholic than the Pope, but
who not only dissolved monasteries, but also dismantled the shrines of the
saints, and clearly threatened all intercessory foundations. The *King's Book*
of 1543, or *A Necessary Doctrine and Erudition for any Christen Man*[1] had
struck a delicate balance. In its final section 'Of prayer for souls departed',
it had declared

> Forasmuch as due order of charity requireth, and the Book of
> Maccabees and divers ancient doctors plainly shew, that it is a very
> good and charitable deed to pray for souls departed; and forasmuch
> as usage hath continued in the church many years, even from the
> beginning, men ought to judge and think the same to be well and
> profitably done . . .

thereby clearly implying the orthodox view that the prayers of the living
were beneficial to the dead. However, the same section then went on to
conclude

> . . . it is much necessary that all such abuses as heretofore have been
> brought in by supporters and maintainers of the Pope in Rome, and
> their complices, concerning this matter, be clearly put away; and that
> we therefore abstain from the name of purgatory, and no more
> dispute or reason thereof. Under colour of which have been advanced
> many fond and great abuses to make men believe that through the
> Bishop of Rome's pardons souls might clearly be delivered out of it,
> and released out of the bondage of sin . . .[2]

Without purgatory, or some equivalent, there was no sense of spiritual
progression among the departed, and consequently no obvious function

---

[1] *STC* 5168.
[2] *A Necessary Doctrine and Erudition for any Christen Man* (1543) in *Formularies of the Faith* by
Charles Lloyd (Oxford, 1825), pp. 213–337.

for intercessory prayer. When Hugh Latimer had argued that the dissolution of the monasteries implied the abandonment of purgatory he had mistaken the main purpose of the *opus dei*, but in a sense he had been right.[3] It is unlikely that Henry had planned either the dissolution or the destruction of shrines for the purpose of undermining the practice of intercessory prayer, but he had been prepared to accept the logic of his own actions, up to a point. His will made generous provision of trentals for the repose of his soul, but an unimplemented Act of his last Parliament confiscated all revenues devoted to the support of such prayers for the promotion of his secular policies.[4]

Although he would probably not have been willing to admit it, Henry was caught in the same dilemma as his old foe, Martin Luther. If the souls of the departed are not in purgatory, where are they, and what is their estate? The Catholic doctrine, for all its amenability to abuse, was both humane and logical. Given the immortality of the human soul, which was not admitted by all who called themselves Christians but was common ground to all the mainstream groups, some doctrine of the status of souls after death was essential. Purgatory was a concept which had evolved in response to the common-sense perception that few human beings merit either heaven or hell at the end of their mortal span. Moreover, once the doctrine of Judgement and General Resurrection had become established, some means of bridging the gap between death and resurrection was equally necessary. The concept of timelessness could be invoked to remove the need for such essentially chronological perceptions as waiting, but such a level of intellectual and spiritual sophistication was always rare.[5] The Apostolic Church had expressed its belief in 'life everlasting', but had left no indication of when it expected that level of existence to commence. It could be admitted without embarrassment that both heaven and hell were in a sense temporary locations, because at the Last Day there would be a new heaven and a new earth, and only then would joy or pain be fully consummated. So there was, within this doctrinal framework, plenty of scope for the idea of purgation and spiritual development after

---

[3] The *opus dei*, or cycle of prayer which was the main purpose of the monastic life, had a general intercessory purpose, but was not particularly connected with intercession for the dead. G. E. Gorrie, *The Sermons of Hugh Latimer* (Parker Society, 1844).

[4] Statute 37 Henry VIII, c.4; 'An Acte for the dissolution of Colleges, Chantries, and Free Chapels', *Statutes of the Realm*, 3, p. 988. Henry VIII's will is printed in T. Rymer, *Foedera, Conventiones, Literae* (London, 1727–9), 15, p. 144.

[5] The theological issues involved in these controversies about the state of departed souls are examined in Norman T. Burns, *Christian Mortalism from Tyndale to Milton* (Harvard University Press, 1972).

death. It was this extension of penance and absolution which gave the concept its lasting appeal. The dead may have departed, but they remained accessible to help and love within an effective bond which gave the invisible Church meaning, and provided a sense of both participation and hope.[6]

The reformers' rejection of purgatory was based on a number of considerations, both practical and doctrinal. At a practical level they were revolted by the spectacle of avaricious clergy exploiting the concern of believers by selling them indulgences and other services alleged to provide comfort for the deceased. They also claimed that it was unscriptural, which was strictly true because the Book of Maccabees was not part of the received canon.[7] More important, however, as predestinarians they rejected the whole notion of spiritual development. Once a man had used the opportunity of this transitory life to testify to the faith which the grace of God had conferred upon him, he could only wait in hope. There was no sense in which the pilgrimage of this life could be extended beyond the grave. In rejecting both purgatory and predestination, the English Church in 1543 was in an illogical and almost untenable position, but there is no sign that that worried a king who was not known for either sensitivity or self-doubt.

Luther's solution had the merit of simplicity, but seems to have been reached by a process of elimination. Purgatory was unacceptable for the reasons mentioned, and he was bitterly opposed to the idea that the soul dies with the body, and shares its resurrection, a doctrine known as thnetopsychism which was taught by a number of the radical reformers with whom he waged such acrimonious battles.[8] By 1524, if not earlier, Luther was teaching that the soul slept, or entered a state of suspended animation between death and judgement. This doctrine, technically called psychopannychism, reappears in a number of his later works, including his commentary on Ecclesiastes of 1532, apropos of the text 'the dead know not anything, neither have they any more a reward'.[9] Luther may have developed a slightly guilty conscience about this line of argument, because

---

[6] This sense of community is strongly emphasized in Eamon Duffy, *The Stripping of the Altars* (Yale University Press, 1992), pp. 134–41.

[7] The first and second Books of Maccabees were declared to be canonical by the Council of Trent in 1546, but the Council's decrees were not ratified until 1563. The Protestant Churches never accepted them, and their status during this period was consequently indeterminate.

[8] Paul Althaus, *The Theology of Martin Luther*, trans. Robert C. Schultz (Philadelphia, 1966), pp. 410–17.

[9] *An Exposition of Salomons Booke, Called Ecclesiastes or the Preacher* (London, 1573), p. 60v. *D. Martin Luthers Werke, Kritische Gestamtausgabe* (Weimar, 1883–), 20, p. 70.

although he was well aware that the Swiss reformers disagreed with him, he never attacked them for doing so, in contrast with his forthright polemicism over the eucharist. Indeed, his whole thinking on the nature of the afterlife seems to have been clouded with uncertainty. In the same commentary on Ecclesiastes, he wrote

> Hell signifieth a pit or grave, but properly (as I judge) that secret withdrawing place, where the dead sleepe out of this lyfe, whence the soule goeth to her place (whatsoever it be, for corporall it is not) so that thou mayest understand hell to be that place where the souls be kept. . . . But what manner of place it is, we know not. . . . For they that are truely holy goe not into hell to suffer anything there. . . .[10]

In what sense any soul could suffer in a place of temporary oblivion is not clear, nor whether the souls of the 'truely holy' sleep elsewhere, or go straight to their reward. In 1542 Calvin explicitly attacked the sleep of the soul, denouncing it as a doctrine of the Anabaptists, but he was aware of Luther's problem, and carefully refrained from linking the German reformer with their common enemies.[11] Heinrich Bullinger, writing in 1548, was equally reticent, but it is clear that the English reformers, who looked particularly to Bullinger for guidance, followed the Swiss line on this issue, as on so many others. William Tyndale and John Frith seem to have been tempted by soul sleeping, because it was such a simple and logical alternative to purgatory, but by 1547 it was associated exclusively with radicalism.

Insofar as there was an agreed perception of the condition of souls departed among the Edwardian reformers, it was probably that set out in Calvin's *Institutes*.

> In the mean while, as the scripture uniformly commands us to look forward with eager expectation to the coming of Christ, and defers the crown of glory which await us till that period, let us be content within these limits which God prescribes to us—that the souls of pious men, after finishing their laborious warfare, depart into a state of blessed rest, where they wait with joy and pleasure for the fruition of the promised glory; and so all things remain in suspense till Christ appears as the redeemer. And there is no doubt that the condition of the reprobate is the same as Jude assigns to the devils, who are

---

[10] *Salomons Booke*, 151v–152r. *D. Martin Luthers Werke*, 20, pp. 162–3.

[11] G. H. Williams, *The Radical Reformation* (Philadelphia, 1962), pp. 581–3, 586; Burns, *Christian Mortalism*, p. 31.

confined and bound in chains till they are brought forth to the punishment to which they are doomed. . . .[12]

Such a doctrine was difficult to express liturgically, because it broke the fellowship of the living with the dead upon which the medieval offices had been based. The dying person had been supported through his last ordeal not only with the sacrament of extreme unction, but also with a continuous round of prayer, involving the whole company of heaven to deliver the passing soul from all danger. The concept of the death-bed struggle, with angels supporting and demons lying in wait, had no place in the tidy eschatology of predestination, but it had bound the living and the dying together with a common sense of purpose. Nor was that purpose relinquished after death, as the solemn rite continued with a service of Commendation, and the preparation of the body for burial might well be accompanied by further psalms and antiphons, where the means of the family could run to such generous provision.[13] The burial service was then accompanied by a requiem mass, at which the priest offered again the supreme sacrifice of Christ for the specific purpose of safeguarding the recently departed soul. During the month which followed Placebo and Dirige would continue to be said in the parish church, and the requiem mass would be repeated on anniversary dates for as long as the funds lasted.

By comparison, the provision of the 1549 Prayer Book, although it retained some of the form, lacked substance. The visitation of the sick, which was supposed to be a rite of comfort, concentrated largely upon the notion of sickness as divine punishment, during which the sick person was urged to 'Take therefore in good worth the chast(is)ement of the Lord; for whom the Lord loveth he chastiseth. Yea (as St. Paul saieth) he scourgeth every son that he receiveth . . .'[14] The point of this, and of the catechism which followed, was to establish in the mind of the sufferer the probability of his own election, which was the most that could be done because the identity of the Elect is known to God alone. The traditional forms of confession and absolution were preserved, and even the anointing of the sick person, but without the sacramental content. The visitation might, or might not, conclude with a Communion. The old rite had included a mass, the main purpose of which was not the reception of the elements by

---

[12] John Calvin, *Institutes of the Christian Religion*, Bk III, ch. xxv, sect. vi, ed. John Allen (Philadelphia, 1936), 2, p. 253.

[13] Duffy, *Stripping of the Altars*, pp. 313–27, 'Ars Moriendi'.

[14] *Liturgies . . . of the Reign of Edward VI*, ed. Joseph Ketley (Parker Society, 1844), pp. 136–7.

the sick person, so much as the special intention of the celebrant. In 1549 the main purpose was reception, partly to emphasize the relationship of the sufferer with God, but more importantly his or her place in the community of the faithful. For that reason it was expected, although not strictly necessary, that members of the family or others would also receive, and that a general confession and absolution would be used, as in church. A household communion was a more difficult matter than a traditional mass because, unless it was held immediately after the main parish communion, a fresh consecration of the elements was necessary. Reservation in the traditional sense was implicitly rejected in the Prayer Book because of the abuses to which the practice had been subjected. The sick person might be close to death, but any implication that this was a crisis in which the soul's fate might be determined was very strictly eschewed.

The burial service itself followed much of the traditional pattern, although considerably shortened. It consisted first of a procession to the church or grave, followed by the actual burial, and then the Office of the Dead, concluding with a special eucharist. This last was a very ancient practice, originally intended to emphasize the belief that the communion of saints extended beyond the grave. Later the emphasis had shifted to a propitiatory sacrifice on behalf of the departed, and Cranmer's intention was presumably to revert to the original purpose. However, this was not entirely consistent with the notion that the dead have entered into a higher state of existence, and there are some other signs of uncertainty in the wording of the rite. For example the burial concluded with the following prayer:

> Almighty God, we give thee hearty thanks for this thy servant, whom thou hast delivered from the miseries of this wretched world, from the body of death and all temptation; and, as we trust, hast brought his soul, which he committed into thy holy hands, into sure consolation and rest: Grant we beseech thee, that at the day of judgement his soul and all the souls of thy elect, departed out of this life, may with us, and we with them, fully receive thy promises and be made perfit . . .[15]

whereas the collect at the eucharist ran (in part)

> we meekly beseech thee (O Father) to raise us from the death of sin unto the life of righteousness, that when we shall depart this life, we

[15] *Liturgies . . . of the Reign of Edward VI*, ed. Joseph Ketley (Parker Society, 1844), pp. 145–6.

may sleep in Him (as our hope is this our brother doth), and at the general resurrection in the last day both we and this our brother departed, receiving again our bodies ... may with all thine elect Saints, obtain eternal joy....[16]

Given the care with which the whole work was prepared, it is hard to believe that this wording was inadvertent, and it must raise some doubts as to the exact nature of the Church's teaching in 1549.

By 1552 these ambiguities had been removed. The visitation of the sick in the second Book of Common Prayer was both shorter and simpler, the psalms being entirely omitted, but it had not changed its nature. The catechism, confession, and absolution remained. The opportunity of unction had, however, been removed, and the Protestant sense of the concluding collect strengthened. In 1549 the priest prayed that the sufferer might '... withstand and overcome all temptations and assaults of thine adversary, that in no wise he prevail against thee, but that thou mayest have perfect victory and triumph against the devil, sin, and death, through Christ our Lord.' In 1552 the corresponding prayer (transferred into the third person), asked '... forasmuch as he putteth his full trust only in thy mercy, impute not unto him his former sins, but take him unto thy favour, through the merits of thy most dearly beloved son, Jesus Christ'.

The whole communion rite had been drastically altered in the second liturgy, to remove any lingering suspicions of a real presence doctrine, and even the brief reservation from the church to the house was no longer permitted by the revised rubrics. Not only did the minister have to consecrate afresh in the sick person's house, but the possibility that the invalid might receive alone was excluded. In 1549 a person too ill to receive could be told that if he repented in faith, and gave thanks to God '... he doth eat and drink spiritually ... although he do not receive the sacrament with his mouth'. That provision, in the same words, remained in 1552, but among the reasons why a person might be unable to receive the elements physically was included 'lack of company to receive with him'. Only in time of plague or similar contagious disease, when the lives of others might be endangered, was it permissible to relax this rule.[17]

The structure of the burial service was substantially modified in the second Prayer Book, to remove all traces of what by then was called

[16] Ibid., pp. 147–8.
[17] Ibid., p. 317.

'Popish superstition'. Both the Office of the Dead and the communion were abandoned, and a small but significant alteration was made to the words of committal. In place of 'I commend thy soul to God the father Almighty, and thy body to the ground', the minister declared 'Forasmuch as it hath pleased almighty God of his great mercy to take unto himself the soul of our dear brother here departed; we therefore commit his body to the ground . . .'. The souls of the dead could not be seen to owe anything to the living; not even a Commendation, which was the last relic of intercessory prayer. The Presbyterians later objected to this form of wording, on the grounds that it implied every departed soul to be in a state of grace, but the reference was to Eccles. 12. 7 ('dust returns to the earth as it was, and the spirit returns to God who gave it') where the meaning was strictly neutral.[18] The soul returned to God for judgement, not necessarily to eternal life.

The duty of the living was to hope in faith, both for the departed and for themselves, and to give thanks to God for whatever his judgement might be. This thinking was neatly and clearly summarized in the words of the final prayer:

> Almighty God, with whom do live the spirits of them that depart hence in the Lord, and in whom the souls of them that be elected, after they be delivered from the burden of the flesh, be in joy and felicity: We do give thee hearty thanks, for that it hath pleased thee to deliver this our brother out of the miseries of this sinful world; beseeching thee that it may please thee of thy gracious goodness, shortly to accomplish the number of thine elect, and to hasten thy kingdom, that we with this our brother, and all other departed in the true faith of thy holy name, may have our perfect consummation and bliss, both in body and soul, in thy eternal and everlasting glory.[19]

There remained, inevitably, a grey area, but it was not reflected in the liturgy. Insofar as God was always open to petitionary prayer, it remained possible for the dead to be named in the pleas of the living, as it always had been. But this sort of memorial, which could provide important psychological relief, also gave Puritans a bad conscience and was never officially encouraged.

The starkness of the 1552 burial service, which was not modified until

---

[18] F. Proctor and W. H. Frere, *A New History of the Book of Common Prayer* (London, 1965 rpr.), p. 635 and n. 1.
[19] *Liturgies*, pp. 319–20.

1661, arose partly from the eschatological expectations of the reformers. Like the early Christians, they believed that they were living in the last days of the world. To have followed some radicals, and set a date for such a consummation, was considered presumptuous, but that did not alter their sense of urgency. The interval between death and resurrection was therefore expected to be brief, and the reunion of the faithful imminent. Moreover, the emphasis in Protestant worship was very much upon the triumph of the elect, and however correct the theological reservations, in practice worshippers were encouraged to think of themselves, and their deceased members, in that light. For the elect prayer was redundant, and for the reprobate useless. This 'sure and certain hope' sublimated any feeling of helplessness, and compensated for the lack of warmth and fellowship in the last rites. The joy of waiting in hope was the first stage of the triumph, and not to be contaminated by thoughts of sleep or unconsciousness, which could easily be represented as a doctrine of pessimism or despair. Article 40 of the 42 Articles promulgated in the summer of 1553, which represented the final brief formulation of Edwardian doctrine, specifically condemned those who taught both the sleep and the temporary death of the soul.[20] This was in the context of condemning a number of Anabaptist teachings. By 1563, when the Articles reached their final form, the fear of radicalism had receded, and that Article, with several others, was withdrawn. It was therefore possible for an Elizabethan Anglican to keep an open mind about the state of the soul immediately after death, but with all intercession strictly proscribed, there was little temptation to depart from the positive stance taken by Calvin and Bullinger, who between them exercised a dominant influence over the late sixteenth-century English Church.

The folklore of the month-mind and the anniversary nevertheless remained, and some concessions had to be made to the need for commemoration. At a popular level these were extra-liturgical, and were tolerated rather than countenanced by the Church. However, liturgical provision was made in Walter Haddon's Latin version of the 1559 Prayer Book, which appeared in the following year.[21] Presumably the literate were thought to be in less need of protection from popish wiles, for this Book, which was loosely based upon a Latin translation of the 1549 rite, also retained a eucharist as a part of its burial service. In 1560 a new form for the commemoration of benefactors was specifically provided, and

---

[20] E. C. S. Gibson, *The Thirty-Nine Articles* (London, 1904), p. 88.
[21] *STC* 16424.

continued in use until the total decay of Latin within living memory. In spite of the traditional language, this was theologically correct in the Elizabethan sense. After the declaration 'Justorum animae in manu dei sunt', it continued with the prayer

> Domine Deus, resurrectio et vita credentium, qui semper es laud-
> andus, tam in viventibus quam in defunctis, agimus tibi gratias pro
> fundatore nostro N. caeterisque benefactoribus nostris, quorum
> beneficiis hic ad pietatem et studia literarum alimur: rogantes, ut nos
> his donis ad tuam gloriam recte utentes, una cum illis ad resurrec-
> tionis gloriam immortalem perducamur.[22]

Commemoration satisfied some of the social and psychological needs which had previously been met by intercession, without the unacceptable implications. It bore the same sort of relationship to the traditional rites as funeral monuments did to the images of the saints. In 1550 the statute of 3 & 4 Edward VI c.10, ordering the destruction of images, specifically exempted tombs, and on 19 September 1560 Elizabeth issued a proclamation protecting such monuments, which clearly reflected the similarity of purpose:

> The Queen's majesty, understanding that by the means of sundry
> people, partly ignorant, partly malicious or covetous, there hath been
> of late years spoiled and broken certain ancient monuments. some of
> metal, some of stone, which were erected up as well in churches as in
> other public places within this realm only to show a memory to the
> posterity of the persons there buried, or that hath been benefactors to
> the buildings or donations of the same churches or public places, and
> not to nourish any kind of superstition . . .[23]

and forbade the breaking or defacing of any such memorial. The distinction between praising famous men and commending them to the favour of God might be clear enough to the theologically trained, but it was not at all clear to the multiplying Puritan laity of the 1570s and 1580s, who suspected all appeals to a religious past which they regarded as irredeemably contaminated. Only the antiquity of the law might be invoked with impunity.

By 1560 the liturgies of Protestant England showed a clear break with

---

[22] Procter and Frere, *A New History*, p. 123.
[23] P. L. Hughes and J. F. Larkin, *Tudor Royal Proclamations*, 2, pp. 146–8. This issue is more fully discussed in Margaret Aston, *England's Iconoclasts* (Oxford, 1988), pp. 314–15.

the past in several important particulars. The eucharist was fundamentally different from a sacrificial mass, and the whole meaning of the last rites had changed. Instead of expressing the solidarity of the living with the dead and dying, in a solicitude which continued legitimately and effectively beyond the grave, they marked the immediate entry of one of the elect upon the first stage of his, or her, reward. The absence of ostensible comfort and support was intended to be a positive theological statement. Death was not a battlefield, nor the commencement of an arduous pilgrimage of uncertain duration in which the living could assist with their prayers and alms. Instead it was a victory already won, the entrée to a short period of happy relaxation prior to the triumph of the general resurrection. It is not at all surprising that traditionalists found the Protestant services bleak and impoverished, but they were nevertheless a reflection of that predestinarianism which was the greatest strength of the Reformed Churches. The souls of the Elizabethans could look forward not to sleep, nor to a form of catalepsy, nor to an interminable slog through purgatory, but to immediate, if incomplete, felicity. Such is the perversity of human nature that men are naturally more inclined to see themselves among the elect than among the reprobate, no matter how strong the evidence to the contrary. When Thomas Cranmer replaced the last collect of his 1549 burial service with the words, 'O merciful God, the Father of our Lord Jesus Christ, who is the resurrection and the life, in whom whosoever believeth, shall live though he die; and whosoever liveth and believeth in him shall not die eternally . . .', he was making a statement of hope which all could understand, and which more than compensated for the loss of the more humane and supportive, but ultimately less optimistic, rites of the medieval Church.

ESCHATOLOGICAL EXPECTATION IN THE WORKS OF J. S. BACH

by JAN R. LUTH

WHEN we look at the texts with which Bach was involved, we discover that eschatology has several meanings. In many texts we find a wish for death, which is the moment in which the body finds rest and the soul is liberated from sin. Dying means also standing before Jesus, not at the day of final judgement, but immediately after death. A difference is made between the body, which is buried, and the soul, which is ascending. Sometimes death is not glorified, because one also knows the pangs of death. However death remains welcome, because all necessities disappear. Dying means going to heaven and enjoying eternal rest. The body is the dress of mortality and is given back to the earth, and then begins the time in which the faithful are with Christ. One can take leave from the sinful world with pleasure. We find this approach—that eternal life starts with dying—much more than eschatology seen as the time of the return of Christ and final judgement. So let us look at the exceptions.

THE CANTATAS

The first exception

There are many texts in which death appears as sleeping until the resurrection—another reason why death is desired. We also find this approach in many German hymns of the seventeenth and eighteenth centuries and, for instance, also in the works of Heinrich Müller, a Lutheran theologian whose works Bach appreciated.

In Bach's cantatas in which death is described as sleeping, we only find by exception the notion of resurrection. One text contains the following thoughts:

> Death is sleeping and resting. But the shepherd will find his sheep again and that will happen when Christ returns.
> This means that death is a sleep until the resurrection at the final day. The believer is resting in his grave until Jesus wakes him.

Here death is glorified because the soul will live with Jesus until he comes back and then he will finally reach the pasture. Here we find eschatology;

the judgement is not mentioned, but a positive judgement by the judge is presumed.

A special case is Cantata 161, *Komm du süsse Todesstunde* (*Come sweet hour of death*). At the end of the first hymn we find the lines:

> Ich hab Lust abzuscheiden
> Von dieser bösen Welt
> Sehn mich nach himml'schen Freuden
> O Jesu, komm nur bald!

'I desire the joy of heaven, Jesus please come soon.' This sounds like the end of the Revelation of St John: 'Even so, come, Lord Jesus.' But the meaning of this sentence in the cantata is otherwise: Jesus comes to take the believer with him to heaven. To be dead is to be with Christ. The body is in the grave, but the soul is in heaven. 'Come soon' means here 'Come, take me soon'. In part 5 of this cantata immortality starts with death. That means the soul is immortal while the body awaits its resurrection. The call for the coming of Jesus is here, as in the first part, also related to dying and not to the eschatological return of Jesus. When he comes, when I die, glory begins and therefore this coming is strongly desired. The cantata ends with the fourth stanza of *Herzlich tut mich verlangen*, with the thought that the body will be woken and glorified.

This conviction that there is eternal life leads to the desire for death, which becomes the last great joy. Thought of death is influenced by the *unio mystica* and therefore it is wanted. The more this is emphasized the less we see the notion of judgement.

We meet thought about death in the same sense in the famous *Actus Tragicus*, BWV 106, and in *Wachet auf ruft uns die Stimme*, BWV 140. In the *Actus Tragicus* we find the sentence from the Revelation of St John, 'Even so, come, Lord Jesus', an expression of desire to the redeemer who will go to meet the faithful. Cantata 140, *Wachet auf ruft uns die Stimme*, refers to the return of Jesus, as the expected bridegroom. In German hymn books we find this hymn in the rubric about the final judgement, but in Bach's time it was still a hymn on the resurrection after death. The readings for the relevant Sunday were Matthew 25 about the ten virgins and I Thessalonians 5 about the day of the Lord which comes as a thief in the night. The cantata *Wachet auf* is most often regarded as a wedding cantata and not as an eternity cantata. The reason is that it contains a great number of references to the Song of Solomon. The final day is not especially mentioned in this cantata, but it is however there in the call to be wakeful, and of course there is the connection with the lessons for the day. The emphasis is on the eschatological joy defined by the union between bride and bridegroom. Eschatology and *unio mystica* go together in this text.

There is also the connection between the shepherd and the outlook of eternity. The Good Shepherd gives his life for the sheep and he rescues them. Paradise and heaven are thus painted as the pasture of life. In this case we see in the music the use of a bar consisting of twelve quavers. This bar is not only used with the shepherd's music but also where the text concerns peace and redemption, which begins with the birth of Christ, the promised salvation, the eschatological last consolation, as in the *Weinachtsoratorium*. A good example of the connection between Christmas and eschatology is Cantata 51 for the third day of Christmas, where this bar is also used: *Süsser Trost, mein Jesus kommt* ('Jesus is coming [that means: he is born] now I am chosen for heaven').

First conclusion: in several texts death is a sleep until the last day, or the gate to the *unio mystica*, the union with Christ. We can call it eschatology but without the notion of judgement.

The second exception

In some texts eschatology is connected with the final judgement and the judge of the world. An example is BWV 162, for the 19th Sunday after Trinity, at which Matthew 22 was read, the parable of the royal wedding. In part 4 we read: 'With alarm I heard that you condemned wedding guests without wedding clothes.' However, the judgement seems to have been passed during one's lifetime, for in part 5 the believer in heaven receives white clothes because during his life he had received the clothes of justice.

Another example is BWV 90, *Es reisset euch ein schreckliches Ende* ('You will have a terrible end'). God's goodness is new every day, but the sins of ungrateful people are growing. Then the poet asks if God's goodness will not lead to penance. The determined sinner will have a terrible end, for there is an avenging judge.

We also meet the judge of the world in the *Credo* of the *Hohe Messe*. The words 'Et iterum venturus est cum gloria, judicare vivos et mortuos' are sung in unison, probably a reference to the voice of the judge of the world.

In connection with this, there is another point we have to mention. In Cantata 104 *Du Hirte Israel, höre* ('Shepherd of Israel, hear'), we find in part 5 the following sentence:

> Beglückte Herde, Jesu Schafe,
> Die Welt is euch ein Himmelreich.

(Happy flock, the world is your kingdom of heaven.)

That means here and now. But the rewards one will receive are deferred until after the sleep of death, which will end at the final day. Judgement is connected with the notion that eternity is experienced here and now. In one cantata, for instance, a contrast is made between misfortune in this world, which will not last for ever, and eternal pain, out of which rescue is impossible. The notion of judgement is obvious in BWV 20, *O Ewigkeit, du Donnerwort* ('O Eternity, you word of thunder'), in which we also see that eternal judgement starts here on earth.

> Die Zeit so niemand zählen kann,
> Fängt jeden Augenblick
> zu deiner Seelen ewgem Ungelück
> Sich stets von neuem an.

(The time which nobody can count starts every moment and leads to eternal misfortune of the soul.)

The irrevocability of eternal misery is threatened. The faithful can, however, look forward with joy.

In recent publications this approach is called 'Eschatology in the present' (*präsentische Eschatologie*), which means that eternity is experienced here in a moment of time and it alarms the soul. Time here becomes a representation of eternal time. In the Baroque this is expressed by the unceasing rumbling thunderstorm in the air with black clouds and a voice speaking from them. Before the judgement is final, there is an opportunity to do penance. Therefore Bach prescribes here in the instrumentation the Baroque tromba, representing the trumpet of doom.

Another example belongs to the already mentioned exception: BWV 127 *Herr Jesu Christ, wahr'r Mensch und Gott* ('Jesus Christ, truly Man and God'), where the trumpet of doom is presented together with the last judgement.

Second conclusion: in some texts eschatology is connected with the final judgement, sometimes in a special sense as a reality in the present.

ORGAN WORKS

There are only a few chorale-based organ works in which we find eschatology. We have seen that Bach uses the bar with twelve quavers representing the promised salvation. An intensified form is the bar which consists of 24 semiquavers. Bach uses it only three times in his compositions for organ. The first is in the partita *O jesu du edle Gabe* ('O Jesus, you precious gift'), which consists of 12 variations of which the second to the eleventh correspond exactly with the ten stanzas of the hymn text. Partita 8 has this bar written in. It is interesting to see to which text this belongs:

> When I die
> Your blood will refresh me
> Then I will die very joyfully
> and will receive life
> Your blood washes my sins
> and will extinguish the fire of hell.

The second organ work in which Bach uses this bar is *Herr Gott nun schleuss den Himmel auf* ('God, now open heaven'). This hymn is a prayer to open heaven and to be admitted to the eternal rest and place of joy.

The third composition with this bar is *Valet will ich dir geben*: take leave of the angry world, but it is good to live in heaven. Stanza 4 is a prayer for entry into the glory of heaven.

Eschatology in these works seems to start with death. But the bar of 24 semiquavers represents 24 hours as the fulfilment of time, and moreover the 24 elders as the heavenly representatives of the people of God.

The meaning of this number is explained in a book about the Revelation of St John which was in Bach's library: 'It concerns the whole Christian Church of the New Testament which is collected from all people and all the faithful of all times, who are redeemed by Christ and made kings and priests, and who will govern with Christ during a thousand years.' I return again to the partita *O Jesu de edle Gabe* ('O Jesus, you precious gift'). We have discussed already the eighth variation; in the following ninth variation we find the resurrection and the last judgement: when the body rises the blood of Christ will wash away its sins and will give it a good judgement. So there we have a reference to the resurrection at the final day. In bar 16 this ninth variation reaches the high *c*, the moment corresponding with the words 'good judgement' in the text, here represented by that *c* as a hyperbole. Because the dead will be woken by the trumpet this is a reason to use the corresponding organ stop.

In the following stanza, the believer enters the joy of heaven in white clothes and with an escort of angels. These ninth and tenth variations both contain a bar consisting of three crotchets. We can find another example of this bar in the *Gloria* of the High Mass, where the bar represents heaven, in this case the joy of the heavenly kingdom of God into which the believer enters. In variation 9 the left hand plays broken chords—a resurrection motif.

The believer being escorted by angels into heaven is represented by the three-crotchet bar and a joyful rhythm. Moreover the accompaniment has the rhetorical figure *circulatio*, a figure which Bach also uses in other works with the words 'cherub' and 'host of angels'. In this case the accompaniment represents the angels and the melody in white notes the believer in white clothes.

The last variation does not correspond with a stanza of the hymn. But it is possible that this variation was added to represent the heavenly Jerusalem. Because it is the twelfth variation it reflects the Revelation of St John, the twelve gates, the twelve angels, the twelve tribes of Israel, and the new Jerusalem.

The tenth variation bears a resemblance to three other organ works, *Komm heiliger Geist*, *An Wasserflüssen Babylon*, and *Schmücke dich o liebe Seele*, in all of which the soul is invited to the Lord's Supper in heaven. The resemblance is very clear, and can be explained when we know the texts.

In the third stanza of Luther's *Komm Heiliger Geist* are the lines

> Let us here valiantly fight
> though death and life oppress us.

In *An Wasserflüssen Babylon*, Psalm 137, the third and fourth stanzas refer to the earthly Jerusalem, but Bach's application of the 3-crotchet bar makes it very reasonable to suspect that there is also a reference to the new Jerusalem.

The last example among the organ works is another partita to the hymn *O Gott, du frommer Gott*. The eighth stanza describes the final day at which the dead will rise and the faithful will join the other elect. In the corresponding partita Bach uses the chromatic fourth as the main interval. In the seventeenth and eighteenth centuries it is the figure which belongs to the *deus-humanus* and his suffering. The meaning of this interval could be as follows: see in the crucified the Lord, in the rejected the elected, in the dead the faithful destined for eternal life. Probably this partita is a prayer for resurrection. The rhythm of joy, *figura corta*, is probably the expression of trust in God, and from bar 17 the dotted rhythm expresses the joy of the faithful which belongs to the elect, mentioned in the text. In bar 12 there is the lowest note of the whole variation, followed by an ascending motif. At that moment the text is: 'and wake my body'. The key is E major, which is used by Bach when the resurrection is involved.

It is a good rhetorical custom to end with the beginning: eschatology in Bach's compositions has many interpretations.

JEWS IN EVANGELICAL DISSENT:
THE BRITISH SOCIETY, THE HERSCHELL
CONNECTION AND THE
PRE-MILLENARIAN THREAD*

by CLYDE BINFIELD

I will add but one word. It is written, 'Shut up the words, and seal the book, even to the time of the end; the words are closed up and sealed, till the time of the end' ([Daniel] 12. 4, 9). If, then, the seal be now broken, the time of the end is at hand.

(Pergamos, 'Prophecies of the Latter Times—Letter VI', *Voice of Israel*, 2. 34 (1 February 1847), p. 167.)

I

C ASTLE CAMPS in the twentieth century is a small, and in the nineteenth century was an entirely agricultural, village close to the borders of Cambridgeshire, Esssex, and Suffolk. It has a United Reformed church which was formerly Congregational and whose members at the close of the nineteenth century included the village shopkeeper. That was not unusual. What is less usual is that he was a Jew.[1]

What was exotic in Castle Camps was unsurprising in contemporary suburban or northern Congregational or Unitarian churches, as any perusal of church membership lists in Bradford, Manchester, Liverpool, or Hampstead might suggest.[2] The reasons for this are probably more cultural, economic, and social than doctrinal. They reflect a conscious process of assimilation. The Nonconformist *minister*, however, who was Jewish is another matter. With him we enter several realms. In addition to

* I must gratefully acknowledge grants from the British Academy and the Research and Foreign Travel Funds of the University of Sheffield towards the preparation of this paper. I am also particularly indebted to Dr D. Bebbington, Mr J. Creasey, Dr Jane Dawson, Dr S. Gilley, Mr F. Keay, Mr G. C. Lightfoot, Mrs S. Mills, Dr I. Sellers, and Mrs E. Wood.
[1] Mark Harris (d. 1901), converted Polish Jew, baptised 1865, grocer and publican, church treasurer, and local councillor. Mabel Evans, 'Castle Camps—A Country Church 1813–1989', *Journal of the United Reformed Church History Society*, 4, No. 8 (May, 1991), p. 484.
[2] Yet was it so exotic in Castle Camps? Rumour had it that the Brown and Goodman families who so dominated the Baptist and Congregational church life of nineteenth-century Huntingdonshire were of Jewish descent, like their famous connection by marriage, Henry Allon the London pulpiteer; and those rumours were more affectionate than malicious.

those of cultural assimilation and the social main chance we might need to add those of 'catholic Christianity' (as it was eirenically called in Revival's high noon) and evangelical mission. We might also need to add those of prophecy and interpretation, for with such men we are likely to encounter the heady universe of eschatological expectation.

Victorians, and their fathers, were naturally fascinated by Jews. Daniel Deronda and Fagin and the Revd Mr Emilius testify to that. For evangelical Victorians, and their fathers, there was a pressing, fourfold fascination. Biblically-minded Christians could hardly ignore Jews or Judaism. Successive decades of exciting current events gave an urgency to evangelistic duty and coloured fresh twists of prophetic interpretation. Science, archaeology, literature, foreign trade, and foreign travel extended the horizons of relatively ordinary men and women in the most suggestive ways, and Jews were among the strange creatures dotted and silhouetted on those horizons. Britons of a Whiggish turn could not fail to be encouraged by the Reform Movement in European and English Jewry. Urban Britons could not fail to register the rapid, even dramatic, growth in Britain's Jewish community, for that faced them with problems quite unlike those posed by immigrant Protestants or even Roman Catholics. Travelling, or at least periodical-reading, Britons were increasingly aware of what was happening to Jews who lived in Central or Eastern Europe and of the slow but cumulative growth in the number of Jews who lived in Palestine itself. Most of those were poor and woefully ill-educated. Where they were Europeans they tended to be Russians escaping from Tsarist persecution (or military service, which amounted to the same thing) or who had arrived in time for the Messiah's expected arrival in 1840.[3] Again and again it seemed to be prophecy which blended with politics and common humanity to fuel the motor of Protestant evangelism. It was consequently inevitable that a society should exist to cope with such concerns.

The London Society for Promoting Christianity Amongst the Jews was well within the mainstream of interdenominational missionary endeavour.[4] It was a child of the famous London Missionary Society. In 1805 J. S. C. F. Frey, a Franconian Jew in his earlyish thirties who had been an LMS protégé since 1801, with an eye to South African service, was set

---

[3] T. Parfitt, *The Jews in Palestine 1800–1882*, Royal Historical Society Studies in History, 52 (Woodbridge, 1987).

[4] See especially R. H. Martin, *Evangelicals United: Ecumenical Stirrings in Pre-Victorian Britain, 1795–1830* (London, 1983), particularly chapter 9, pp. 174–88.

apart to conduct a mission to Jews in Britain. Relations between Frey and his employers became more and more difficult. The London Missionary Society could not afford the revenue-consuming facilities which Frey advocated for his converted Jews. There had to be a parting of the ways. The London Society, started in 1808, was incorporated in 1809 and by 1810 the remaining Jewish work of the London Missionary Society had disintegrated. At first this had seemed to be as sensible as it was painful. Leading Dissenters continued to support the new society without lessening their backing for the existing Baptist or London Missionary Societies, while Anglicans who had been put off by the latter's Dissenting tone now felt able to join the new body. By 1815, however, the Anglicans had taken it over. There had been two stumbling blocks in the way of such practical catholic Christianity. One was money. This had already exercised the parent London Missionary Society in its tussles with the enthusiastic Frey. The other was polity. For the new society was a *missionary* society. Its brief was not so much to publish the Gospel as to present the Gospel and make sure of the consequent conversions. But to what were Jews to be converted? The society's answer was that they were to be converted to Christ as Messiah. For most evangelical Dissenters at least that was enough. All else was secondary. But the point at which an *institution* appeared, with a *chapel* as part of its complex, meant that questions could no longer be avoided about the licensing of the chapel, the nature of its officiating ministry, the shape of its liturgy and the theology which informed its rites, not least baptism. That point occurred when Palestine Place opened in Bethnal Green in July 1814. The Bishop of London could not contemplate licensing a chapel in which Anglicans officiated huggermugger with Dissenters. No doubt the society's Dissenting supporters would have adjusted to that tiresome situation, but the society's debts forced the issue. A godfather (perhaps 'angel' is a better word) appeared in Lewis Way who was prepared to cope with the debt if the society was reconstituted on Anglican lines. Just as the once interdenominational London Missionary Society had become wholly Dissenting and largely Congregational by 1815 so its difficult child, the once interdenominational London Society, had become wholly Anglican.

This is an important part of the prehistory of the society with which this essay is first concerned: the British Society for the Propagation of the Gospel among the Jews. Like those other products of the 1840s, the YMCA and the Evangelical Alliance, the British Society was a last fruit of Revival. Like them it was indisputably evangelical and like them it managed to sustain an interdenominational thrust with what amounted to interdenominational support, although the core of the British Society's support, unlike that of the YMCA or the Evangelical Alliance, was always Dissenting. The Society was literally British: its initial sphere of operation was the cities of the United Kingdom and although it was founded in London it was almost as much a Scottish as an English initiative.

There were three threads to its prehistory. The first was the proto-evangelist, Christian Frederick, formerly Joseph Samuel, Frey. His methods and dreams were theirs and some of their supporters had backed his London Society in its interdenominational dawn. The second thread was Presbyterian. This was an English outworking of the Church of Scotland's deputation of 1839 to investigate the condition of Jews in Palestine and of the Irish Presbyterians' 'first little company of missionaries to seek the lost sheep of the House of Israel' in 1842.[5] The Church of Scotland's deputation was doubly transmuted: by ill-health and physical accident it became a mission to Jews in Hungary rather than Palestine,[6] and by ecclesiastical disruption it turned into the Free Church of Scotland Jewish Mission. The vital spark (and already burning himself out) in extending this evangelistic fire to England was Robert Murray McCheyne.[7] He had been with the Scottish deputation of 1839, he had pleaded the Jewish cause to the Irish Presbyterian Synod in 1841, and in November 1842 he was in the vestry of the National Scotch Church in Regent Square, London, when the British Society was formed. McCheyne was one of two Scottish observers; of the nine attending ministers with English congregations four were Presbyterians, four were Congregationalists, and the ninth was in effect a Congregationalist. He was Ridley Herschell, whom the British Society saw as the third thread in its formation and on whom the second half of this paper will concentrate.[8]

The Society flourished sufficiently for its jubilee publicity to display helpful statistics in the approved Victorian fashion. By 1892 it had a head-quarters near the British Museum, a long-established monthly called *The Jewish Herald*, and twenty-six paid agents and missionaries. Its work had extended from Britain's cities to cities in western, central, and southern Europe, and along the Mediterranean coasts of Africa, the Middle East,

---

[5] J. Dunlop, ed., *Memories of Gospel Triumphs Among the Jews During the Victorian Era* (London, 1894), p. 13.

[6] One of the deputation fell off a camel's back and was invalided home via Budapest.

[7] Robert Murray McCheyne (1813–43), *DNB*.

[8] In fact five of the nine 'English' ministers were Scottish; Mrs Ridley Herschell was Scottish; and £500 of the new society's income of £927 in its first year was given by the Church of Scotland.

and Asia Minor.[9] It might not have converted all of the United Kingdom's 3,000 Jewish Christians living in 1892, let alone the 100,000 thought to have been converted in the Victorian era, but it felt sufficiently confident of its part in that work to note those figures.[10] For a few years it had run a small training college at Blackfriars Road, and since all its missionaries— Naphtali, Zucker, Jaffé, Cohen, Brunner, Lowitz, Liebstein, Hershon, Gottheil—were converted Jews from mainland Europe they were wanderers with stories to tell. For many the British Society was a staging post. For some there were periods in the Congregational or Baptist ministry. One of the Baptists was Issachar Flecker, kinsman of James Elroy Flecker the poet. The most widely known was Dr Laseron, who was one of the first students at the British Society's Mission College before he turned to the medical work (and non-denominational Brethrenism) which cul-minated in his remarkable Protestant Deaconesses' Institute and Training Hospital.[11]

If the British Society had surmounted the problems which had beset and shaped the London Society and had successfully cut its coat according to its financial cloth, its progress had none the less not been one of cumulative advance. The training college was wound up in 1857; there were only three more missionaries in 1892 than there had been in 1867; its claims did not figure large in the denominational year books; and its jubilee notables were less glittering and on the whole more conservative than those who had preached, lectured, or generally starred in earlier years; even its jubilee volume was entitled *Memories of Gospel Triumphs among the Jews during the Victorian Era*. The momentum had not been main-tained.

This needs examination. In 1892, as in 1842, the society was supported by Evangelical Anglicans, Wesleyans, Baptists, Brethren, English Pres-byterians, and Congregationalists. In 1892 as in 1842 the core and clout of its support was Congregational. But, even allowing for the fact that any society worth its salt secured the big names more for their names (and their subscriptions) than their time, those of the first rank cluster in the lectures and sermons of the society's first two decades: William Arthur, William Maclardie Bunting, and J. H. Rigg, the Wesleyans; Francis

[9] Lyons, Paris, Strasbourg, Frankfurt, Nuremberg, Breslau, Vienna, Tunis, and Beirut as well as London, Manchester, Birmingham, and Hull; already by 1867 the society was a Cook's tour of gospel endeavour with twenty-three missionaries, eight of them in London. At various times Amsterdam, Rotterdam, Dresden, Marseilles, and Algiers also had agents.

[10] Dunlop, *Memories of Gospel Triumphs*, pp. 19–20.

[11] Ibid., pp. 355–6, 336–40.

Augustus Cox, John Aldis, Baptist Noel, and Charles Haddon Spurgeon, the Baptists; James Hamilton, John Cumming, J. Chalmers Burns, and Thomas Archer, the Presbyterians; John Pye Smith, Thomas Binney, John Leifchild, Thomas Raffles, Henry Forster Burder, Josiah Viney, Henry Allon, John Harris, Richard Alliott, James Bennett, Samuel Martin, and Ralph Wardlaw, the Congregationalists. These men were the established or up-and-coming pulpit princes, college principals, and movers and moulders of their denominations. Some, like Dr Raffles, Dr Bennett, and Dr Pye Smith, had been members of the London Society. The only questionable credentials were Anglican ones: several clergymen supported the society and some even preached for it; wealthy and ecclesiologically innocent (or obstinate) laymen contributed to its funds; but the former tended to be out of active charge and the latter were often crypto-Congregationalists.[12] Thus the jubilee sermon was preached in Eccleston Square Congregational Church by the *former* rector of All Saints, Dorchester; and such men as John Dean Paul, the Strand banker and the society's first treasurer, or Sir Culling Eardley Eardley Bt, who moved from the treasureship to the presidency, were as well known in Congregational as in Low Church circles. W. G. Habershon, the architect, who succeeded Eardley as president, came from a Congregational family and had superintended a Congregational Sunday school in London for several years; George Williams, the London wholesale draper and founder of the YMCA, had been a Congregationalist before becoming the lowest of Low Churchmen, while his father-in-law, George Hitchcock (Issachar Flecker's benefactor), balanced his equally low Anglicanism with a wide family circle of LMS, that is to say Congregational, missionaries.[13]

That was to be expected. Yet even among the mainstream names of the earlier years the balance lay more with the elder statesmen of their bodies than with the social or political activists. The society's support in the 1840s and 1850s was that which also bolstered the YMCA or sustained the credibility of the Evangelical Alliance as well as working for the BMS or LMS or stage-managing petitions against Sir James Graham's proposals for factory education or even testing the temperature of the Liberation Society. But where in the 1890s was the support of R. F. Horton, Joseph Parker, C. S. Horne, John Clifford, or Hugh Price Hughes? Instead there

[12] A notable exception was Edward Henry Bickersteth (1825–1906), later Bishop of Exeter, who joined the committee in 1856.
[13] For this see C. Binfield, *George Williams and the YMCA: A study in Victorian Social Attitudes* (London, 1973).

was the provincial activist, such a man as F. W. Brown, perhaps, the Congregational minister who was secretary of the Bristol and Clifton Auxiliary. Brown combined this with presidency of the Hotwells Branch of the Bristol Protestant League (established to curtail the encroachments of ritualism) and fuelled it with a repertoire of lectures on matters scientific, biographic, and historical. 'His entire nature bubbles over with cheerfulness . . . always fresh and forceful, extemporaneous in delivery, every sermon gives due sign of fitting preparation. He is a master of alliteration, and with a copious vocabulary is vigorous and fluent. Evangelical in doctrine and fervent in spirit.' The type is unmistakable.[14]

The society's jubilee president, Dr Hiles Hitchens, was Brown held down by metropolitan *gravitas*. Thirty-four years a Congregational minister, Hitchens had been at Eccleston Square, 'in the very midst of fashionable Belgravia', for twenty-one of them. There, Geneva-gowned and 'the very beau-ideal of a popular preacher', Hitchens 'looks all the Puritan, and he speaks with an ease and dignity which always commands the ear of a large and intelligent congregation'. Certainly the restrained classicism of Eccleston Square was awash with activity. Its chapel had a library, a soup kitchen, 'Clubs for Cricket, Cycling and Swimming', a large Sunday school for children 'of a superior class', and a Young Men's Association whose patron was the Duke of Westminster (since this was estate-agents' Belgravia) and whose vice-presidents were Archdeacon Sinclair and W. Burdett Coutts MP. Hitchens himself had preached in London theatres, lectured in Spurgeon's Tabernacle as well as the Birkbeck Institute, and written a procession of books and booklets on such matters as *Jesuits* or *Ritualism* or *The Young Men of Scripture*. He was not denominationally prominent, though his extramural committee work included the Protestant Alliance, the National Protestant Congress and the Christian Evidence and Instruction Societies. He was an Evangelical Alliance man. He had several times been pressed to become an Anglican and had once been offered a living. All this he had declined, though he liked to mix with Low Church deans and canons and to persuade Low Church parsons to enter his pulpit. The Dorchester rector was not the first.[15]

The conservatism of all this is clear, its tenor clinched by George Williams's deceptively incoherent and wholly characteristic effusion when he chaired the society's first jubilee meeting in the Exeter Hall. By

[14] Dunlop, *Memories of Gospel Triumphs*, p. 475.
[15] Ibid., pp. 454–6.

1892 Williams was two years away from his knighthood and already the grand old man of a clutch of good causes with the YMCA chief among them. Indeed, since 1881 the YMCA had maintained the Exeter Hall, the Evangelical hot-house where all seriously successful societies still liked to hold their annual meetings, preferably in May:

> I remember fifty years ago—I was comparatively young. (*Laughter*). I had just come up to the Metropolis from the West of England. In 1841 I came from the West of England. I had been in London just one year when this Society was formed, and have been here ever since. (*Cheers*). Now, I have observed a little of your growth from time to time. I have heard of you, and have known some of your most excellent agents, and something of the great work they have been doing for their dear Lord and Master. Now, as Gentiles, how indebted we are to the Jews. What could we have known of the Creation, but for the Holy Scriptures? What should we have known of the constitution of the Christian Church? What comfort the Scriptures, which have come to us through the Jews, have been to our hearts! Only think: what should we have done without the Scriptures? What noble examples we have set before us in the Scriptures of some of the Jews; and there is one great advantage too, we have their defects pointed out to us to warn us, as well as their good qualities to guide us (*Cheers*). Now, beloved friends, we are familiar with the Old Testament saints—Abraham, Isaac, and Jacob—oh, what a list of splendid men we have in the Word! Then, how often have we sung the sweet songs of David. What should we have done without the Jews? For, to crown all, have they not given us a Saviour, a precious Saviour, a dearly beloved friend—surpassing every other friend that we can possibly have in this world? Now, this dearly beloved Saviour I am sure is with us for another period of time and work. I am very glad it has happened to me to be with you on your Jubilee day—(*cheers*)— and if I had a silver trumpet, and could play it, I would make it sound out so that it should gladden all our hearts. (*Renewed cheers*). However, we have so many silver trumpets on the platform, and therefore we shall have a really good Jubilee service (*Cheers*).[16]

Harmless, undemanding stuff. The speaker, however, was an eminently successful city businessman whose position in the ragtrade neces-

---

[16] Dunlop, *Memories of Gospel Triumphs*, pp. 451–2.

sitated innumerable contacts in the daily run of business with Jews;[17] he was also the representative founder-figure of an equally successful international youth movement. It may not, therefore, be quite enough to explain the British Society's relative lack of momentum by its religious conservatism or even by the hot-potato questions raised by a Jewish immigration that was suddenly far more intense than any in the previous fifty years. Neither may it be enough to put it down to the options defined by the patterns of those past fifty years, or even to the unwillingness of most religious activists to act undenominationally. All these played their part, but there is also a surprisingly hidden thread which had none the less to be part of the warp and woof of any Jewish-Christian missionary enterprise: that 'darkest mystery of prophecy', millennialism, and especially *pre*-millennialism.

II

Millennial concern has a respectable history in the long and scholarly tradition which has seen the key to human history in the books of Daniel and Revelation. That tradition, which is probably inextricable from Christian belief and is as old as the early Church, burst into long, luxuriant flower with medieval heretics and Protestant reformers. Its English variant, building on the conviction of Protestant Reformers that Rome was the ultimate evil within the four world empires of prophecy, concentrated on the chronology developed in the seventeenth century by Joseph Mede and subsequently accepted in the highest quarters (Isaac Newton among them) that there were to be 1,260 years of the Pope's rule as Antichrist. If those 1,260 years began with Justinian's recognition in AD 533 of the Pope's universal jurisdiction, then they were due to end in 1793. The coincidence of that date with the French Revolution and political and social unbalance of a quite new kind gave an urgent relevance as well as excitement to such interpretation, while calculations that the years between 1793 and 1867 would see God pouring the full judgements of Revelation on to an apostate humankind turned it into more than some passing scriptural flavour of the month. Evangelical Protestantism's reawakened apocalyptic mentality was fine-honed by Bible study and minute recalculation as empires and political systems shuddered, the twin

[17] His politically ambitious youngest son, Alfred Thomas Williams (1866–1908), a few years later tried to capitalize on East London's anti-Semitism.

Antichrists of Rome and Infidelity exploded, and simple artisans took the Gospel to islands new found in the southern seas.

Millennialism, therefore, was Protestant orthodoxy. It took, however, two forms.[18] *Post*-millennialists believed that gospel evangelism would inaugurate the Kingdom of God which was to last for a thousand years, after which Jesus would return to earth. This was a standard and in many ways a forward-looking attitude which could take overseas and home mission in its stride and contemplate social or political activity as appropriate for spirit-empowered Christians. This holy worldliness, which could slide wholly into worldliness, tended to be the mentality of Clapham Evangelicalism and of the Dissenting generality.

Pre-millennialists, however, had an increasing purchase on Evangelical emotions. They believed that Christ's second advent would precede and not follow the thousand-year Kingdom of God and that the period between Christ's first coming and his second—that is to say, the period in which Christians were now living—was the 'last days', at once of grace when the elect could be saved and of evil as the world collapsed into the abyss from which Christ's coming would deliver it.

It can be seen that if post-millennialism allowed for a Christian strategy based on cumulative usefulness, pre-millennialism could allow for no such thing. Any protective strategy under so arbitrary a dispensation was really a matter of temperament. The post-millennialist could see the Spirit at work in the world and be caught up in that work. The premillennialist was world-denying save in a general fascination with such current events as might confirm prophecy. Pre-millennialists were not necessarily conservative or *laissez-faire* and some could be disconcertingly radical and reactionary in successive breaths—Lord Shaftesbury comes famously to mind—but the pressures were clear even though, in the world of politics at least, the most lasting reform is often the issue of pessimism.

Pre-millennialism was not a mainstream Non-conformist preoccupation in the 1890s. Neither had it been a prime preoccupation for most Non-conformists in the 1840s. It had, however, been a stronger preoccupation than their subsequent historiography has made out, and across the British Evangelical board as a whole it was a very much stronger preoccupation yet, and it remained so.

Millennialism, especially in its pre-millennial form, has several occupational hazards. One is a fascination with calculation, and therefore a

[18] See J. M. Gordon, *Evangelical Spirituality* (London, 1991), pp. 137–8.

vulnerability to miscalculation. Another is unfulfilment; while the trouble with fulfilment is that the whole enterprise will have served its purpose anyway. It is not a momentum sustainer for practical activists even if it can be a powerful momentum inducer for nature's initiators. For them, indeed, it is the ultimate realism. For those of a nervous or conservative disposition, however, it bypasses realism for pessimism. Intellectually, for similar reasons, it leads to backwaters. For a while at the cutting edge of academic biblical study and theology, it was then decisively outstripped. Hence its virtual disappearance from subsequent historiography. Yet by no means all its adherents were cranks, autodidacts or under-educated. The Evangelical and philanthropic world of the 1840s, for instance, was firmly pre-millennial in tone and those who peopled its committees held that tone in succeeding years however much they moderated it or even kept it to themselves. If it rapidly ceased to be the dominant tone for most Congregationalists, Presbyterians, and Wesleyans, and probably for most Baptists as well, it remained one to which many responded. It explains many networks within and across the denominations and sometimes out of the denominations into the still largely uncharted (and perhaps unchartable) contradictory world of doggedly non-denominational sectarianism. George Williams, for instance, was a pre-millennialist. It was probably that rather than upward social mobility (and marriage to his boss's daughter) which explains his transition from the City Congregationalism of The King's Weigh House to the West End proprietary Anglicanism (it can hardly be called episcopalianism) of the Portman Chapel.

Such purchase as pre-millennialism held among English Nonconformists had an increasingly Scottish accent. It was the influence of Edward Irving and then of R. M. McCheyne and the Bonar brothers, Horatius and Andrew, which brought pre-millennialism home to Dissent.

Until recently Edward Irving's spectacular collapse into glossolaly and exuberant ecclesiology has damned him.[19] Yet he was as much the representative as the victim of his Christian age, as brilliantly prone to its manifold heresies and contradictions as others who have fared better. This anti-Romanist with his sympathy for Catholics and his grasp of Catholic doctrine and liturgy; this pessimistic illiberal with his democratic instinct

---

[19] For this section I am particularly indebted to the important paper by Dr S. Gilley, 'Edward Irving, Prophet of the Millennium', first given in Regent Square United Reformed Church, 9 December 1984; since revised, under the same title, and published in Jane Garnett and C. Matthew, eds, *Revival and Religion since 1700: Essays for John Walsh* (London, 1993), pp. 95–110.

for need; this strangely practical visionary who, because his chief path lay with London Presbyterianism and thus with the pulpit princes, spoke most tellingly to individual Dissenters, was a key influence, even if an ultimately disintegrative one, in the Evangelical world of the 1820s and early 1830s and, through his admirers, for some years after his death. His life was instinct with the millennium. He was born in 1792, as the Reign of Antichrist ended and the Last Days began. He lived through political, social, and religious upheaval on an international scale. He came to Christian prominence at the point where English Evangelicalism, which should have been in the position of defining the direction of English religion for the foreseeable future, was losing a whole generation of its most natural leaders to the charms of broad or Catholic churchmanship and was finding its precariously pan-denominational consensus channelled into a series of separate and often competing denominational apparatuses. His influence found its power less through his pentecostalism or his theological illiberalism than through his millennialism.

Irving's formation was in the post-millennial evangelical activism of Thomas Chalmers, the Scottish counterpart of the world of Clapham and William Wilberforce. He moved into pre-millennialism at a time of great personal loss between 1824 and 1826, chiefly influenced by James Hatley Frere. Post-millennial Evangelicalism now seemed 'the optimism of the philosophers' for in all stark reality the Church was as lost as the world. The situation was humanly and literally irredeemable. Redemption could come only with the Second Coming. Irving brought much more to this than the allure of a romantic temperament and great physical charm. He super-added several distinct approaches. To the Protestant, historicist, 'orthodox' view that the world had already experienced its 1,260 years of Babylonish rule by the papal Antichrist he added a futurist dimension: those 1,260 past years were now to be reflected by the 1,260 future years of an infidel Antichrist. There was a further strand: the conviction of up-to-date scholarship that Revelation described events in the first Christian century. This allowed Irving to admit that prophetic interpretation might change. It gave his biblical literalism considerable sophistication—or at least a modish mysteriousness.

As minister of the Scotch Church in Hatton Garden and then in Regent Square Irving was a man of note in both kingdoms. His congregation eventually became one of the chief supports of the Free Church of Scotland's most sympathetic English ally, the Presbyterian Church in England. This explains the influence of McCheyne and the Bonars, men who, though pastorally the heirs of Thomas Chalmers, were set spiritually in pre-millennialism.[20] They were this-world-denying in Christendom's long apocalyptic shadow, but they were future-world-affirming in the light of the advent hope. Consequently they were suspicious of contemporary liberal thinking, for the whole of life was provisional—until He come—yet they knew that the whole of life witnessed ineluctably to God's purpose in the consummation of all things. When Irving returned to speak in Edinburgh in 1829, McCheyne was there to note down the burning words and Horatius Bonar continued the search in his *Quarterly Journal of Prophecy*, firm in the imminence of 'The curse removed, Paradise restored, Israel gathered, the Gentiles converted, creation blessed, and Jehovah in the person of Immanuel taking up his everlasting abode with the children of men.'[21]

Israel gathered.... The end of Moslem power, the return of the Jews to Palestine and their conversion to Christ as Messiah, were part of the premillennialist's scheme of things. When Irving preached in 1825 to the Continental Society on 'Babylon and Infidelity Foredoomed of God', he paused to speak of the restoration of the Jews to Palestine, and when, a year later, the most select Evangelicals conferred at Albury Park the company included that fascinatingly unappealing portent, Joseph Wolff, the German Jew turned Catholic priest turned Protestant explorer turned pre-millennial missionary who eventually turned High Church parson and earl's son-in-law.[22] Wolff fused all that the pre-millennial mind found irresistible and Irving capitalized on it when he translated and popularized the pre-millennial work of a converted Latin American Jew, Juan Josophat Ben-Ezra.[23] But how much of this was in the forefront of the minds of those fathers and founders of the British Society gathered in the vestry of Regent Square Scotch Church (not yet Presbyterian Church in England) on 7 November 1842?

III

At first sight the answer, at least as refracted in the Jubilee *Memories of Gospel Triumphs*, has to be disappointingly muted. Certainly the prophetic element is a sustained motif. Indeed the careful reader might see it as a prime introductory motif, for it is there in the references to Woodrow,

[20] Gordon, *Evangelical Spirituality*, pp. 121ff., 137–45.
[21] Ibid., p. 139.
[22] For Joseph Wolff (1795–1862), see *DNB*.
[23] Who was in fact a Chilean Jesuit, Manuel Lacunza y Diaz. Gilley, 'Edward Irving'.

the Glaswegian who first urged the Church of Scotland to look into the condition of Palestinian Jews and was the 'author of a solid book on unfulfilled prophecy'; or to Horatius Bonar, 'one grand characteristic' of whose ministry 'was his unwearied setting forth of the blessed hope of the Lord's Premillennial Coming'; or to McCheyne's sermon of November 1839 on 'Our Duty to Israel', that race 'ready to perish—to perish more dreadfully than other men. The cloud of indignation and wrath that is even now gathering about the lost, will break first upon the head of guilty, unhappy, unbelieving Israel.'[24] That element certainly surfaced in Dr Adams of Dorchester's public jubilee address of November 1892 when he spoke with mercifully ignorant accuracy of how 'We are probably on the eve of a conflict such as the Church of God has never yet witnessed. The Jews were the earliest and the bitterest foes of the Christian faith. They will be its last and most formidable antagonists. For this struggle they are themselves preparing.'[25]

The weasel word was 'probably'. For all its brave certainty, pre-millennialism 1890s- and British-Society-style was carefully imprecise. Thus John Dunlop, the society's full-time secretary and the *Jewish Herald*'s editor, rallied his troops:

> Astronomers inform us that the heavenly bodies, with moon revolving round planet, and planet round sun, in obedience to some mighty cosmical force, are all moving forward century by century, as on direction, to a definite point in space. Even so, the speculations of philosophy, the discoveries of science, the achievements of art, the march of armies, the preservation of the Jews amid unspeakable persecutions, the propagation of the Gospel among them, these and similar events, under Divine propulsion, consciously or unconsciously, to the agents themselves, are all moving forward to a fixed period, even the time when every one of the prophecies concerning Israel's glory and joy shall be fulfilled. . . . Just as sure, then, as the events which happened yesterday, the supreme mission of the Jewish nation, namely the evangelization of humanity, will be realized by and by, through faith in a crucified, living, loving, coming Christ.[26]

That was whistling in the dark of the most unobjectionable kind; and it was entirely consistent with the line taken over the past fifty years by the

[24] Dunlop, *Memories of Gospel Triumphs*, pp. 11, 36, 31.
[25] Ibid., p. 23.
[26] Ibid., p. XII.

society's distinguished annual preachers and lecturers. Richard Alliott, the
Jewish Herald's first editor and one of the short-lived Mission College's
honorary tutors as well as a leading London Congregational minister and
college principal,[27] made that clear in his first editorial on New Year's Day
1846: all questions of prophecy, strategy, and chronology, all matters
about the restoration and conversion of the Jews, were to be treated as
open questions. The British Society's sole object was 'to diffuse among the
Jews the great doctrines in which true believers in the Lord Jesus are
agreed'. He recognized that such an aim brought together people with
'different views with regard to the interpretation of unfulfilled prophecy'
and consequently he proposed to leave, 'as out of our particular province,
to other publications the promulgation of doctrines which only part of
the true church receive as Scriptural'; and he referred firmly to one of the
two proof texts of the millennialist armoury: Romans 11. 25–6.[28] 'Still,
some will say that the time has not yet come. But how do we know that it
is not come? "Blindness", indeed, "in part, is happened to Israel, until the
fulness of the Gentiles be come in"; but to what fulness is reference
made?'[29]

Thus was stretched the tightrope which most of the British Society's
publicists managed to tread. They concentrated on the gospel imperative,
or on the magnificent, appalling paradox of Jewish uniqueness; but they
preferred to leave prophecy to fend for itself, aware that the nuances of
their stance would be evident to close students of form without alarming
chance subscribers or casually interested hearers. Thomas Raffles, the
veteran Liverpool Congregational pulpiteer, who in his early twenties had
preached a 'Demonstration Sermon' for the London Society, preached
when he was sixty for the British Society.[30] His theme, 'A Man that is a
Jew' (Acts 10. 28), was illustrated by a surprising but missionary-directed
anecdote about the Pope which was wholly to the Pope's credit.[31] His
thrust was that the British Society 'simply seeks the conversion of the Jew,

---

[27] Richard Alliott (d. 1863); *Congregational Year Book* (1865), pp. 217–18.
[28] 'Blindness in part is happened to Israel, until the fulness of the Gentiles be come in. And so all
Israel shall be saved.' The other text was Luke 21. 24: 'Jerusalem shall be trodden down of the
Gentiles, UNTIL the time of the Gentiles be fulfilled.'
[29] Dunlop, *Memories of Gospel Triumphs*, p. 240.
[30] Thomas Raffles (1788–1863), *DNB*.
[31] The Pope, no Antichrist he, was about to pass a Jew who was having a seizure in a Roman
street. To the horror of onlookers ('He is a Jew!') the Pope rushed to help ('He is a man!').
Raffles then drew the moral: 'Alas! we boast a purer faith, but had he fallen thus in the streets
of London, how few there are who would have been disposed to go and do likewise.' But then
it was April 1848 and Pio Nono could still be seen in an amiable light.

as you would seek the conversion of any other man . . . it offers no interpretation of prophecy flattering to Jewish pride or succumbing to Jewish
prejudice. It proposes no expedition to Palestine, no colonization society
for the Holy Land. All these things it eschews, as a Society, leaving them to
men's private judgments.'[32]

That line was identical to the one taken in Burkean vein the preceding
year by Henry Allon, then still young at Union Chapel Islington.[33] In 'The
Religion of Moses and the religion of Jesus essentially the same', Allon too
concentrated on the gospel call and the unique fascination of Jews:

> It will not advantage us that you become Christians. We wish it
> simply because we believe Christianity to be true, and because you
> have souls for which it proffers a salvation. . . . We repudiate the
> Christianity that does not love and reverence you. *We honour your
> name.* None has so proud a heraldry, so glorious an ancestry . . . we
> accord to you the privilege and honours of primogeniture. . . . *We
> reverence your Scriptures. . . . We reverence your land.* . . . All that is
> precious to us—Moses and the prophets, Jesus and the apostles—all
> are of the Jews; and veneration, gratitude, yearning affection, are our
> emotions at your name. . . .
>
> We will add that . . . Judaism, by its ceremonies, typified His work
> as a Saviour, His death as an atonement; and that when He appeared
> the Jewish system came to an end; there was no longer need of type,
> for He was the Antetype; of symbol, for He was the thing signified.
> Hence when He had come, the temple was overthrown, sacrifices
> ceased, and, because of their wicked rejection of Him, the Jewish
> nation was scattered. . . .
>
> . . . And now you are scattered; your genealogies are destroyed; you
> have no means of recognising a Messiah, even should one come. You
> could not prove Him of the seed of David, of the tribe of Judah. . . .
>
> Look at the facts of His history. . . . And then act upon your con-
> viction, whatever it may be. Salvation is a momentous matter; the
> soul is a thing for eternity; and it is purely a personal concern. You
> will not be saved by being nationally either Jew or Christian. . . . Reli-
> gion is a thing solely between God and yourself. No one else can in
> this sense meddle with it. . . . You may be saved, a member of an evil
> nation; or lost, a member of a holy one.[34]

[32] Dunlop, *Memories of Gospel Triumphs*, p. 305.
[33] Henry Allon (1818–92), *DNB*.
[34] Dunlop, *Memories of Gospel Triumphs*, pp. 251–3.

The society's lecturers liked to hang their rhetoric on such fretworked pegs. When the septuagenarian James Bennett[35] lectured on 'The Present Condition of the Jews' he reflected—while noting that there were perhaps as many Jews in London as in all Palestine—that they 'exhibit, in their present state, the strange confounding enigma of a people who have received from heaven a law which they cannot obey'; and in that state he discerned their future.[36] For the United Presbyterian, Thomas Archer, lecturing on 'The Dispersion of the Jews', there was the excitement of a nation which was itself a prophecy, 'a people whose movements were mapped in minutest detail, with perfect circumstantial accuracy, ages before they have been realized!'

> The Jews, scattered indeed ... have outlived the dynasties that enslaved them, and now rise among the ruins of ancient thrones ... themselves a ruin, but lofty, noble, and indestructible ... an eloquent enforcement of the great truth that nations, *as such*, are responsible, and that having no future social existence, this earth is the only theatre of developed responsibility and felt retribution.[37]

Yet there were matters that the British Society's supporters wanted to know about, however knotty. None doubted the call to convert Jews, but what about their restoration? Archer's fellow Presbyterian, though more Free than United, Regent Square's James Hamilton,[38] who built his lecture about 'The Destination of the Jews' on the proof texts Luke 21. 24 and Romans 6. 25–6, admitted that the 'New Testament allusions to Israel's last return are cursory and few, but it is enough that there *are* allusions', and he proceeded to prove both that the Jews were to be restored to Palestine and that they were to be converted. *En route* Hamilton visited Nineveh, Babylon, and Petra[39] and then, with marked optimism, he set Jerusalem alongside them: 'No city was ever honoured thus.'[40] For Hamilton the reason could only lie 'in the purposes of God' and the outcome

---

[35] James Bennett (1774–1862), *DNB*.

[36] 'The theme allotted to me ... calls me to exhibit them as the visible monuments of God's displeasure against their sins—but reserved for a display of sovereign mercy and final restoration to favour'. Dunlop, *Memories of Gospel Triumphs*, pp. 159, 161.

[37] Thomas Archer (1806–64), ibid., p. 144.

[38] James Hamilton (1814–67), *DNB*.

[39] 'They were not exterminated, and yet they have vanished. Merged in the nations, and mutually commingled, there is no precipitate which can decompose them and bring them out in their original distinction again.' Dunlop, *Memories of Gospel Triumphs*, p. 82.

[40] That 'city whose case is quite peculiar ... though eighteen centuries have passed, and strangers still tread its hallowed soil, that city is still the magnet of many hearts'. Ibid., pp. 82–3.

must correspondingly be held in prophecy ('I prefer quoting, without comment, the sure word of prophecy') and viewed through the optimistic lenses of Spirit-empowered missionary endeavour. The Jews would be restored and they must be converted:

> Looking to the present languid and withered aspect of the country, it may be a question with some whether a literal restoration to Palestine would be a blessing to the Jews. . . . Let but the seed of Jacob people it once more, and its pastures will be clothed with flocks, and its valleys with corn. . . . I doubt not that the Jews are to be the possessors of Palestine and the people of God again. This is their destination. . . . [F]oreign missions have exerted a most quickening power on domestic Christianity, . . . every triumph of the Gospel abroad has pioneered a corresponding victory at home. . . . In reading the prophecies I see many proofs that regenerate Palestine is to present the world with a living epistle largely written of this first-rate Christianity.[41]

Hamilton's hearty approach to prophecy echoed that of F. A. Cox, the Hackney Baptist,[42] whose lecture on 'The National Characteristics of the Jews' ('A Jew is nowhere to be mistaken') likewise moved from history to futurity: 'There is one history, however, which is free from . . . defects, being written by an inspired pen . . . the nation of THE JEWS . . . having their peculiar destiny linked by a predetermining Providence, with the ultimate conditions of all the other communities and tribes of mankind. They are thus associated with all people and with all time.'

As for their restoration, 'This is as wonderful a fact, embosomed in prophecy, as any portion of their past history. . . . We have heard of no resurrection before from the entombment of a national ruin. . . . The Jewish nation is in fact a miracle in the mighty system of human existence.' Then he drew back. He admitted that the 'general restoration of the Jews, by conversion to Christianity, seems to be an event universally admitted and anticipated; so clearly it is written on the page of Scripture'. He further admitted that it 'is intimated that the universal conversion of mankind will occur about the same period with that of the Jews' and that this had been linked with 'the further question as to the personal reign of Messiah on the earth'; but were these things to be taken literally, or spiritually, or both? 'It may not be wise dogmatically to pronounce on these points of

---

[41] Dunlop, *Memories of Gospel Triumphs*, pp. 84–90.
[42] Francis Augustus Cox (1783–1853), *DNB*.

controversy ... but ... the one does not necessarily involve the other. If the return of the Jews to their own land be assumed, we are not compelled to decide on the personal reign.'[43]

There spoke Hackney man, a representative Dissenter of the older, more sober school. Cox's ponderous Congregational Hackney neighbour and contemporary, Henry Forster Burder, who could at times be intolerably magisterial,[44] lecturing on 'Our Debt to the Jews', also turned his attention to 'the disclosure of the purposes of God to bring the Jewish people into the Church of Christ':

> I am fully aware that it is not in predictions of the future, that we are usually to seek a guide to duty or a directory of conduct. Over many of them there is intentionally thrown a veil of obscurity, one object of which may be to prevent any agency on the part of man, with an express design to impede their accomplishment. Disclosure, however, of the purposes of God may be given with so much clearness, and may be so obviously interwoven with intimations of our duty, as to be evidently designed for our practical guidance and encouragement. Such, if I mistake not, are the revelations which are given us of the future history and destinies of the Jews, and especially of their conversion to the Christian faith. . . .
>
> The conversion of the Jews, as a nation, to the faith of Christ, is to be effected, as soon as the fulness of the Gentiles is brought into the Church. And here let me observe, that we should guard against exaggerated notions of the extent of that preparatory fulness which might induce us to place it at too remote a period. Is there sufficient reason to suppose that, even during the millennium itself, the *entire* population of the world will be truly converted to God? If that supposition be entertained, let me ask, out of what materials and under what circumstances, could arise that awful outbreak of wickedness which will *succeed* the millennium, as is clearly set forth in the twentieth chapter of the Book of the Revelation? It is enough, I conceive, to suppose that the *mass* of the people, *during* the millennium, will be real Christians.[45]

Such matters of restoration and conversion powerfully exercised that older generation. Ebenezer Henderson of Highbury College was the

[43] Dunlop, *Memories of Gospel Triumphs*, pp. 136, 139–41.
[44] Henry Forster Burder (1783–1864), *DNB*.
[45] Dunlop, *Memories of Gospel Triumphs*, pp. 56–7.

British Society's second honorary secretary.[46] His lecture on 'The Conversion of the Jews' grappled not with the future fact of their conversion and restoration, for that was certain ('a conviction produced by an impartial study of the prophetic oracles' as well as by 'the impossibility of their obtaining a settlement in any other country under heaven'), so much as with its timing and nature. Would the Jews be converted before or after their return to Palestine? And would they be converted 'by the blessing of God's Holy Spirit upon the use of ordinary means, or by the intervention of renewed miraculous agency?' 'The practical bearing of these questions upon the efforts of Christians to promote Christianity among the lost sheep of the house of Israel must be obvious.'[47]

These were the musings and worryings of judicious and unfanciful men speaking, often powerfully, to a brief and bound to take prophecy seriously whether they tended to post-millennial optimism or pre-millennial blues. It was not always so agonized or so organized. When Craven Chapel's Dr Leifchild[48] arrived at the Freemasons' Hall for the British Society's 1847 annual meeting he found himself faced with a resolution about starting a Mission College, of which he had been entirely ignorant until his arrival and yet which he was expected to propose. So he turned to the ladies. 'When I listened to that Report, and looked at this assembly, and considered what a number of Christian females were here present ... I felt that you were greatly on the advance. If so many Christian females will elicit their sympathies on behalf of this subject, then you cannot fear, but you may go forward and take courage.'

And he too affirmed his belief 'in the approaching accomplishment of scriptural prophecy'.[49]

There was always the bluff layman to let the cat out of the bag. In 1892 it was George Williams. In 1860 it was Sir Culling Eardley, whose wealth, and therefore his title, derived from the banking prowess of Jewish ancestors.[50] He had been stirred by reports of Jewish attitudes to the current crisis in the papacy:

I am not a great prophet, neither do I say how such and such things are to be accomplished, but I believe, looking to the passing events of our day, that the Jews will be ours; that God intends to use them as a

[46] Ebenezer Henderson (1784–1858): secretary of British Society 1842–58, *DNB*.
[47] Dunlop, *Memories of Gospel Triumphs*, pp. 73–6.
[48] John Leifchild (1780–1862), *DNB*.
[49] Dunlop, *Memories of Gospel Triumphs*, pp. 268–9.
[50] Sir Culling Eardley Bt (1805–63), *DNB*.

mighty machine for the conversion of this world to Christ. . . . I, for one, regard this rising feeling amongst the Jews against the papacy as corresponding with what is said by Paul in the eleventh chapter of Romans. . . . It is a remarkable fact that that warning is addressed . . . to Romans. It does seem to me to indicate a possible purpose in the mind of God that it is by that great heresy, which has its centre at Rome, being overthrown, that the Jews are to be materially helped to come to the Truth of the Gospel. Nothing, I think, strikes the Jews so much throughout Europe as the evident passing away of the papal power.[51]

Laymen charged in where fathers and founders feared to tread.

If from the first the British Society's platform face carefully turned aside from the whirlpools of millennial speculation, at best regarding them as jacuzzi for those who liked to be braced by that sort of thing, there remains the matter of its representative public face. This was less that of Sir Culling or the Dissenting doctors and more that of the Herschell connection.

IV

The Herschell connection offers genealogical vistas as suggestive as any provided by the twelve tribes. Ridley Haim Herschell (1807–64) was the third son and fourth child of a Polish Jewish brewer.[52] He was the grand-son and brother-in-law of Polish rabbis but a series of adventures sustained by a marked self-reliance which he combined with an equally marked sense of race as well as family, refreshing reserves of wit as well as wits, intelligence as well as clarity of mind, and a genius for useful friend-ships which was never allowed to outweigh his liking for those made vulnerable by life, took him from Jewish orthodoxy of the most pious, chassidic-accented kind, through the University of Berlin[53] to Hamburg, London, Paris, and London again. His orthodoxy fell away. In Paris he came agonizingly close to conversion to Rome but in London he was baptized by Bishop Blomfield and came very close to preferment in Canterbury. In the event he became a Congregational minister, first in

---

[51] Dunlop, *Memories of Gospel Triumphs*, p. 218.

[52] *DNB*; the fullest source is *Memoir of Ridley Haim Herschell, late Minister of Trinity Chapel*, by his daughter (Edinburgh, privately printed, 1869).

[53] His intention was to read medicine. It is unclear how far he completed his course; it was certainly interrupted for prolonged intervals as only wandering students know how.

Islington and then in Marylebone where Trinity Chapel was built for him just off the Edgware Road.

His story shapes itself into several modes. The modern reader is strongly tempted to see it as that of the blissfully eternal student with London and Paris as his Kabul or Khatmandu and Edgware Road as his tryst with reality. For Evangelical contemporaries and admirers it fitted with pattern-book ease into the standard improving biography, striking testimony to the workings of Providence. Others, with novels in mind, might have discerned a disconcerting eye for the main chance—the ability to chat up prosperous strangers on long coach journeys; to secure introductions (admittedly seldom taken up) to important people; when conversion to Catholicism is at issue it is through the joint agency of a French archbishop (not named) and the Duke of Bordeaux's Jew-turned-Jesuit secretary-cum-librarian; when conversion to Evangelical Protestantism is achieved, the world of drawing-room prayer-meetings and invitations to serious country seats opens up and the Eustace diamonds seem to glitter before the eyes of Trollope's Mr Emilius.

The upward mobility is certainly impressive. Herschell married twice and well, each time to an older woman. His first wife, Helen Mowbray, was a Leith merchant's daughter: 'you may picture me sitting in what I have now learned to reckon a large room; that is one about 22 feet by 16', she wrote soon after marriage of their home in Woolwich, which was virtually a hostel for Jewish vagrants.[54] Herschell's second wife, Esther Fuller-Maitland, the daughter, sister, and aunt of MPs, came from the cream of the cream of the older mercantile Dissent. The Maitlands were an interrelated cousinhood of bankers, merchants, and landowners conscientiously working their way through Burke's *Landed Gentry* onwards and upwards into the *Peerage and Baronetage*.[55] They had combined and increased several fortunes as adroitly as they moved between Dissent and the Establishment. The historians S. R. Maitland and F. W. Maitland were part of the clan, and knew it. So were the Whitaker-Maitlands of Loughton Hall in Essex and the Maitland-Wilsons of Stowlangtoft Hall in Suffolk. The Whitaker-Maitlands were several times connected with the Fuller-Maitlands of Stansted Park in Essex and Park Place, Henley, who were the branch which retained its Dissent the longest. While the first

[54] R. H. Herschell, ed., *'Far Above Rubies'. Memoir of Helen S. Herschell By Her Daughter* (London, 1854), p. 134.
[55] G. H. Rogers Harrison, *A Genealogical and Historical Account of the Maitland Family* (London, privately printed, 1869).

Mrs Ridley Herschell was virtually disowned by her family (in her first years of marriage she contributed to the household budget by acting as a daily governess and giving singing lessons), the second Mrs Ridley Herschell was a rich woman in her own right.[56] When her stepson, Farrer Herschell, the future Lord Chancellor, married into a Dorset county family, it was into a family already doubly connected with the Maitland-Wilsons and the Fuller-Maitlands: the new Mrs Farrer Herschell was her stepmother-in-law's great niece.

That solid marriage, which ensured the Herschells their abiding place in Burke's *Peerage*, was complemented by those of Farrer's sisters, Mary and Ghetal. Ghetal married John Scott Burdon-Sanderson, the physiologist, who became Waynflete Professor at Oxford in 1883 and a baronet in 1899.[57] The Burdon-Sandersons, like the Fuller-Maitlands, had sufficiently benefited from real estate and mercantile marriages to find themselves in county circles, in their case in Newcastle and Northumberland as well as London and the Home Counties. They too were Dissenters, if of a slightly quirky kind. John Burdon-Sanderson's grandfather on the Sanderson side was a London banker and hop merchant, twice Lord Mayor and therefore a baronet, who had sat in the younger Pitt's parliaments for Malmesbury and Hastings. Since Burdon-Sanderson's great uncles on the Burdon side were Lord Stowell, the judge, and Lord Eldon, the Lord Chancellor, and his nephew was R. B. Haldane, who was also Lord Chancellor, the political not to mention the intellectual gyrations of this stretch of connection are almost beyond suggestion. Perhaps only Providence could have brought a Polish rabbi's great-grandson into so strange a trinity of English Lord High Chancellors as Eldon, Herschell, and Haldane: that, or the millennium.

Mary Herschell married equally well since her husband, John Cunliffe of Lancaster Gate, on his death in 1894 left £629,394, the bulk of it to her.[58] He was a banker whose family of confusingly repetitive Rogers, Jameses, and Johns banked in Blackburn and Manchester as well as London. The Cunliffes too were Dissenters. In Lancashire Cunliffes had been early benefactors (and treasurers) of what became Lancashire Independent College, grandly sited on land provided by a Cunliffe partner, Brooks. In London Cunliffes were prominent at Henry Allon's Union Chapel and married into the family network which included Allon

---

[56] She left £18,000 when she died in 1882; *The Times*, 5 August 1882.
[57] Sir John Scott Burdon-Sanderson Bt (1828–1905), *DNB*.
[58] *The Times*, 9 November 1895. Will dated 30 May 1891, proved 21 February 1895.

247

and a powerful complex of Fenland Dissenting activists. John Cunliffe's own loyalties lay with Paddington Chapel, the spiritual home of the Barretts of Wimpole Street. Like the John Burdon-Sandersons, the John Cunliffes were childless but they too had spiralling connections. The Manchester Cunliffe Brookses swiftly married into grandly impoverished aristocracy and their own name vanished into a peerage and a Scottish castle, while John Cunliffe's nephew, Walter, became Governor of the Bank of England.[59]

These were the grandest Herschell connections, but they were not the only ones. Five of Ridley's younger brothers followed him to England and were converted to Evangelical Christianity. One fell by the way and emigrated under a cloud to the United States where he died repentant. The other four became parsons. Louis and David Abraham became Congregational ministers in London; both worked at various times for the British Society although it was David Abraham whose flair and energy came closest to Ridley's.[60] Louis too married helpfully. Gulielma Holmes was the daughter of a Horsham Quaker who kept a pack of beagles, translated Schiller and Goethe into English verse, was regularly distrained for non-payment of tithes and delayed three months before consenting to the marriage of Gulielma's sister Mary to a man who was both a brewer and the son of an Indian Army general. Louis Herschell, though also a brewer's son, by comparison posed no such problems. Their son, George, became a Harley Street specialist in diseases of the digestive organs.[61] That leaves Victor and John Francis Israel. The former trained for the Congregational ministry, quickly left it for the Church of England after a bruising experience in Northamptonshire and went as a missionary to Jamaica, where he was murdered.[62] The latter went to Queen's College, Cambridge, in 1838 and thence into Anglican orders; his son, another George Herschell, became a solicitor.[63] Thus are the professional classes steadily enlarged. Ridley's was not the only generation of Herschells to settle into English

[59] Walter Cunliffe, 1st Baron Cunliffe (1855–1920), *DNB: Missing Persons* (Oxford, 1993).

[60] David Abraham Herschell (1823–1904), E. E. Cleal, *The Story of Congregationalism in Surrey* (London, 1908), pp. 305–9.

[61] For Louis Herschell (1821–90) see Cleal, *Congregationalism*, pp. 124–5; for the Holmes family, kin to the family of Ridley and Belfort Bax, see B. Thistlethwaite, *The Bax Family* (London, privately printed, 1936), pp. 364–6; for George Herschell MD (1856–1914), see *Who Was Who 1897–1916*.

[62] His English career can be deduced from *Congregational Year Book* 1854, p. 181; 1855, p. 194; 1857, p. 156. T. Stephens, ed., *Album of The Northamptonshire Congregational Churches* (Wellingborough, 1894), p. 107.

[63] Venn, *Alumni Cantabrigienses*, 3, p. 342.

Protestantism. In the 1850s two sons of his brother Jesia also left Strzelno for Britain. Adolph became an African merchant in Liverpool where his family were members of Presbyterian and Congregational churches on the Wirral. His son Arnold married into Timpson's shoes, which were Baptist in Northampton but Congregationalist on Merseyside, and tended to neglect the African export trade for lawn tennis and other sports.[64]

By any standards this far flung connection of Herschells, Timpsons, Holmeses, Burdon-Sandersons, Haldanes, Cunliffes, Goodmans, Fosters, Browns, and Maitlands is a remarkable testimony to social and professional assimilation and advancement; the more so for being through such consistently unfashionable channels. Despite all the evidence of shrewd eyes for the main chance and their undoubted family solidarity the weight of that evidence falls firmly on the side of consistency, probity, and sheer attractiveness of character and intellect. It might indeed be urged that the good marriages reflected more of Esther Fuller-Maitland's or Helen Skirving Mowbray's or Gulielma Holmes's eyes to the main chance than Ridley or Louis Herschell's. They were intelligent women who found in their unorthodox marriages the outlets that might otherwise only have come with the foreign mission field. Helen Herschell ran households that as often as not were hostels for enquiring or converted and certainly wandering Jews. In addition to her singing classes she undertook translation and editorial work for her husband and one suspects that the felicities and clarity of his style were in fact hers. Those things approached drudgery; they were certainly not ladylike, but they stretched the mind and multiplied the usefulness of a cultivated and talented early Victorian woman. Esther Herschell was middle-aged when she married. One suspects that it was her money which allowed Ridley to buy on impulse the cottage in Essex where he had missioned as a young man and enlarge it into a summer retreat where he could entertain the whole of 'D' division police force and their families. It was certainly thanks to her that on other occasions Park Place could be used for such a treat. Thus her philanthropies could be channelled and disciplined. Indeed, was that concern for a policemen's mission (sailors, soldiers, cabmen, and navvies, all had their missions; why not that most socially isolated species, the police?) hers or his?[65]

---

[64] Arnold Herschell (1872–1956), Chairman of the Lawn Tennis Association 1937, son of Adolph Herschell (d. 1913). I am indebted to Mr G. C. Lightfoot and Dr Ian Sellers for information about this branch of the Herschell family.

[65] *Memoir of R. H. Herschell*, pp. 285–7.

But what was the thread to such connection? Was it purely tempera-
mental chemistry, or chance, or even Providence? Here we return to this
paper's theme: the thread was millennialism. It was this shared concern
which brought together this significant social and professional connection and which accents their variously shared Dissent. It is this which
should colour the carefully distanced tone of the British Society's annual
platform party, for with this we come to the heart of the British Society.

V

Ridley Herschell met his first wife at a weekly meeting for Bible study and
conversation often attended by Edward Irving and members of his congregation; she was visiting London and had been taken to one of those
meetings by a family friend whose brother had been a sponsor at Ridley's
baptism the previous year. He first met his second wife while on honey-
moon with Helen. They were at Henley (quite by chance); Ridley was
invited to preach at the Congregational church: 'After service, a lady of
the name of Maitland, a person of large fortune and great consequence in
the neighbourhood, came into the vestry, and invited him to come next
day and see the pleasure grounds, which are a sort of lion for miles
around.'[66] That was Esther's mother, whose Fuller and Ellis banking
fortunes had been so usefully added to the Maitland banking fortune. The
most striking thing about Ridley, and the most carefully sustained, was his
Jewishness: he was a Christian *Jew*, not a Jew who had become Christian.
Such matters greatly exercised the Maitland network. Mrs Fuller Maitland's first cousin by marriage, S. R. Maitland, was the author of an
*Enquiry into the Grounds on which the Prophetic Period of Daniel and St John has
been supposed to consist of 1260 years* (1826), a work intended to undermine
millennialist notions which in fact added fuel to the millenarian fire by its
argument that Revelation was yet to be fulfilled.[67]

As for the Cunliffes and the Burdon-Sandersons of the next generation, John Cunliffe remains a discretely shadowy figure, though in 1860
he laid the foundation stone, and presumably gave generously to the
building fund, of D. A. Herschell's new chapel at Loughborough Park,
Brixton.[68] The quirk that makes sense of the Burdon-Sandersons' Dissent

[66] *Memoir of R. H. Herschell*, pp. 285–7.
[67] Samuel Roffey Maitland (1792–1866), *DNB*; Maitland's work, much debated and canvassed
at the Albury Park conferences, influenced both the emergent Catholic Apostolic Church
and J. N. Darby.
[68] Cleal, *Congregationalism*, p. 306.

has to be millenialism, for they are almost impossible to place denominationally. The churches in Hampstead and Newcastle with which John Burdon-Sanderson's father and brother were most closely associated were Baptist. John's sister, Elizabeth, was latterly a member of Lyndhurst Road Congregational church in Hampstead. There was also, however, a strong family stream of Plymouth Brethrenism. John's father, Richard, seems to have become a Plymouth Brother in 1837 and his friendship with the Haldane family of Scottish Congregational, Baptist, Evangelical, and *Recordite* fame, and the marriages of his son Richard and his daughter Mary Elizabeth to Isabella and Robert Haldane, emphasize the firm but non-denominational evangelicalism of the connection. But there was more to it than that. The Burdon-Sanderson Dissent was out of the mainstream, but it was decidedly unquiet. Richard Burdon-Sanderson was politically advanced and pamphleteeringly noisy. As the nephew of Lords Stowell and Eldon (and the son of Newcastle's Sir Thomas Burdon, who was a Tory brewer), Richard Burdon, not yet Sanderson, had been assured of a glowingly safe career. Oriel College, Oxford, confirmed this intellectually but jeopardized it in worldly terms since it was at Oriel that he caught Evangelical religion.[69] His marriage coloured such imputations, for although Elizabeth Skinner Sanderson was the orphaned heiress of a Tory City baronet there was Quakerism in her background and she was the stepdaughter of that notorious 'Cranbrook derelict and Thames Ditton Coalheaver', William Huntington, Sinner Saved, author of *The Bank of Faith* and builder of Jireh Chapel, Lewes. That strange alliance is not referred to in Burdon-Sanderson's biography, but when Elizabeth's mother was buried it was in an unconsecrated plot belonging to her dreadful husband, with Richard Burdon (now Sanderson) to read the committal service, innocent of any benefit of clergy.[70]

Thus in every case there is the apparently unusual phenomenon, although common to this connection, of considerable landed property,

[69] The fullest background is to be found in G. B.-S., *Sir John Burdon-Sanderson: a Memoir* (Oxford, 1911); this can be supplemented by R. Welford, *Men of Mark 'Twixt Tyne and Tweed* (Newcastle, 1895), 3, pp. 345–50 for Richard Burdon-Sanderson (1791–1865) and pp. 352–5 for Richard Burdon-Sanderson (1821–76). See also R. Coad, *A History of the Brethren Movement* (Exeter, 2nd ed., 1976), pp. 81, 181; F. Buffard, 'James Castleden (1778–1854) Bethel Baptist Church, Hampstead', *Baptist Quarterly*, 31. 3 (July, 1975), p. 118. Elizabeth Burdon-Sanderson (1823–1908), sister of Sir John, joined Lyndhurst Road Congregational Church, Hampstead, 2 April 1885 (Church Book 1880– ; in Dr Williams's Library).

[70] William Huntington (1745–1813), *DNB*; his marriage to Elizabeth, Lady Sanderson (1765–1817), is racily described in T. Wright, *The Life of William Huntington S.S.* (London, 1909), esp. pp. 157–63, 223–9, 301.

CLYDE BINFIELD

promoted by commercial fortunes, moderated into the professions, held together by marked intellectual acumen and reflected in a millennially nuanced Evangelicalism, generally mainstream yet embracing considerable, even apocalyptic, extremes and mostly fighting shy of firm denominational expression for all the elements of Quakerism, Brethrenism, Congregationalism, Baptism, and Presbyterianism to be found among them. For all the oddities, it is cultivated and socially well-bred, even classy. It is this which suggests that such a connection is a last outlier of the 'catholic Christianity' of Revival's golden age: the atmosphere breathed perhaps at Oriel by Richard Burdon at the very time that the London Society was set on foot. It is this which explains the ease with which Ridley Herschell moved in town and country house prayer meetings—family prayer at Park Place, Bible study at Worlingham in Norfolk or Brampton in Huntingdonshire. This was how he became a missioner for Lady Olivia Sparrow, earl's daughter and duke's mother-in-law,[71] among her fisherfolk in Essex and her farm labourers in the Cromwell country where also he encountered a sturdily independent race of prosperous tenant farmers with irons in commercial fires far removed from farming and with surprising tentacles in Essex, Cambridge, and the north-east, and their own views as to mission, polity, and destiny.[72] It is here that such gleams illuminate each other. Those Huntingdonshire farmers and millers, with their wary respect for Lady Olivia and their periodic tussles with her, were firm in their Dissent and distinctive in their understanding of its polity. Their origins were Quaker, so they were weak on the ordinances though they tended to believer's baptism; yet they were happiest with Congregationalists, consequently they promoted Union Churches and liked to get their metropolitan kinsman, Henry Allon, up for great occasions. They were also hot on evangelism and corresponded with the Americans C. G. Finney and Asa Mahan, and hosted them on their British preaching tours. Theirs was in fact the religious temper that came closest to Ridley Herschell's. He too wavered on the ordinances, especially baptism. Indeed he found it hard to fit his views on the matter anywhere, and while at Leigh-on-Sea he secured birth notes for his daughters from Witham Friends Monthly Meeting.[73]

---

[71] Lady Olivia Sparrow (d. 1863), daughter of 1st Earl of Gosford, widow of General Sparrow of Brampton (d. 1805) and mother-in-law of 6th Duke of Manchester (1799–1855).

[72] This can be followed in H. Bell, *A Jubilee Memorial of the Union Chapel, Houghton* (Cambridge, 1890); B. Brown, *Reminiscences of Bateman Brown J.P.* (Peterborough, 1905).

[73] Birth notes dated 3.6.1835 and 25.1.1836. The records of Witham Monthly Meeting are with Essex Record Office, Chelmsford. D/NF 1/1/9.

Throughout the network there are references to a fascination with Bible study and meetings for reading and conversation, with prophecy as part and parcel of such meetings. Lady Olivia's son-in-law, Manchester, was known to be a millennialist duke, and the subscribers in the 1840s to Herschell's new Trinity Chapel have give-away names: Sir Culling Eardley (who bought the site and had paid for Herschell's recent visit to Palestine) and John Dean Paul, the British Society's first treasurer, were among the first trustees; Unwin, who printed and published for Herschell; Spicer Brothers, who were Unwin connections and made Unwin's paper; George Hitchcock; the Fuller Maitlands; Joshua and Joseph Wilson, who were Fuller Maitland connections; John Remington Mills, who was a Wilson connection; W. Alers Hankey, whose hereditary philanthropy was the London Missionary Society and whose hereditary church was the Weigh House; Thomas Piper, another Weigh House man; Mrs J. J. Gurney, from the Quaker banking set; Morton Peto, the Baptist; William Wilson, the Nottingham-turned-Sheffield-turned-Torquay Congregationalist; C. J. Metcalfe of Roxton, the Congregational squire from Bedfordshire; Dr Keith, the Scottish millennialist and missionary to Jews; and a small remnant of the old Evangelical aristocracy—the Earl of Gainsborough, Viscountess Acheson, Lady Olivia Sparrow, the Honourable Mrs O'Brien.[74] There was at least one name from the early days of the London Society, that of Miss Parminter of A La Ronde in Devon, since Lewis Way, who had taken over that Society for the Church, had caught something of his passion for converting Jews from visiting the Parminters and seeing how they expressed their own enthusiasm in their quaint Devon chapel of Point-in-View.

These are gleams, but they kaleidoscope into a pattern. For its consistency we need to return to Helen and Ridley Herschell.

VI

The background of each was, in its way, prosperous, educated, and orthodox. Helen Mowbray's formation was Church of Scotland as stamped by Thomas Chalmers, 'our excellent friend'.[75] In comparison with her later life, it was worldly—that is to say, it encompassed travel, music, good clothes, painting, and an easy social life. These fitted her

---

[74] The progress of Trinity can be followed in *Voice of Israel*, 1. 12 (1 April 1845), p. 116, through to 2. 44 (1 December 1847), p. 288.

[75] *Far above Rubies*, p. 43.

station and her temperament. Even at her most intense she never lost her common sense or her sense of the ridiculous. Come that change of heart 'which the Scriptures tell us must take place in every one before he can become a child of God',[76] and which in her case came in 1821–2, she put aside worldly things with an asceticism which in later life—perhaps having experienced the simplicity enforced by slender means—she sensibly retracted. She defended her new stance with reasoned vigour: 'for they who hold the opinions I have been defending (I reject the term *evangelical*, and all other *technicals* in religion), will always be found to live a more pious and virtuous life, than any self-righteous despiser of these opinions'; but then she added: 'If you knew me better than you do, you would know that enthusiasm forms no part of my composition.' At this point classic Protestantism pushes through. She urged Doddridge's *Rise and Progress* on a correspondent and, reflecting on the impact of TB on her own family, she wrote with more than an echo of William Law's *Spiritual Call*, 'Remember the time is short. Remember the many warnings we have had in our family. . . . It has frequently been my custom to remind those whom I have addressed on the subject of religion, that it might, perhaps, be the *last* time God would send a warning message to them through any of His creatures.' She was, in short, ready for Edward Irving, whom she heard whenever she was in London. 'I hear Mr. Irving with increased delight every Sabbath. He is a very different person from what the generality of People in Scotland suppose him', she wrote late in 1825; and again, in 1830: 'I am enjoying to the full my beloved pastor's preaching, which is superior now to what I ever heard it previously.'[77]

This was at the time of Irving's espousal of pre-millennialism. It was also, as will be recalled, a time of sharp mortality in his immediate family. Helen was stirred by such notions:

> She was led to turn her attention seriously to the subject of prophecy. She saw clearly stated there the predictions of the 'great and terrible day of the Lord', and of the second coming of Christ. . . . She saw set forth, with equal distinctness, the promises made to the Jews, and the honour reserved for them, and was thereby led to take a peculiar interest in God's chosen people. This also induced her to begin the study of Hebrew.[78]

[76] *Far above Rubies*, p. 4.
[77] Ibid., pp. 15–16, 29–30, 113–14.
[78] Ibid., p. 104.

She made lists of Old Testament texts on prophecy and gave them to her friends. By 1827 her Wednesday afternoons when in London were spent with the Irvings to 'hear Mr. I[rving] and Mr. F[? Frere, or Farrer] converse on the subject of prophecy'. In March 1828 she described 'a delightful day with the author of the *Cry from the Desert*, and his wife. They are a most interesting couple, of much spiritual discernment, and seem to live habitually under the influence of those glorious hopes which should animate all those who are "waiting for the Coming of the Lord".'[79] Certainly she feared 'that this holy doctrine will cause great divisions in the Church of Christ', but she expressed with engaging clarity the release that Irving's scriptural literalism provided for those who felt like her:

> Some of the young believers at that time, were brought in con-
> nexion with a school which taught the possibility of fleshly perfec-
> tion. After this they were therefore striving, alas! how vainly; and
> great was their disappointment to find themselves still enclosed in a
> 'body of sin and death', and to see how far the Church of Christ
> was from enjoying those blessings which they believed she ought to
> experience, if her members were walking consistently with God. It
> was, therefore, a great relief to be enabled to believe that the
> predictions refer to a period still future, and that the full joy and
> blessedness predicted will only be experienced by the Church when
> Christ comes as the Bridegroom to claim His Bride. A new light was
> now shed upon the whole of prophecy, and with joy could these
> young believers look forward to the time of the literal fulfilment of
> all the glorious promises contained in it. It was no marvel, there-
> fore, that he who was the instrument in God's Hands, of bringing
> forward so important a truth, should be revered and looked up to
> by them.[80]

Irving's pentecostalism, however, was too much. Helen found it un-
biblical. As she admitted in 1833: 'You know how fully I received those
things, at one time, as the manifestations of the Holy Ghost. Long and
tenaciously did I cling to this opinion, but the doings at Mr. Irving's
Church have for a long time appeared to me so contrary to the *written
Word* in many respects, that I cannot conceive them to proceed from the
same source.' To paraphrase an earlier letter of hers, she had discovered

[79] Ibid., pp. 113, 110.
[80] Ibid., pp. 112–13.

'the *saints* are not *angels*'.[81] But Irving's views on prophecy remained hers until she died.

In two other respects her common sense triumphed. She, who in her twenties dressed only in black and put aside all she enjoyed, in her forties ensured that her family had a singularly sunny home life in which not even church or Sunday school were enforced and in which the Trinity manse rang with Sabbath laughter. She phrased her enlightenment severely:

> The experience of many years has disabused me of my early prejudice. I have had ample proof . . . that where intellect slays its hundreds, uncultivated *animalism* slays its thousands. I have seen, among the children of religious parents, who have been sedulously kept from the gay pleasures of the world, an eager grasping after worldliness in its lowest and most revolting forms—the uncultivated and empty mind seeking to fill the craving void with any garbage within its reach.[82]

By the same token she recognized the occupational Sunday hazard of such religious views as hers:

> It seems to me to have been truly one of Satan's devices for some years past, to set people to try and find out the precise apostolic form of a church, all parties arguing upon uncertain inferences, and too many of the best and most able agreeing in nothing except the impossibility of worshipping in any place with pews and pulpit. My dear husband and I have had our share in the delusion and in experience of its consequences, and I can say for my own part, and I believe his also, that I never found anything less profitable than *coterie worship* with some twenty individuals in a room where the want of selection was only more glaringly apparent from the smallness of the company.[83]

That reference to her husband, whom she met at a time when the coterie worship of a Jewish church was engaging his mind, brings us to the remarkable partnership that was effectively her professional career.

Pre-millennialism was reasonable. That was its charm for somebody in Helen Mowbray's circumstances. That was also its charm for somebody of Ridley Herschell's temperament, brought up among orthodox Polish

---

[81] *Far above Rubies*, pp. 116, 119.
[82] Ibid., p. 192.
[83] *Memoir of R. H. Herschell*, p. 133.

Jewry, who remained committed to the place of his race even when he rejected its religious practices for those of Evangelical Protestantism. The place of Jews in the Christian dispensation was of vital importance. That stood to reason. It was on this that the minds and faith of Helen Mowbray and Ridley Herschell met.

VII

Herschell's background was devoutly orthodox. Orthodox Judaism never lost his sympathy or, in a traditional sense, his loyalty. Naturally the Jewish Reform Movement interested him. There was much in it to admire and more to understand. Its leaders had experienced the intellectual and cultural tensions which had hit Herschell in Berlin when his fellow students found him *alt modisch* in his ways and made it clear that this was not how the *aufgeklärten* lived.[84] But such 'enlightenment' struck at the root of Judaism. In 1844, while travelling on a Rhine steamer, Herschell got into conversation with a young, Catholic-educated Jewish wine merchant. The Rhinelander was convinced that his generation of Jews must soon become Christian 'or some other mighty change must take place':

> I asked him whether he had ever studied the prophecies? He said, 'No'. I asked him whether, if the governments of Europe offered to protect the Jews and place them in Palestine, he would like to go there? 'No', said he; 'I assure you nearly all the young men would rather be baptized than be forced to go there'. . . . He was very much astonished when I told him that many Christians pray earnestly for the restoration of the Jews; and that I also believe that the time is approaching when great changes will take place among them . . .[85]

That conviction among the younger, assimilated or assimilable generation was as much a problem as an opportunity in the eyes of one so orthodoxly reared as Herschell. One of the charms of Trinity Chapel, Edgware Road, was that the area was popular with London's Reform Jews. But Reform was not necessarily the thin end of a Christian wedge. Reformed Jews were just as likely to have 'Jew' hissed at them in the streets as orthodox Jews, but they had let slip the very part of their inheritance that Herschell saw as common ground. It disturbed him, however

---

[84] R. H. Herschell, ed., *Jewish Witnesses that Jesus is the Christ* (London, 1848), p. 3.
[85] *Memoir of R. H. Herschell*, pp. 207–8.

understandable it was, that 'we neither expect nor wish a Messiah who will lead us back to Palestine. We know no other country than that to which we belong by our birth and our civil relations'; 'the European Jews have no desire for a Palestine state'.[86] Consequently he stressed in his writing the positive points of the orthodox Judaism of his birth, the reasons behind its customs, the communal values which they exemplified, the consistent way of life which they promoted. The Jews Herschell carefully described in his *A Brief Account of the Present State and Future Expectations of the Jews* (1833, 5th edn 1841), were not benighted; it was the Polish Catholics and Lutherans among whom they lived who were benighted and who aroused the bitterest animosity in true Jewish hearts. Among such people it was the intellectual inconsistency and the mix of images—not a cross-roads without its crucifix—that was so distasteful. Even among 'real Christians' there was the dangerous tendency to see the Old Testament simply as a record of past events and its prophecies as mostly already fulfilled:

> by spiritualizing away what they admit to be yet future, from their true meaning, [they] cast additional stumbling blocks in the way of enquiring Jews, by throwing a degree of doubt and absurdity over all their interpretations of Scripture. To tell a Jew that Zion and Jerusalem mean the Gentile Church, and that 'the land where their fathers have dwelt,' means Heaven, is at once to tell them what is false, and what is glaringly absurd.[87]

What otherwise was to be made of the fact 'that several thousand Jews of Poland and Russia have recently bound themselves together by an oath, that as soon as the way is open for them to go up to Jerusalem, they will immediately go thither, and there spend their time in fasting and praying unto the Lord, until he shall send the Messiah?'[88] That was a testimony which greatly moved Herschell and he feared lest Christians downgrade such things. In a piece on 'The Sure Word of Prophecy' Herschell called Russian Jews as witness:

> What should we think of the Russian Jew of the present day, who should maintain against the infidel, that all the promises made to Israel have been fulfilled; who should insist that Palestine means Muscovy, and returning to Jerusalem signifies not being sent to

[86] *The Voice of Israel*, 1. 7 (1 November 1844), p. 53.
[87] R. H. Herschell, *A Brief Account of the Present State and Future Expectations of the Jews* (London, 5th edn, 1841), pp. 14–15.
[88] Ibid., p. 39.

Siberia, and that 'sorrowing no more at all' is descriptive of the peace and prosperity enjoyed by the Jews under the gentle sway of the Czar? Is this absurd . . .? Less ludicrous, perhaps, but equally remote from the truth, are the numerous attempts that have been made to accommodate the predictions of Scripture to the existing state of things, whether in the church, in the world, or among the Jews. . . . Now, we believe the Church *will* visibly be one; when it is so the world will believe the Father hath sent Christ. That is *not* so now. . . .[89]

And he feared that Christians were now doing what the Jews did when Jesus first came. As the Jews had overlooked the prophecy of an intermediate time, when the Messiah would appear to 'have laboured in vain, and spent his strength for nought', so now the Christians saw only the Church's glory at the expense of its actual humiliation. With this we come to the heart of Herschell's prophetic message to Christian and Jew alike:

O, it is fearful to think of the accumulated load of guilt that lies on the head of that which calls itself the Christian Church! Let not those few of her members who are truly spiritual, lull themselves asleep by saying, 'Peace and safety', while sudden destruction is about to come upon her. Let them not point to her Bible and Missionary Societies, as if these could now redeem a character ruined by centuries of ungodliness. . . . Say not that the *real* Church of Christ is not chargeable with the sins of the visible Church. . . . No; in such proportion as you have connived at the world's calling itself the Church, you are guilty of the consequences that have flowed from this fatal error. I know that those whose hearts are right with God, will be saved, when the wood, and hay, and stubble, which they have built on the true foundation, shall be burnt up; but I believe that they will then know what it is to be saved 'as by fire'.[90]

Herschell the Jew who was also Herschell the Christian could not fail to be Herschell the prophet, or at least the student of prophets, with judgements for Israel and Christendom alike:

The Jews have an indescribable horror of death; and perhaps it is only one of them, who has been brought into Christ's marvellous light, that can fully understand how the work of Christ in the flesh delivers

---

[89] 'The Sure Word of Prophecy', *The Voice of Israel*, 1. 5 (2 September 1844), p. 33.
[90] *A Brief Account*, pp. 23–4.

them who, through fear of death, were, all their lifetime, subject to bondage. . . .

The whole world presents at this moment a melancholy spectacle of sin and misery; but there is this important difference between Israel and Christendom, that, while in the horizon of the former, we perceive the faint dawning of that morn which shall terminate in a glorious day, in that of the latter, we behold the sun declining, and the lowering clouds quickly gathering, that shall soon envelope the whole in the blackness of darkness. . . . [I]t is impossible for a Christian . . . to avoid seeing the present evil state of things. . . . [G]lorious days are yet awaiting our nation; but remember, Zion is to be redeemed with judgment, and her returning ones with righteousness: and the rebels are to be purged out of her . . .[91]

For the first eight years of his Christian life Herschell was convinced that his call was to be an evangelist to Jews. Although that call remained, he became equally convinced of a call to minister to a settled congregation. How, given his low view of the state of the Church, and without falling into the trap of 'coterie worship', were those calls to be answered and reconciled? He had come very close to the trap of coterie worship when he met Helen Mowbray. He had been lodging at the London Society's Jewish Institution, and with a group of fellow converts and encouraged by the Institution's superintendent, Erasmus Simon, he conceived the idea of forming a Jewish Church. The Institution's committee was alarmed by this and there was some warmth between Herschell and his grandest protector, Bishop Blomfield; but that was recompensed by the sympathy of Edward Irving. As Herschell's daughter put it:

the period in question was one of great excitement among religious people. The followers of Edward Irving were looking for a return of the miraculous gifts of the Spirit to the Church, in answer to their prayers; and many who were studying prophecy believed that the 'signs of the times' indicated that the 'end of all things' was approaching. What more natural, then, than that there should also be a movement among the Jews—that they should gather themselves together preparatory to their expected restoration to their own land. . . .[92]

Here seemed to be a true recreation of apostolic times for, spurned by the Institution's committee, the group left for a house in Kensington

[91] *A Brief Account*, pp. 128, 131–2, 148.
[92] *Memoir of R. H. Herschell*, p. 75.

where they lived communally, sleeping on the floor and holding weekly Scripture meetings; Irving attended some of these and it was at one of them, introduced by Miss Farrer, that Herschell met Helen Mowbray. The Jewish Church came to nothing; its disciples went their different ways; and when, from time to time, the idea was revived, Herschell kept aloof.

Though he was now in Irvingite circles Herschell also kept aloof (and saw that Helen did the same) from Irvingite pentecostalism. When he acted as locum for six weeks in 1832 at an Oxford Dissenting chapel where glossolaly had broken out and brought Herschell's friend, its minister, to the point of breakdown, he quelled the gifts with magisterial ease. In the middle of his first sermon a woman began to speak in tongues. Herschell paused until she had finished but he was aware that other women were on the verge of rising and he was even more aware that there was a ringside audience of undergraduates visibly enjoying the fun. He acted. 'I too have a message from God; let me deliver mine, that all things be done in order.' And he finished his sermon, at which point he returned to the issue of the hour. Unbelievers were present, he observed, referring to the undergraduates. It was unseemly to speak in unknown tongues in their presence; let them retire and then 'we will hear whatever message any of you have to deliver'. The spell was broken. No more messages were delivered that morning.[93]

Tongues were not prophecy. For Herschell prophecy was bound up with his people. Hence his concern with the British Society, whose founding resolution he moved, seconded by that fiery millennialist, Dr Cumming of Crown Court. In Herschell's eyes the British Society had a breadth denied to the London Society by the latter's Anglican limitations, but the two societies complemented rather than competed with each other, rather as the new society was to work in tandem with the Church of Scotland's society. Above all, the new society was based on sound views of prophecy. Hence the resolution at its first public meeting: 'That while deeply sympathising with the Jewish people in the unparalleled sufferings to which, in consequence of their rejection of the Messiah, they have been subjected, the Society joyfully contemplates, in the predictions of Holy Writ, and in the signs of the times, the approach of a brighter period in their history. . . .'[94]

---

[93] It is not clear which chapel this was; the circumstances fit neither the situation of New Road Baptist Church at that time, nor what became George Street Congregational Church. *Memoir of R. H. Herschell*, pp. 92–4.

[94] J. Dunlop, *Memories of Gospel Triumphs*, p. 17.

For the past five years Herschell had been ministering to an independent congregation. At Chadwell Street in Islington from 1838 (very close to where Irving had lived) and then at John Street, Edgware Road, from 1846, he therefore had a base which could also act as a Jewish mission station, providing the sort of work that Frey had urged on the London Missionary Society forty years earlier. On Sundays he was restrained. He increasingly disliked the long prayer that was habitual among Dissenters and he disapproved of their glorification of the sermon. He also disapproved of random sermonizing. First and foremost on Sundays he was the pastor of a diverse congregation:

> There were some parts of Scripture on which he never preached, because he was undecided as to their significance. Though he had given much attention to the prophetic Scriptures, and was one who 'watched the signs of the times', he very seldom made unfulfilled prophecy the subject of his discourses—never unless he could bring it to bear on the actual condition and necessities of his hearers. At the same time his sermons contained frequent allusions which showed what the bent of his mind was on this subject. He did not sympathise with those who have mapped out all God's future dealings with the world according to their own views; and he decidedly objected to any attempt to fix 'the times and the seasons which the Father hath kept in His own power.' But he earnestly and prayerfully studied the writings of the prophets, and was thereby led to believe that the Lord Jesus will come again to 'reign on the earth', and that the Jews will be restored to the land of their fathers; 'I fully believe in the prophecies relating to Israel, to Judaea and Jerusalem', he wrote, when he was in the Holy Land, 'but I assuredly believe also that to the believer every spot is hallowed ground. . . . I tremble for those who having become interested in the subject of prophecy, try to fulfil it by plans of their own contriving. It is altogether a mistaken idea. Now is the time for a spiritual testimony to be given; and an upper room in Jerusalem, or in a desert, becomes a temple, if disciples are praying there for the outpouring of the Spirit of Truth.'[95]

That commonsensical approach intensified with his two visits to Palestine, in 1843 and again in 1854. The emotion of such visits is obvious,[96] but they had a practical outcome in a determination to found

[95] *Memoir of R. H. Herschell*, pp. 227–8.
[96] There was a convenient belief in the Herschell family that they descended from Jews who,

an agricultural colony for European Jewish converts to Christianity. His backers included the Bishop of Jerusalem and that city's British and American consuls as well as the Earl of Shaftesbury; and a model farm and agricultural school were started at Jaffa. Thus, at the end of his life Herschell saw the practical outworking of what in mid-life he promoted editorially in his short-lived monthly, *The Voice of Israel*.

VIII

If neither the pulpits of Chadwell Street and Trinity nor the platform of the British Society were places for prophetic exuberance, the privately run *Voice of Israel Conducted by Jews who Believe in Jesus of Nazareth as the Messiah* was another matter. That voice was heard monthly from May 1844 to December 1847. The first issue ran to eight pages, the last twelve. The size of its readership is not known; the Congregational Library's bound copy, presented by a member of the family who printed and published it, was uncut until the present writer consulted it.[97]

Its contents fall into three main types, mostly, one suspects, written or ghosted by the editor and his wife: *information*, that is to say about the beliefs, customs, and past of the Jews; *contemporary*, that is to say news of Jewish events and issues in Europe and elsewhere; and *prophetic*. *The Voice* was unashamedly 'millennarious': in that respect 'we side with the few, rather than the many', and while it recognized that the 'positive fixing of dates, and minute description of details, have done much to prejudice sober-minded Christians against the study of unfulfilled prophecy' yet, as that subject 'is intimately connected with the future destiny of the Jews, we think it very suitable to *The Voice of Israel* that a portion of its columns should be devoted to this interesting topic'.[98]

That portion grew. It embraced reviews of books, letters of enquiry or exposition, lectures and accounts of lectures, flavoured with judicious controversy, often from America. Thus Thomas Watson's *Shiloh's Sceptre; or the Signs of the Times* was noticed as a 'sober and scriptural . . . truly

---

after the Babylonian captivity, had moved to Spain, and thence to the Netherlands and Poland rather than back to Jerusalem. So they at least had no part in the events of the Crucifixion. None the less he wrote of his Palestinian visit under the title *A Visit to My Father-land: Notes of a Journey to Syria and Palestine* (1844).

[97] Published by Jacob Unwin of 31 Bucklersbury, the volume, bound but uncut, belonged to George Unwin, and was included in 'Mrs G. Unwin's Donation'.

[98] *The Voice of Israel*, 1. 7 (1 November 1844), p. 54.

spiritual and practical' treatment of unfulfilled prophecy well up to Edward Bickersteth's standards of sound sense. Thus again, 'A Layman' commended T. R. Birks's *The Four Prophetic Empires* and E. B. Elliott's *Horae Apocalypticae* for their masterly evaluations of the prophecies of Daniel and St John, though the vicar of Great Canfield (J. P. Gurney) was unhappy at Elliott's conviction that Napoleon's dethronement of the Holy Roman Emperor fitted the fourth vial and 'Yours in the love of the truth, J.K.' was yet more critical of Elliott.[99] Controversy could never be far from the surface in such matters. *The Voice* was delighted, for example, with A Protestant Nonconformist Layman's *The Second Advent Introductory to the World's Jubilee*, because it was 'a cause of thankfulness that the glorious truths brought forward in this seasonable publication are gaining ground in quarters where, for a long time, they were reviled'. Unfortunately that pamphlet was in fact a rebuke to Thomas Raffles whose new 'Jubilee Hymn' provoked Protestant Nonconformist Layman by its inconsistency. Raffles assumed that the Messiah would return when the whole world was converted—a view taught neither by Christ nor the apostles:

> I am writing to you with the map of the world suspended before me. The map of this world, of which Satan is the god, and whose right to it, *de facto*, the Bible does not dispute. . . . Will you, in your study, travel with us over the map or ground plot of the great usurper's dominions, and tell me where it is that you have discovered the cause of such jubilant acclamations as your hymn so joyfully, so sweetly breathes. . . .[100]

Herschell did his best to encourage variety. A Macclesfield Congregational minister, G. B. Kidd, wrote 'On the Posture of the Messiah Now in Heaven'. William Rigby wrote in from Killashee, Ireland, about 'The 70 Weeks and 2300 Days of Daniel'. The persistent 'Pergamos' wrote a series of letters on 'Prophecies of the Latter Days . . . Daniel II and VII', with which Herschell could not agree. One contributor speculated as to whether Gypsies were the remnant of the ten tribes of Israel, but the consensus was that they were more likely to have been Hindustanis. W. W. Pym, another frequent contributor, asked whether the saints would escape the Great Tribulation and found comfort in the Great Rapture: 'the great tribulation of the last days will not be poured out, until

---

[99] *The Voice of Israel*, 1. 6 (1 October 1844), p. 52; 1. 10 (1 February 1845), p. 91; 2. 38 (1 January 1847), p. 215.
[100] Ibid., 1. 13 (1 May 1845), p. 128; 2. 14 (2 June 1845), pp. 139–40.

after the saints shall have been caught up in the clouds to meet the Lord in the air'.[101]

Inevitably there was intense speculation about events in Palestine. 'It is not at all unlikely', began 'Letter from Jerusalem' in August 1845, 'that should the Pope be made to resign his temporal powers, and confine himself solely to his spiritual office, to the effect of which a proposal is said to have been made to the Pope by the Austrian Government, Jerusalem may become, under such circumstances, the residence of the Roman Catholic Church . . .'.[102]

That was heady stuff but headier far was the report of a lecture given in New York by Judge Noah. Herschell was careful to distance himself from much of Noah's approach[103] but the excitement of Noah's analysis is patent. First he surveyed the 'great revolution' which in the past quarter century had drawn Turkey, Greece, Egypt, Syria, Russia, India, China, France, and England into its vortex; then he described the beckoning role of those Jews who in so many countries were natural farmers in that least conserved yet most fertile of countries, Palestine:

> Russia, with one arm on the Mediterranean, and the other on the North Sea, will nearly embrace all Europe. The counter balance of this gigantic power will be a firm and liberal union of Austria with all Italy and the Roman States down to the borders of Gaul: but the revolution will not end here. England must possess Egypt . . . then Palestine, thus placed between the Russian possessions and Egypt, reverts to its legitimate proprietors . . . the descendants of Abraham. . . . This is our destiny. Every attempt to colonise the Jews in other countries has failed; their eye has steadily rested on their beloved Jerusalem. . . . The valleys of the Jordan will be filled by agriculturalists from the north of Germany, Poland, and Russia. Merchants will occupy the sea ports, and the commanding positions within the walls of Jerusalem will be purchased by the wealthy and pious of our brethren. Those who desire to reside in the Holy Land, and have not means, may be aided by these societies to reach their destined haven of repose. Christians can thus give impetus to this important movement

---

[101] Ibid., 2. 40 (2 August 1847), pp. 235–6; 2. 34 (1 February 1847), pp. 160–1; 2. 30 (1 October 1846), pp. 114, 118–19; 2. 28 (1 August 1846), pp. 92–4.

[102] 1. 16 (1 August 1845), p. 156.

[103] 'An excellent illustration of a most anomalous state of mind . . . in which . . . we must understand them to believe that Christianity is neither true nor false!' Ibid., 1. 9 (1 January 1845), p. 71.

and emigration flowing in and actively engaged in every laudable pursuit, will soon become consolidated, and lay the foundation for the elements of government and the triumph of restoration.[104]

Noah's dream was a century in the making. Such dreams were not confined to Noah. The English Lt Col. Gawler's *Tranquilization of Syria and the East* also advocated Jewish agricultural colonies, although his vision placed them under Great Britain's benevolent aegis. Herschell, however, was clear-eyed as to the practicalities. In his experience most Jews were not agriculturalists and the likeliest settlers in any Jewish colony would be lame dogs and failures. What was the use of transporting those who teemed between Cheapside and Thames Street to the wastes of Tyre and Sidon? Of course, matters might be different if 'some Jews of wealth and education would . . . forego the comforts of a European home, and settle among them as the guides and counsellors of the infant colony . . .'[105]

Herschell's role of practical millennialist was not an easy one. Far too few Christians were alert to 'juster views of the destiny of Israel'. Far too few had any sense of the Church's peril.[106] Far too many works on prophecy turned when it came to Jewish restoration from literal belief to some sort of mystical explanation. Far too many Jews indeed spiritualized prophecy into that future time when 'the whole world shall be their Palestine, every city their Zion, and every synagogue their Temple'.[107] And far too few read *The Voice of Israel*.

Such blindness wearied an editor's patience. Herschell was no chronology cruncher but he was bound to note and thus set forth the 'wonderful coincidence' of opinion among prophetic commentators:

> the whole amount of the difference in the calculations of the numerous writers, of all ages and of all countries, is but thirty years. In different periods of political excitement, it is true, there have been those who, like the fifth-monarchy men of the seventeenth century, conceived the event to be near their own times; but of the students who have calmly made the calculation in their closets, there are scarcely any who have fixed it earlier than the year 1836 of the

[104] *The Voice of Israel*, 1. 9 (1 January 1845), p. 73.
[105] Ibid., 1. 17 (1 September 1845), pp. 168–9.
[106] 'So far, then is it from being the case, that the world is gradually to slide into the Church, until it be entirely absorbed in it, that we find the wickedness of the world is to be most rampant, and its oppression of the children of God, most grievous, at the time when Christ comes to deliver his Church.' 2. 22 (2 February 1846), p. 14. Also 2. 21 (1 January 1846), p. 1.
[107] Ibid., 1. 4 (1 August 1844), p. 31.

Christian era; nor (with the exception of a very few who from love of round numbers fix the year 2000) are there any who make it later than 1866 or 1867. When it is known that these calculations are made from different data, and by men entertaining opposite opinions on the nature of the millennial glory, the measure of coincidence is surely much more remarkable than the degree of discrepancy.

Why could not more Christians see that?

The man of the world perceives the rapidity with which the events of this earth's history are developing themselves; the infidel journalist enters on the new year with the expectation that it is to bring forth momentous occurrences and shall the Christian be found in the ranks of the ignorant who say, 'All things continue as they were from the beginning of the creation'?[108]

IX

It was not easy for a pre-millennialist to be a strong churchman of any kind. It might follow, therefore, that the last of the older-school 'catholic Christians' were likely to be pre-millennialists. Ridley Herschell was never a denominationalist. His daughter's biographies of her parents nowhere refer to their Congregationalism or that of their churches. Yet his closest and most consistent denominational circles were Congregational ones. Congregational ministers preached at the opening of his chapels and Congregational ministers buried him. He was listed in *Congregational Year Books* and so was Trinity. But that was a general listing. Though Congregationalists recognized him as one of them and his church as one of theirs, Trinity was a member neither of the London Congregational Union nor the Congregational Union of England and Wales, and its minister was in no Congregational fraternal and had no personal membership of any Congregational Union. He had found that he could not be an Anglican since he did not believe in a priesthood; he could not subscribe to any sort of canonical obedience; and he considered the Church's baptismal and burial services to be 'equally repugnant in Scripture and reason'.[109] But then he could not belong to any sect because he could find no sects in Scripture. On the other hand his views must immediately commend him to Congregationalists. Trinity's stated

---

[108] Ibid., 1. 9 (1 January 1845), p. 70.
[109] *Memoir of R. H. Herschell*, p. 140.

doctrines were firmly evangelical: the corruption of human nature, justification by faith, sanctification through the Holy Spirit, the whole to be found in Scripture which was 'the sole rule of faith and practice':

> My views are very simple. . . . As believers multiplied in different localities, they could not all 'come together in one place', and were therefore necessarily separated into different communities, each of which, without any disunion from the whole body of believers—the Church of God—was a complete church in itself, governed by suitable office-bearers, and instructed and watched over by one whom the Holy Ghost had called to the office of overseer or bishop, (Acts XX.28), the church, or body of believers, participating in the consideration of all matters connected with their own well-being. In short, the early church government was strictly congregational, each one being entirely independent of external authority. . . . That the order of these early churches was at first uniform or nearly so, I do not doubt; and I believe that the apostles strove to prevent unseemly innovations, (I Cor. XI.6–16); but this was not seeking uniformity for uniformity's sake, but order for order's sake. There may have been and probably were, at a very early period, different local arrangements, that did not for a moment interrupt the unity of the Spirit. . . . We believe the sin of schism . . . to consist in . . . such an alienation from other churches of Christ . . . as to prevent all union and co-operation with them.[110]

That was certainly the basis on which Thomas Binney opened the renovated Chadwell Street Chapel on Herschell's behalf in April 1839. Some of Herschell's firmest supporters were connected with Binney's King's Weigh House Church, and the weight of Binney's name was used at the inception of the British Society even though he had to send his apologies to its opening meeting and was never able to attend the Committee to which, in his absence, he was elected. The sermon Binney preached for Herschell at Chadwell Street, *Conscientious Clerical Nonconformity*, was a celebrated one. It was massive, shot through with a searching humour, and it was several times reprinted. That is because although it was a very fair account of where Herschell stood it could also serve very well as a general counter to Puseyism or, as republished nine years later, to the Gorham Judgment affair, or, as republished twelve years later still, as a commentary on Binney's experiences with Anglicans in Australia. The

[110] *Memoir of R. H. Herschell*, pp. 142–4.

one thing it did not refer to was pre-millennialism and it barely referred (save in the title) to the most obvious aspect of Herschell's ministry, his Jewishness. Binney began ringingly with a quotation:

> Evangelical Nonconformity 'is a stand not merely for the claims of Scripture, and the supremacy of Christ—not merely for the liberty of all to consult his will, and to follow their convictions, and thus to render to Him a reasonable service; but it is a stand for the recognition of all as Christian brethren, "who hold the head", it is a stand for mutual indulgence to secondary differences, grounded on agreement in what is supreme; it is a stand for substantial and visible unity, by being a stand for universal Christian communion—for the unrestricted intercourse of ministers and churches, in spite of the diversity of forms of discipline'. This is the spirit of Evangelical Dissent. It is equally opposed to imposition and exclusiveness; to the dictates of power, and the selfishness of party....[111]

There indeed was catholic Christianity, but could that continue in Ridley Herschell's new chapel? Binney anticipated a day when the sacraments might be observed in it, a *membership* gathered, an order evolved. He implied that that would be a proper development. Certainly if the cause were to endure it would be a necessary development, and perhaps he was wise to make no reference to prophecy or the future state of Jews, for such matters were powerful solvents of the denominational principle.

And so things turned out. Trinity Chapel did not long survive Ridley Herschell's death. For a while it strove to keep its distinctiveness under Abraham Schwartz, but by 1869 neither he nor it was anywhere to be found in *Congregational Year Books* and the premises were taken over by Baptists,[112] as those in Chadwell Street are at the present day (1993). Pre-millennialism was not sustained by the next generation, who of course long survived the rigours of 1867. Farrer Herschell,[113] the future

---

[111] T. Binney, *Conscientious Clerical Nonconformity. A Discourse, Delivered at Chadwell Street Chapel, Pentonville, on Monday, April 15, 1839, On Occasion of Its Re-Opening for the Use of RIDLEY H. HERSCHELL, a Converted Jew* (London, 1839), p. 4.

[112] *Baptist Handbook* (1889), pp. 141–2, 146–7.

[113] Farrer Herschell, 1st Baron Herschell (1837–99), *DNB*; see also R. F. V. Heuston, *Lives of the Lord Chancellors* (Oxford, 1964), pp. 85–127. The political Liberalism of the connection is worthy of note, given the presumption that the pessimism inherent in pre-millennialism might be conducive to conservatism. Esther Herschell's nephew, William Fuller-Maitland, was on Asquith's list of possible Liberal Peers should the 1909–11 Parliament crisis have demanded it: R. Jenkins, *Asquith* (1964), p. 542.

Gladstonian Lord Chancellor, became a churchwarden at the unmistakably High Church St Peter's Eaton Square. R. B. Haldane, the future Liberal and Labour Lord Chancellor, though he had for kindness' sake been baptized by immersion (it was hardly *believer's* baptism),[114] moved quickly into agnosticism. The son and heir of Alexander Haldane, the *Recordite* and sternest Evangelical of them all, by contrast became a High Churchman and a notable Bishop of Argyll and the Isles.[115] Sir John Burdon-Sanderson moved into Broad Churchmanship. Not all forgot their roots. Mary Cunliffe, for example, remembered in her will James Oswald Dykes, successor of James Hamilton and Edward Irving at Regent Square and first principal of the Presbyterians' Westminster College, Cambridge, where is to be found in the dining hall's east wall a window depicting Christ gathering children around him, the gift of the childless Mrs Cunliffe.[116] And Arnold Herschell, the tennis-playing African exporter from Liverpool, retained contact with Jewish cousins now living in Berlin. He visited them in the 1890s and in 1938 he saved the lives of two of them, a mother and daughter, by getting them out of Germany and across to England where he paid for the daughter's education at Benenden School.[117] That piquant cultural transition from the holocaust world to gymslips brings one back to the world of prophecy:

> I will add but one word. It is written, 'Shut up the words, and seal the book, even to the time of the end; the words are closed up and sealed, till the time of the end'. ([Daniel] XII.4,9). If, then, the seal be now broken, the time of the end is at hand. . . .[118]

[114] In 1876, D. Sommer, *Haldane of Cloan* (1960), p. 47.
[115] James Robert Alexander Chinnery-Haldane (1842–1906): Venn, *Alumni Cantabrigienses*, 2. 3, p. 192.
[116] Will dated 7 November 1894; R. B. Knox, *Westminster College, Cambridge: Its Background and History* (Cambridge, 1979), p. 19.
[117] Information from Mr G. C. Lightfoot.
[118] *Voice of Israel*, 2. 34 (1 February 1847), p. 167.

INDEX

Index

Bernard of Clairvaux
on coming of Antichrist 8–9
and earthly Jerusalem 174–82
and heavenly Jerusalem 172–4, 176–9,
181–2
Beza, Theodore 114, 118
Bible
and Bernard of Clairvaux 176
decline in medieval scholarship 29, 31–
2
in Durham 125–9
infallibility 157
and Joachim of Fiore 17–19, 21, 25
and literalism 32, 36, 122, 128–9, 173–
8, 236, 255
and Marian exiles 77–9, 90–1
medieval Franciscan commentaries 29–
37
and Müntzer 71, 72
Sentences-commentaries 31–2
symbolic interpretation 135–6
and Wyclif 49–53
see also allegory; chronology; Daniel;
hermeneutics; Revelation
Bickersteth, Edward Henry 230 n.12, 264
Bierman, Johannes 161
Binfield, Clyde viii
Binney, Thomas 230, 268–9
Birks, T. R. 264
Blackfriars Council 1382 39
Blomfield, Charles James 245, 260
Bloomfield, Herbert 29
Bochart, Samuel 154
Bocskai, István 96, 99
Bohemia, seventeenth-century revolts
106–8
Bohemian revolt, and influence of
chiliasm 97–102
Bonar, Andrew 235, 236
Bonar, Horatius 235, 236–7, 238
Bonaventure, St 31, 32–3
Boniface VIII, Pope 77
Bonnet, Gisbertus 165
Book of Common Order 77–8, 89
Bossy, John 203
Boswell, Sir William 114
Boubereel, Cornelis 145
Bradford, John 84

Bredero, Adriaan H. viii, 184 n.5
Brethren *see* Plymouth Brethren
Brightman, Thomas 119, 122, 161
British Society for the Propagation of the
Gospel among the Jews 227–8, 244–
5, 268
and Herschell 261, 263
leadership 229–33
Mission College 229, 239, 244
and pre-millenialism 237–41, 244, 250
Brown, F. W. 231
Brut, Walter 43 n.24
Bucer, Martin 118
Budovec, Václav 97–9
Bullinger, Henry 85, 208, 213
Bunting, William Maclardie 229
Burder, Henry Foster 230, 243
Burdon-Sanderson, John Scott 247, 248,
270
Burdon-Sanderson, Richard 251, 252
burial service
and medieval gilds 192–3
in Prayer Book of 1549 210–11, 215
in Prayer Book of 1552 211–13
Burns, J. Chalmers 230
Burr, David 30
Byfield, Nicolas 117

Cabbalism 132, 136, 155, 162, 166
Calvin, John, and sleep of the soul 208–9,
213
Calvinism
and chiliastic prophecy 94, 97, 99, 107,
116, 128
in Netherlands 142–3
in Scotland 123, 126
Cambridge, chantry colleges 189–91, 197,
198
Cambridge Platonism 131–40
Capelle, Louis 154–5
carmina Burana 12
Carstairs, John 124
Cassiodor 6
catechism, Dutch Catholic 144–7, 148–50
Chalmers, Thomas 236, 253
chantries 184, 189–91, 198–201
Chapman, John 196–7

Index

Cunliffe, Mary 247, 270
Cunliffe, Walter 248
Cyprian, Henry 199

Daniel
 and evangelical Dissent 233, 264, 270
 and Marian exiles 78, 81, 89, 91
 and periodization of history 5, 6–7, 25–6, 52 n.55, 161
 in seventeenth-century Protestantism 96, 120, 140
Davenant, John 116 n.21
De Dieu, Ludovicus 112–13, 114
De Leo, Pietro 26 n.45
death
 in Bach 217–19, 220
 and memorials to the dead 214
 and Prayer Books of 1549 and 1552 205–15
 pre-Reformation fellowship with the living 183–204, 206–7, 209, 215
Delumeau, Jean 141–2
Diers, Michaela 171–2, 174
dirige for the dead 191, 193, 196–7, 200, 209
Dissent
 and conversion of Jews 226–33, 237–46, 250–3, 256–7
 and interest in Jews viii, 225–6
 and pre-millenialism 234–7, 238, 244, 250–7, 265–7, 269
Doddridge, Philip 254
doles, anniversary 202
Drabík, Mikuláš 107–8
Dunlop, John 238
Durham, James 123–9
Durie, John 137, 140
Durkheim, E. 192 n.50
Dutch Mission, devotional literature 141–2, 145
Dykes, James Oswald 270

Eardley, Sir Culling Eardley 230, 244–5, 253
Easton, Adam 43
Edward VI, King of England 83–5
 and commemoration of the dead 198, 202

Ehrle, F. 29
elect, the
 in Müntzer 69
 in Prayer Book of 1552 213
 in Victorian Dissent 234
 in Wyclif 53
Eliot, T.S. 151
Elizabeth I, Queen of England
 and memorials to the dead 214
 and the True Church 88–9
Elliger, Walter 66
Elliott, E. B. 264
England
 apostasy 83–5, 88
 as new Israel 43–4, 84–5, 88–9
enthusiasm, in More 131
Erghome, John 44
eschatology
 and creation 151–66
 Dutch Roman Catholic 141–50
 and evangelical Dissent 226
 and history 3–13
 in J. S. Bach 217–23
 and medieval monasticism 3, 5
 present 220
eucharist
 and commemoration of the dead 189
 and real presence 145–6, 211
 in Reformation Prayer Books 210–13, 215
 in Wyclif 39
 see also mass
evangelicalism, British
 and Jews 225–33, 237–46, 250–3, 256–7
 and post-millenialism 234, 236, 244
 and pre-millenialism 234–7, 238, 244, 250–7, 265–7, 269
Evans, R. J. W. 94
exiles, Marian
 influence 75–8
 and People of God 78, 84–6, 88–9, 91
 and True Church 78–89, 91

faith, in Müntzer 66–7, 70, 71, 74
family, and commemoration of the dead 184–7, 197, 201–3, 209
Fifth Monarchism 139–40, 266

274

2

Index

Herschell, Arnold 249, 270
Herschell, David Abraham 248, 250
Herschell, Farrer 247, 269–70
Herschell, George 248
Herschell, George (son of John) 248
Herschell, Ghetal 247
Herschell, Jesia 249
Herschell, John Francis Israel 248
Herschell, Louis 248
Herschell, Mary 247, 270
Herschell, Ridley Haim 228, 245–6
    and Dissent 250, 252–3, 267–9
    family connections 246–52
    and Judaism 257–61, 269
    as minister 260–2
    and Palestine 263–4
    and pre-millenialism 256–7, 265–7,
        269
    and prophecy 261–5
    and *Voice of Israel* 263–7, 270
    wives *see* Fuller-Maitland, Esther;
        Mowbray, Helen Skirving
Herschell, Victor 248
Hildegard of Bingen 45–6, 51
Hildersham, Arthur 117
Hilten, Johannes 96
Hirsch-Reich, Beatrice 23, 25 n.37, 26
history
    and chronology of creation 3–4, 151–
        60, 162–5
    periodization vii, 4–13, 25–6, 33–4, 49,
        78–9, 81, 153, 160–1
    of Protestantism 78–82
Hitchcock, George 230, 253
Hitchens, Hiles 231
Hoberweschel, Andreas 100
Hoccleve 62
Holl, Karl 66
Holmes, Gulielma 248, 249
Holy Land
    and crusades 173–4, 180–2
    as place of pilgrimage 169–70
Holy Spirit
    and Age of the Spirit 16, 21, 34
    in Müntzer 70–1, 72–3
    in Van Laren 118
    in Victorian Dissent 234, 244, 268
Hooper, John 85

Hoornbeek, Johannes 100
Horne, C. S. 230
Horton, R. F. 230
Hudson, Anne 39
Huet, Pierre Daniel 154
Hugh of Digne 30
Hugh of Fleury 11
Hugh of St Victor 176
Hughes, Hugh Price 230
Hughes, Jonathan 44
Hughson, Nicholas 186
Hungary, seventeenth-century revolts
    106–8
Huntingdon, William 251
Hus, John 72–3, 98

identity, corporate 187, 188–9, 192
idolatry, and Marian exiles 85–8
imitatio Christi, in Wyclif 49, 52, 53, 54–5
Incarnation, as initiating final period of
    history 4–5, 165
individual
    in Dutch Catholicism 143–6, 148
    and medieval eschatology 3, 5
indulgences 194, 207
Ingaldesthorp family 185, 186
Innocent III, Pope 57
Innocent IV, Pope 45
interdenominationalism, and conversion
    of the Jews 227–8
Irenaeus 129
Irving, Edward 235–7, 250, 254–6, 260–1,
    270
Isidore of Sevilla, and eschatology 4

Jacobsz, Heyman 145
Jerome, St
    and Jerusalem 169, 171
    and periodization of history 5, 25–6
Jerusalem
    earthly 174–82, 241
    heavenly city 5, 170, 172–4, 176–8,
        181–2, 222
    as place of pilgrimage 169–71
    recapture 170–1, 180
Jews
    in Bernard of Clairvaux 177, 178, 179,
        181

276

Index

Index

Lubac, Henri de 29–30
Luther, Martin 98
  and Müntzer 65–6, 70–1
  and purgatory 206, 207–8

Mahan, Asa 252
Maitland, F. W. 246
Maitland, S. R. 246, 250
Maitland-Wilson family 246–7
Makeblyde, L. 144, 148
Malachy, archbishop 8
Manchester, 6th Duke 253
Manselli, Raoul 29, 35 n.10
Map, Walter 12
Marinius, Samuel 101
Marsilius of Padua 43, 53 n.56, 60 n.89, 62
Martin, Samuel 230
martyrdom
  in Durham 127
  in Foxe 79
  and Marian exiles 79–80, 82
  in Wyclif 40–1, 55–7, 62–3
Mary of Egypt, St 169
Mary Tudor
  and commemoration of the dead 202
  and Protestant exiles 75–91
mass
  commemorative 184–5, 189–97, 199–200, 202, 209
  and Marian exiles 85–6
  requiem 193, 200, 209
  for the sick 209–10
Masse, John 194, 195
mathematics, and apocalyptic 25, 90
Mathew of Albano, Cardinal 9
McCheyne, Robert Murray 228, 235, 236–7, 238
McGinn, Bernard 31, 45 n.32
Mede, Joseph 90, 111–15, 118–19, 122, 161, 233
  Clavis Apocalyptica 111, 112–15, 119–21, 126–9, 139
  Commentarius 112, 113–14
  and More 132–4, 136–7, 139–40
Meier, Johannes 166
Melito of Sardis 169
Melville, James 91

memorials to the dead 214
Metcalfe, C. J. 253
Middle Ages
  attitudes to death 183–204
  and periodization of history 3–13, 122, 153
milleniarism
  in Durham 127
  in evangelical Dissent 233–7
  and history vii–viii, 5–6, 165
  in Mede 111–15, 119–21, 132
  in More 131–40
  in Van Laren 115–22
  see also apocalypticism; chiliasm; post-millenialism; pre-millenialism
millenium
  and role of the Church 6, 135
  spiritual interpretation 128–9, 136–9
Mills, John Remington 253
modernity, and signs of Antichrist 10–13, 34
monarchy, in Wyclif 42, 61–2
monasticism
  and dissolution of monasteries 205–6
  and earthly Jerusalem 171
  and eschatology 3, 5, 9, 24
  and heavenly Jerusalem 5, 172–4, 178–9, 181–2
  reforms 9, 24
More, Henry 131–40
  and Joseph Mede 132–4, 136–7, 139–40
mortmain licences 184, 189, 194
Morwin, Thomas 77
mourning, rituals of 200
Mowbray, Helen Skirving 246–7, 249, 250, 253–7, 260–1
Müller, Heinrich 217
Müntzer, Thomas 65–74
  and chiliasm 68–9, 72–4
  cohesion of interior and exterior 70–2
  and Luther 65–6, 70–1
  mystical influence on 66–8, 69–71
  and the Spirit 70–1, 72–3
mysticism
  in Müntzer 66–8, 69–71
  of Bernard of Clairvaux 171–2
  Roman Catholic 147

278

Index

Index